THE WAR WE WON APART

Also by Nahlah Ayed

A Thousand Farewells: A Reporter's Journey from Refugee Camp to the Arab Spring

THE WAR WE WON APART

THE UNTOLD STORY OF TWO ELITE AGENTS WHO BECAME ONE OF THE MOST DECORATED COUPLES OF WWII

NAHLAH AYED

VIKING

VIKING

an imprint of Penguin Canada, a division of Penguin Random House Canada Limited

Canada • USA • UK • Ireland • Australia • New Zealand • India • South Africa • China

First published 2024

www.penguinrandomhouse.ca

LIBRARY AND ARCHIVES CANADA CATALOGUING IN PUBLICATION

Title: The war we won apart : the untold story of two elite agents who became one of the most decorated couples of WWII / Nahlah Ayed.
Names: Ayed, Nahlah, author.
Description: Includes bibliographical references and index.
Identifiers: Canadiana (print) 20230561187 | Canadiana (ebook) 20230561225 | ISBN 9780735242067 (hardcover) | ISBN 9780735242074 (EPUB)
Subjects: LCSH: Butt, Sonia. | LCSH: D'Artois, Guy. | LCSH: Butt, Sonia—Marriage. | LCSH: D'Artois, Guy—Marriage. | LCSH: World War, 1939-1945—Secret service—Great Britain. | LCSH: Women spies—Great Britain—Biography. | LCSH: Spies—Great Britain—Biography. | LCGFT: Biographies.
Classification: LCC DS810.S7 A94 2024 | DDC 940.54/86410922—dc23

Book design by Matthew Flute
Typeset by Daniella Zanchetta
Cover design by Matthew Flute
Cover image: © Portman Press Bureau

Printed in the United States of America

10 9 8 7 6 5 4 3 2 1

Dedicated to the women and men—and their children—
forced to contend with wars that never end.

CONTENTS

PROLOGUE: LUNCH IN PARIS, 1944 1

PART I: ON THE HOME FRONT

1 SEEKING REFUGE 7
Sonia • *English Channel, late summer 1939*

2 FINDING A WAY 19
Guy • *Montreal, September 1939*

PART II: OFF TO WAR

3 LEAVING HOME 31
Guy • *Atlantic Ocean, January 1940*

4 FINDING HOME 43
Sonia • *London, May 1941*

5 A CHANGE OF DIRECTION 50
Sonia • *London, November 1941*

6 ANOTHER DETOUR 61
Guy • *London, December 1941*

7 COG IN A LARGE MACHINE 67
Guy • *Near Oshawa, October 1943*

PART III: SPECIALLY EMPLOYED

8 AGENTS-TO-BE 73
Sonia and Guy • *London, early December 1943*

9 LOVE IN A TIME OF WAR 87
Sonia and Guy • *Scotland, December 1943*

10 FIRST DISAPPOINTMENT 109
Sonia and Guy • *London, April 1944*

PART IV: BEHIND ENEMY LINES

11 FROM THE HEAVENS — 117
Dieudonné • *Over France, May 23, 1944*

12 A "GIRL" COURIER — 133
Blanche • *Le Mans, May 23, 1944*

PART V: D-DAY

13 THE MOMENT HAS ARRIVED — 145
Michel le Canadien • *Charolles, June 1944*

14 MOTHER OF ALL MAQUIS — 154
Guy • *Sylla, June 6, 1944*

15 HIDING IN PLAIN SIGHT — 163
Blanche/Madeleine • *Le Mans, June 6, 1944*

16 OPERATION CADILLAC — 173
Guy • *Sylla, July 14, 1944*

17 AWAY — 186
Sonia • *Le Breuil Saint Michel, July 20, 1944*

18 TRIUMPHANT MINUTES — 200
Guy • *Charolles, August 1944*

19 CONSTERNATION — 204
Guy • *Sylla, August 1944*

20 LIBERATION — 209
Sonia, Guy, and Sydney • *Paris, September 1944*

PART VI: GOING HOME

21 WAR BRIDE — 221
Sonia • *Atlantic Ocean, December 11, 1944*

22 THE LIMELIGHT — 229
Sonia and Guy • *Canada, December 1944*

23 LETTERS — 244
Guy and Sonia • *Canada, 1945–46*

24 NORTH 252
Guy • *Moffet Inlet, October 4, 1947*

PART VII: WAR AGAIN

25 GOING EAST 261
Guy and Sonia • *Korea and Quebec City, March 1952*

26 REUNIONS 274
Sonia and Guy • *Werl, Germany, 1955*

27 SURGERY 284
Sonia • *Montreal, 1960*

28 HOME 287
Sonia • *Como, 1961*

PART VIII: PEACE AT LAST

29 ONE FINAL VISIT 299
Guy • *Charolles, June 9, 1984*

30 REMEMBRANCE 306
Sonia • *Normandy, France, 1994*

31 ÇA FAIT LONGTEMPS 313
Sonia • *London, December 2001*

32 SONIA'S WAY 320
Sonia • *Salt Spring Island, March 2002*

EPILOGUE: NEVER TOO LATE 323
Montreal, 2007

A Note on Sources 325
Notes 331
Bibliography 385
Acknowledgments 393
Photo Credits 397
Index 399

PROLOGUE: LUNCH IN PARIS, 1944

It was a late September day, around lunch hour, when a woman barely out of her teens strode into what was once one of the most popular tearooms in Paris, near the Champs-Élysées. Like the tearoom itself, her face showed signs that the war had taken a toll. She'd lost more than thirty pounds in four months. You could see it in her ever so slightly sunken eyes and in the way her slender frame strained against tanned and tired skin. Yet somehow Sonia Butt still glowed, her chestnut eyes glittering as they always did, even when scanning for danger.

Paris was battered and war-weary, and yet it too glittered, still tipsy weeks after it had gone mad with celebration. The German garrison's surrender had marked the end of France's occupation and the start of a new phase in Europe's bloodiest war. "Paris is liberated!"—words thrilling to hear but difficult to fathom after four years of Nazi occupation. The latest battle had been won partly on the backs of young men with guns whose lives had been painfully interrupted, and in no small part on the backs of impossibly young women who had put themselves, body and mind, in harm's way.

And just as the Allies counted a major triumph in a terrible war, Sonia—only twenty—could also righteously claim victory. She had done her part at great peril, parachuting in behind enemy lines to wage a secret war that would pave the way for D-Day. She'd seen death up close. She had beheld the power of an air strike and that of a single bullet: she'd pulled the trigger herself. She had also experienced the worst that can happen to a woman in a theatre of war. Known at times as Suzanne, Madeleine, Blanche, Ginette, or Tony, depending on who was speaking and when, she'd amassed names and personae just as other women of her years and beauty amassed admirers. And she had amassed those, too. As the war began its long fade, Sonia's necessarily compartmentalized life was divided between two men from opposite sides of the Atlantic.

Sonia had learned early on how to navigate the obstacles complicating her path. Her place in the world, right up to the moment when she had parachuted into France, had frequently shape-shifted—and she along with it. Her life thus far had been a series of disruptions, separations, and reunions: with her abusive and neglectful mother, with her adoring and itinerant father, with her protective brother, and with her loyal circle of friends. Her wartime experience was no different. And now her final battle of the Second World War promised to be a disruption, a separation, and a reunion all at once.

For the first and only time, she was bringing the two men in her life together for a frank conversation. The three of them had all known each other just a moment ago, when they were agents-in-waiting for the British Special Operations Executive (SOE), back before the war transformed them. But so much had happened since their training had ended and they dropped into different parts of occupied France to help the impending Allied invasion.

When the country was finally liberated, the SOE had called in its agents from the field. It was here, in Paris, that they had converged on the makeshift French Section office for a debrief on their triumphs, their disappointments, and their exorbitant mistakes.

Sonia's personal debrief with Guy and Sydney would happen over lunch.

She had unilaterally predetermined the outcome of the encounter, already decided how she would spend the rest of her life and with whom. There was no changing her mind now. But that didn't make it easy.

The encounter would be "the most depressing moment" in their young, eventful lives. They would all walk away from war-torn France heartbroken—but lucky to be alive.

Sonia and Guy had won their war apart. But it was a victory that came at great cost.

PART I:

ON THE HOME FRONT

1

SEEKING REFUGE

Sonia • *English Channel, late summer 1939*

The ferry lumbered across the watery corridor connecting France to England, cutting through troubled blue-grey waves livid with movement. Its passengers were packed in so tight they swayed with the waves as one, many of them seasick, and though the conflict had yet to tangibly start, already war-sick. These hulking vessels regularly swept back and forth between Calais and the Dover Cliffs across the English Channel, a distance of about 50 kilometres; cutting through fog and foam and passing by the occasional gannet flying a well-trodden route. But on this day the wind was too violent and the climate too uncertain for such familiarity to offer the passengers any comfort.

Europe was again at the threshold of war, and people were frantically scrambling to leave the mainland. Aboard one of the last ferries to cross before hostilities would halt them indefinitely, apprehension swathed the passengers like the invisible droplets of water saturating the air.

Among this cohort of the uprooted stood Sonia Butt, all of fifteen years old, tired, dishevelled, and alone. Still, as a bit of a tomboy, being tired and dishevelled was just part of being Sonia. Being alone was second nature, too. But it hadn't always been that way. Her older brother, Derek, had almost always been there. Back when they could spend endless sun-kissed days at the beach, she and Derek had been virtually inseparable. But on this late summer day, centuries into her young life, Sonia had boarded the ferry without Derek, without anyone or anything really, save the toothbrush tucked in the pocket of her blazer.

It was a small miracle that she'd made it on board at all. The little travel attaché case she'd started out with fell casualty to the chaos and the crowds she'd encountered on the first leg of her solo journey from the south of France to England. It took her three days just to get to Paris— "a horrendous journey." Then, at a Gare du Nord café in Paris, she'd spent the last of her money on a coffee and a croissant served by a waiter who, at the dawn of a world war, sharply pointed out that "*Mademoiselle*, the bill does not include tip."

It was 1939. And, on the other side of the agitated Channel, Britain too was in a petulant mood.

September 3 was a Sunday. At a quarter past eleven o'clock that morning, Prime Minister Neville Chamberlain declared war against Nazi Germany. Only months earlier he'd chosen, in the name of peace, to swerve in the face of Europe's greatest threat. Yet now, in a curt announcement on BBC Radio, Chamberlain declared that Hitler could only be stopped by force. "We have a clear conscience," he intoned. "We have done all that any country could do to establish peace. But a situation in which no word given by Germany's ruler could be trusted, and no people or country could feel itself safe, had become intolerable. And now that we have resolved to finish it, I know that you will all play your part with calmness and courage."

The speech ended with a peal of Bow bells, sounding somehow more sombre and urgent than usual. A presenter then read a government decree announcing the closure of places of entertainment. It urged listeners to avoid gatherings, to stay off the streets as much as possible, and to always carry their gas masks. The reader counselled all members of each family to carry their names and addresses on their persons, even sewing them into labels on children's clothing so that they too would never be without identification. The instructions ended with a thin instrumental rendition of "God Save the King."

The government appealed to more than God to save the country's children. For months the nation had been preoccupied with the threat of attack, gripped by the prospect that its cities would be the prime target. So even before its official declaration of war, the government had launched Operation Pied Piper. Hundreds of thousands of children, as well as pregnant women and some mothers, were moved out of urban areas and, the hope was, out of harm's way in what would become the largest mass movement of people in the country's history. At train stations all over London, parents lined up with their children, kissing them goodbye, sending them off to be billeted in the countryside with strangers whose kindness could not be guaranteed. The motive was to spare children the trauma—and possible injury—of living under bombardment. Yet the disruption would still leave countless in a generation with injury or trauma of another kind.

Sonia knew trauma early, the way one knows a longtime neighbour. She'd grown up with separation, instability, and abuse long before war upended her life. Born in England to British parents, she was only three when they separated, after which her mother moved them to the south of France. Her father lived abroad and returned only for rare, short visits. Her mother, too, occasionally disappeared. Derek, at first, was the one constant: her best friend, schoolmate, and a source of endless hand-me-downs that she gladly wore in lieu of girly dresses. Derek was always there—at least until they were pried apart and sent to boarding schools in separate towns. In those long, wet winter months, Derek and Sonia would write each other letters in which he'd enclose part of the allowance that he received and that she was, for some inexplicable reason, denied.

Now, as she swayed with the waves that carried her back to the country of her birth, there was no Derek, no letters, and no words of comfort, never mind a half-allowance. Sonia was on her own and on the move.

"You're completely alone, aren't you?"

"Yes," Sonia told the older gentleman who started a conversation on the ferry.

What would she do, he continued, once she arrived in London?

After disembarking from the train at Victoria Station she'd head directly to the Grosvenor, a palatial railway hotel a short walk from Buckingham Palace, where she had been with her mother many times before. "I'm going to go there and see the manager," Sonia explained. She figured he would remember her, and she could ask him for a loan to get her on a train to Horley, near Gatwick, where her mother lived when she wasn't in France.

The gentleman seemed satisfied with the answer. "It sounds as though you can take care of yourself," he remarked. Still, he promised to make sure she got there safely.

After Chamberlain's declaration of war, London was in a bewildered, cheerless state. The crowds and queues disappeared, save for those waiting for necessities or fuel. Theatres and cinemas were closed, some schools and sports venues shuttered. Blackouts were already being enforced. People were building shelters in their gardens if they had them; others were taping their windows shut against possible poison gas attacks. The city already seemed shell-shocked, prematurely grey against the perpetual green.

There was the war at hand, of course, but the country was also still reeling from the latest bomb attacks by the Irish Republican Army. The IRA had declared its own war against Britain in January of that year. The first bombings of 1939 came not from the air, but from invisible men on London's streets. Nothing, it seemed, was immune: the attacks targeted banks, post boxes and offices, bridges, underground stations, and just recently, the cloakroom at Victoria Station, Sonia's destination. By the time Britain declared war against Germany, the IRA had mounted the equivalent of one attack every other day somewhere in or around a major British city in an effort to end British control of Northern Ireland.

As Britain prepared for yet another world war, it was also quietly laying the groundwork for its own campaign of irregular warfare—one that would use "sabotage and subversion" to undermine Nazi Germany, inspired in part by the urban sabotage tactics of Irish nationalists after the turn of the century. And so, as early as the spring of 1939, small groups of select British civilians were training in the "elementary theory" of guerrilla warfare. But those first steps were tentative at best, taking a distant backseat as the familiar war machine ramped up.

Hundreds of thousands of men signed up to wear the uniform and fight, some for the second time in their lives. Males too old or too young for military duty joined the local defence volunteers—later the Home Guard—for defence duties at home, protecting factories and preparing for possible invasion. Women joined civil defence units too, driving ambulances or painting sidewalks to help drivers navigate the roads obscured by blackouts. Others answered the call to join the newly re-formed Women's Land Army to replace the men in local agriculture and food production.

Women who wished to serve in uniform could choose one of the auxiliary services available to support the army, navy, and air force. Beginning in 1938, the Auxiliary Territorial Service had become the women's branch of the army. The Women's Royal Naval Service, disbanded after the First World War ended in 1918, was dusted off and reopened in 1939. Then there was the Women's Auxiliary Air Force, which started up in June of that year. Hundreds of thousands of women signed up and put on a uniform to do their part.

Much as she wanted to pitch in, fifteen-year-old Sonia Butt was still too young for any of it. But in her own personal war—the first of many—she was already fighting a pitched battle.

Sonia's life, like her mother's, was charted by war. Both were born to military fathers; both spent their teenage years in the shadow of a world war. Both would also marry military men and chafe against the constraints of life as military wives. They were both strong-willed and independent—and impeccably fashionable and beautiful. But that is where the similarities between mother and daughter seemed to end.

Thelma Esme Florence Gordon, Sonia's mother, was only fourteen when the first guns of the First World War were fired. But she was raised in India, a long way from the Western Front. Even during the war, to be British in India was to live with all the trappings of colonial excess—money, opulence, servants, and the life of leisure that comes with all that. Laurence George Frank Gordon, a British colonel, and Florence Juliet Walters had only Thelma, and no other children. That afforded her an especially charmed life, and she was denied little. She learned to dance exquisitely. She learned to ride beautifully. She learned how to play tennis—and how to win. She grew into a tall, slim, striking young woman who was as beautiful as she was erratic, and later, at least where her daughter was concerned, cruel.

In her youth, Thelma also proved to be impetuous. At just seventeen, with the war still ongoing and her father out of the country, she married without his consent. Her new husband was much older, and a man Sonia would later understand to be a "gambler and a playboy." The arrangement didn't last long. When Thelma's father returned from abroad he insisted on having the marriage annulled; to his relief, they went their separate ways.

The man Thelma married next was a much more conventional choice. Leslie Acton Kingsford Butt was only four years Thelma's senior, a charming, handsome, well-dressed officer who was serving in the Royal Flying Corps, a man who had career prospects and a promising future. He had a temper, but he also had an infectious, genuine smile. Like Thelma, he was a wonderful dancer. But Leslie came from more modest means, his early years far less charmed than those of his new wife.

Leslie was only thirteen when a railway worker found his father, Harry Percy Butt, dead on the train tracks at Bracebridge Cutting in Sutton Park, just north of the city of Birmingham. It happened in 1909 between Christmas and New Year's, a day after his thirty-eighth birthday. He had, according to a local paper, just had a "happy Christmas with his family and friends." The *Sutton Coldfield News* reported that the "news of his tragic death came as a terrible blow to his relatives and friends, who at present are utterly in the dark as to how the affair happened." Family lore and one newspaper report hinted at financial difficulties and a subsequent breakdown.

An inquest ruled it "suicide while temporarily insane"—a condition, one paper reported, possibly brought on by influenza, which "had caused many unhingements of the mind." Whatever the cause, Harry left his young wife, Sarah, to writhe under the significant social stigma of a family suicide, with five children and no means of support.

Harry's parents, who were comfortably off, stepped in to offer an education for the eldest of the children. And so Sonia's father-to-be became the only one of his siblings given a chance at a life better than the tragic circumstances allowed.

Leslie went to live with his grandparents and attended the Royal Military Academy Sandhurst, after which he moved abroad to join the Indian Army. It was a turn of events that would forever divide the siblings by distance and by class. That gulf was sealed by Leslie's marriage to Thelma.

Leslie and Thelma's children arrived between the wars. Derek was first, in India. Thelma and Leslie subsequently moved to England, where Sonia was born on May 14, 1924, at Eastchurch, Kent, where her father was posted at the RAF station as a flight lieutenant.

They were a happy family at first. But Thelma and Leslie's relationship grew tumultuous, and it didn't take long for the marriage to go completely off the rails. Leslie once came home to find Thelma gone and the children left in the care of nannies. Eventually, as he became exasperated with living in a troubled home, he bundled the children up and took them to a rented house on the airbase. Only three years after Sonia was born, the couple separated. What followed were years of drama involving adultery, a prison spell, and petitions for divorce from both sides.

Leslie filed the first petition in 1928, accusing his wife of adultery at a hotel. The judge in the case, Justice Hill, rejected the petition based on Thelma's personal past—"I see nothing to be gained by allowing her to marry a third time"—while also calling out Leslie for his own indiscretions: "The wife goes off with another man. Within a month the husband is committing adultery with his children's governess, who appears to have been up to that time a decent girl. . . . and he does not propose to marry the woman."

And so, thanks to Justice Hill, Leslie and Thelma remained married in name only, and the children were drawn into a torrent of scandals and chaos, shuttled back and forth and back again. The scandals had lasting consequences that would, even beyond the psychological damage, alter the course of Sonia's life. Just weeks after being publically called out for adultery by the court at which he requested divorce, Leslie resigned his commission "by his own request."

Thelma's interest in her children seemed to depend on her relationship status. She once swooped in and grabbed Derek from kindergarten, took Sonia from home, and immediately boarded a flight for Nice, to a house nearby that she'd set up with her then lover. The children had no recourse. Thelma's occasionally desperate attempts at keeping them seemed at odds with one constant where Sonia was concerned: her inexplicable antipathy for her daughter.

Right around Sonia's fifth birthday, she was taken to hospital in Nice with signs of malnourishment and injuries that suggested physical abuse. A household staffer had called the police to report the maltreatment of the little girl. The police arrested Thelma and her partner at the time, a Captain Grey Patrick Baldwin, and held them in prison for five weeks on accusations of "beating and starving Sonia Butt." Given Thelma's status as the daughter—and still nominal wife—of a high-ranking British officer, it was scandalous and public and unfortunate for all involved. Sonia was unaware of the wider consequences of the hurricane around her. She withdrew into herself.

Furious, Leslie dispatched his then live-in girlfriend, Flavia, to France to take Sonia away and bring her back to England. At the hospital, the beautiful red-headed lady found the little girl all alone. Flavia reassured her that everything was going to be all right, that she was going to take her back to her father. As Sonia recalled, she "just went along with it. I was so afraid, and so insecure, and so unhappy . . . I was just letting anybody do whatever they wanted." Flavia spirited the child away, and "the next thing I knew, I was in London."

Leslie, however, had uncertain employment after leaving the military; he bounced from selling encyclopedias to vacuums until he landed employment with Caltex Oil in West Africa, a posting that took him abroad for extended periods and, more crucially, one that didn't allow children. Leslie had little choice but to hand Derek and Sonia to his father-in-law, Thelma's father, Laurence Gordon, who was by then living near Salisbury. Gordon's first wife, Thelma's mother, had died of an illness, and he was now married to his childhood sweetheart, a woman who became known to the children as Auntie Vi. Sonia flourished in their home: "I was quite happy with that arrangement. I loved it there." Gordon wasn't blind to his daughter's erratic behaviour, and promised Leslie not to allow her to take the children. Yet when Thelma and her partner were acquitted by a French court of maltreating her daughter, she swiftly returned and took the children back to France anyway. Sonia despaired, but there was nothing she could do. Derek was her only ally; he provided the only balm to wounds that grew deeper with time.

"He was very protective. But there [were] certain things . . . he just couldn't prevent," said Sonia. Derek had an entirely different experience of their mother. But as far as Sonia was concerned, "She was a cruel woman."

Still, life in southern France suited the children, who were often left to the beach and their own devices. It suited Thelma, too, who spent most of her time showing, breeding, and selling champion dogs.

Leslie, Sonia's father, sometimes visited. On one of those visits, despite the depth of the acrimony, he attempted a reconciliation with Thelma. The result was Thea Ivy, nicknamed Bunny, a sickly child born "with a hole in her heart." In 1933 Sonia and Derek surreptitiously watched her birth from the treehouse outside their home. Sonia was duly impressed by the events of that day, but her teachers were less so when she related the story to her schoolmates. By then, Sonia was attending a strict boarding school at a French convent run by nuns just over the border in Italy. They were so strict that the girls weren't allowed to have a bath in the nude. But after Sonia told the story of Bunny's birth someone snitched on her and she was, mercifully, kicked out. She would salvage her education at her next school, Pensionnat de Jeunes Filles, in Saint-Paul-de-Vence.

But there was nothing left to salvage in Leslie and Thelma's marriage. Thelma eventually met the man who would become her third husband on a trip to Monte Carlo to attend a dog show. She'd taken along the children, who noticed that their mother was staying out later and later every night and wondered what was going on. Finally Thelma returned to introduce them to the man behind all the late nights. Sonia privately cringed.

"Oh my God, it's going to happen again. Here we go," she thought.

Sure enough, Leonard Coventon, a dog handler, quickly became a fixture in their lives, moving into their house and taking up most of their mother's time. When, on the eve of war in 1939, Thelma and Leslie finally divorced, her father insisted that she marry Coventon. They tied the knot and made a home together in England, where they spent their summers.

Sonia was left at boarding school in Saint-Paul-de-Vence, even in summer, and happily so. The old medieval town on the French Riviera was achingly beautiful—longtime home to artists like Marc Chagall, and later the American writer and civil rights activist James Baldwin, who lived there for seventeen years. Sonia flourished in the relaxed environment of the school, where in contrast to the convent, the teachers were friendly and nurturing. There, Sonia could be herself: tomboyish, curious, fun-loving, and not particularly scholarly. By the age of fifteen Sonia spoke French like a native. She knew France better than she knew England. It had implanted itself in her heart, having become as much a "home" as any.

In the summer of 1939 Sonia was again one of the few students left on the premises; with war in Europe seeming inevitable, those still there were glued to the radio. Sonia watched as, one by one, her schoolmates were picked up by frantic parents and taken away. She was among the last to remain unclaimed. Finally, word came from Thelma that Sonia should be released to make her own way, with one caveat: that she first visit the family's house and ask their dog keeper to put all their dogs to sleep, with the exception of Pride, their beloved old fox terrier, whom he was to keep. Worried for Sonia, the headmaster gave her some money to carry her through. She packed the small travel attaché that she'd soon lose—and left.

Some fourteen hundred kilometres later, Sonia arrived in London and made her way from Victoria Station to the Grosvenor Hotel, where the manager duly recognized her. He gave her enough money to get her on the train and called ahead to let her mother know she was on her way "home."

But no one met Sonia at Horley Station. To get to the house, she walked nearly five more kilometres, alone.

It was just the beginning of her journey.

2

FINDING A WAY

Guy • *Montreal, September 1939*

The SS *Athenia* was just two days into its voyage across the Atlantic to Canada when the German submarine *U-30*, operating in the Western Approaches, attacked it with a torpedo, causing an almighty *boom* that shook the hulking liner and extinguished the lights just as first-class passengers were being served their main course. The explosion instantly claimed several lives. Then, as the ship began to sink, hundreds of the Canadian, American, and British passengers clambered into the lifeboats. Frigid, terrified, and exhausted, at the mercy of the waves and unprotected from an infinite sky, they waited hours for rescue. Some of them died waiting. Eventually other ships would arrive and, under the watch of British destroyers, begin lifting the survivors from the ocean. Many of those on board the stricken ship were refugees trying to escape the impending war. Instead, they inaugurated its casualty list.

It was a frightful start to a conflict still in its infancy, and for many on both sides of the Atlantic the attack marked the opening act of the Second World War in the West. It was September 3 and, only hours into the war, Germany had its first U-boat kill, Britain its first sunk ship, and Canada its first casualties.

For Canadians, the war suddenly felt disturbingly close. That September alone, nearly sixty thousand of the nation's men signed up to serve—some out of a sense of obligation and others as a chance to escape hopelessness, boredom, and desperate unemployment, to seize an opportunity that would provide regular meals and pay. Still others did it for the promise of adventure.

Among them in the lineups was twenty-two-year-old Guy d'Artois.

Guy was a slight, wiry thunderstorm of a man, turbulent and impatient. He had hazel eyes and short-cropped dark hair; he wore a moustache and had an air of certainty that eluded most men his age. His mind was lightning fast; he was seldom without an opinion or a burning cigarette between his fingers. Nothing about Guy was shy. He was agile, athletic, playful, combative, and brash—though he could also be effortlessly charming. He wasn't the sort who could possibly sit out the war; it called out to him like a long-lost friend. For every generation there is a defining, life-altering event, and for Guy and his like-minded cohort, it was this war. It was, to be sure, a gross interruption to their young lives, a nightmare intruding on possibility, on hope, on the beautiful pain of ordinary life. Still, it was not to be missed.

Guy was just a year older than the peace that held between the wars. Bookended as it was by the two great wars, Guy's life seemed forever destined to be shaped by them.

At five-thirty in the morning on April 9, 1917, Easter Monday, as many as twenty thousand Canadian soldiers charged into driving sleet and a storm of machine-gun fire to attack a strategic high point on the northern tip of France, which was being held by the occupying German forces. In the Battle of Vimy Ridge, the Canadian Corps—made up of four divisions of men, average age twenty-six, from across Canada—was pitted against three divisions of the German 6th Army, in a diversionary attack aimed at allowing the French forces to punch through the German lines in the south. By the time it was all over, on April 12, the Canadians had taken the ridge—a badly needed victory for the Allied troops. But that one victory cost a shocking thirty-six hundred Canadian lives, many of them cut down within minutes of charging out into the open, their blood tingeing the mud red. Politicians and military men back home would much later see symbolic unity in the moment when the four divisions fought together for the first time to take the ridge, describing it as "the birth of a nation." But for the mothers and families of the fallen soldiers, it was instead an end—an anti-birth, a tragedy of incalculable proportions.

That same Easter Monday, in the Quebec town of Richmond, Antoinette Dufort d'Artois, a twenty-two-year-old Canadian of French descent, gave birth to her second child, a healthy baby boy.

Antoinette was a porcelain-skinned brunette whose deep brown eyes seemed to convey an indefinable sadness. In 1912 she'd married Joseph Valmore d'Artois, thirteen years her senior and an ambitious lawyer with the means to give her a good life. He was a tall, broad man whose family could trace its history all the way to the 1700s, when some of their early ancestors left a place called Artois in France and settled in Quebec. Their pride in the old country immigrated with them and was passed down through several generations.

The couple decided to etch that pride permanently into their lives by naming their two children after the border region—Alsace-Lorraine—that France had reluctantly ceded to Germany in 1871 following the Franco-German War, to the outrage of French citizens. They named their eldest daughter Lorraine, born in 1914, the same year the First World War began. They then named their second child Calixte Lionel Alsace d'Artois. He later went simply by Guy.

When Britain declared war in 1914, Canada, as a dominion, was naturally drawn in. The first contingent of the Canadian Expeditionary Force (CEF) was soon crossing the Atlantic. Some thirty thousand men, mostly English Canadians, were eager to answer the call of the old country. When the volunteer base began to dwindle, the government allowed the creation of Irish and Scottish units in an attempt to renew interest. After pressure (and an offer of funding), Prime Minister Robert Borden promised to create a French Canadian infantry battalion named the Royal Canadien-Français to encourage French Canadian participation. Recruitment specifically for this unit began in Montreal and Quebec City. Posters exhorted French Canadians to sign up: "*Enrolez-vous dans les régiments Canadiens-Français.*" The 22nd Battalion was soon deployed abroad as part of the second division, as the first and only French unit in the CEF. Once in France, the 22nd Battalion fought with zeal, earning a reputation as brave and tough—but rowdy. They distinguished themselves in several harrowing battles on the Western Front: Ypres, Passchendaele, the Somme, and the Battle of Vimy Ridge, where they ruthlessly mopped up pockets of German resistance that survived the Canadian wave of attacks. But all those successes came at a heavy cost: more than eleven hundred who had fought with the battalion would perish in the Great War, many of them interred in place, in the land of their ancestors but far from home. After the war, the battalion was disbanded, but elements of it would become part of a permanent unit called the Royal 22e Régiment. They would come to be informally known in English as the "Van Doos," a play on the French *vingt-deuxième* or "twenty-second."

By the time Guy was baptized on April 15, Vimy Ridge was in Allied hands and news of the victory and the losses was beginning to trickle back home. Canadian troops were busy burying their dead in hastily dug graveyards, sometimes marked only by wooden crosses fashioned by harried regimental carpenters. Etched on those crosses were names like Legault, Rousseau, Roussin, Beauchamp, and Gaudet—Quebecers and other Canadians who had fought with the 22nd Battalion. And sometimes, in the chaos, their names were misspelled, sending their individual stories down the road to being altered forever and forgotten.

The war was finally ended by armistice at the eleventh hour on the eleventh day of the eleventh month of 1918. By the end of that hideous conflict, more than sixty thousand Canadians—nearly one in ten of those who fought under the British standard—had been killed in the carnage, and more than a hundred and seventy thousand wounded, some disabled for life, physically, mentally, and often both. Families were struggling to adjust to life without husbands, fathers, brothers—too many of them just barely out of their teens when they'd gone to war. The dead and the many missing were mourned at home as heroes, never to return, connecting Canada and Canadians to Vimy Ridge, the Somme, Passchendaele, forever. Thousands and thousands of veterans returned with injuries—visible and otherwise—to pick up interrupted lives, with mixed success. The following year, Germany was forced to hand Alsace-Lorraine back to France and the Spanish flu pandemic was well into its deadly campaign around the world, claiming mostly young adult lives, just as the war had done.

Guy and Lorraine d'Artois and their generation of children grew up in a young Canada that was deep in mourning, traumatized by the magnitude of the losses from war and disease and heartbreak.

Still, as the children of a prospering lawyer, Guy and Lorraine led a privileged life for the times. The family lived in a large home and moved about in a chauffeur-driven car. Their life revolved around their father's career and around the church, where Antoinette took the children every Sunday. As it was for countless other francophone families, Christmas was a religious affair at the d'Artois home, and acting in a school nativity play was a rite of passage. One year, in a letter presumably from boarding school, Guy informs his father that he's in the play. "I would like you to be present to see your little Guy," he writes on a sheet of paper adorned with a depiction of a pirate.

"Kisses from your Petit Guy."

In September 1929, at twelve years old, Petit Guy was among the first students to walk the halls of the newly opened Jesuit private boys' school Collège Jean-de-Brébeuf. The stately school in Montreal's Côte-des-Neiges district was named after a French Jesuit missionary who'd lived among the Huron-Wendat people in the seventeenth century and learned their language and culture. Along with a number of Huron people, he was captured in one of a series of raids by the rival Haudenosaunee, then tortured and killed. Nearly three hundred years later, just as the school was starting up, he was canonized as a saint. The school quickly became a prestigious destination for the boys of Quebec's French elite—including future Canadian prime minister Pierre Elliott Trudeau, who attended three years after Guy.

Guy enrolled in classical studies as a boarding student, and while he proved himself a multitalented athlete, his marks weren't always quite as impressive. In the 1931–32 year he failed the "Syntax A" level with a mark of 294 out of 900. The following year he performed far better, especially so in English and Latin. He also displayed physical agility and strength. He learned to fence and ski, played lacrosse, and was a good skater and hockey player. It was likely in his days at the college that he developed an interest in photography—later setting up a darkroom at home—and possibly where he learned to play chess, a pursuit he would cherish into old age. He also spent a great deal of time reading. Despite the mostly serious face he put on for the many school pictures, he was known to be a good practical joker. Otherwise, he spent much of his time staring out the windows, watching planes take off and land from the nearby airport.

But then the unexpected happened: just over a decade after the Great War ended, the Great Depression arrived, and it soon caught up with the d'Artois home. Guy's father lost everything. The situation steadily worsened until, at fifteen, Guy withdrew from Brébeuf.

In 1933 he switched to the Séminaire Saint-Charles-Borromée in Sherbrooke, another private school but closer to home, where in his first few months he performed terribly. While still being noted for good conduct in an October report card, of the thirty-one students in "Syntax B," Guy came dead last.

In an attempt to improve their fortunes, the family relocated to Montreal, where Valmore tried to re-establish a legal practice, but clients were few. Antoinette was forced to take in lodgers at their rented home in the city's Plateau area. Though still young, Guy was terribly aware. "I knew the hard times, the sorrow—it affected me greatly," he once said. "So I started to ask myself: 'and what about tomorrow?'"

He began to look beyond school to prepare himself for the working world. He took a night course in repairing aviation engines. Then, in 1934, at the age of seventeen, Guy joined the militia through the Université de Montréal.

Like many young men his age, Guy was also on a serious march for work at a time when work was scarce. His dogged search impressed his former *préfet des études* from Brébeuf, who in 1937 agreed to write him a letter of recommendation. "He's a bright, hardworking, ambitious young man," wrote J. Paré, who noted that Guy was able to handle himself in English as well as French. He praised "the courage and tenacity he has displayed while looking for an occupation during this time of high unemployment among our young people."

Guy did luck out, working at one point in construction, lending a hand in the building of a monastery in Saint-Eustache, where he was noted as "a good worker, very energetic, serious." He then worked as a researcher, and also as an assistant to a chemist in a lab at the École des hautes études commerciales at the Université de Montréal for sixty dollars a month. All the while, he participated in the Corps-école d'officiers canadiens (Canadian Officers' Training Corps) attached to the university. It was there that he demonstrated ease in the military world and showed an aptitude for leadership, starting out as a cadet and then quickly rising through several ranks all the way to company Sergeant Major.

The biggest test of Guy's young life, however, would come on June 29, 1938, when his father suddenly passed away at age fifty-six. The cause was cholecystitis, a gallbladder affliction likely brought on by gallstones. Guy, only twenty-one, had the disagreeable task of picking up his father's body and transporting it on a train back to Sherbrooke, where he was buried. It was likely Guy's first experience with premature, unexpected death, but it would certainly not be his last.

That same year, the country was abuzz with talk of another war in Europe. Many Canadians, especially in Quebec, were wary, especially given that the government had imposed conscription later in the First World War. In an attempt to allay those concerns, Prime Minister

William Lyon Mackenzie King promised in a speech to the House of Commons in March that if the country went to war again, conscription would be completely off the table. It was a strategy that, when the time came for a vote, had mollified apprehensions enough (for the time being) to smooth the way for a decision in favour of war.

After Britain's declaration on September 3, 1939, in a show of independence, the Canadian Parliament was brought back early to debate the country's participation. Both Parliament and the Senate approved Canada's own declaration of war on September 9. It became official with royal assent the following day, a full seven days after Britain's.

Thousands of volunteers signed up to go abroad, among them Guy. He did it despite its being optional, and despite being Antoinette's only son and she, as a widow, his dependant—to the tune of fifty dollars a month.

But Guy was determined, and like thousands of other Canadians, he voluntarily lurched across the ocean, leaving life as he knew it behind.

PART II:

OFF TO WAR

3

LEAVING HOME

Guy • *Atlantic Ocean, January 1940*

Nearly five months into the world war, on the thirtieth day of the New Year, Guy was finally on his way to Europe. On that day, four luxury passenger ships pressed into war duty quietly slid out of Halifax's Pier 21 and into the vast darkness, carrying 7,350 Canadian soldiers headed to war. It was an agonizingly slow departure by any measure, and certainly by the measure of an eager young man impatient for his overseas adventure to begin.

Men had been gathering near the waterfront for days, many of them sleeping in the makeshift barracks at Pier 21. Others had been circling for weeks in the chaos of Halifax, that familiar wartime departure lounge, some with their wives and children clinging on, jostling with thousands of other servicemen for rental apartments, restaurant seats, even theatre tickets, all of it teeing up long, messy farewells drenched in tears.

It is a colossal undertaking to coordinate the movement of that many men, even if they are military men. On the appointed day, against the cacophony of shouts meting out orders and directions, the men, weighed down by whatever kit was available, began to shuffle on board, quiet with apprehension. At length, the slow-motion procession would fill the four ships. With the soldiers aboard, the *Empress of Britain*, the *Aquitania*, the *Monarch of Bermuda*, and the *Empress of Australia*, joined by the Polish ship SS *Batory*, became Canadian Troop Convoy No. 3—a flotilla of stories and hopes and tragedies-yet-to-come, of young soldiers both scared and spoiling for a fight. It was accompanied by a medical brigade complete with field hospital and casualty clearing station, its own men both reluctant and ready to pick up the pieces.

The men of No. 1 Convalescent Depot had first started gathering on January 26 at Montreal's Grand Union Hotel on Notre-Dame Street West. They held morning parade as the sun rose and then marched to Bonaventure Station to board the train leaving for Halifax at nine a.m.

The journey widened the aperture on Guy's view of the country and gave him a ground-level glimpse of Eastern Canada at its winter bleakest. They travelled alongside the fabled St. Lawrence River to Quebec City, then through Moncton, Amherst, and Truro before finally landing at Pier 21, the gateway to Canada for many an immigrant, including the ancestors of numerous Canadians of French, Scottish, and English origin who were now "returning" in uniform to the part of the world from which their families hailed. In signing up, they were all acquiring an instant new family, as well as friends—and purpose.

Immediately upon arrival in Halifax, at four the following afternoon, Guy and his fellow soldiers were directed to board the *Empress of Australia*. From then on, leaving the ship was forbidden. By the time the convoy started its journey, Guy had been on board the docked ship for three mind-numbing days. The next time his feet touched solid ground would be thirteen days later, on the other side of the ocean.

When the war started back in the fall, Guy had hoped to become a pilot with the Royal Canadian Air Force. Even the regular army would have been a satisfactory, if distant, second choice. The infantry rejected him, though, apparently because of a childhood bout of mastoiditis, an infection behind the ear that had necessitated surgery in his late teens. But Guy was the sort of young man who wanted a place at the table—and if there was no place, Guy was the sort of young man who would still find a way.

In his search for a way, Guy discovered that his interest and experience in physical fitness could be his passport. He would go over not as a pilot, nor as an infantryman, but as a member of the newly formed No. 1 Convalescent Depot, a unit put together to provide long-term rehabilitation and therapy support to injured Canadian troops abroad. On January 20, 1940, he signed up as a private, and on the very same day he was promoted to acting sergeant. Ten days later he was on board the *Empress of Australia*, making for Europe.

Guy's search would eventually earn him the unlikely wartime position of physical training instructor.

In crossing the ocean there was always the risk that, even before they arrived in the theatre of war, those young men could become its casualties. By January the Battle of the Atlantic was in full swing, with German U-boats and aircraft stalking the ocean waters to defy a French-British naval blockade. Just a few days before Guy left, the

German submarine *U-22* torpedoed and sank the British destroyer HMS *Exmouth*, leaving not a single survivor.

And so, to give ships the best chance at arriving safely, convoys to and from North America accompanied by warships became the norm. The convoys were often escorted out of Canadian waters by Canadian destroyers and then handed off to British ones at the western edges of the danger zone threatened by submarines. Troop Convoy No. 3 was escorted by three battle cruisers and seven destroyers that the men of the convalescent hospital judged as looking "very capable." En route, security was paramount, and the men were briefed on the dos and don'ts of how to avoid drawing enemy fire.

On the second day of travel, a terse message came through from the commander of the naval escort:

> LIGHTING MATCHES AND SMOKING ON THE UPPER DECK AT NIGHT IS MOST DANGEROUS, AS LIGHTS CAN BE SEEN, FROM A GREAT DISTANCE. THIS MUST CEASE FORTHWITH.

All departures and arrivals of convoys were "closely guarded secrets." But there were no guarantees on the high seas. Added to the U-boat menace were the ordinary risks inherent to such a crossing. As T.C. No. 3 left harbour all was calm, but on their fifth day out the heavy February Atlantic conjured up relentlessly high waves that tossed the ship about, afflicting dozens of the men with seasickness and threatening a far worse outcome. On the seventh day the convoy was joined by a British navy escort. On the eighth the sea finally calmed and the soldiers began preparing to disembark.

On the ninth they lost their escort for more than seven hours, facing the ocean's perils, including U-boats, alone.

They remained so until they were joined by three British destroyers that brought them into port. The ships finally swept into the busy Clyde Canal at the doorstep to Glasgow and dropped anchor just after noon.

War had not yet arrived on British soil. There had been no aerial bombardment and no immediate threat of ground invasion. The nation had been on a war footing for five months—complete with blackouts and rationing, and with round-the-clock unease starting long before that. It was tedious and exhausting bracing for a war slow in coming, but the arrival of the third and largest contingent of Canadians seemed to help lift the mood.

Crowds of people gathered at the quayside. Men of the Royal Navy lined up at the rails of their own docked ships and cheered as the Canadian ones pulled up. An official welcoming party also appeared to meet them: Major-General Andrew G.L. McNaughton, General Officer Commanding of the 1st Canadian Infantry Division in the U.K. and a trained physicist and engineer, was there, along with the British undersecretary of state for the dominions under Prime Minister Chamberlain. McNaughton marched up to the deck of the *Empress* to welcome the men who'd lined up en masse to salute him. As the soldiers began to disembark, a "wee girl" handed out chocolates, a notable gesture of gratitude—and generosity—given that the troops were arriving at a time of strict rationing.

The Canadians "sang themselves hoarse" as they arrived, echoing across the harbour and making headlines throughout the country.

"Canada is calling again, sending out its welcome news that another big contingent of the Dominion's overseas army has arrived in this country," said the February 9th *Daily Record and Mail.* The *Daily Mirror*'s front page carried a photo of disembarking Canadian troops in uniform, one of them predictably carrying "a pair of ice skates over his shoulder," with no explanation of precisely where or how he planned to use them. Another report optimistically predicted that the new troops would deploy to France "as soon as the British High Command considers the time suitable."

It took two days for everyone to disembark. When Guy finally set foot on solid ground, he was one eager young man among a sea of them, many wearing their First World War ribbons, relieved to have survived the deadly obstacle course that was the Atlantic Ocean and ready for the next.

Worn out from the roiling waters, the men filed onto trains destined for Aldershot, far to the south, where most Canadian troops were based. Four days later, after they had taken their posts at the makeshift convalescent hospital there, Guy was among the first group to finally be given leave to recover from the exhausting journey. For the first time, he laid eyes on London. It was St. Valentine's Day, 1940.

After the excitement of arrival and settling into a new place, life for Canadian troops in and around Aldershot became one interminable wait, punctuated by flurries of intense activity—training, exercises, sports, more training—that were inevitably followed by more waiting. But as life for Canadian soldiers in England was slowing to a crawl, in the rest of the world life seemed to be speeding ahead.

The war itself was evolving fast. By mid-March, the Winter War that had erupted following the Soviet invasion of Finland was over. In April the Nazis invaded Denmark. On the same day Denmark surrendered, German forces then invaded Norway, and a longer fight there began. Meanwhile, in France, the British Expeditionary Force was bracing for a battle. And yet, for the most part, the Canadian Army overseas was forced to remain in place. The frustration and boredom started to show.

Locals in the Aldershot area submitted "numerous" complaints about the "unseemly conduct" of some Canadian soldiers. Growing numbers of them had been "seen in an intoxicated state in the public streets" in towns nearby. There were also complaints of trespassing on private property. In his daily orders, the depot's commanding officer, Lieutenant-Colonel A.P. Plante, advised his officers to mete out the severest punishment for the worst offenders, who were ruining it for the rest.

Guy seemed to steer clear of such trouble. By April 20, after ninety days of holding the acting rank, Guy was confirmed as sergeant. Still, like thousands of Canadian troops who'd come to see action, he remained grounded by an unexpectedly long wait.

The events of May 10, 1940, however, punched through the monotony.

Neville Chamberlain resigned, and Winston Churchill suddenly became Britain's new wartime prime minister. An even more momentous development occurred the same day, when German forces began a new, sweeping offensive: invading Belgium, Luxembourg, and the Netherlands. In short order, German forces began to pour from Belgium through the border into France. A clash with Allied forces seemed inevitable.

At Bordon, Hampshire, Guy's new home, rumours cascaded through the ranks about possible troop movements. All leave was cancelled. The Convalescent Depot's Lieutenant-Colonel Plante rushed up to London for meetings.

"The German Army struck at Holland and Belgium. This should cause some action. Our troops are very fed up with the inactivity of barrack-room life," Captain D.L. Darey, writing in the unit's war diary, noted succinctly.

But the Canadians remained in their barracks. The only excitement for the No. 1 Convalescent Depot was an impending move to a rented property on the shores of the English Channel near Brixham in Devon. It was a welcome diversion.

There were many, many worse places than Dolphin Holiday Camp for a Canadian to live out the wait for action. Until recently it had been a popular seaside resort, a collection of neatly arranged wooden huts built right on the water, less than a kilometre from Brixham—a fishing town popular with tourists and home to a horseshoe-shaped harbour. Within a healing view of the sea and a short distance from Devon's lavishly green fields and rolling hills, the camp offered an ideal location for recuperation. In those early days, the resort was mostly out of harm's way and had little more than a few sandbags and a single row of barbed wire protecting the coastline. Despite sitting right across the Channel from mainland Europe, Dolphin Camp seemed as far away from the frontlines as one could get.

"This is a wonderful camp, much too good for military troops," wrote Captain Darey as they arrived.

Yet even with that breath-taking view, the living was austere. Each of the romantic little white chalets intended for lovebirds now accommodated two Canadian soldiers and their kit. On the cold days the huts were uncommonly chilly, so the men were furnished with oil stoves. In warmer temperatures, the new tenants hung their laundry on a drying line out front that, from afar, looked like bunting.

There was enough food around, but luxury items like chocolate, cigarettes, and gum came only occasionally in shipments of "comfort" from the Canadian Red Cross. Or, for the lucky, in lovingly assembled packages mailed by family back home. Antoinette once sent Guy chocolate, cigarettes, a *Life* magazine. He sent her a picture of himself and another sergeant in uniform smiling broadly outdoors.

"I remain in good spirits and good health," Guy wrote his mother on a postcard that fall. "I wish you the same. Nothing new here. Did you hear me on a radio programme broadcast from England to Canada? . . . I said my name and said hello to you. It was about a month ago. Goodbye. Do write to me."

Although Canadian soldiers in Britain hadn't yet engaged in combat, the hospital experienced a steady influx of patients that spring—mostly victims of road accidents and training mishaps. Since the unit to which Guy belonged had been assembled in Montreal, many of the officers were francophone, including the commanding officer, Lieutenant-Colonel Plante. Their camp would have had a familiar feel from the start, easing Guy's separation from home. And as noted in Plante's daily orders, Guy was on a regular rotation: one week on guard duty, another on orderly duty.

Sergeant d'Artois's time was otherwise taken up by a heavy training schedule. After a course qualifying him as an instructor in physical and recreational therapy, the colonel in charge praised Guy for showing "energy and keenness throughout the course." Guy had done "remarkably well," even if he was "handicapped" by imperfect English. "Is a good leader," the colonel concluded. "Keen, intelligent, and very popular," wrote another one of his superiors. And on and on the training went.

Even as the complicated move to Dolphin Camp was underway, however, Guy and his fellow Canadians were seized by news from the front. At that moment, the German offensive had forced the British Expeditionary Force, as well as thousands of French soldiers, to retreat, pushing them to the beaches of Dunkirk, where they would likely be eviscerated if they remained. Evacuation was the only option. Churchill demanded and oversaw a huge rescue operation that brought more than three hundred thousand Allied soldiers across the English Channel, using British and Canadian and other Allied navy vessels, as well as civilian ones. Once complete, Churchill hailed it as a "miracle of deliverance." Yet he warned against giving it "the attributes of a victory," acknowledging that "Wars are not won by evacuations."

Germany's steady gains, meanwhile, culminated with thousands of its troops marching into Paris on June 14, 1940. France officially surrendered and became two zones. Maréchal Philippe Pétain would lead a collaborationist government from the "unoccupied zone." In the rest of France, a humiliating life under German occupation began.

With no foothold left on the mainland, Britain no longer had the means to fight German forces on the ground there. Only the angry grey waters of the Channel separated Hitler's army from Britain, which was now directly under threat of invasion. Still, Churchill insisted, there would be no British capitulation.

"We shall fight on the beaches, we shall fight on the landing grounds, we shall fight in the fields and in the streets, we shall fight in the hills; we shall never surrender," a fiery Churchill intoned after Dunkirk.

Shortly thereafter, fighting began in the only theatre possible for British forces under the circumstances—in the skies.

Among the Canadians, unless you were a pilot or aboard a ship, you were still not going anywhere. At Dolphin Camp, the only evidence of war was the ominous growing number of enemy aircraft flying overhead and the arrival of injured airmen, who came to the facility to recuperate.

When Guy did finally come face to face with the conflict, it was on later visits to London, where he experienced life under German bombardment. He was awed by the magnitude of the explosions, describing them as "enormous," like nothing he'd ever seen before. He was startled by the damage left behind, and by the palpable fear among ordinary citizens for whom air raid sirens and dashing to shelters were a daily reality. "You faced certain death if you didn't reach one of the shelters," he once explained. "Even then, we found so many of those makeshift shelters totally leveled, and those who sought safety there squashed like flies!"

In time it became the norm for German aircraft to pass over Dolphin Camp on their way to targets farther inland, meaning that alerts would sound at all hours, disrupting routines and jangling nerves day and night there, too. One day, at nine-fifteen a.m., right in the middle of morning parade, Dolphin Camp finally drew enemy fire. First, two German aircraft dropped bombs on the nearby town of Brixham, killing seven people and causing "considerable" damage. Then, on their way back, their machine guns suddenly strafed sleepy Dolphin Camp itself. Men ran in all directions as they scrambled for cover. No one was injured, but it was the closest brush with the conflict they'd yet experienced. A few days later, a visitor from Canadian military headquarters in London expressed concern that the camp might well be serving "as a guide for enemy aircraft." He recommended that the white chalets be camouflaged with green paint, and that the soldiers be trained on guns that would protect the camp.

The options for striking back were limited, and Dolphin Camp's relaxed atmosphere had changed for good.

Following the invasion of France and the withdrawal from Dunkirk, Britain's options for a concerted response were also severely curtailed.

In France, however, with many ordinary citizens refusing to accept German occupation, a quiet, spontaneous resistance movement began to stir. As one French resistance organizer would later write, the "spirit which inspired the resistance was there, in the French people, even at the moment of defeat and humiliation." Many French soldiers who landed in Britain after Dunkirk also began to agitate and organize resistance, either from London or from back in France.

Behind the scenes, Britain itself began to build a secret army to support Europe's nascent resistance forces. It was named the Special Operations Executive. And the SOE's first order of business was finding young, fit recruits willing to go to a new and invisible front.

4

FINDING HOME

Sonia • *London, May 1941*

On her seventeenth birthday, Sonia set off with her father on a train bound for London, intending to mark the occasion by enlisting in the armed forces. Given the recent news out of the city, she was well aware of the risks in taking such a journey. But by then Sonia was no stranger to air raid sirens and life under bombardment. Besides, she was eager to "do war work" and had been counting the days until the moment she was old enough to sign up, to do her duty.

Just a few days before Sonia arrived, London had lived through one of those Saturday nights that Londoners would talk about for decades. Apart from the light of a near full moon, the city was enveloped in darkness, under curfew and with a blackout order in effect until 5:27 the next morning. German raids that night were particularly ferocious, the airborne terror cloaking the metropolis with shadows and flames. Since the beginning of the Blitz in the fall of 1940 the German Luftwaffe had bombarded London countless times—the Palace of Westminster alone had sustained more than a dozen attacks—but on that Saturday night through to the early hours of Sunday "a constant procession" of some five hundred bombers "roared across a moonlit sky," unleashing a fury of fires that would consume seven hundred acres in the capital and take the lives of at least fourteen hundred people.

It was, said *The Daily Herald*, "the most wanton raid of the war."

It was also in retaliation to the Royal Air Force attacks that two days before had brought down ten German aircraft and, more injuriously, carried out the most sustained bombing campaign yet over German cities—in Hamburg, in Bremen, and, notably, striking targets in the heart of Berlin. The tit-for-tat raids claimed the lives of scores of civilians and disrupted many others in both countries.

But unbeknownst to the British civilians below, and possibly even to the German pilots above, the night of May 10 would mark the last major Blitz attack on London.

On the first anniversary of Churchill's becoming prime minister, six high-explosive bombs landed on the Houses of Parliament that night. The chamber itself—the seat of the country's power—was on fire, nursing a pile of smoking debris. Fire also threatened Westminster Hall, the oldest building in the palace complex, ravaging its roof of high arches held up by beams of oak. Amid the devastation, an unexploded bomb went through the floor of the House of Lords while others damaged the precious British Museum. Even Big Ben suffered a direct hit, shattering its glass and starting yet another blaze—though its timekeeping mechanism remained intact. The seat of government, however, was no longer usable. From May 13 onward lawmakers would sit at the Church House Annex, next to the grand Westminster Abbey—which had also been attacked that night, leaving it "open to the sky," the roof "crashed on the spot where, for more than 900 years, Britain's Kings and Queens have been crowned."

London was reeling, dented and, in places, irretrievably broken. The rubble was so plentiful that it rivalled the city's spring blooms. The lively, bustling city dotted with overflowing corner pubs, streams of tourists, and overexcited, lavishly dressed theatregoers sauntering by—all of it had vanished. People didn't walk through the city now so much as scurry along with a wary eye to the sky before disappearing into a whole other city that now thrived underground. Thousands retreated to the tube stations at night, huddling fully clothed under blankets on the platforms in long rows together, their feet pointed to the tracks—some even slumbering between the rails below. This was still the London of the stiff upper lip. But it was also a London in mourning, a greyer-than-usual London pinned down by an unrelenting storm of war.

This was the London that greeted Sonia as she arrived with her father in the wounded city to enlist.

She was, of course, constrained by the gender norms of the time, which prohibited combat roles for women. Their options for serving in the armed forces were still limited to the three auxiliary services that supported the air force, the navy, and the army: the Women's Auxiliary Air Force (WAAF), the Women's Royal Naval Service (WRNS), and the Auxiliary Territorial Service (ATS). Sonia was at a loss about which service to join.

But she'd come to London with a plan for how to decide. She made her way to a branch of Moss Brothers Clothiers. At a time of widespread shortages and rationing, even contemplating a purchase at a high-street clothing store was a luxury most people could not afford. But Sonia was shopping for something else altogether: Moss Brothers had opened several locations during the war to serve the armed forces, and there she would try on each of the uniforms available for women—and judge for herself which one suited her best.

The khaki ATS uniform didn't appeal to Sonia much. Then she tried on the WRNS uniform, with its double-breasted navy jacket and gold buttons. As did many women at the time, she liked it immediately, but she was under the impression it wasn't easy to join without a family connection to the navy. Next came the WAAF uniform: first buttoning up the light blue shirt, finishing it with a tie, then pulling on the form-fitting jacket, cinching it by the wide belt at the waist. It looked as though it was made for her. Sonia thought it flattering, and so, then and there, she made the decision to join the WAAF—based not on her father's history in the Air Force, but, by her own admission, largely on the look of the uniform. In the dearth of accessible information on how best to contribute to the war effort, she wasn't the only British woman to decide in exactly this way.

Sonia then stood in the lineup at the recruitment office and contemplated the motley crew of women who'd made the same decision. Behind her, she discovered to her amusement, was Sarah Churchill, the prime minister's daughter and celebrated stage actor. In front of her was a woman she described as a "Piccadilly commando," a prostitute who walked the streets of Soho and Piccadilly. In a society obsessed with class, war had become an equalizer—your life was as dispensable as everyone else's. Sonia signed the forms, underwent a physical exam, and then made her way to the train station to head home for the six-month wait for the call. On the journey back, Leslie Butt beamed upon learning his daughter's decision to apparently follow in his footsteps. "Good show, old girl," he said. "I knew you'd come through."

Sonia, by then, had settled in at her father's place, safe and wanted perhaps for the first time in her life. It was a hard-won state of affairs.

Shortly after she returned from France, the air raids had become so frequent that she and her sister Bunny were evacuated to their grandfather's home in Salisbury, where she was still nominally her mother's responsibility. But one day her father, Leslie, and his new wife, Mina, came to visit and told Sonia that they wanted her to live with them in southern England—if that was what she wanted. Though she enjoyed living with her grandfather, she agreed, wanting to escape her mother's orbit for good.

Leslie launched a classic custody battle. Sonia was nervous before the hearing, knowing that her mother would fight it tooth and nail and might just succeed. Mina tried to assuage her fears, promising her that it would all turn out in her favour. She had an ace up her sleeve: if it became necessary, she told Sonia, she would show the judge the newspaper articles about her mother's scandalous imprisonment in France after five-year-old Sonia was found to be malnourished and neglected. Surely that would be enough to persuade the judge that Thelma was unfit to care for her teenage daughter.

Ultimately, none of that was necessary. The judge simply asked Sonia directly where she wanted to live. She answered that she'd prefer to stay with her father and stepmother. Her mother shot her a look of daggers across the courtroom. It was a courageous decision, given her mother's threats: "No matter how far away you go, you'll never be able to go far enough to get away from me. I'll always come and hurt you and haunt you," Sonia recalled her once saying. Now, in choosing to leave her domineering mother behind—something for which she'd long wished—Sonia was finally charting her own path.

Even at sixteen, she knew enough to make decisions about her own education. She chose to forgo the classic British boarding school education, partly because she felt that her international upbringing, her bilingual and bicultural experience, made her different.

She would never fit in with the other British girls. She also knew deep down it was a challenge for her to focus. Instead she would study at the Wiltshire School of Domestic Science, enrolling in, among other things, a "dairy course," which taught her such skills as the making of butter and cheese. She also took a course in home nursing with the British Red Cross Society, and then she volunteered until it was her turn to put on a uniform.

So much had changed since Sonia had crossed the English Channel alone nearly two years earlier.

Derek had enlisted and, in July of that year, 1941, had already left to serve in India. Leslie was back in uniform and at the Air Ministry, having begun as acting squadron leader, on the day Britain declared war, then moving up to acting wing commander. The country was awash in uniforms; everywhere you turned there were people—and mannequins, and movie stars, and toys—in some kind of military garb. There was no escaping the war. If you didn't wear it, you lived in its shadow, and it dictated how you lived, what you ate, what you couldn't eat, where you could go, and even whom you might fall in love with or marry.

The country swelled with new residents. Thousands of refugees came from all over Europe, but especially France, many of whom were Jewish, escaping the ominous and increasingly glaring evidence that they were in the crosshairs of the Nazi regime. There were also tens of thousands of Commonwealth soldiers in uniform, including Canadian, New Zealand, and Australian ones, who made themselves at home as they waited to wage war on behalf of the British Crown. Add to all that the French military men who'd been evacuated from

Dunkirk or had fled Vichy France, some of whom opted to try liberating their country from the relative safety of London. Among them was Charles de Gaulle, a recently promoted French general who'd left France immediately after German troops marched into Paris. Upon the French government's surrender, the British recognized de Gaulle as leader of the Free French, the part of the French nation that refused to capitulate to German occupation and vowed to overthrow it. He made his first address to the French people, from a BBC studio in London, on June 18, 1940.

"Speaking in full knowledge of the facts, I ask you to believe me when I say that the cause of France is not lost. The very factors that brought about our defeat may one day lead us to victory."

"Whatever happens," he went on to say, "the flame of French resistance must not and shall not be extinguished."

He gave two more speeches that week, both of which amounted to a call on French citizens—in uniform or not—to strive for the liberation of their country. Thousands and thousands of people heard the call and acted, just as de Gaulle had hoped.

It was also just as the British had hoped.

5

A CHANGE OF DIRECTION

Sonia • *London, November 1941*

It was exactly six months after her seventeenth birthday when Sonia was finally called up and ordered to report to basic training at the seaside town of Morecambe in Lancashire, in the northwest of England. A steady procession of young women, many of them, like Sonia, still technically teenagers, had already been making the journey to the newly opened training centre at Morecambe, answering the WAAF exhortation to "take the road to victory." Some of them had never taken any road to anywhere too far from home, never mind a train journey clear across to the north. But then Britain had never been so far down this road either; it had never signed up so many women into service. The war machine required all hands on deck. For the young women whose lives were upended by the compulsion to serve, it was a transformative and exciting time.

Even before arriving at the leading edge of the home front, Sonia had been undergoing transformational change. Out from under her mother's shadow, she was blossoming into a beautiful and adventurous young woman, one who felt a strong urge to pitch in. As she waited for the call she'd joined the Land Army, working on a farm. Later, she volunteered, behind her father's back, to spray-paint army trucks and serve food to recovering pilots. Now she was excited by the opportunity to finally do "real" war work.

But for many young women—as well as many young men—those first days in a military setting were a disorienting, maybe even terrifying experience, and some of them coped badly. Sonia remembered at least two women among her cohort attempting suicide, and a third who was struggling with addiction. Few of the new recruits were old enough to remember living at war, and fewer still would have ever worn a uniform or slept away from home. Now, though, in the grip of an exceptionally cold winter, Sonia and a whole army of newly recruited WAAF women sporting that flattering fitted uniform were caught up in a whirlwind of medical checks, inoculations, lectures, and drills. To say that it was all an eye-opening experience for Sonia would be underplaying the culture shock. And yet she embraced her new environment. She loved the thrill of doing something worthy. She loved the marching, the uniform, the obstacle courses—all of it.

Near the very end of basic training, just as Sonia prepared to leave for her first posting, the war swerved in a dangerous new direction.

On Sunday, December 7, 1941, Japan mounted a surprise attack on American military installations at Pearl Harbor in Hawaii. The death toll was in the hundreds and rising. More than a hundred and eighty aircraft were destroyed, nearly twenty naval vessels wrecked or badly damaged. The number of servicemen killed was steadily rising. The world collectively held its breath.

It was still dinnertime in Britain when the news broke. Churchill happened to be dining with the American ambassador, Gil Winant, and Averell Harriman, President Franklin D. Roosevelt's special envoy to Europe. Like so many throughout the country, the three men leaned toward the radio. Churchill called Roosevelt, who said, "We are all in the same boat now."

Word spread quickly through ordinary households as well as through the ranks of women and men in uniform all over the country. These events brought a new uncertainty, a heightened unpredictability to the war. It was no doubt a terrifying escalation, but it was one in which Churchill saw opportunity.

Churchill had long understood that Britain could not win the war against Germany without the United States, which had hitherto remained at least publicly neutral. Now that American help was all but assured, in Churchill's mind, so was victory. At the end of that night, he would later write, "I went to bed and slept the sleep of the saved and thankful."

Less than twenty-four hours later Roosevelt addressed a joint session of the Senate and House of Representatives, proclaiming December 7 a "date which will live in infamy" and asking Congress to declare a state of war with Japan. In the days that followed, Germany in turn declared war on the United States, which, inevitably, declared war against Germany and Italy, too. The course of the war had patently changed. The conflict was now truly global.

That same year also saw Nazi Germany entrench its systematic campaign for the mass murder of Jews. By then, the Nazi regime had set up concentration camps in Germany and then Poland early in the war, and Jews were regularly being deported and killed en masse. In 1941, the first permanent extermination camps were also established. In early December, the day after the Pearl Harbor attack, the killing operation began at Chelmno, northwest of Warsaw in Poland, the first fixed Nazi camp dedicated to mass murder of Jews. Others followed, and in the war years to come, the Nazi regime would round up and murder millions of Jews in an unprecedented campaign of horror. The war had not only become global, it had also become a genocide-in-progress, inflicting incalculable damage on—and entirely eliminating—whole families and communities, damage that would have terrible consequences for generations to come.

In Britain, it had been a long, trying year. London was still in mourning, still jittery and wounded from the relentless air raids. By that December German bombardment of major British cities had largely ceased and life had improved dramatically since the previous year, when Christmas was celebrated mostly underground. Still, the British people were hardly in a festive mood. But with the Americans joining the effort against Axis powers, that Christmas brought a whiff of hope that the war could turn in their favour.

Sonia too had officially become part of the Allied effort. After basic training she was posted to RAF Cosford, near Birmingham, to serve at the lowest rank, as an aircraftwoman, 2nd class. It was a position well within the accepted roles for women, who were now acting as stand-ins for the men going off to do the hard work on the frontlines. She was mostly tasked with administrative work, "filling in forms, filing, mailing, recruiting and signing people up." There was much more excitement to be had spending time with some of the Free French soldiers based nearby.

Also on the definite upside, Sonia met Paddy, whose real name was Maureen O'Sullivan, a tall, Dublin-born woman about six years her senior, a former nurse who'd joined the WAAF a few months earlier. Paddy had lost her mother when she was only a toddler, and at the age of seven she was sent alone to live with an aunt in Belgium. That afforded her the opportunity to become fluent in French, and to Sonia's delight, the two of them would often speak it to each other. They bonded over their experiences abroad. And though their circumstances were different, the two shared a history of early self-reliance and cross-border ease as well as the yawning absence of a loving mother during their formative years.

Sonia and Paddy became inseparable, both at work and at play. Together they dabbled in the wartime social scene, frequenting events and dances put on for the entertainment of bored soldiers. Giving in to their youthful impulses, they would sometimes take the short train ride to Wolverhampton to party. After changing into civilian clothes in the train's bathroom—evading the sergeants who might corral them—they would dance the night away, then rush to return before their eleven o'clock curfew. They didn't always make it. As punishment, especially when they missed the last train back and completely blew curfew, they'd be ordered to peel mountains of potatoes, wash floors, or worst of all, march with heavy kit up and down the parade square, rain or shine. This Sonia did not appreciate. She wanted to do her part, but she also wanted to have as much unfettered fun as life during wartime would allow.

Sonia took great care with her attire and hair and overall looks. The camera adored her and the impeccable way in which she dressed. There she was in a plaid jacket over pinstriped, cuffed, rather masculine trousers, hands in pockets and in mid-stride in well-shined shoes. There she was again, smiling and windswept, a scarf tightly wrapped around her head and tied at her neck. There she was once more, smiling broadly, wrinkling her nose in the way she reliably did when something or someone made her genuinely smile.

Men also adored Sonia. Those who knew her and her father would look her up when they landed at Cosford. There was also no shortage of eligible young men around, and given that she was at an Air Force station, they were often pilots—the highly desired heroes of the moment. One pilot who pursued her, Sonia recalled, was named

Michael Todd; he'd survived after being shot down. She thought him a hero and felt sorry for him. She danced with him on a few occasions. Their romance became serious, and then one day Michael presented her with a ring. They even met each other's parents and discussed marriage arrangements. Mina, Leslie's wife, liked him a lot. And yet Sonia was as unsure about him as she was about the role she'd been assigned in the war effort thus far.

The WAAF uniform might have suited her slender five-foot-six frame, but Sonia realized that the job itself, the tedious clerical work, was ill-fitting and far from what she'd imagined. Paddy was marginally better off when she was promoted to section officer. Sonia herself would be promoted to leading aircraftwoman, but she had no interest in becoming a commissioned officer—she didn't want the responsibility. As the two young women entered their second year in the WAAF, it began to increasingly take on the feel of a dead end.

By the summer of 1943, they'd had enough. Despite all the initial excitement, Sonia had to admit to herself that she was "bored and bored and bored." Now she and Paddy put their heads together to seek out more interesting war work. Could they ask for a transfer? Could they get closer to London, and perhaps act as interpreters for the Free French there?

It occurred to Sonia that her father might pull some strings at the Air Ministry, so she took a forty-eight-hour pass and visited Leslie with a request. "I'm asking for two of us," she said before giving him Paddy's name and coordinates. Leslie promised he would look into it.

Two weeks later Paddy received a request to report to London for a conversation about possible new employment. She was instructed not to discuss the details with anyone, and that included Sonia—hard as that might be. Sonia was immensely frustrated. She called her father again: Why had she been left behind?

Eventually Sonia too received a call, asking her to report to an address in London's Marylebone district. There she was interviewed by an American officer who spoke terrible French—and she too was instructed to keep the details to herself. Leslie quizzed her afterward on some specifics that betrayed he had some idea of what she was getting into.

Only years later would Sonia learn that Leslie was aware of an organization in the Ministry of Economic Warfare that could use French-speaking British women. His exact link with the Special Operations Executive is a mystery, but he was already helping to recruit on their behalf. "He had a direct connection with SOE, and I didn't know anything about this," Sonia would recount. "And naturally, he was hesitant to put his own daughter's name forward."

Nonetheless, Sonia was called in for further interviews that culminated in a life-altering conversation with one Maurice Buckmaster, a man who for two long years had been quietly steering the French Section of the SOE.

March 1941

In a bare fifth-floor office in the heart of London, Major Maurice Buckmaster sat at his desk making a detailed list of every snippet of information he could remember about the factories he'd visited while he lived in France. It was a first attempt at fulfilling a vague job description in what his new commanding officer described as a "highly embryonic" war effort for which he'd just been recruited. Slowly he managed to construct a kind of annotated map of France's industrial landscape: which factories were likely to be commandeered by the Germans to produce war materiel, which had owners who were likely to cooperate with the British. As he listened to German planes picking off targets in London, he was assembling a list of possible targets in France.

At thirty-nine, and as a non-professional soldier, Buckmaster had lived a whole other life before the war. Eton-educated, he'd spent years in France—first as a private tutor to a young boy, then as a reporter, then a banker, then an executive with the French branch of the Ford Motor Company. A tall, fit man with a penetrating blue-eyed gaze, he had just walked away from a job as an intelligence officer in favour of a position that, in theory at least, would better draw upon his knowledge of France and his fluency in the language. Yet everything about the office at 64 Baker Street—the lack of staff and guidance, the fact that he doubled as an off-hours security guard—spoke to him of an organization that had yet to find its footing.

With German occupation a suffocating reality, resistance in France had spontaneously emerged using whatever means were available, further galvanized in the wake of de Gaulle's call to action. But they lacked organization, weapons, money. After the humiliating Dunkirk retreat, British leadership became persuaded that what was needed was a special underground organization that could use "many different methods, including industrial and military sabotage, labour agitation and strikes, continuous propaganda, terrorist acts against traitors and German leaders, boycotts and riots" to undermine the occupying German forces and give the *résistants* a hand. Hugh Dalton, head of the newly established Ministry of Economic Warfare, asserted that it was a job better left to civilians.

Churchill was enamoured of the idea. And so, on July 16, 1940, he put Dalton in charge and directed him to "set Europe ablaze." Six days later, in his final act as Lord President of the Council, Neville Chamberlain, the former prime minister who had once tried to make peace with Hitler, signed a document creating an organization "designed to bring Hitler down." The War Cabinet approved it on July 22, and on that day, the Special Operations Executive officially came into existence. The idea was to first train and then clandestinely send in lone agents who could work behind enemy lines to support local resistance groups in sabotaging German efforts. Targets would include factories, rail lines, and communications.

It would ultimately become Buckmaster's job to build the French, or F, Section part of the organization from the ground up, and to recruit the (mostly) men, and later women, who would put the plan into action.

The F Section of the SOE necessarily started small. On May 5, 1941, its very first agent landed by parachute, with a wireless radio, on a large private property near Valençay. The agent, George Noble, and a group of aristocratic French brothers would become something like godfathers to the SOE in France. With George's help, they received the very first SOE drop of supplies and weapons into the country: two containers that held Tommy guns, plastic explosives, knives, and limpet mines. It proved a successful trial run. "For the first time, the British had sent us the tools for real work. The resistance, or our small part of it, was armed," one of the brothers, Philippe de Vomécourt, later wrote.

In France, there were a variety of groups with different allegiances, each operating under the constraints of occupation with whatever means were at their disposal. After the occupying Germans prompted a new law in 1942, the Service travail obligatoire—a compulsory forced-work scheme in factories and construction projects for German benefit—countless young French men ducked the order by running to the forests. Many of them formed loose bands of *résistants* called the *maquis*, meaning "underbrush." For the SOE, they would eventually be the most fertile terrain for recruitment.

For Buckmaster the biggest challenge was finding suitable candidates to send into France to help undermine the occupation from within. It became particularly challenging because Charles de Gaulle was displeased with the SOE for recruiting French citizens to send in. F Section was therefore restricted to a much smaller pool of British or other non-French nationals who spoke French like natives and were open to working behind enemy lines. Over time, these agents would come from all segments of British society; among their ranks were students, nurses, teachers, and a former American diplomat with a wooden leg. That pool would inevitably include French Canadians, too. As Buckmaster himself would later put it, SOE agents were mostly ordinary people trained to do extraordinary things.

When Sonia walked into Buckmaster's office, she was under the impression that the job for which she was interviewing would, much like her current one, be clerical. Her father believed that as well. Buckmaster had other plans in mind. He asked if Sonia would be interested in work that would put her behind enemy lines in France, the country she had once called home. Sonia was momentarily taken aback. She did not fully understand what she was getting into, but she blurted out a hasty yes: "I would be delighted to go to France."

Her next thought came out quickly: "How do you get there?"

The wheels were put in motion. There was paperwork to be filled out in duplicate and signed before she could be transferred out of the WAAF. Now-leading aircraftwoman Butt, service number 454240, was to become a FANY—a member of the First Aid Nursing Yeomanry—the charity-in-uniform that became the preferred cover for women of the SOE as they became "agent[s] in the field after training." Sonia's transfer, based on her having "the necessary linguistic and geographical qualifications," had immediate effect. The official transfer date was set for December 4, 1943.

Spurred on by her imminent departure from Cosford, Sonia made the decision to break her engagement to Michael Todd.

But he wouldn't hear of it, stubbornly refusing to take his ring back. She knew it had to be done. So, one night shortly before she left, Sonia broke his heart publicly. She gave him back his ring on the dance floor, right in front of all his friends. She hoped that this way they could help pick up the pieces.

Sonia did not know precisely what was ahead, but she did not look back. She was all of nineteen. And fuelled by the courage of youth, she wasn't afraid of much.

6

ANOTHER DETOUR

Guy • *London, December 1941*

As hundreds of thousands of young American men prepared to wade into the Second World War, Guy, at twenty-four, was marking the end of his second year in the U.K. with a new post. Having completed a slew of training courses, he was leaving Dolphin Camp and the No. 1 Convalescent Depot for good. He'd just been transferred to No. 1 Canadian Division Infantry Reinforcement Unit when the Pearl Harbor attack happened. Then, in the spring of 1942, he would be transferred to the storied Royal 22e Régiment as a sergeant, nearly three years after his first attempt to enlist in Montreal. It was the closest he'd come to seeing combat since the war started.

Guy had already marked two birthdays waiting for war. And as he celebrated his second Christmas in Britain, the country's prime minister was in North America, meeting with his American and Canadian counterparts to plot the defeat of the Nazis. On the heels of that meeting, on Boxing Day, Churchill addressed a joint session of Congress, lauding the United States for drawing "the sword for freedom." It was one more reason, he added, that "led the subjugated peoples of Europe to lift up their heads again in hope."

Several days after Churchill arrived in Washington, and after several nights of drinking into the early hours of the morning, he made his way to Ottawa. There he delivered a twenty-two-page speech in Parliament that, with the lawmakers' enthusiastic interruptions, took thirty-seven minutes to get through. In it, Churchill addressed all those Canadians in the United Kingdom who had "chafed" in the absence of a fight with the enemy.

"In a few months, when the invasion season returns, the Canadian Army may be engaged in one of the most frightful battles the world has ever seen, but on the other hand their presence may help to deter the enemy from attempting to fight such a battle on British soil."

He derided the Vichy French generals who'd told their prime minister in 1940 that "In three weeks England will have her neck wrung like a chicken."

"Some chicken; some neck," Churchill scoffed. Something of that defiance was captured moments after the speech in what would become an iconic photograph, dubbed *The Roaring Lion*. And Churchill's words rang like a bell among Canadians overseas, most of whom hadn't seen action, home, or loved ones for more than two years.

In the weeks that followed, it was becoming clear that Guy was destined for something grander than just a steady rise through the traditional ranks of the Canadian military. Guy himself seemed to be more definite about his ambitions. That spring, just before he joined the R22eR, he was interviewed by a Lieutenant J.D. Lemay, who duly recorded that Guy's primary goal was to do "secret service." Lieutenant Lemay also noted that Guy "would like to be in paratroops," an ambition that Guy recalled he'd had since he was in the militia. Lemay seemed to agree that Guy had special potential: "Very fine type of man. Suggest he should be sent to OCTU [Officer Cadet Training Unit]. Good material for an officer."

It wasn't long before a superior ordered Guy to return to Canada to become a commissioned officer—a next step toward realizing his dream of becoming a paratrooper.

His road to war had taken a temporary detour. Guy was officially posted to Brockville, Ontario, and as the summer of 1942 began, he was crossing the ocean back to Canada without ever having faced the enemy.

On August 3, 1942, at nine in the morning, Guy d'Artois was on a troop train again, this time heading to the Canada–U.S. border. The train was carrying more than three hundred soldiers and would take three days to arrive at its destination—Fort William Henry Harrison in Helena, Montana—finally pulling in around noon. After a desperately needed shower, the group gathered around Lieutenant-Colonel John G. McQueen, their commanding officer, who had flown in earlier, and Colonel Robert Frederick, the American in charge, who briefed the men on the plan for the coming weeks. It was an early night. Training would begin at six-thirty the very next morning.

These were no ordinary soldiers. The men were among the fiercest the Canadian Army had in its ranks, chosen for superior physical fitness, aggressiveness, and self-reliance. When word went out that the army was recruiting men to join a "second" Canadian parachute battalion, many soldiers, both at home and abroad, showed intense interest. But there was no second parachute battalion; the name was used as cover for the Canadian element in an elite joint force of American and Canadian soldiers that was being put together for special operations. Recruits were required to have outdoor and winter experience and to be willing not only to work in hazardous conditions but also to parachute out of a plane. Guy's superiors saw him in the description, and so, apparently, did he. The brass had also been keen to find qualified French Canadian candidates. In more ways than one, Guy seemed an obvious choice.

"Son, in 1937, you wrote that you wanted to be a paratrooper," Guy recalled a Lieutenant-Colonel Bernatchez telling him. "You will be one. You're going with the American army. Goodbye."

Guy had been in Canada barely a month before he joined the very first Canadian cohort—some twenty-seven officers and just over three hundred soldiers—to participate in the cross-border experiment. It was a direct descendant of Churchill's idea to assemble commando units—an idea, like the SOE, born under duress when Germany overran France. This North American version was named the First Special Service Force (FSSF), informally known as the Devil's Brigade.

It was supposed to be kept secret. But it was difficult to resist publicity, given what it could do to raise public morale. On August 6, 1942, both the American and Canadian governments trumpeted the news of a joint unit specializing in offensive warfare, elite men trained in "parachute training, marine landings, mountain fighting, and desert warfare." The press was riveted.

In an article that featured Guy, Odette Coupal from *Le Petit Journal* described him as "elegant, distinguished, and fine-featured, he appears at once thoughtful and cheerful, and his eloquence betrays a quick-witted, sharp mind." She asked Guy how much longer he would remain in the U.S.

"Your questions are too precise for me to answer. I'm sworn to secrecy!" he replied.

"Whether I'm sent to face the Germans, the Japanese, or the Italians, I'll fight to kill with all the ardour and know-how gained with the First Special Service Force. My zeal, and that of millions of soldiers fighting with the Allied forces, will soon, [I'm sure], lead us to victory." It's just the kind of language that would have surely pleased Guy's superiors.

During those months in Montana, Guy was promoted to lieutenant, and he began acquiring the skills that would carry him through the rest of his war. The unit had a tight deadline—to have men trained and ready to be deployed by December 15, 1942. So Guy's training schedule was relentless: a 4:45 a.m. start to the day, a two and a half kilometre run. Long marches, night and navigation exercises, calisthenics, and hand combat, at which Guy excelled. Survival in hostile terrain. All of it was aimed at developing the mental resilience to keep going even when the odds were against them.

Guy also learned how to blow up bridges and rail lines. The key skill he acquired, however, was parachuting. Guy's very first jump was likely on August 14, just one week after he arrived.

"In spite of all the cold-bloodedness we believed we had . . . and displayed, we feel the uncontrollable prickle of fear," Guy said of his first jump. The pace was so accelerated that within just two weeks of arriving Guy had qualified as a parachutist, entitled to draw extra "parachute pay" of two dollars per day.

Pay was just one of several tension points for this first group of Canadians serving alongside the Americans. Every one of them knew that Americans were paid more for the same work. Worse, within weeks of arriving they had to line up to be measured for a new American uniform—an equally ill-fitting idea for some of the brass back in Ottawa. Plus the men were living in close quarters, with two Americans and two Canadians to each hut. Inevitably, the tensions led to international scuffles. The Canadian commanding officer nodded to the strain in his daily war diary when he described a particularly cold, frostbitten day that winter: "The next Yankee to refer to Canada as a land of cold, ice and snow is likely to be shot."

Guy stayed long enough to finally realize his ambition of becoming a paratrooper. He also stayed long enough to participate in the very first FSSF combat mission, dubbed Operation COTTAGE, in August of 1943. The unit set out on rubber assault boats for Kiska, one of the Aleutian Islands in the territory of Alaska, only to learn after their arrival that the Japanese forces had withdrawn. It was nevertheless a test run, and one more detour on Guy's journey to war.

After that, it was time for another break. Guy sent a telegram to his mother in Montreal on September 4, 1943: "LEFT SAN FRANCISCO LAST NIGHT EXPECT ME AROUND 15-."

During that visit home, Guy received an unusual invitation from an officer with a British accent asking him to attend an interview at the Sun Life building in Montreal. The officer offered Guy what sounded like an enticing proposition: a special assignment that would take him back to Europe, and to the heart of the growing conflict. Guy did not have to think long before he answered in the affirmative.

His life was once again caught up in a whirlwind of change. He cut his vacation short and left for Toronto. There he met a woman who drove him to a spot near Whitby, Ontario, a fenced-off area that looked like a military camp in the middle of nowhere.

7

COG IN A LARGE MACHINE

Guy • *Near Oshawa, October 1943*

Like many recruits before him, Guy arrived at "Camp X" as a passenger, bewildered but intrigued. They pulled up to the camp's main and only gate, stopping at a rudimentary guardhouse where a man in uniform checked his papers before waving the car through. Only the odd wooden sign along the perimeter gave any hint of what went on inside: NO TRESPASSING. Or, PROHIBITED AREA—DEPARTMENT OF NATIONAL DEFENCE.

All recruits had to wear a uniform during working hours on site, a requirement spelled out in the instructions for new arrivals.

> *This is a military establishment. For the benefit of local inhabitants and visiting tradesmen, it is considered advisable for the military appearance of this Camp to be consistently maintained. . . .*

The nondescript site on the shores of a cold but placid lake had once been a farm owned by a family by the name of Sinclair. It took just a few weeks, in late 1941, for it to be quietly but hurriedly transformed into a school for irregular warfare. Even so, the facility still looked much like the farm it once was, with the original fences and barns intact. A single jeep patrolled the area at all hours of the day and night. If anyone did get close enough, which people did on occasion, they were sent away with dispatch and told never to return. The large antenna that eventually went up on the site was explained away as a station for the Canadian Broadcasting Corporation.

Mystified by the secrecy surrounding it all, the locals would take to calling the place "Camp X." In reality, it was Special Training School 103, one of only a few SOE schools operating outside Britain. STS 103, which did not officially exist, opened in December 1941 to prepare would-be SOE agents for subversive work in Europe and beyond. It had been the brainchild of William Stephenson, a Winnipeg-born Canadian industrialist. He was sent to New York by the Secret Intelligence Service as head of British Security Co-ordination, headquartered in New York; its aim was to gather intelligence and disseminate propaganda to help protect British interests and promote American support of the war.

The camp itself, across Lake Ontario from New York State, was also home for Hydra, a system that allowed Canada, Britain, and the hitherto neutral United States to share signals intelligence secretly and securely. While Canada provided most of the potential recruits at STS 103, Britain paid for the program and dispatched the instructors who presided over training.

As the war stretched on, the SOE had been experiencing a shortage of British volunteers who were fluent in languages that could be useful in the secret war against Axis powers. As a result, it looked to multicultural Canada for help.

By the time Guy arrived, the Camp had graduated operatives of numerous nationalities, among them Yugoslav, Italian, Hungarian, Romanian, Bulgarian, Chinese, Japanese, and British. It also trained U.S. operatives and instructors who would go on to join the American Office of Strategic Services (OSS). The sheer diversity of recruits was an indication "of the extent to which the war was becoming a global affair." They came from all walks of life and included, for example, a geologist, a shoemaker, a journalist, a blacksmith, and even a priest.

With D-Day purportedly around the corner, the SOE was particularly interested in recruits who spoke French in the fall of 1943. After an appeal from London, forty-nine French Canadians, all military, had been identified by superiors as potential agents, including Guy. If any of them met the very high bar they would be dispatched for final training in Europe, after which they'd be sent to France to join Churchill's secret army.

After only a few days, the vast majority of the forty-nine Canadians who had arrived at "Camp X" that fall were sent packing, deemed "unfit for the physical and psychological strain of clandestine war." Astoundingly, only three of that particular cohort, including Guy, were deemed promising enough to put through an initial training course, then forward to Britain for further training.

Hints of D-Day were already in the air. The opening address in a series of lectures designed specifically for the students of STS 103 explains that irregular warfare was moving from a "pre-invasion phase" to an "invasion phase" that was "beginning."

You will be a cog in a very large machine whose smooth functioning depends on each separate cog carrying out its part efficiently. It is the object of this course to clarify the part you will play and ensure the efficiency of your performance.

Guy was already well versed in many of the skills they taught at "Camp X," but he still had much to learn: the arts of subterfuge and of counterespionage; how to build contacts and train local resistance; how to maintain a cover story; how to disguise himself if necessary. Most importantly, he had to learn how to live and behave like a French citizen. In other words, he would have to learn to pass as French.

That would all come later. Guy remained at "Camp X" for just over four weeks. Still, Hamish Pelham-Burn, the tough chief explosives instructor and kilt-wearing officer in charge, would later say that Guy was the highest-graded soldier in all his time there, and that he "couldn't wait to tell Britain." Guy was exactly the kind of "soldier of fortune" the SOE was looking for.

By late November Guy was again saying his farewells and making his way to the familiar departure lounge that was the port of Halifax. On November 23, 1943, he boarded the SS *Mauretania* to make his second arduous journey back to the U.K. This time he knew that his long-awaited war was finally coming. But first he had a date with London.

PART III

SPECIALLY EMPLOYED

8

AGENTS-TO-BE

Sonia and Guy • *London, early December 1943*

A few steps away from the Saturday night bustle of Marylebone High Street, bundled deep away from the rain-slicked sidewalks and curious passersby, an eclectic group of fifteen young people gathered in a small room, waiting for instructions. They knew enough not to speak of the purpose of their presence, and exchanged small talk about mundane things instead. Undoubtedly there was excitement, barely contained, behind the courteous nods and furtive looks around the room, though surely none of them would have knowingly let that show. They had, after all, been hand-selected for special work, every one of them. It would be difficult in such circumstances not to have felt, along with the apprehension, an inflated sense of their importance, a renewed sense of purpose, perhaps even of indispensability in a war effort where everyone felt dispensable.

It had taken a lot of behind-the-scenes work, word of mouth, phone calls, secondments, transfers, favours, cajoling, and paperwork to get party 27AG, as this latest cohort of potential SOE trainees was called, assembled and ready for the psychological assessment designed to test whether they were indeed suited for secret agent work. Like the dozens of others who'd preceded them, they came from various backgrounds and experiences, in one way or another ordinary people who had lived extraordinary lives. But now, as 1943 was drawing to a close, marking more than four years of the war, getting SOE agents to France had taken on new urgency.

The SOE had evolved significantly since the days of the "ministry of wishful thinking." F Section, or "The Firm," as its people came to call it, had more staff and more resources in London than ever. Several active SOE *reseaux* were already operating in France, discrete "circuits" or "networks" each with its own SOE-parachuted organizer, wireless radio operator, even couriers, training, receiving parachuted weapons, and, when possible, leading sabotage action against German forces. But there was increasing pressure to focus on preparing for D-Day, the Allied invasion of mainland Europe, whose date was still unknown but constantly rumoured to be imminent. The SOE would soon have effectively two masters: the Ministry of Economic Warfare and the Supreme Headquarters Allied Expeditionary Force (SHAEF). Once Allied troops did finally land on French shores, it would be up to the resistance forces, supported by the SOE, to slow down German reinforcements from reaching the front.

Reflecting the urgency, the SOE would have many more flights at its disposal to send in more agents and more weapons to the French resistance—Sten guns, ammunition, grenades, and explosives to be hidden in French garages and attics or buried in holes in forests until the Allied invasion began.

The new cohort, now gathered in London, would become a microcosm of the Allied powers: they came from the U.S., France, Canada, Poland, and the U.K. (although almost immediately one Englishman backed out, deciding that "the racket," as they called it, wasn't for him). They'd signed up for the vague assignment "behind enemy lines" for a variety of reasons. Many simply despised Nazi Germany and wanted to contribute to its defeat in whatever way possible. There were men with military experience who believed they had much more to contribute to the war effort beyond training and waiting. There were civilians drawn by allegiance to France and by alarm over the deportation and murder of Jews in Europe.

Looking around that room that night in London, it would have been hard to pinpoint exactly what they all had in common beyond command of the French language. Many SOE recruits were young, idealistic, and good-looking. Often they were straddling two or more cultures—one of those cultures invariably being French. Many had grown up in a country that was not their own, and so had never felt they belonged firmly in one or the other. The SOE, to some of them, might have provided an opportunity to escape that uncertain status. "They were needed now, both by the country of their nationality and by the country of their upbringing," one F Section agent would later write. "Through accepting the risks of underground service they stilled the conflict within."

Among party 27AG, Guy might have been one of the few exceptions to such generalizations—he was there for the promise of adventure. He was also one of the best trained and most experienced of the group. His days at "Camp X" were still fresh in his mind; he had several years of military service under his belt; and his parachute jump record was enviable, for those who cared to count. He wasn't out of place among this cosmopolitan group either. He had, after all, been to England twice and had served in the U.S. and on the Aleutian Islands, which made him well travelled compared to most of his Canadian peers. His arrival at the F Section offices was the culmination of hard work, and Guy was eager to demonstrate what he knew. It didn't escape him that his audience included a number of attractive women. He was well spoken, had a commanding presence, and exuded confidence. In every possible way, in that room, Guy was in his element.

Sonia, at least in terms of experience, was at the opposite end of the spectrum. At nineteen, she was the youngest would-be agent in the group—so young that later in their training, when what remained of their cohort formed into a tightly knit group, they would come to call her "baby." She'd never learned to shoot a gun, had never imagined handling explosives, and certainly would never have contemplated leaping from a plane for anything—not since her dear brother Derek pushed her off a diving board when they were children and forever instilled in her a fear of heights. It would be some time before Sonia understood precisely what was being asked of her at the SOE. But she already desperately wanted to be there. Whatever it was, it would beat the monotony of working in the WAAF.

What Sonia did have, in addition to fluency in French, was highly valuable experience living in France like a young Frenchwoman. She easily navigated borders of both the physical and the metaphorical kinds. The others in her cohort had wildly different upbringings, but somehow they had all demonstrated a degree of malleability, inventiveness, and creativity in problem solving; self-reliance; and the ability to talk their way out of tough spots. Sonia had one more advantage, though: from the Firm's perspective, one of the most important attributes of a good agent was the ability to operate on their own despite any risk.

Sonia knew precisely how to operate on her own. She'd almost always had to.

As the F Section welcomed its latest cohort, one of its largest circuits in France was unravelling, undoing months of lonely, painstaking work.

Arrests, imprisonment, torture, death—all were inevitably part of the SOE story from the beginning. In the early days Vichy police stalked a key safe house in Marseille and ensnared even the very first F Section agent to land in France. Other agents were picked up after their IDs failed to stand up to scrutiny. Yet others were given away by double agents or infiltrating German operatives, or, more mundanely, discovered at routine checkpoints.

But the spectacular collapse in mid-1943 of a pivotal and sprawling circuit named PHYSICIAN, also known as PROSPER, laid bare the many weaknesses of the F Section. Terrible security lapses, both in the field and at HQ, led the German Gestapo to round up several agents and hundreds of French recruits in the crucial region in and around Paris.

As party 27AG settled into their first few days at the SOE, several PROSPER agents in German custody were enduring brutal treatment. Then two Canadians, Frank Pickersgill and Ken Macalister, were captured and violently interrogated and tortured at the hands of German intelligence at the notorious Gestapo headquarters at 84 Avenue Foch in Paris. So was Noor Inayat Khan, the Moscow-born daughter of a Sufi master and an American mother, who had become F Section's first female radio operator in the field. Later, as party 27AG entered formal training, she and others were taken to Germany and left to languish either in prisons or in fearsome concentration camps, their fates unknown in London.

Also as a result of PROSPER's collapse, German forces were operating at least two of their radios, impersonating SOE agents and endangering the life of every new agent who arrived behind enemy lines. Some of those commandeered messages arriving at HQ contained signs that something was amiss, omissions of agreed coding practices that should have alerted London that someone other than their agent was operating the radio. But those signs were repeatedly missed—Buckmaster once even ordered a reply to the sender telling them to "be more careful next time." And while London eventually discovered the German *Funkspiel* and engaged in its own "radio game," the early lapses would cost several lives and threaten the F Section project at the most crucial time.

From the moment of its creation, the SOE had many detractors. It was seen in some quarters as no more than "a hopeful improvisation devised in a really desperate situation." With its every misstep the SOE would be questioned repeatedly by rival organizations, including the existing secret service, which accused it of being "amateurish" and "irresponsible" for sending ill-prepared young agents to their deaths. It was even accused of deliberately sacrificing agents to protect D-Day. The criticisms came from its own agents and members of the resistance movements it was supposed to serve. And yet, reportedly, flawed as it was, the SOE had Hitler's attention.

"When I get to London," he's quoted as once saying, "I am not sure who I shall hang first—Churchill or that man Buckmaster."

Worrying about and tracking every detail was Vera Atkins.

She was born Vera May Rosenberg in Galatz, Romania, the daughter of a Jewish couple from Germany and the United Kingdom. Young Vera spoke several languages and had a distinct worldliness about her, polished to brilliance at finishing schools in Switzerland

and France. As life became more perilous for Jews in Romania and the rest of mainland Europe, Atkins adopted her British mother's maiden name and moved with her to the U.K. Even four years later, when she accepted work with the SOE, she hadn't acquired official British citizenship, and yet she exuded Englishness with every puff of cigarette smoke she exhaled. She also had a commanding presence that rivalled that of any man at the Firm, Buckmaster included.

Atkins joined the SOE at 64 Baker Street in April 1941, back when it was called the Inter-Service Research Bureau to obscure its real purpose. She'd first walked through its sandbagged entrance as a civilian secretary to Buckmaster, but by watching over the agents they sent behind enemy lines, she distinguished herself behind her humble desk. Working six to seven days a week, she became involved in every aspect of the work—from payroll and research to gathering intelligence, briefing agents before departure, and orchestrating the BBC radio messaging used to communicate with agents in the field—and she soon became the F Section's intelligence officer. Although subordinate in title, she ran her own show, and some among the female agents contended she *was* the SOE.

Unsurprisingly, Atkins was an early believer in the advantages of sending women behind enemy lines. "They were not as suspect as men, they had very subtle minds when it came to talking their way out of situations . . . and they performed extremely well," she once said. Women, she added, were "very conscientious."

Women at the time were not permitted in combat roles. Within the Firm, aside from a handful of early exceptions, they'd been mostly confined to the ranks of the secretarial staff. But it didn't take long for F Section to understand that women agents were a huge advantage, and to begin, very quietly but actively, to recruit them. It wasn't until 1942, however, that F Section acquired Churchill's explicit permission for doing so. The Prime Minister had asked the F Section's then chief recruiter, Selwyn Jepson, about the SOE's use of women.

"What are you doing?" Jepson recalled him asking.

"Don't you think it is a very sensible thing to do?" Jepson responded.

"Yes" was Churchill's apparent reply. "Good luck to you."

The SOE was a front-runner on the cutting edge of gender equality, but for years the rest of the world wouldn't know it.

Yet even within the Firm there was pushback. Some of the instructors seemed to resent the idea of training female agents and consistently provided HQ with dismissive, sometimes insulting and blatantly sexist feedback about female recruits. But the leadership would often cast that feedback aside.

Given the mores of the time, and the prohibition on deploying women to combat zones, it was certainly revolutionary. But there was no illusion about the motive; the decision had ultimately been a tactical one. A woman, especially a beautiful one, was simply less likely to arouse suspicion in the field.

And yet, even as they were actively sought by the SOE, it was still impossible for Sonia and other women like her, no matter their abilities, to completely escape being seen and cast in sexualized roles, treated as objects of desire, and if not, then treated to ridicule. Even Colin Gubbins, who had risen to the rank of major-general and director of the entire SOE, and was in favour of adding women as agents, was still described by at least one staffer as "a lech" to be avoided.

Like Sonia, the women recruits were often beautiful, intelligent, and single, though even married women couldn't escape harsh judgment or undue attention based on their looks. It's obvious even in the physical descriptions included in their files. On Sonia:

"Square face, regular good features, very even teeth. Scar on right eyelid. Attractive looking."

Atkins took charge of female agents and looked after their welfare as a kind of den mother. She'd help them prepare their wills before they left and to stay in touch with their families afterward, often by sending the occasional card with little more than a line or two to reassure them that all was well. She also often insisted on accompanying agents to the airfield, and when she did so, she wouldn't get home before the wee hours of the morning. She was so secretive about her role that her own mother was completely in the dark. On one of those early mornings, when Vera returned at dawn, her mother remarked, "I hope one day he'll make an honest woman of you." Vera took that as the best evidence yet that she was excelling on the security front.

By December of 1943, several women were already deployed and active in the field for the SOE. And in party 27AG, there were four more women who might soon join them—but first they had to get past the SOE psychologists who would gauge their suitability for clandestine work.

After gathering in London, the recruits were sent by train to Surrey to attend the so-called student assessment board. Upon arrival, they were gathered in a roomful of desks, each of them assigned a number that would identify them throughout their training. Names were forbidden, at least at the start. As they settled in, Guy scanned the room in appreciation. With all the "pretty girls" in the group, he later recounted, "I told myself that happy days lay ahead."

That very first day the instructor gave them an odd assignment. He asked each of them to write down the number assigned to a person in the room with whom they would most like to spend a weekend in London.

Sonia looked around at the men in her cohort, each wearing a number in lieu of a nametag. They barely knew each other but she had already noted Guy's presence—hard not to with his bold demeanour and his overexuberance—and his American uniform with the various insignia on his chest. "He looks like a Christmas tree," she thought. She also thought he was a "good looking chap." So she arbitrarily wrote down his number: 13.

Unbeknownst to her, Guy, it so happened, had scribbled down Sonia's number: 14.

Only the instructor would have been privy to the charming coincidence. If it had any significance, that remained the purview of the staff of Winterfold House.

On the green heath of the Surrey Hills, southeast of the town of Guildford and perched a few hundred metres above Cranleigh village, Winterfold House had been welcoming SOE agents for most of the war as STS 4, a preliminary school for the Dutch and Belgian sections. It was just one of the fifty or so private estates that the SOE had requisitioned for their purposes during the war. So many of these were grand mansions with sprawling acreages that among its growing alumni of agents and instructors the SOE was jokingly referred to as standing for "Stately 'Omes of England."

Winterfold House wasn't the grandest among them, but it sat on a huge private property and offered its lodgers a warm, comfortable refuge from the December cold. As the demand for agents in France grew, the weeding-out process was streamlined and shortened to maximize output. And so Winterfold was repurposed as STS 7, the home of a new student assessment board—one that would decide the fate of members of party 27AG in less than a week. On staff were two majors who were also psychiatrists, a captain and a lieutenant who were psychologists, and three sergeants who were testers. Through a series of tests and observations, they determined whether recruits were psychologically suited to survive and thrive as lone-wolf agents.

Sonia recalled that, from the moment her group arrived that December afternoon, they were under vigilant watch. After they settled in, it wasn't long before the instructor started with the questions, in some variation of the following: *As you walked down the stairs to the dining hall, how many portraits did you see along the way? In the east wing of the house, how many windows are there? Where are the exits?*

Each unanswerable question was a rebuke, an *aide-mémoire* about the importance of observation.

The students were still in the dark about the organization that had recruited them. This was, after all, a weeding-out exercise. The less the potential agents knew, the better. Those who chose to leave or failed to meet the minimum standards were dispatched to a mystery location called "the cooler," where they were assisted in "forgetting" what they'd learned. In what manner that forgetting was encouraged, beyond the passage of time, isn't clear.

The students were also still mostly in the dark about each other. Guy might have seemed exotic to the rest, having come from so far away and, unlike Sonia and some of the others, having never seen Paris once.

But they all quickly found common cause, and friendship, as they delved deeper into their shared, mysterious endeavour.

Over the subsequent few days they watched each other through a series of tests they performed under the eyes of the staff, men who had clipboards in hand but provided zero feedback. Some of the tests were downright baffling. In one of them, a psychiatrist showed Sonia a piece of paper with a large ink blot and asked her what she saw. She was thrown by the question, made something up, and hurried from the room. On the way out she warned Nancy Wake about what to expect.

Nancy, a nurse and journalist raised in Australia, was married to a Frenchman and until recently had lived in Marseille. She'd already been active in helping the resistance—and when she was found out, she escaped on foot over the Pyrenees Mountains and then joined the SOE in an effort to return to France and find her husband. Nancy loved to drink and had a wicked sense of humour, along with a defiance that often got her in trouble. She had strong opinions, too. "I hate wars and violence but if they come then I don't see why we women should just wave our men a proud goodbye and then knit them balaclavas," she once said. At Winterfold House, Nancy and Sonia were becoming friends. When it was Nancy's turn to contemplate the ink blot, she told the psychologist that she saw an ink blot and that he should stop wasting his time and hers.

The students soon took to calling the place the Mad House, or the Looney Bin. They would all dine together, and all conversation was to be in French, and behaviour was expected to conform to that of the French. After all, these would-be agents must pass as French. So, beyond the tests, the staff also monitored the recruits' behaviour. Every little thing mattered. How did they handle their cutlery at lunchtime? Did they cut or break the bread? Did they use expressions unfamiliar in France? How did they behave after a few drinks? The wrong behaviour in each case could potentially give them away.

Once, after an evening spent drinking, Sonia woke up in the middle of the night and was startled to find an officer sitting on the edge of her bed. It was something they did to all the recruits—not only to listen and verify whether they spoke in their sleep but also to determine whether they'd default to English if they were suddenly woken up.

Just two days into their baffling week, the recruits were ordered outside for a test likely intended to be as much a measure of their physical strength as it was of their ability to assess their own limits.

They were taken to two trees connected by three cables at different heights and asked to traverse one of the cables in whatever way they saw fit. Almost everyone chose the highest cable, twenty feet above the ground. Guy had performed a similar exercise before and breezed through it. Almost all the others struggled to get across. When it was Sonia's turn, she too took on the highest rope, and Guy surmised that she too looked unlikely to make it all the way across. Suddenly she let go and fell, landed hard on the ground, and blacked out. When she woke up she felt intense pain in her back—something serious had happened. It was serious enough that she was taken to see a doctor from the nearby Royal Surrey County Hospital.

The doctor sent back a report. "I have fully examined your patient," he wrote. Based on X-rays, he'd concluded that there was no spinal injury, nor had he seen any sign of organ damage or headache to be concerned about. "Although severely shaken by her fall," he concluded, "I think that she has done no organic damage to herself." Sonia's pain would later subside, but it would return, time and again, for years to come.

It was a relentless few days in close quarters, a crash course in recognizing their limits, as well as pushing them. The recruits would just be finishing one exhausting exercise when they'd be asked to perform one more. It was as though their assessors were asking, *Could you keep going, despite exhaustion, in the field? Could you still keep your wits about you and make sound choices? Could you keep running if someone was in pursuit?*

Still, there were lighter moments all the way through. Nancy Wake was once trying to jump through a hanging tire in an obstacle course and got herself stuck inside. They had to pull her out. She chuckled about it with good humour, drawing laughter from those around her.

Cheerfulness was certainly not required, but resourcefulness, initiative, endurance, and creativity were. To test for those qualities, recruits were asked, for example, to find a way in and out of a locked attic or to steal a hidden document. In another challenge they were divided up into teams and asked to build a raft to transport an important item across a river without getting it wet. For most of a week the tests went on and on, until finally the notes on the clipboards became reports back to HQ.

At the end of the assessment period, the observers described Sonia as "A self-willed thorough tom-boy with a definite 'devil may care' streak in her veins. She is tough and self-reliant and game for risk and adventure. Physically quite reckless and fearless."

However, that first written assessment cast doubts on Sonia's intelligence—she was rated at 4, which is below average. She also seemed impossibly young to be undertaking such a grave mission.

"She has little use for any job calling for serious reasoning. Though determined and self-assured she still lacks maturity and balance. Has a good sense of security. Quite unsuited for W/T [radio]. Might make a courier with careful training.

"Probably would be at her best as a saboteur."

Her overall assessment was put at a "D," meaning "low, but pass."

Nonetheless, two days later, HQ—meaning Buckmaster—ruled that she could move on to the next phase.

9

LOVE IN A TIME OF WAR

Sonia and Guy • *Scotland, December 1943*

At platform one in central London's Paddington Station, a larger-than-life figure of a soldier reading a letter has kept watch since 1922, erected to commemorate the twenty-five hundred Great Western Railway employees who died fighting in the First World War. Like almost all such monuments, the bronze depiction had, just two decades later, taken on new meaning. Presiding over the energetic churn of a new generation of uniformed youth, it spoke very much of the moment: of the sacrifices, the lives lost so far, yes, but if one looked closer, it now perhaps also spoke of the unique loneliness and emotional toll of entering a fifth year at war, the letter a silent reminder of the sustaining power of connection, of relationships, of love in a time of protracted crisis.

In the blur of steady-gazed soldiers marching by the memorial—now joined by their American counterparts—the SOE's newest recruits wouldn't have prompted a second look. They were, as Roosevelt had said after the attack on Pearl Harbor, all in the same boat. With D-Day looming, everything in late 1943, even that inert bronze memorial, whispered of the inordinate cost still to be borne by the young. After two days of rest in London, members of party 27AG boarded a train at Paddington heading north to Scotland. They would have switched trains in either Edinburgh or Glasgow and then eventually boarded a small bus before finally arriving in Arisaig, on the west coast of the Scottish Highlands. It was a long way to go for a training course. But with its crisp, wet air, its enormous grey sky full of clouds with character, its quiet, unforgiving terrain with startling emerald outcrops, and its dark, bottomless lochs, the Scottish Highlands were an ideal setting in which to train and hide a secret army. And so the SOE had requisitioned several private homes in Arisaig and Morar and turned them into special training schools, closing off the area to keep intruders out.

For the recruits, the stately Meoble Lodge, their home for the next several weeks, was a welcome sight after such a long trip. And when they arrived, the commanding officer of STS 23 was there to greet them wearing a kilt, just as he would for the duration of their stay, no matter the activity or the weather.

Away from the bustle of London, the demands of family, the constraints of the WAAF, and the ennui of ordinary life, the weeks ahead would be some of the most peaceful Sonia had known since the war began. As Christmas approached, in the silence and the serenity of the Highlands—incongruously perhaps, given their purpose in being there—the war seemed to fade to near nothingness.

Their first day, and every day thereafter, began with physical exercise in the morning frost, purely as a warmup. The rest of each day was then divided between intensely physical work and classroom lectures. Here the recruits started to learn the nuts and bolts of surviving and operating alone in the field. And since much of the work they did took place outside in the rain, almost every day they'd return to the house soaked. It was commando and survival training rolled into one. Ultimately they had to learn how to inflict harm on the enemy while protecting themselves, no matter the circumstances or the terrain.

Nineteen-year-old Sonia hadn't grown up around guns. And now she was faced with a multitude of weapons—British, American, French, and German—and expected to learn not only how to tell the difference between them but also how to dismantle and then reassemble them even in the dark. She did manage to learn all that, and became fairly adept at shooting, doing "quite well with pistol." To the dismay of more experienced colleagues like Guy, she was also ambidextrous, and could outshoot some of the men no matter which hand she used.

Each layer of training opened up a whole new world far removed from her own. She learned the basics of raids and ambushes and silent killing using only her hands; the latter was taught while having to contend with "the inability to practice and see the results on a live person, although holds, blows and knife thrusts were practiced with full fury on special dummies." Sonia hadn't yet learned to drive a car, but here she was at a local train station, learning how to drive a locomotive—and how to blow one up, too, including where to place the charges and when. France's rail network was essential in the movement of German troops and materiel. Sabotaging it would help slow down any German reinforcements responding to the planned Allied landing. But that bigger picture had yet to be explained fully to the recruits. Sonia was having a grand time in the outdoors learning new things, but for some others, it was a bewildering experience that led one woman, after four weeks of training, to ask, "What *ARE* we being trained for? I answered an advertisement for a bilingual secretary."

As the training progressed, the recruits were sometimes divided up into smaller groups that competed against each other. There was no denying Guy's abilities; he was seen as having "very great drive" and as being "practical" and "sharp-witted," and so instructors often put him in a leadership position to help guide some of his less experienced colleagues. At one point his group included fellow Canadian Jean-Paul Archambault—a Montrealer and another able Camp X graduate—as well as Sonia Butt and twenty-nine-year-old Lilian Rolfe, a beautiful woman who'd caught Guy's eye from the start.

Lilian was Jewish, the daughter of a British chartered accountant, and had grown up in France; and she carried a burden of heartbreak, of a tragic story that could come about only in wartime. She'd been married to a Dutch man who'd supposedly lost his first wife in the war. His wife, meanwhile, was actually alive and well, and had managed to also escape to the U.K. to track down her husband. After a dramatic reunion, the man had no recourse but to have his marriage to Lilian annulled. Since then she'd been in constant mourning.

Back in Montreal, Guy had been dating one May Talbot, a young woman who apparently held a beauty pageant title. He was so enamoured with May that he once bought all her dance tickets at the White Shoes Ball at the grand Windsor Hotel, meaning he could dance with her all night. His mother approved of May and invited her to family gatherings, believing that Guy intended, as he'd apparently promised, to marry her upon his return from the war. But that didn't stop him from becoming intensely interested in Lilian, his beautiful fellow trainee, even if she did cry easily and even if she did so in Guy's company.

In such close quarters, it was inevitable that some of the recruits would fall in love with each other—it was practically an SOE training course rite of passage. Some would later admit that it was impossible not to, no matter their relationship status. Stanislaw Makowski, a Polish officer who joined this cohort, was constantly concerned about his wife, Alice, who'd been ailing since a miscarriage. Yet that didn't stop him from pursuing Sonia early during their time in training. She showed interest in him, too—thought him "a lovely guy"—until she learned he was married, after which she steered clear.

Meanwhile, alongside all the flirtation—maybe even complementary to it—there was a healthy amount of competition.

Guy quickly established himself as the class know-it-all, opinionated and verbose. The instructors were still unsure about his promise as an SOE agent. He was a "restless, impulsive, intensely active man, intolerant of discipline and lacking in judgement and perseverance." Further, he was labelled as "self-centred and ruthless in his relations with others."

In class, he could also be an occasional disruptor who liked to draw attention to himself. He wasn't beyond flicking spitballs at the women in the room. On one occasion Guy launched an entire barrage of them and Sonia reacted with an audible giggle. Both were punished, the instructor assigning them extra study while everyone else went off to enjoy happy hour together.

Sonia was indeed behind on navigation, a skill that required the use of a map and compass and was crucial to their exercises on survival in the outdoors. The recruits would be dropped in a remote area, given basic supplies, and told to safely find their way back to the lodge. Guy's punishment was to bring Sonia up to speed, and they were banished to a room with a big couch and a fireplace. But within minutes they abandoned the map reading and started fooling around, making their own fun. Neither of them thought much of it then—it was just an opportunity, and they happily seized it. Guy would have admitted then that Sonia was beautiful. But he thought all the women there were beautiful too.

If anything, Sonia and Guy seemed to be developing a somewhat antagonistic relationship. Guy was disdainful of what he described as Sonia's occasional lack of confidence. "He was very tough on me," she remembered. He called her a "weak little girl." The teasing escalated. Though she did find him attractive, she also found him arrogant and even obnoxious, and yearned to put him in his place. So once, during an exercise, she pushed him into a river. He emerged soaking wet and seething; in retaliation he pushed her face into the mud. And on it went. All the same, they also flirted "outrageously," yet in hindsight maintained that it was all "innocent."

Despite the seriousness of their task, the overall atmosphere at the school was light and playful. In class, one female recruit would ask the Scottish colonel what was under his kilt, prompting uproarious laughter. All would be forgiven by the time they gathered for happy hour, a daily ritual after the long, frigid hours at work. After dinner they'd play games and drink and laugh late into the night. Sonia and Guy would inevitably end up dancing together, and she thought him a wonderful dancer. Throughout, the candidates were actively encouraged to have fun. Some of the more raucous evenings would end up with everyone gathered around the piano, instructors included.

These were, admittedly, most unusual circumstances. The recruits were not yet aware that their chances of survival in France had been assessed at fifty-fifty. For wireless radio operators, life expectancy in France in 1943 was only around six weeks, vulnerable as they were to being detected by German surveillance. The recruits knew none of that, yet. But they instinctively understood that they must live in the moment, that there was every chance they might never return alive.

After two intense weeks, Acting Lieutenant Gordon sat down to record his initial assessments of this latest cohort of recruits.

Sonia, he wrote, "is very nice, very popular. She has I think, a very strong determined character, and it appears is very anxious to do this work, I imagine, from motives of romance."

But there were already signs that the instructors believed young Sonia might be out of her depth. And she wasn't the only one judged so. But the SOE was not rushing to dismiss recruits on the eve of a decisive battle.

Christmas Eve arrived quickly, bringing with it a welcome change of pace. Some of the recruits decided to attend midnight Mass at a church across the lake. In those winter days, the sun set no later than three-thirty in the afternoon, so by the time they left Meoble Lodge, with a waning moon and so little artificial light about, it was dark, cold, and silent.

To get across the lake, they filed onto an old cabin cruiser. Guy helped Sonia on board, and she quickly huddled inside the cabin to shield herself from the cold. Guy left her there and joined the others on the deck. He didn't last very long, feeling compelled to return to beautiful Sonia, who was still sitting alone inside. And it was in those moments that the two of them first held hands.

They arrived at the church and settled in. There was a world-at-war's worth of reasons to pray.

And so Sonia and Guy held hands for the rest of the church service. They held hands against all that was ahead, against the loneliness that comes from staring into an opaque future. They held hands in acknowledgment of their common predicament, and of whatever fears they might have shared. They held hands against the cold, against the uncertainty. But perhaps most of all, they held hands against the unknown.

President Roosevelt's Christmas Eve address to the American nation was carried around the world. In it he announced the appointment of General Dwight Eisenhower as the Supreme Commander of the Allied Expeditionary Force, whose mission was to defeat Nazi Germany. That Christmas, nearly four million American servicemen were overseas, each representing a potential casualty, a life cut short, a family forever dismembered. In Italy, Canadian and German troops were engaged in the battle of Ortona. In Berlin, hundreds of Germans, as many as two thousand, were killed in some of the heaviest raids on the city yet, an armada of Allied aircraft leaving swathes of the city burning on Christmas Eve. And yet Roosevelt still predicted that "'peace on Earth, goodwill toward men' can be and will be realized and ensured. This year, I can say that. Last year, I could not do more than express a hope. Today I express a certainty, though the cost may be high and the time may be long."

It was peaceful, in that moment, in the Scottish Highlands. But everyone knew by then what must yet come before a more permanent peace settled on earth. And Sonia and Guy knew they were likely to be in the thick of it.

That evening marked a turning point in Sonia and Guy's relationship. It was clear to both that they had deeper feelings for each other than they'd thus far realized. They were embarking on the very beginnings of what could be, if one imagined for a moment, a whole lifetime together. One that, if it came together, would straddle continents, endure long separations, and bring many children into the world. They were not to know any of that then. They were not to know whether they would even survive this war, whether they would return with their faculties, their bodies, their futures intact.

In that moment, though, they were alone in a world very few others could possibly comprehend. Their chance meeting had been so unlikely.

Without the war, without this candlelit night, their hands might have never touched. She a Briton raised in France, he a francophone born and raised in Canada. It was war that brought them together. And it would be the outcome of the war that would determine whether they could make something lasting of it.

But it was early going then. In subsequent days, they would begin to spend a lot of time together. They would begin to learn about each other, about their families, about the history that had brought them to this peculiar moment. They would discover that they'd been within striking distance of each other when Sonia was recovering from what was likely tuberculosis at the RAF Convalescent Hospital in Torquay, right across the bay from Canada's No. 1 Convalescent Depot at Dolphin Camp on the English Channel. She would learn that Guy had a velvety baritone and could beautifully carry a tune. He would learn that she smiled when she was nervous. She knew about the distinctive mole on his left arm. Still, it was a relationship very much in its infancy.

As they counted down to the end of a pivotal year, it was back to the strenuous training, and back to the antics and mischief. Despite Guy's own troublemaking tendencies, there was a mischievous streak in Sonia's personality that irked him. On New Year's Eve she conspired with others to smear everyone's beds with peanut butter and corn flakes. Another time, Sonia joined forces with Jean-Paul Archambault on a more dangerous prank, setting off some leftover explosives, a "tiny" bomb, to scare the others. It turned out not to be so tiny, and it shattered every window in the building. The next day the colonel told the group that if no one owned up to it they'd all be made to pay for the damage. Sonia was forced to sheepishly put up her hand. Money would be docked from her pay. For days afterward, Guy refused to speak to her.

Sonia's apparent immaturity worried Guy as well as her instructors. Acting Lieutenant Gordon added to her file at regular intervals while she was in Scotland. On December 30, a day before the New Year's Eve shenanigans, he described her as "self confident, rather with the self confidence of post-adolescence, considering herself an experienced woman, whereas in reality she is immature and not awkward but very young."

"She has, I believe, been engaged twice," he added, rather judgmentally, as part of what appeared to be a list of shortcomings. A subsequent, unsigned assessment holds that she seemed to have "determination and reliability" and yet "has remarked that she cannot concentrate."

"From the beginning has shown a definite interest in the opposite sex and is now spending a lot of time with d'Artois. There appears to be some sort of an understanding between them."

There was an understanding. But even to Guy and Sonia, it was still vague and unarticulated. They may well have been falling in love, but there was no question of making commitments. Not now. They were well aware that the world could turn on a dime. There was a war on, after all. Agents who'd gone before them had already paid with their lives. Given the circumstances, it was not a relationship that would follow a straight line.

The New Year brought a new spate of bad news for the SOE's F Section. January saw German forces capture a highly successful Canadian agent, a Montrealer named Gustave Biéler, along with Yolande Beekman, his circuit's wireless operator. Subsequent months would bring similar news.

At a French prison north of Toulouse, however, the new year also brought F Section a badly needed lucky break.

In the spring of 1943, F Section agent Sydney Hudson was confined in cell 101 of the Maison centrale d'Eysses, in southwest France north of Toulouse, grappling with the loneliness of solitary confinement in what was only the start of a five-year prison sentence.

Sydney was a tall, handsome, older SOE agent with gentle blue eyes and chestnut hair—a former Olympic skier who'd grown up in Switzerland and spoke fluent French. Only a few months earlier he and a radio operator had been dropped by parachute with plans to start a new circuit, one of the many networks the SOE was now operating in several corners of France. But then, just two weeks in, Sydney was arrested at the safe house where he was staying. During his interrogation, and in a serious indictment of the SOE's methods, police inspectors who'd picked up Sydney could see right away that his identification had been forged. He decided to confess that he was, as they suspected, a *parachutiste anglais*, a British agent who had arrived by parachute. Sydney was charged with entering France illegally. After what was a trial in name only, he was ultimately sentenced to a five-year jail term, with hard labour, and transferred to the French-controlled maison centrale. Though his situation was already dire, a greater concern constantly weighing on him was the possibility of being handed over to German forces, at whose hands he would almost certainly face torture and execution.

In a rare good twist of fortune, however, by June 1943 life had improved dramatically for Sydney Hudson at the maison centrale. He was moved out of solitary confinement and could mix with the other prisoners, many of whom, he learned, were members of the French resistance. He also happily discovered that other SOE agents were among them, including a man by the name of Philippe de Vomécourt—one of those aristocratic brothers who were part of the original group of SOE agents credited with getting the organization up and running in France. The two began to plot an escape.

The French prison guards were far more relaxed than they'd been at first, and a few even appeared to be sympathetic to the resistance. Sydney felt confident enough to approach some of them for help. One of the guards joined their plot. Another declined but agreed to lend his tacit support—and his set of keys—while pretending he was overpowered. In the early evening of January 3, 1944, Sydney, Philippe, and two dozen other men they had recruited ran for their lives and melted into the countryside. Then, sheltered among the local population, they managed through another agent to send word to London. HQ ordered Sydney and Philippe urgently to get out of the country and report to London, and to bring along the men they had recruited.

Their only option was to walk over the border to Spain, a treacherous trip on foot through the Pyrenees Mountains and in uncomfortably deep snow. But with the help of a Spanish guide and then British diplomats in Barcelona, Sydney and Philippe made it all the way back to London with their new recruits in tow. It was a miraculous escape—one that, upon arrival, was promptly rewarded with Sydney's arrest.

Sydney was dismayed. After a year and a half's absence, he was eager to reconnect with his parents and the daughter he'd left behind only a day after she was born. But having been in the custody of the enemy, he had to remain under arrest until he was debriefed; it was obligatory.

Once the formalities were completed, Sydney finally reunited with his wife and family. Yet he no longer felt that he belonged. Instead he felt "a sense of belonging to a different world—the world of the underground struggle, of life-and-death loyalties and treacheries, or resistance and the Gestapo. I felt that one day, perhaps very soon, the Allies would invade France and that I must be there."

Sydney met with Buckmaster and told him he wished to return to France on another mission as soon as possible.

Buckmaster agreed. It was March 1944. After some extra training and health checks, Sydney repaired to the SOE hostel at 32 Weymouth Street to wait for his second run.

On January 7, Acting Lieutenant Gordon sat down to size up the recruits again. He was still highly critical of Sonia's abilities. Reading between the lines, however, one could be forgiven for suspecting that at the same time he too was personally taken with her.

"My natural chivalrous instincts and politeness about pretty girls must here be suppressed," he begins.

"Mss [*sic*] 14 is very nice, wholesome and full of animal vitality, she is interested in men, and susceptible to their attentions, probably without exercising her critical faculties, being obstinate and lacking in subtlety, this is rather a drawback."

"I don't see that she would get by on sex appeal alone," he adds.

What follows is a litany of complaints that culminate in Gordon's bluntly levelling with HQ, the presumed intended audience, about what underlies his discomfort with her: "the qualities she possesses would really be more helpful if she were of another sex."

In the final report on her time in Scotland, the school commandant then concluded, "I do not think that her heart is truly in this work."

And yet Buckmaster, the ultimate arbiter, seemed to understand that Sonia had more potential than either she or the instructors imagined. So he called her in for a meeting. She could do better, he told Sonia gently. Despite her young age, she needed to act more maturely.

Buckmaster's advice had an impact. Like the instructors, Sonia had little confidence that she could pass all the tests they put her through. But "I knew deep down that I would never, never waver; I was sure of myself in that."

Guy, meanwhile, had become one of the most thoroughly trained Canadians in the SOE. Yet even he, according to Acting Lieutenant Gordon, was "young enough for anything energetic and like the others unsuitable for anything else." But by the end of his time in Scotland, the instructors were warming up to him. They noted how helpful he was toward other students, Sonia included, describing him as a man who "grows on one," who "certainly appears the most natural leader here."

"The armies of General Wallenstein probably contained many men like him, if he had lived in the era of the professional soldier he might have been one," wrote an instructor.

And yet, "I do not think young French people would gather round him as an inspired leader, with joyful and exuberant acclamations, his values being different to theirs, and his mind working in a different direction."

Despite their mixed reviews, both Guy and Sonia were given the green light to proceed to Ringway Airfield in Manchester for parachute training.

It was nearing the end of January, and with each day Guy and Sonia were drawing closer: to each other, and to becoming full-fledged agents. And so shortly after they arrived at Ringway, on January 24, they were each given a single sheet with the heading "Declaration" to sign: "I declare that I will never disclose to anyone any information which I have acquired . . . as a result of my connection with this department . . . that disciplinary proceedings under the Official

Secrets Acts . . . may be taken against me if I at any time or in any way contravene the terms of this declaration."

Their signatures underlined the gravity of what they would soon be asked to do. They couldn't be further, however, from knowing what the long term would hold. But perhaps in this extraordinary suspended moment removed from all that was ordinary, it didn't matter. As they prepared to be schooled on how to drop into enemy territory, they were gradually falling for each other.

Ringway was a place where most parts of the SOE intersected, meaning that many agents crossed paths there who might not have otherwise. Sonia's time there overlapped with that of Violette Szabó, a stunning young British woman—and a mother—who was then a promising SOE recruit. Sonia would come to know her quite well, thought her "a lovely, lovely person, good fun, warm, gutsy, wasn't scared of anything." Violette, Sonia, and Nancy Wake became a trio to be reckoned with and at every opportunity would spend a lot of time partying together.

This was another place that offered a natural opportunity for Guy to shine—as the experienced paratrooper he was, and also as a mentor to the others, especially Sonia. All agents had to complete several clean jumps before they could move on to the final part of their training. For some of the agents—possibly most—it would be the very first time they had ever been in an airplane. Guy, meanwhile, had plenty of jump experience, so it didn't take long before his training was complete and his jumps assessed as "first class." Sonia, on the other hand, didn't relish parachuting, and that was clear from the start. Instructors would note that she was "quite nervous throughout the course."

In the weeks past, she had done many tasks she'd likely never contemplated. Guy was there all along. For nineteen-year-old Sonia, those exhilarating days would be seared in her memory, becoming inextricable from Guy. They were paired up again when it was time for Sonia to make her first practice jump out of a real, moving aircraft. Given the time they had spent together, and the early omen of their mutual desire to share an imaginary weekend in London, this decision by the instructors was likely no accident.

The plane reached the required altitude. As Sonia prepared to propel herself into the rushing wind, she was grinning from ear to ear. "She kept looking at me and laughing," said Guy, and he knew instinctively that she was nervous. He watched her as she grappled in real time with a lifetime fear of heights.

Then the jumpmaster gave her the signal: Go! As though Sonia had heard Guy's thoughts, she once again did the unexpected: she waved, smiled, and winked at him—and then turned around and dropped into the sky. Guy felt his heart leap. "I suddenly realized I might never see her again . . ."

In her instructors' estimation, Sonia made an average landing. Not bad for someone afraid of heights.

In that moment, Guy made himself a promise: "I decided to ask her to marry me."

Just as Sonia and Guy were about to embark on the last—and arguably most important—round of training, at what was described as the SOE's finishing school in the south of England, the SOE lost yet another agent. As far as HQ knew, twenty-one-year-old Roméo Sabourin—one of the youngest agents to be dispatched so far—had landed safely to begin his mission. In reality, HQ, thanks to one of its missing radios, had fallen into yet another German trap, and

Sabourin, another Canadian, had parachuted straight into the hands of the enemy. When he realized it, Sabourin engaged in a gunfight with his would-be captors, killing two of them before he was arrested and taken away, eventually to a concentration camp.

Throughout their training, the recruits would get wind of such hair-raising stories—hush-hush accounts of agents rounded up, interrogated, beaten, imprisoned in chains at concentration camps, having their toenails pulled to extract answers. "We always did hear the rumours," said Sonia. "We weren't supposed to but we would. And they were people that we'd just been with two or three days before."

The SOE nonetheless made sure its recruits had some idea of what it was like to be captured by the enemy. One night, it was Sonia's turn to be dragged from her bed by dead-serious men dressed as Gestapo agents. They questioned her roughly for hours. According to an instructor, she "stood up to interrogation very well."

At STS 33, at Beaulieu in Hampshire, much of the training was about trying to avoid that fate. And it was only there that the recruits finally learned the precise nature of their roles in France. Several revelations were made in the very first lecture there.

> *The purpose of the Organization to which you and I belong is subversion. Subversion, properly applied, is one of the most potent weapons one can use; it is the fourth arm in modern warfare.*

Home for the next few weeks was a romantic country house right on the beach in Beaulieu, aptly named The House on the Shore. That first lecture very quickly raised the enormous risks involved.

> *We shall be discussing with you every kind of measure for your own safety—the importance of having the right story to tell, the right*

> *kind of job to do, and how to lead your life most in accordance with those facts. We shall teach you how to build up your organization from zero. There is only one word of warning I wish to make here. If you follow conscientiously in the field all that we teach you here, we cannot guarantee your safety, but we think that your chance of being picked up is very small.*

The recruits were free to back out at any time, and many did. It was a wonder any of them hung in after the opening address at Beaulieu. There was no significant financial incentive—apart from a small raise—for being an SOE agent, no guaranteed fame. The public would know nothing of their sacrifices, and everything was done to ensure it would remain that way, possibly for decades. There was also every chance they would never return.

And yet both Sonia and Guy remained. As did dozens of others, among them a total of thirty-nine women deployed by F Section.

It was at Beaulieu that the recruits were introduced to the real spycraft that would help them operate as SOE agents behind enemy lines. They learned the more subtle arts of clandestine life: organization, recruitment, how to disguise themselves, how to lose a tail, how to organize a parachute reception committee. And most importantly, they learned how to hide in plain sight. In a lecture on "Cover" the instructor explained how:

> *Before your departure, with the assistance of your Section Officers, you will probably prepare a story of your past life up to the time of your arrival.*

This was where acting came in. They had to inhabit that new French persona, memorize everything about it, and forget everything about who they used to be.

To test their knowledge near the end of the course, each recruit had to complete a ninety-six-hour exercise that mimicked a real-life scenario.

Sonia's involved pretending to be a widow, and her mission was to gather information about a factory in the area of Nottingham. There she carried around a photo of a young boy whom she claimed was her son. (In reality it was a photo of her newest sibling, Leslie and Mina's two-year-old son, Michael.) To bolster her story, she went to Marks and Spencer and bought an inexpensive wedding ring. Sonia's performance in Nottingham did not go perfectly, and her instructors noted many failings that would have given her away—including carrying a spectacle case with her real name on it, and the speed with which her story unravelled when she was questioned by Nottingham police.

It was at Beaulieu, however, that one Ensign Davenport gave Sonia what was perhaps the most positive assessment since her training began. She wrote that Sonia had "plenty of personal courage," was "extraordinarily worldly for her age," and that she'd been no trouble during the course, "being completely wrapped up in d'Artois, who has helped considerably in her work."

In conclusion, the feedback on Sonia returned to the same themes: inability to focus, lack of concentration. Not "much head for book learning," Davenport wrote. "I think she would be good for a job that would require more physical toughness and courage, rather than anything which would need much brain-work."

There was one more training stop for Guy and Sonia. "Cookery school" appealed to them both, and they chose to sign up for it together. They learned how to make explosives using basic household products that could be easily purchased; these included acetone, paraffin wax, and different types of fertilizer. Both Sonia and

Guy enjoyed the course, and Sonia seemed to have an aptitude for it, "memorising the ingredients and tricky quantities as though she were baking a cake." In an orange military-issue school exercise book, Sonia kept meticulous notes in pencil. In recipe style, ingredients followed by method, she jotted down three ways of making ammonium nitrate and how to make homemade grenades using explosive material, paraffin wax, sawdust, and tins. Upon completion, Sonia was noted for working "well but had a tendency to let her partner do most of the work."

And yet with training officially over, HQ declared that Sonia "has done well in training and is now operationally ready." She and Guy and the others returned to London's Marylebone neighbourhood, and to the limbo that was Halfway House on Weymouth Street, where they awaited their deployment.

The hostel certainly lived up to its nickname. Its inhabitants were emphatically back in the "real world," and yet unable to fully embrace it. They knew they could be ordered to deploy to enemy territory at any moment, suddenly forced to become someone else. They checked in every day. If it was not yet their turn, they withdrew again into the suspended existence of their confined world. They remained constrained, unsettled, and necessarily anonymous.

Any repressed anxiety would inevitably find an outlet in the late nights of drinking and dancing. Together, Sonia, Nancy, and Violette spared no effort in seeking out comfort in the big city's wartime nightlife.

It was sometime during this period at 32 Weymouth Street that Sonia crossed paths with Sydney Hudson, the blue-eyed, serene-looking agent who'd escaped from a French prison. She was sitting around with some of the others in the hostel lounge one day when Sydney walked in and caught her attention. It was shortly after he had returned from his epic journey. Somehow, they started talking, but even before they said a word, they had so much in common: growing up abroad with British parents; learning French early; the lives they were living that very moment, as agents-in-waiting.

Their connection was instantaneous.

With no iron-clad commitment to Guy holding her back, Sonia decided to meet Sydney for a date. It was no doubt a detour from where Sonia and Guy seemed to be heading, but something compelled her: Was it a minor rupture with Guy? An inordinately strong attraction to this calm, quiet older man? Did Guy know? Was he also dating someone else in the interim?

There was no doubt that this development presented a challenge to the relationship Sonia and Guy had formed, that it must have threatened its steady progress. Sydney, for his part, was instantly smitten with Sonia. Though a fourteen-year age difference stood between them, they met more than once: he the experienced older agent, she the untested younger agent-to-be, engrossed in an unexpected meeting of minds.

"We liked one another a lot," Sonia explained. "It was one of those things that you know, you look at somebody and it just clicks right away." It was one of those things that she could not have foreseen, and that he, newly detached from everyday life, could only have hoped for. But in wartime, anything was possible.

Over the course of their conversations, however, Sonia learned that Sydney was married. She was taken aback, and even more so when she learned that he had a young daughter. Sonia recalled Sydney trying to explain that his marriage was all but over. But with the history of her own parents' turbulent marriage in mind, she divested herself of the relationship before it went too far. As she put it, "There was no way I was ever going to be responsible for breaking up a marriage."

Sonia swiftly moved on. It had been a momentary infatuation. Maybe it had been necessary to meet Sydney in order to be sure about Guy. Maybe the brief test brought them closer. Maybe in the spring of 1944, as the war was about to reach a crescendo, relationships simply couldn't go in a straight line.

10

FIRST DISAPPOINTMENT

Sonia and Guy • *London, April 1944*

In the cool early spring days of April, several of Sonia and Guy's friends began to disappear. On the night of April 5th Lilian Rolfe dropped into France as a radio operator for the HISTORIAN network. The same night, Violette Szabó left for her assignment in the Rouen region. Hot on her heels was Montrealer Jean-Paul Archambault, who was sent in to organize the resistance in a corner of the Saône-et-Loire region with the DITCHER network. And on the night of April 8th, Stan Makowski, the Polish officer who had briefly pursued Sonia, also left. On the very same flight was Sydney Hudson, who was leaving for his second stint in France, this time to establish a new circuit from scratch near Paris.

For those agents-in-waiting still at 32 Weymouth Street, the narrow, unassuming building they called Halfway House, the only requirement was to visit HQ once a day for updates, briefings, or new equipment, instructions, or fittings for their tailor-made French wardrobes. The exact date of D-Day was still a matter of utmost secrecy, yet with such a flurry of deployments there was little doubt it was near. The ever-dwindling group knew their turn was coming. In the interim, they partied as only one could on the eve of battle: with abandon. These were memorable, emotional nights. But they were also ephemeral.

With Sydney relegated to a minor distraction in Sonia's life, she and Guy carried on. If the diversion had any lasting effect, they had somehow put it behind them. They did have some hiccups, though. Guy once found Sonia smoking a pipe and was so angry about it that he shut her out and wouldn't speak to her, until the night ended in tears—and a real marriage proposal. Now it was only a question of when they would tie the knot.

They waited together, hoping to be deployed to France as a team. And eventually, they learned they would. The SOE was assigning Guy to help organize the maquis in the Saône-et-Loire region. Sonia would act as his courier.

It was as good a moment as any for the young couple to seriously deliberate marriage. Guy liked the idea of marrying once they arrived in France. Sonia, on the other hand, preferred that they tie the knot right away, before they were deployed. It was a hasty decision, but they ultimately opted for a London wedding.

With curfews, blackouts, and shortages to contend with, planning a wedding in wartime London was an exercise in tempering expectations. Guy and Sonia had little money, and so they agreed to keep it simple. They would marry in their military uniforms. Sonia's only nod to luxury would be silk stockings and a khaki-coloured pure silk shirt to wear underneath her uniform. She wandered all over London looking for such a shirt, until she found it at Lilywhites. For a ring they'd use the Marks and Spencer band that Sonia had bought for her final exercise in Nottingham. As another cost-saving measure, they would defer buying Guy a ring, just for now. There would also be no flowers.

Sonia also told Guy she would not be inviting her mother.

She broke the news to her father while the two of them were attending the wedding of a family friend. Leslie was dismayed at receiving such short notice—how would he find the alcohol to throw a wedding party? He approved of Guy but told Sonia to "tell him to learn English."

There was also the matter of May Talbot, Guy's intended, who was waiting for him back home. Sonia encouraged him to break the news to her sooner rather than later. Guy went to the telegraph office and dictated a heartless single line: "L'HOMME PROPOSE, ET DIEU DISPOSE." Something like "A man's heart plans his way, but the Lord directs his steps."

One final but pivotal hurdle was securing Buckmaster's permission.

Even during training, Sonia and Guy's relationship was a matter of debate. Opinion was divided among their instructors about whether such a love affair would be a help or a hindrance in the field. Some believed that Guy had a positive influence in bolstering Sonia's confidence and improving her skills. But others were less certain of the benefits.

"If she works with him it is doubtful whether the arrangement would be good for either of them," one instructor wrote. "If, on the other hand, she is separated from him, she would not prove at all efficient. In these circumstances it is doubtful whether she would be employed."

In Ensign Davenport's view, "If they went over together, I would hate to think what would happen if ever he found someone else who interested him more."

Yet in a third assessment, this one in Guy's finishing school report, another instructor opined that their relationship "might prove a serious advantage were they to work together."

Buckmaster, it appears, wasn't so certain. He was apparently uncomfortable with the impending union, knowing as he did the perils of sending a husband and wife together into the field—and the potential for harm if they fell into enemy hands. As a way to extract information or encourage cooperation, one could be tortured or one's life could be threatened in front of the other. And so Buckmaster summoned Sonia and Guy, separately, to his office. He first explained to Guy why it was a bad idea. Guy emerged from his office to where Sonia was waiting her turn. By then Buckmaster was adamant about talking Sonia out of the wedding. But then, as Sonia recalled, he saw the look on her face. He knew how stubborn and determined she was. So apparently he decided it wasn't even worth trying.

With only days or at most weeks left before the young couple would deploy, Buckmaster couldn't in good conscience stand in their way. Instead, he would attend the wedding and stand witness to their union. Along with those who predicted Guy and Sonia's marriage wouldn't last, Buckmaster now kept his opinions to himself.

On April 15, 1944, Sonia and Guy walked into St. James's Church at Spanish Place in the Borough of St. Marylebone wearing uniforms and easy smiles. The Gothic stone church that regularly welcomed hundreds of Catholic worshippers was now in the service of a modest wedding. To cut costs, Sonia's stepmother, Mina, had made the wedding cake from scratch and Sonia had carried it herself on the train from Woking all the way to London. She'd invited some of her civilian friends as well as some of the staff at the SOE, and Mary Hackett, another longstanding friend she'd made in the WAAF, was her maid of honour. Several agents also attended, including Canadians, and Nancy Wake, whose very presence virtually guaranteed that it would turn into a rocking party. Following the ceremony Buckmaster disappeared when it was time to take photos outside.

Guy and Sonia linked arms for a snap, the closest to an official wedding-day photo, just outside the church. As the photographer pressed the shutter, Sonia, wearing her FANY uniform and beret, stepped forward, as if propelling herself into an uncertain future. And yet she was genuinely beaming. Her childlike cheeks pressed against eyes brimming with joy; next to her was an equally cheerful Guy. One frame couldn't possibly contain all their hopes and their shared romantic view of that day, the coming days, the entire future they had imagined together. They were defying the war, thumbing their nose at it, and for one fleeting moment it bent to their will. After the formalities, the party moved to the Royal Air Force Club on Piccadilly, where Leslie, thanks to his connections, had managed to arrange on short notice for a rare open bar. The young couple and their friends would later bar-hop into the early morning hours, just as they had all along since their training had ended.

Only now they were Mr. and Mrs. Guy and Sonia d'Artois, a change that the SOE bureaucracy put in motion a day before the wedding. The couple had a short honeymoon in the beautiful port town of Penzance in Cornwall. And when they returned they were no longer waiting for their mission at Halfway House; instead the SOE had arranged more suitable accommodations at a small hotel on Half Moon Street. Guy and Sonia arranged for a formal photo together, a beautifully lit one in a professional studio—again in uniform. This time, Sonia had added a borrowed military shoulder patch that read "Canada."

It was only a handful of days after their union that the happy couple received unhappy news.

The debate over their deployment together had raged on in the background, and Buckmaster and the SOE had made a final decision. Now that they were married, they were going to France separately. For their own protection.

Sonia and Guy were fated to fight their wars apart.

PART IV

BEHIND ENEMY LINES

11

FROM THE HEAVENS

Dieudonné • *Over France, May 23, 1944*

The captain gave his first warning at twenty minutes out. He knew nothing about the agents hitching a ride on his plane that early, moonless morning, nothing of the stories that had brought them to this singular moment in those battle-worn skies. Still, he joined them in the awkward confines of the fuselage to share some cognac and cigarettes—a final indulgence before the agents would jump into France, and into the possibility of no return.

"[Are these] our last cigarettes and our last drink?" Guy rhetorically asked the British captain presiding over this Allied gathering in the sky. The co-pilot was Australian, and among the agents were two Canadians and one British. There were also two radio operators: one was American; the other was French and the lone woman on board.

Madeleine Lavigne had already had a harrowing maiden stint as a courier for an SOE circuit in her home city of Lyon, where she'd also helped forge identity cards for agents, downed pilots, and members of the resistance. She had been betrayed, then she'd escaped, and then she was tried and convicted of terrorism in absentia. After that she went through some training with the SOE in the U.K. and was now on her way back to France, this time as a radio operator—a partially trained one. Demand for them in the field was such that she'd never finished her course. She hadn't seen her two boys since she'd been evacuated to England four months earlier.

It was close to two in the morning. This was Guy's second foray into French skies and into the anxious realm of the unknown. The first time he'd flown with the Carpetbaggers, one of the American bomber units now working overtime out of Harrington Airfield, east of Birmingham, to ferry agents and supplies into France ahead of D-Day. But that night a thickly overcast sky had intervened. After three hours of flying the crew couldn't see the intended drop zone, nor could they spot the lights that would have signalled the presence of the reception committee. They circled for eight minutes before turning back toward British airspace, frustrated but safe. Under the circumstances, that alone counted for a lot.

Just over a week after that aborted attempt, Sonia and Guy's farewell ritual was repeating itself.

Sonia was distraught. She had been shocked when Buckmaster summoned her to say she wouldn't be going to France with Guy. She made a rash decision to refuse deployment, declaring, "I'm not going to go if I can't go with my husband." She then walked right out and slammed the door behind her.

Despite this, Sonia and Buckmaster were together again at the RAF Tempsford airfield, their gazes lingering on Guy as he prepared to take off a second time.

Guy was dressed head to toe in a camouflage jumpsuit. In a money belt strapped to his body he'd stashed half a million francs—a substantial amount, given that it reportedly took 600 francs a month to maintain one member of the maquis. Guy also carried a knife, a .32 pistol, and the same air of confidence he always carried, but nothing else of his previous life. The closest he had to personal possessions were clothes and suits made by a French tailor in London expressly for this assignment and handed to him to change into at the airport, and forged papers that identified him as a local. Even his watch was forbidden. In those final few minutes Buckmaster reached out, took it off, and handed Guy a French-made one. Then, instead of wishing him good luck, Buckmaster offered him the preferred French version: "*Merde*!"

Guy then said his goodbyes to Sonia, his new bride of only five weeks.

In the short period they'd known each other, Sonia and Guy had lived a whole lifetime: celebrating their first Christmas together, their first New Year's Eve, and each other's springtime birthdays, only five weeks apart. They'd had their wedding, their honeymoon, and, upon being denied the chance to serve as a team, their first disappointment. And now they were embarking on their first separation.

They joined countless young couples who were brought together by the war, only to find themselves pried apart by it. Many of those marriages, like Sonia and Guy's, were hasty affairs, ushered down the aisle by the urgency of wartime and a desperation to seize happiness while they could—while they were still alive. Who knew what would come in a month, or a year, or under the wrath of the next air raid? For the legions of women sending lovers off to the battlefield, there was at least the theoretical possibility of sending a heartfelt letter, a food parcel or a picture to connect and help raise morale. For Sonia and Guy there would be none of that.

After weeks of being inseparable, they had to contend with zero contact. It was forbidden. Nothing. Nothing about the dangers they might face, the people they would meet, the lives they would lead apart. It was as though it had all been a dream, and now they were waking up to reality. Or maybe it was the other way around. Their marriage would now effectively be on indefinite pause. In their final embrace, there was a strong conviction that one day they'd pick up where they had left off and carry on. There was also profound fear that they might never lay eyes on each other ever again. That farewell, Sonia would later say, was the hardest thing she'd ever had to do—twice over.

This time Guy would fly over in a British RAF Halifax bomber. He climbed aboard the plane with four other agents, and with no idea when he might see his new wife again. They took off at 10:24 p.m., and once airborne, Guy was en route to the country of his ancestors—just a few dozen kilometres from the Alsace-Lorraine border region that had inspired one of his names.

Left behind, Sonia was inconsolable. After years of aimlessness Guy had become an anchor, an address, a kind of home. And now he was gone.

"I felt absolutely bereft," she once recalled. "It had all been such an adventure. As long as we were together, I always felt we'd make it. Now he was gone and I didn't know if I would ever see him again."

High above France, the bomber that carried Guy and his fellow agents was nearing its target. Cognacs drained and cigarettes smoked, the agents started to get into position.

Of the group dropping into France, it would be the youngest and least experienced who would jump first: the outlandishly young American Joseph Gerard Litalien, who was on the journey of a lifetime a month shy of his eighteenth birthday.

Joseph, code-named Jacquot, had been a student when his life was irrevocably interrupted, a teenager who hadn't yet settled into a career when he signed up, listing his part-time "shipping clerk" and "theatre usher" roles as previous employment. Early on at the SOE he was judged "too young and immature for useful work in the field." Still, with only one year of naval service and three months of SOE training behind him, he was now about to land as the new, desperately sought radio operator for the DITCHER circuit, to which Guy had also been assigned. Beyond his age and inexperience, there was one other problem: although Litalien's parents had been born in Canada, and with names like Germain and Antoinette were likely francophone, he was born and raised in the town of Leominster, Massachusetts, and his French was mediocre at best. Still, as far as DITCHER was concerned, Joseph was, along with his radio, arguably the most precious cargo on this flight: together they would become Guy's only lifeline to the outside world.

Guy would drop next. As a seasoned jumper, he knew what to expect when he received the signal to propel himself out of the plane. But he hadn't always been so self-assured.

"There are minutes in life that count like hours, but those preceding a first parachute jump count like generations," he once told a reporter, describing his very first jump. It was a moment in which he felt "the uncontrollable prickle of fear."

"Neither pride, prestige, nor bravado, nothing helps, only the very human instinct for self-preservation remains. It was impossible to forget the danger."

Guy's imminent jump into France was a whole new level of danger. He was leaping into darkness, into unfamiliar, occupied territory—he knew not a soul on the ground—and he was doing so on the eve of a major flare-up in a global war. His entire mission was fraught with peril, but perhaps there was no more perilous moment than the arrival. And yet, to Guy, it was all "an adventure," as he once said. "Something new."

If Guy was more self-assured than Joseph about the jump, he was less so about the assignment and the ultimate objective; these were as yet only words on paper. SOE agents didn't know the exact date of D-Day, but they sensed it was coming, soon. It was foreshadowed right there in the personalized typed instructions Guy was handed before leaving:

> *Our most important single objective at the present stage is to make sure that our D-Day programme functions with the maximum effectiveness.*

Guy's primary task was to enable a sabotage campaign that would hamper German forces from responding to an Allied landing from D-Day forward. The instructions, dated April 26, 1944, refer to an agent, code-named Tiburce, who was already operating in the Saône-et-Loire region and had been tasked with leading the vast DITCHER circuit and organizing the resistance for action on D-Day. Ten days earlier, Guy's instructions explain, Tiburce had made a specific request for "a lieutenant" to lead a party "600 men strong."

> *Your mission is to act as lieutenant to* TIBURCE *the purpose of taking charge of the body of men mentioned . . .*

If there was anything resembling an ideal prototype for an F Section agent, then the man code-named Tiburce came rather close. Flight Lieutenant Albert Browne-Bartroli's life skated across three cultures—he'd been raised in Marseille, the multilingual son of a bourgeois Catalan mother and a British father in charge of installing telephone lines between Marseille and Barcelona. Before the war, Albert had been a "chemist with a penchant for poetry." There was no shortage of eclectic personalities among agents of the SOE.

Albert, it just so happened, also had a sister deployed in France for the SOE. Eliane Plewman had parachuted in two months ahead of him to work in the Marseille region where they were raised. But after a laudable start Eliane had disappeared, and Albert had gone weeks without news of her. He didn't yet know that back in March she'd been captured by the Gestapo.

For the moment, Albert had more immediate concerns. The local men he'd recruited and organized were having to lie low after a series of devastating German reprisal attacks that had begun just weeks after he arrived.

In addition, Albert's predecessor—who'd been doubling as the radio operator—had left in February and returned to the U.K. The local man trained to replace him initially struggled at staying in regular touch with London. That meant delays in the parachuting of arms at a crucial moment.

The Halifax en route to France that night was carrying the re-inforcements Albert needed: Joseph would be Albert's new radio operator, and Lieutenant Guy d'Artois would take charge of the resistance in the Charolles region in eastern France, more or less without oversight. For a military man who was nevertheless "intolerant of discipline," it was the perfect assignment. Guy was code-named Dieudonné, meaning "God-given," or "a gift from God." And he would come to inhabit that description, in the eyes of his most loyal followers and in his own, later likening his role to a "Rex Imperator," or king emperor. It seemed far removed from the "cog in the wheel" role he'd been promised back in training at Camp X. Emperor or not, in the estimation of his trainers, Guy would bring "great drive" and "self confidence" to the far grander role of helping to turn the war around.

Ten minutes out, the agents at the back of the plane received another warning. Guy prepared the equipment chutes.

For the SOE, the instructions said, discipline was a matter of the "highest importance." But it wouldn't be easy to impose discipline on people desperate to drive out an occupying force.

> *This is going to be an extremely difficult task since not only will there be general excitement, but they may see other groups with different directives—or no directives at all—taking action all around them.*

Given the "probable shortness of time" before D-Day dawned, Guy's instructions were to prioritize attacks on railways—the lifeline that brought in supplies, personnel, and ammunition for the German occupation. Next on the target list were telephones and roads. Guerrilla activities came last.

At three minutes the men attached their parachutes to the line.

> *You will be parachuted into France accompanied by Jacquot,*
> *who is to be W/T operator for Tiburce, to a point*
> *12 ½ kms. N.N.W. of Amberieu*
> *3 ½ [kms.] W.N.W. of Pont d'Ain.*

At two minutes they were standing in position, waiting for the signal.

"You have to act quickly, like thought," Guy said, finding words for the intensity of every parachuting experience.

"It takes tremendous effort to control one's nerves. But as the call of duty kicks in, so does a relative calm with which you approach the abyss."

Joseph, Guy, Madeleine, and the two others, each waited their turn, walked up to the trap door open to the abyss, stared at the red light, and, when it turned green—"GO!"—they dropped.

Then silence.

"Once in space, an extraordinary clarity guides our descent. Eight to ten feet from landing, the wind stops affecting the parachute, and we're suddenly projected to the ground. You run through your muscles to try to find your feet first."

Quoting Voltaire on finding the ground, Guy adds: "Once done, you feel like 'it's only the first step that costs.'" It's only the beginning that's difficult.

Guy landed within seconds. Then he took his first few steps on French soil, breathing in the muted, humid air.

"When that plane flew off and left me alone in the dark French countryside, I felt some funny tugs at my heart," Guy once said in a newspaper interview. "I was all alone from there on in."

On the ground, Albert was growing impatient. He and his men had spotted the Halifax as it flew by, and there they stood, ready with their lights, following it with their eyes as much as the darkness would allow. The drop zone was a wide field of green stretching into the distance, punctuated by hedges, framed by lush wheat farms and a vast, cloudy sky. There wasn't a single house in sight—not that you could tell for sure in the pitch darkness. After a few moments, the plane circled back, but it was still too high in the sky for a drop to make sense—surely it couldn't have happened from that altitude. The plane skirted the horizon a final time, went out of view, and then disappeared.

At least two full hours passed and still there were no signs of any agents. Two of Albert's men wanted to hightail it back to Lyon before sunrise. They were ready to give up.

Just then, Albert recalled, a woman staggered into the car's headlights, "white as a ghost." Madeleine Lavigne was so disoriented she could barely speak. The men understood right away that the drop had indeed been made—and at such an unconscionable height! While some of them tended to the woman, the others rushed into the fields, wading chest deep into the wheat to look for the rest. They had to find them before someone else did.

As luck would have it, Guy had missed the landing field by about three kilometres. He hit the ground and then, somehow in the fog that had settled over the darkness, found Joseph. Together they dragged their parachutes to nearby mounds of hay, hid them underneath, and then started walking. After two fruitless hours in the countryside there was still no sign of their reception committee. Guy had a backup plan—he'd memorized an address where he could find refuge if he failed to find the welcoming party—although going that route would be much harder, much more perilous.

Then Guy and Joseph heard men speaking French in the distance. The voices drew nearer. Guy couldn't be sure it was the reception committee, so he hid behind a wall, and then he yelled out, "Halt!"

The group stopped cold.

Albert remembers seeing a figure in a trench coat appear with a pistol pointing at his chest. It was Guy.

"Who are you?" the man with the gun, speaking in French, asked drily.

"It's me, Toto," said Albert, using his local nickname. "Quickly, quickly we must call everyone, look for the others."

"I don't know Toto."

They went back and forth. Finally, the man with the dry voice asked, "Do you know Tiburce?"

"Yes, it's me."

Now in English, the man said, "What's [the] name of your bloody circuit?"

"DITCHER."

Guy was relieved, and so was Albert. He had found the rest of his missing agents.

His men quickly bundled off the agents: Guy and Joseph were taken in one direction and Guy never saw those other agents on the ground again.

They rushed a short distance, along the winding farm roads through verdant hills Guy would come to know well. But as they drove on, the euphoria of arriving in one piece would have eventually made way for the sinking realization that there was no turning back, no way out—not easily, anyway. Guy had no uniform, no trained army to help him in this fight, and no Sonia. There was only France and its people, chafing under occupation. It was daunting: a well-entrenched, brutal occupation would have to end before Guy could go home again.

They pulled up at a safe house. Guy and Joseph, finally indoors and out of view, were then bombarded with a hail of questions about Allied intentions: When would D-Day come? How soon? They were served wine and food that they devoured as Albert watched. He was amazed that the SOE had sent him an actual teenager for a radio operator—one who admitted he was drinking wine for the first time. Albert was also irritated by Joseph's mediocre French—and decided then and there to find him an escort and keep him mostly indoors, away from cities or villages where his bad French could quickly expose him.

At the same time, Albert had triangulated Guy's identity in short order by noting his wiry body and short-cropped hair: he was unmistakably army.

He recognized his accent, too. It was just like Jean-Paul's: another Canadian, who'd been parachuted to him in April to take over operations in nearby Ain and as a result missed Sonia and Guy's wedding. It also wouldn't take long for Albert to detect Guy's hostility toward oversight and his impatience with slow progress. But he'd also be pleased with this young soldier who'd been chosen to take control of the Charolles region. After his initial assessment and a little small talk with the men, Albert walked out into the darkness and left them to rest.

The following day Guy and Joseph were taken to a terracotta-roofed farmhouse on the edge of Ferme la Breuille—the home of Pierre Jandeau, nicknamed Dédé. The property was a regular stop for members of the resistance, "no matter the hour of day or night," a quiet place where they could rest and collect themselves before moving on.

Mme Jandeau, the matriarch, now welcomed the men with a meal and the obligatory wine. Soon she came up with a new name for the sharp, handsome Canadian now in their midst: she anointed him Michel, apparently in reference to the archangel, because Guy had "come to us from the heavens like St. Michel." Before long it would become Michel le Canadien, and for many in the region it was the only name they knew for the man who'd dropped from the sky to help them.

Guy took the corner bedroom off the kitchen, which looked out into the green valley. When he saw the countryside in daytime, he was struck most by the red terracotta rooftops, which were unlike anything he'd seen in Canada. He slept nearly the entirety of that first day, then woke up anxious to get to work.

All vestiges of Guy's old life receded except for whatever he smuggled in by memory. He was one of the few agents permitted to keep most of his original name, at least at the start. His forged identity papers christened him Robert Guy d'Artois, and like him, Robert was also a military man. Guy kept the same birthdate in the same year. But he did not inhabit that identity for long—locals told him the name conjured up a despised historical figure. He had a pile of others handy, with such names as Pierre Desbrosses and Henri Faubert, all with different birthdates as well as a variety of callings: driver, labourer, wine merchant—the latter a common occupation in a region known for its vineyards. Guy made it a habit to start each day by asking himself, "Who am I today?"

The training back in Scotland had started to kick in. But even with all the briefings about France and French habits, on the ground there were still plenty of pitfalls. His first test came shortly after he arrived, on foot, for the first time in the town of Charolles. He almost gave himself away at a small hotel when he asked about the whereabouts of the bathroom. He followed the proprietress's directions but couldn't find it and went back to ask again. Perplexed, she guided him there. He had simply failed to recognize a squat toilet, he'd never seen one before. Guy could tell that the woman understood he was likely a foreigner. Luckily, he learned that she was sympathetic to the resistance and wouldn't expose him.

Charolles, a humble town of ancient walls, shuttered windows, imposing trees, and a modest church, was already a hub of resistance activity, and would soon be central to Guy's new life. First, he had to find his main contact.

Guy spotted the woman as soon as her kerchief hit the ground and followed her all the way down rue de la Condémine to a two-storey house with large arched windows at the front, porthole windows on the sides, and a small, walled-off garden shuttered by a gate out front. Her name was Madame Laure Sarrazin, although everyone called her Maman Lucienne, and she was a *résistante de la prèmiere heure,* from the start. She was small, elegant, and stern, and along with her ruddy-faced husband, Jean, a real wine salesman, served as a linchpin of the local resistance movement. They owned a café in the centre of town that was frequented by members of the resistance looking for a meal and a few glasses of wine in a safe place.

Behind closed doors, Maman Lucienne gave Guy a full briefing on the state of the local resistance. The maquis groups were scattered and they were in need of supplies: clothing, vehicles, and arms. Especially arms. They also needed training. It was thus far hampered, Albert explained, because there was a "great shortage of ammunition, owing to the small number of receptions being carried out," and "secondly, because the noise would attract attention to the maquis."

It was crucial in this pre-invasion phase to keep action to a minimum. There were, after all, the occasional German convoys still passing through. Guy began practising the habit of sleeping in different places every night. But Maman Lucienne's house, tucked just steps from the cobblestoned place de la Balance and the local hospital, was an ideal hiding place for Guy; it became both an occasional home and a de facto resistance headquarters. It was smartly furnished, and somehow, no matter the circumstances, had impeccably polished floors.

In time the house on rue de la Condémine earned the name "Villa des Alliés": a meeting place, a hiding place, an underground headquarters for the SOE. Maman Lucienne herself would become everything to Guy—a protector, a banker, and crucially, a wise adviser. Although local German forces suspected that she and her husband harboured resistance figures, they never turned Guy out. She was, according to Guy, "the best woman I have ever seen."

With the Sarrazins' help, Guy got down to work. As he later recalled, he found that many in his district "talked much, everybody wanted to do something, but nobody tried very hard to do anything at first." Even more challenging was that "everyone was a chief." Too many leaders, not enough followers. But there were still many willing to work with him. Along with the Sarrazins, early on there was Jean Tabourin (also known as Jean Morin), a twenty-six-year-old local who'd served in the French military, knew the terrain like no one else, and had deep contacts among farmers in the area. He brought Guy his first nine men—volunteers Jean had persuaded to work with him. Guy trusted Jean, and in short order he became his first lieutenant and confidant.

There were plenty more young men hiding in the forests, including Maman Lucienne's own son. She promised to help Guy recruit the men he needed, with only one request in return: to do whatever it took to keep her son safe. Guy promised he would. And so Maman Lucienne and Jean Tabourin spread the word among trusted contacts, emphasizing that the newly arrived agent was Canadian, not an "*anglais*," a distinction Maman Lucienne felt would help their cause.

Except for a handful of men in his tight inner circle, Guy kept everyone guessing about his identity and whereabouts. For most of those he interacted with, Michel le Canadien wasn't necessarily

Guy, and Guy wasn't Michel le Canadien. It was a minor detail as locals prepared for a long-awaited battle to throw off an intolerable occupation.

On the tarmac after watching Guy leave, Buckmaster asked Sonia if there was anything he could do. Despite her earlier threats to resign, she replied without hesitation.

"Yes. You can get me a mission as quickly as possible."

Buckmaster had another conundrum where Sonia was concerned. Even before all this, the SOE office was concerned about sending Sonia into the field—not because of her performance, but because she was not at all well. Just a day before Guy's departure the SOE had asked a doctor to examine her. He found "evidence of loss of weight, rather pale colour, enlarged gland on the left side of the neck."

His conclusion left little room for discussion:

"This girl is at present in poor physical condition. It is recommended that she be given three to four weeks rest in the country and her case reviewed at the end of this time. She certainly will not be fit for active work in the field for some weeks." Signed by "A.G./Med."

Below that, someone else had written in pencil:

"I gather she is very keen to go to the field, but the risk seems to me a big one for herself and others if we sent her in her present condition and she cracks up—On the other hand it may be just what is needed to put her right.

P.S. I think I should take the risk."

And ultimately, Buckmaster decided he would.

12

A "GIRL" COURIER

Blanche • *Le Mans, May 23, 1944*

The same night Guy successfully parachuted into Charolles in eastern France, Flying Officer Edmund Elie La Porte, also from Quebec, was in mid-flight in the skies over the northwestern part of the country. The Halifax III LK810 was just one of more than a hundred aircraft in a sprawling Bomber Command operation to bomb key transport infrastructure all over France. The pilot and his six-man crew, all Canadian except one British, were en route to target the railway yards in the strategic city of Le Mans.

Their average age was just over twenty-two. La Porte was all of twenty.

Down below, Le Mans was blanketed in darkness, forcibly muted under the twin thumbs of curfew and blackout. Suddenly the sirens blared an alert, disturbing the calm and waking residents from their sleep. Witnesses who dared to look outside saw tracer shells flying up at the phantom aircraft streaking across the dark sky. Explosions followed, ending the anxiety of the wait but amplifying the terror.

It was nearing three o'clock in the morning. The Halifax may or may not have delivered its payload when it began a terrifying unplanned descent. The men may or may not have had time to register the fright of learning that their aircraft had been fatally wounded. There might have been a desperate attempt to keep the plane flying, a shouting of instructions. There might have been only last-second prayers. Thoughts of loved ones. Howls about the unfairness of it all. Or maybe it was instant silence. We will never know. When the plane hit the ground all but one of the men were killed. Gone forever. Struck from the strength of their generation of Canadians and all generations thereafter.

The lone survivor was the rear gunner, Sergeant Robert McGowan, who was as lucky and unlucky as you could possibly get in a theatre of war. He was gravely injured but feverishly clung to life, only to be captured by German forces. After a hospital stay in Le Mans he was taken to a prisoner of war camp inside Germany.

Locals recovered the bodies of the rest of his crew and buried them under wooden crosses in the cemetery just north of central Le Mans. It wasn't the end these men had expected. With all the families, the lovers, and the suspended lives waiting for them at home, they had every intention of returning. But they had come to stay.

Beyond the railyards and factories on the edge of town, the city of Le Mans had largely been spared the kind of wide-scale damage wrought by Allied bombers. In the narrow streets of the old town and in their tiny, timid houses, Le Mans, in spots, felt like a quaint and insignificant small town. But during its latest episode of war it was home to somewhere around one hundred thousand people—plus all the Germans who'd also come to stay. The imposing, ornate Saint-Julien Cathedral and the busy rail station added to the feel of a capital city—a role Le Mans had played for various inhabitants of the region since Roman times. It was also home to some of the best-preserved Roman defensive walls anywhere, lending the place a sense of timeless significance.

In the 1940s, Le Mans became a German stronghold. The SOE described it as an "important junction": a strategic town not only in being a key centre of communications and rail transport for German forces but also in being situated about two hours from so much that mattered in this war: from Paris; from the coast, where the Allied forces would eventually land; and where German Field Marshal Erwin Rommel kept his Normandy headquarters. In Le Mans itself that year, Rommel's officers and attendant soldiers were everywhere—in the châteaus and the opulent apartments, in occupied or commandeered private homes, in the several bunkers that sprang up lightning-fast out of nowhere all over Le Mans, and in the black-market restaurants crawling with Gestapo, along with their loyal French *miliciens* and civilian hangers-on.

Still, in a nod to the city's strategic importance, in the spring of 1944 the SOE embarked on establishing HEADMASTER, a new circuit in Le Mans and the wider Sarthe region. An agent codenamed Albin parachuted into a nearby area in early April, just ahead of Easter; then, a few days later, he cycled the one hundred kilometres to position himself in one of the most challenging areas for the SOE to operate in France.

The Sarthe was, after all, one of the regions caught up in the ill-fated PHYSICIAN circuit, also referred to as the PROSPER circuit, whose collapse had ensnared hundreds of local resistance men and women and led to their wholesale execution in November of 1943. That brutal history—one that had left many among the local population afraid, if not outright hostile—along with the heavy presence of Germans, meant that building a new circuit would be doubly challenging. Vera Atkins and Maurice Buckmaster had given Albin a detailed briefing about that history. He had reason to be extremely wary. The quiet British agent nonetheless agreed to take it on.

Albin had a very bumpy start. On precisely the same day the Halifax fell out of the sky, he lost a colleague, Muriel Byck, the daughter of British-French Jews, who had been sent in as a radio operator for a neighbouring circuit. Albin had parachuted in with her, and he well remembered the moment they finally found each other in the dark, and when, in euphoric celebration of their safe landing on French soil, he gave Muriel an unsolicited—and likely unwanted—kiss. Now he would never see her again. Far from home, she had died, not at the hands of the enemy, but from meningitis. She was just days shy of her twenty-sixth birthday.

Albin and his radio operator, codenamed Gaston, had made some contacts, identified safe houses, and reconnoitred drop zones for the arms and munitions they needed for the work required of them. They had established contact with London and had already received Sten guns and explosives, now stashed away until it was time. But they suffered a major setback when a planned drop was executed several kilometres away from the intended target zone, right at the edge of a village. They rushed over to try to salvage the materiel but it was too heavy, their attempt too dangerous, given the proximity to homes. They abandoned the effort, leaving German troops to round up the weapons the next day.

"If the Gestapo had not been alerted before, they certainly were now," Albin said.

With D-Day approaching, like Albert in Saône-et-Loire, Albin needed more SOE agents on the ground.

"I sent a message to Buck and his staff asking for a capable organizer and for a girl courier. I felt that a girl could pass unnoticed in the town or the countryside much more easily than could a man and on other occasions could accompany me when visiting our contacts in Le Mans," he recalled.

Five days after Guy fell from the sky—and two weeks after her twentieth birthday—Sonia, HEADMASTER's new "girl courier," parachuted behind enemy lines.

28 May, 1944

As she did with many female agents leaving on a mission, Vera Atkins likely accompanied Sonia in the "Black Maria" gliding toward Harrington Airfield. Sonia took a liking to Atkins and would come to "almost worship" her. Although she cut a stern and stoic figure—she terrified some among the staff—in moments like these Atkins provided comfort and words of advice to the women heading to the field, some of them leaving home for the very first time. Then, in their final moments together, she'd check their pockets once more to ensure there was nothing—not a train ticket, a cigarette pack, a note—that could reveal their point of departure.

"I was also involved with the personal side of the people who were leaving for the field," Atkins would later explain, "including getting them to write a will and all that kind of thing—getting to know the family situation."

Earlier, Sonia had visited the flat that F Section maintained at Orchard Court in Marylebone one final time for a briefing. Buckmaster had a few traditional last-minute parting gifts for Sonia: a small silver compact and a silver cigarette case. He also gave her an envelope with a handful of pills. The white ones, he explained, were stimulants and would give her more energy. The single blue one would kill her within three minutes, should it come to that. Worried she might forget which was which, Sonia flushed them all down the toilet before leaving for the airfield.

"I wouldn't trust myself. It was too dangerous. I would rather rely on my wits," she said.

Leading up to her departure, Sonia was nothing if not fragile—even the doctor said so. But watching Guy leave for his mission seemed to have renewed her resolve. And although she wasn't going with him as planned, she wouldn't be venturing behind enemy lines entirely alone. Two other agents were joining her on the same flight: Eugène Bec, code-named Hugues, a nervous thirty-eight-year-old British-French officer and a trained weapons instructor; and Pierre Raimond Glaesner, code-named Alcide, a lieutenant who hailed from the Alsace region and had also trained as an instructor. Both were slated to work with Albin for the HEADMASTER circuit and would therefore have significant roles in Sonia's new world.

"Your mission is to act as courier to Albin, and you will take all your instructions from him." Her official instructions, dated the 24th of May and typed out in sparse paragraphs, gave the particulars of what was expected. Albin would be her circuit leader.

"He will help you establish yourself and assist you in every possible way." Her instructions added, *"Although at the same time you are expected to be as self-reliant as possible."*

Once established, she was to support Albin's assignment to "*organize groups to attack on or about D-Day the railway lines and telecommunications converging on the important junction of Le Mans.*"

Sonia's new identity papers carried the name Suzanne Jacqueline Bonvie. Her London-given code name was Blanche, but on the ground she sometimes went by Madeleine or, later, Ginette. As Suzanne, her birthdate remained the same—May 14—but she was aged by six years, placing her birth year in 1918 instead of 1924. She was also given a note from a Doctor Emile Bardy in Paris, stating bluntly that Mlle Bonvie, Suzanne, needed "total rest" and extra nourishment, providing the pretext for her presence near Le Mans. Given Sonia's physical state when she left for France, this part, at least, was not a fabrication.

If for some reason she failed to locate her reception committee, she was to make her way to a place called Château des Bordeaux. The password: *Avez-vous du chèvre à vendre?* (Do you have cheese for sale?)"

The weather was cooperating that night. Sonia was dressed in ski boots and a thick flannel divided skirt, both designed to keep her warm and protect her skin from the rough brush she might encounter on the ground in the dark. She was to drop with two trunks of clothing containing a beautiful designer wardrobe, one that appealed to the part of her that loved fashionable clothes. It reportedly contained "four afternoon frocks, two sports outfits, six pairs of real silk stockings, gaudy wedge shoes and fluffy underwear, all made in France and in keeping with the upper-middle-class standards to which she supposedly had been raised." She would also go in with two hundred thousand francs for her personal spending purposes, with instructions that, "*for security reasons, your expenses should be kept as moderate as possible.*"

Their ride into French skies that night was American, a B-24 Liberator painted a glossy black, one of dozens of American bombers refitted and painted for exactly this purpose. "HEADMASTER 4" was another Operation Carpetbagger mission aimed at inserting agents and equipment by air into France ahead of D-Day. This particular flight would drop two "Joes," one "Josephine," and eight packages.

Two hours into the flight, American pilot Emmanuel Choper was in the target area. At first, no signal lights were to be seen. But then they spotted the white lights dancing below. The plane circled twice. On the first run, at one-eighteen in the morning, Sonia was the first to jump through the "Joe hole" that had once held a ball turret, from an altitude of six hundred and twenty metres. She had insisted on going first out of fear that she'd lose her nerve if someone else hesitated to jump.

On the second run, six more packages were dropped and the aircraft headed for home. Sonia, Eugène, and Pierre were the last agents that plane would transport to France until midsummer. Upon its return to Harrington, flight 470A, piloted by Choper, had a rough landing.

At the other end, Sonia too had a bumpy arrival. By that time she had four jumps under her belt and had nailed every one. But this time, against instructions in her training, as she left the aircraft and neared the ground she couldn't help but look down. It was a harsh crash as the ground rushed up to meet her, and she tumbled right into a ditch. She couldn't breathe, and for a moment she blacked out. She came to tangled in her parachute, her back and shoulder throbbing with pain, her senses quickly tuning in to an ominous distant rumbling sound.

Unable to liberate herself from the parachute, she pulled out her .32 Colt pistol and proceeded to walk on slowly, dragging the parachute behind her. Eventually Sonia came within earshot of a group of men.

"André?" she called out, tightening her hold on the gun.

"My God. One of them is a woman," someone among the group said.

Once she saw them up close, she realized that they were older men. One of them wondered aloud how badly the Allied effort must be going for them to send in a woman. Then they explained matter-of-factly that André had recently been killed. They helped untangle her from the parachute and bury it, then urged her to get moving quickly—they could still hear the rumble of what was a large German convoy on the move. They took Sonia to a safehouse nearby, where she and her fellow agents would be left to sleep after a glass of local apple brandy.

Sonia's clothing trunks were nowhere to be found. If the Germans got to them first, the packages, with parachutes attached, would be an unmistakable sign that a female agent—a young female agent of a particular size—had arrived.

Should anyone ask, Suzanne Jacqueline Bonvie's story was that she worked at the French luxury handbag and goods company Lancel, a fact that explained her exquisite wardrobe, now lost. She was visiting the Sarthe region to stay with a cousin to recover. One look at the Château des Bordeaux, the address listed on her identity papers and where she planned to convalesce, and it would be difficult to refute her claim. The property in Amné, about twenty-five kilometres from Le Mans, an hour's bike ride, was of breathtaking beauty, surrounded by the kind of soothing green and healing air that could cure any ailment.

The Château des Bordeaux was a grand, imposing home with tall windows, a moat out front, stables at the side, a fountain and a wide forest thick with young oak trees at the back. The main entrance to the property was marked by an ornate archway in the middle of the forest, the building itself not visible from the main road at the other end of the property. It was owned by Edmond Cohin, a young, well-connected bachelor whose father was Jewish and whose mother was the sister of l'Abbé Chevalier, treasurer of the Catholic Church in the diocese of Le Mans. Edmond also owned the land and forest surrounding the château and had put it all at the disposal of the resistance.

On that first day Sonia, along with Pierre and their escorts (Eugène was taken to another safehouse), walked for hours from the farmhouse to the château in the daytime heat, and she found it disconcerting to lay eyes for the first time on the German convoys driving by. But the property would prove to be one of the safest and most luxurious refuges she'd have during her time there. As such, inevitably it also attracted Germans, who would occasionally stop by for rest and food. It appears to have happened often enough that the staff were instructed to keep a duster in the window to signal that the coast was clear; its disappearance meant that agents should stay away. But sometimes they were caught by surprise and had to escape by climbing through the large windows. That's why the agents mostly avoided altogether sleeping in the building, instead camping out in the forest and savouring the château's comforts only at mealtimes.

"We enjoyed a very pleasant existence in the Château des Bordeaux," said Albin. "The rooms had marvellous views over the grounds and, an even greater privilege, there were mounds of butter and cream cheese on the table for breakfast every morning—this at a time when strict rationing was the rule in France!"

Albin hadn't been there to receive the new agents, being otherwise busy with his latest recruitment efforts. The following day he appeared at the château to meet them.

His eyes fell upon a face he had already much admired. Sonia too felt the sudden shock of familiarity. She was face to face with Sydney Hudson, the married man for whom she'd briefly fallen before marrying Guy. Now he was her circuit leader.

At that moment in that château, Sonia had one overriding thought: "My God, how am I going to handle this?"

PART V

D-DAY

13

THE MOMENT HAS ARRIVED

Michel le Canadien • *Charolles, June 1944*

In a tiny car repair shop on avenue de la Gare, across from the train station on the outskirts of Charolles, Louis Lapalus loaded his wheelbarrow with three machine guns, three revolvers, six grenades, and a modest pile of ammunition he'd just unearthed from hiding. He had only fifty metres to traverse to reach his neighbour, a reliable twenty-year-old volunteer who was to train younger fighters in the use of unfamiliar weapons parachuted from Britain. When he was sure the coast was clear, Louis started his deliberate dash across.

Within moments a man called out to him, and he reflexively winced. Looking over, Louis recognized him straight away—he was an SS officer, in charge of a lookout post in his city of Charolles. Louis reluctantly set his wheelbarrow down before trotting over to exchange small talk about the state of the war.

In the window of his house, the neighbour, Louis Charnay, was watching furtively, gesticulating from time to time in an attempt to get Lapalus's attention. Finally Louis Lapalus also noticed that one of the bags on the wheelbarrow had slipped and a machine gun was protruding. Now he made to leave, turning the conversation to the weather. When the chat was finally over, Louis gratefully continued on his way. He pushed past Charnay's house and into a small garden, hiding the cache inside a huge lilac bush, where his neighbour safely retrieved it later that night.

Years later, Louis Lapalus painted this scene in a book he wrote to record his wartime memories in Charolles for his family. But in early June 1944, countless similar scenes were secretly unfolding all over France.

For a while now the resistance fighters who'd opted to work with "*les anglais*" had been lying low, waiting for the moment when they could finally stir. Then, in the first few days of June, they received word that the moment had arrived. The first phase of the D-Day preparation plan could finally go ahead.

The weather, however, seemed to have no sense of occasion. It was rainy, and hurricane-strength winds were conjuring up inconveniently high waves on the coastline. Meanwhile Allied forces were amassing on the British side of the English Channel, awaiting the order to cross and begin the battle to liberate France. In all, some two million Allied soldiers would eventually take part. German forces had picked up signals that something was afoot, and yet their commander in France, Erwin Rommel, left his post in Normandy and headed home to Germany to celebrate his wife's birthday, which happened to fall on June 6. Rommel had apparently put his faith in the crummy weather. Surely a landing on French soil was impossible in such soupy, blustery conditions.

As the Allies' chief weather forecaster, Group Captain James Stagg had been watching the weather ceaselessly. And, like Rommel, he was certain that conditions ruled out action in the immediate future.

American forecasters disagreed. Nonetheless, Allied leaders, who'd hoped D-Day would be launched on June 5, decided to postpone the operation yet again. But then Stagg spotted a thirty-six-hour window—imperfect, but a window all the same—in which the weather might allow the multi-front landing to proceed in the early morning of June 6. General Eisenhower seized the opportunity and issued the order to proceed.

In France, acquiring weapons was the priority. Those lucky enough to have already organized them received drops via London; they would stockpile the weapons and hide them in barns, attics, cellars, cemeteries, and forests, even burying them underground or concealing them under brush, foliage, or rocks. They were also stepping up training with the maquisards, sharing what they knew: how to ambush a convoy, how to cut a rail line, how to put the weapons to use.

They were restless with impatience, anxious for the signal that the wait was truly over. They listened religiously to BBC Radio's "Ici Londres," a London-based French-language service that broadcast hope daily into France. The SOE used the *messages personnels* segment to communicate with agents in the field using prearranged cryptic phrases that meant nothing to anyone else but to those in the know would provide information and instructions for SOE action on the ground. Listeners would tune in to hear reliable news about the war aimed at countering German propaganda. Timpani beats would drum out "V" for victory in Morse code. Then the announcer would read a list of personal messages in which SOE instructions were interspersed with entirely fake ones, deliberately designed to mislead German intelligence.

By June 1944, the SOE's use of the BBC in this way had become routine. Every night, despite German edicts forbidding it, members of the French resistance would huddle around radios across France, waiting for a "personal" message that might herald national salvation. And at around nine-thirty on the evening of June 1, leaders of the DITCHER circuit heard a message that spoke directly to them. "Tell fourteen the Queen's terrace is wide." They would have understood it to mean that D-Day would arrive within the next fifteen days.

There was so little time. Guy had barely stopped since he'd landed. Now there was even more urgency in coalescing the politically disparate, ill-equipped groups into a coherent force that would execute one central mission: keep German reinforcements from reaching the front.

And so, after that initial warning from London, Guy began a round of visits to the resistance leaders in the area, discussing how to organize, fund, train, and arm resistance fighters as quickly as possible.

One of Guy's stops was a small, lone garage on avenue de la Gare, right across from the train station on the outskirts of Charolles. In a large serif font it was identified as a place of "Vente & Réparation" under the direction of "L. Lapalus." In reality, ever since he'd become involved with the resistance in the spring of 1942 and long before Guy arrived, Louis's workshop and the adjoining home where he lived with his wife and two girls had been pivotal to the resistance in Charolles. And then, when the SOE set up shop, Louis lent his attic to radio operators from nearby circuits to transmit and receive messages—men whom Louis explained away to his daughters as cousins visiting from Lyon. The garage was also a regular meeting place for resistance leaders and a hiding place for the growing stockpile of weapons.

When Guy asked Louis Lapalus to start unpacking and distributing the weapons hidden on his property, Louis began by handing over limited numbers to trusted men so that they could start training the volunteers. That's how he ended up in the absurd position of parking a wheelbarrow full of weapons mere metres away from an SS officer—and a hair's breadth away from losing it all.

Everyone who worked in the resistance—especially those who aligned themselves with "*les anglais*"—was at enormous risk. And now, with the Allied forces soon arriving, the danger was particularly acute. Men like Louis and Pierre Jandeau—who'd sheltered Guy in his early days in France—were risking everything. Their families, their neighbours, and their coworkers were also, by association, exposed to danger. But Louis was aware of the bitter divisions within the French resistance: the Gaullists, the communists, the independent maquisards. It was those divisions that drove him to work with the SOE. Only the resistance elements organized by the Allies, he believed, "could give a certain and apolitical result."

Sometime in those early days of June, Guy's pre-invasion tour also took him back to Pierre Jandeau's farm. Guy would revisit the farm time and again, seeking the serenity of that place, the calm and discretion it offered. With D-Day imminent, this time he returned with his trusted first lieutenant, Jean Tabourin, to draw up an organizational chart of the growing fighting force they had at their disposal. Guy's plan had his host taking on the role of "steward of services," or in military parlance, quartermaster: handling all the provisions, food, health care, and finances for a nascent maquis force still in the making. It was a weighty assignment. But Pierre was disappointed, saying he "would have preferred to have taken charge of a combat unit"; after all, he'd been trained as a saboteur and on how to command a unit. Still, it was no time to be choosy. Pierre agreed to the assignment and got to work.

Meanwhile Guy continued his meetings with maquis leaders: Taking stock. Handing out money. Counting heads.

One of those meetings took place at an isolated farmhouse perched on a rolling green hill in the village of Saint-Julien-de-Civry. It was the home of René Fléchard, a thirty-four-year-old father with beady eyes and a warm smile who, as a youth, had been anti-war and "rather anti-military" before 1939 came along and war became an unavoidable necessity. He was actually from nearby Saint-Bonnet-de-Joux, where for years he'd been an accomplished resistance figure. He had helped smuggle gas stolen from the Germans to the resistance. He hid students trying to evade the *service travail obligatoire*, even providing them with forged identification documents to help them duck the order. He assisted the Gaullist resistance, later leading sabotage operations against the German occupiers. Eventually, to escape the German authorities pursuing him, Fléchard was forced to leave his home and move around until he settled in nearby Saint-Julien-de-Civry, at the farmhouse he nicknamed his "personal" maquis. It became a refuge for other resistance figures, including Albert, the DITCHER circuit chief, and Guy; they were both there on June 4 when more BBC messages indicated that D-Day was imminent.

Also present that night were Joseph, DITCHER's new wireless operator, and Gaston Lévy, a Jewish *résistant* who was wanted by German authorities and had recently taken refuge with his family nearby. After hearing the messages on the radio, he cracked open a bottle of champagne saved for just such an occasion. Everyone, including René and Gaston's families, joined in a toast to the moment.

Sensing their coming salvation, the men couldn't help feeling elated. "After the shadow of years of occupation, the light finally returned to our unfortunate country," said René.

The following day, Guy was again on the move. In Saint-Bonnet-de-Joux he visited René's "*petits gars*," or his "little guys"—about a hundred men willing to fight under Michel le Canadien's orders. Guy briefed them on what to expect over the coming crucial days, and before he left he handed René a hundred and twenty thousand francs to help cover expenses. René was thankful—they desperately needed the money—but it was weapons that everyone was after.

In Albert and Guy's hurried effort to build trust in the region, making good on delivering weapons would be a significant down payment. After weeks of spotty communications with London, the weapons shortage in Saône-et-Loire had become critical. Joseph, now operating his radio in various farms, always under the protection of a bodyguard, was key to changing that. And as radio traffic intensified in the run-up to D-Day, Joseph also had some additional help.

Alcide Beauregard had been a signaller with the Canadian Army when the SOE began urgently seeking volunteers to train as radio operators behind enemy lines. He was recruited, and quickly his SOE assessors had been unimpressed, describing him as "a man of very limited intelligence" who "becomes listless and bored." Perhaps even more callous, the SOE student assessment board reported that he was "just worth using as a very short-term W/T operator, but under no other circumstances." Still, in the desperation of the time, he was fast-tracked to parachute training, skipping parts of the usual curriculum. And even when he sprained his ankle while learning to parachute, they still sent him in—delivering him directly to the ground by Lysander.

Then, when his circuit organizer failed to establish a sub-circuit to DITCHER as he had been assigned, Alcide moved to Lyon to help handle the deluge of messages to and from London ahead of D-Day.

Together with Guy and Jean-Paul Archambault, he lent a Canadian flavour to the DITCHER circuit.

On the ground, Alcide was proving capable and reliable—"conscientious and faithful," according to Albert—but there was one major hitch: against accepted protocol for SOE radio operators, Alcide had been working from the same house in Lyon ever since he arrived. And so Albert, concerned about his safety, went to Lyon ahead of D-Day to meet with Alcide at a café.

Albert felt that his confidence was misplaced, that a circle was gradually tightening around him. German forces had become ruthlessly adept at picking up radio signals by using mobile detectors. But Alcide would not be dissuaded, and despite the heavy German presence he continued to send and receive messages from the same spot. In any case, as the big moment approached, DITCHER could hardly afford to work without him.

Alcide's location was only one of many concerns and shortcomings. On the eve of D-Day, the SOE operation in France was far from perfect. There were some two hundred and twenty SOE agents deployed in France—all of them waiting for London's instructions in various states of readiness, wishing for more weapons, more money, and more time.

That night, June 5, the *messages personnels*—three hundred and six of them—sounded as random and nonsensical as they always did, except that night they contained no fakes, not a single decoy. Every message was a specific instruction to a specific circuit for action on the ground: destroy a railway line, cut a telegraph wire, blow up a bridge. Dozens of men and women, visitors to French villages and cities, readied themselves for an unconventional battle from behind enemy lines, one in which many lives would be lost—maybe even their own.

And yet, as Albert admitted, in those first few days of June there were also "shivers of celebration in the air in the approaching spring evenings. . . . We feel drunk before we have had anything to drink."

As France settled into sleep that night, Operation Overlord had begun.

14

MOTHER OF ALL MAQUIS

Guy • *Sylla, June 6, 1944*

Very early on the morning of June 6, thousands of Allied soldiers descended over occupied France in silent, synchronized flight, dotting the horizon with parachutes and gliders. Among them were hundreds of Americans and British, plus five hundred and fifty members of the First Canadian Parachute Battalion, all of whom arrived via a seemingly endless convoy of planes just touching the edge of French airspace before circling back again. Once on the ground, those men were tasked with paving the way for the others who would follow by air and by sea.

In the meantime, hundreds of Allied bombers unleashed a barrage of explosions on the beaches of Normandy, to help ease the way for the tens of thousands of Allied ground troops who then poured onto the beaches in landing craft, firing on German defences in an effort to penetrate "Fortress Europe."

Some fourteen thousand young Canadian men would land on the shore between the villages of Courseulles and Saint-Aubin-sur-Mer, an eight-kilometre waterfront stretch code-named Juno Beach. It had been nearly five years since Canadian troop convoys started arriving in Britain. But now, for dozens of these men, the fight for which they'd waited lasted mere minutes. More than three hundred and fifty Canadians were cut down in an instant as German defences came to life. About four thousand other Allied soldiers met a similar fate, killed in the fighting on Normandy beaches that first day.

Across France, news of the landings spread quickly. In Charolles, Jean Sarrazin, Maman Lucienne's husband, rushed over to Louis Lapalus's garage early in the morning with the monumental news. "They have landed! This morning at dawn on the Normandy coast!" The resistance could now come fully to life.

Guy, who was also in Charolles that day, sent word around to resistance leaders, summoning them to an important meeting for that night. Various *résistants* made their way to Sarrazin's impeccably kept house on rue de la Condémine.

Around eleven-thirty that night Guy called for silence. In a "firm tone" he asked that the German observation post in Charolles be attacked the following day. His request was met with total silence. No one said a word.

Then Louis asked the obvious: "With whom and with what?" It was a fair question. Guy's proposed attack, especially now, without the proper means, could well be suicidal. Louis knew that these observation posts were "small forts," each with an eight-metre-high watchtower and a menacing machine gun to keep people away. Installed every fifteen to twenty-five kilometres, they were also equipped with radios with which "they could be notified of everything on the roads." The watchtowers had "no blind spot, an unobstructed view for 500 metres," and an entrance that was "solidly fortified and inviolable with our means." An attack would almost certainly mobilize German reinforcements, and "Charolles would be set on fire."

But it had to be done. "I'll take care of it," Louis volunteered.

There were other observation posts. Guy tasked René Fléchard with removing the one just south of Saint-Bonnet-de-Joux, in Suin, which was located in a key area for the maquisards. For René's *petits gars*, that became their first military mission.

With those orders, Guy was laying the groundwork for slowing the German advance to the front. His men were guarding the strategic western flank of Saône-et-Loire with the ultimate goal of hampering German troops coming from the south and southwest from reaching Normandy. And in the following days and weeks Guy's men would conduct ambushes, cut highways, sabotage rail lines, and sever communications lines in pursuit of that goal—and, when necessary, fight.

Gaston Lévy and his men, meanwhile, blew up the Paray-le-Monial–Lyon rail line, halting rail traffic and blocking sixteen trains. Guy messaged London, asking "the airforce to bomb them" from the air, but the reply came that "Paray-le-Monial was not Berlin." Still, some of the rail lines that were disabled in these first hours remained inoperable for the rest of the war.

Guy's other priority was to establish a base and staging ground for his fighters, a place where they could gather, prepare for attacks, and resupply. Guy also wanted the mother of all maquis to provide refuge for those young fighters who had escaped forced labour. "The point here was to protect them first," said Guy. "They were wanted by the authorities at home to go to work in Germany. So, they had to leave their homes."

Locals in the know, like Louis Lapalus and Jean Sarrazin, nicknamed Le Gros, Maman Lucienne's husband, encouraged him to consider Sylla.

Seen from above, Sylla looks like a large wooded bowl up a winding road from the town of Martigny-le-Comte. It is in fact the fifty-hectare site of an old quarry, dotted with piles of broken rock, said to have been the source of some of the beige granitic stone used to pave the roads of Paris at the turn of the century. The local resistance, according to Louis, had long recognized Sylla's suitability as a potential base—it had "natural means of defence" in its uneven terrain and its concavity, and dense woods. But with German patrols often in the area, they had abandoned the idea. Now, though, with the Allied forces in France and German convoys increasingly harassed in the region, things were different. Guy recognized Sylla's potential, and he decided to use it as a vanguard base for the men following his lead.

As Sylla began its transformation, word of mouth started to spread about the Canadian who was helping to organize and arm the resistance. Men were now appearing spontaneously at the old quarry: former miners, who were numerous in Montceau-les-Mines; farmers; and even men who'd been gendarmes. In the first week, there were two hundred and fifty men there. By D-Day, just over two weeks after Guy arrived, that number had grown to more than eight hundred. All were directly under Guy's command, and, as he would later note, "They were strong men, I can tell you that."

But because of severe shortages during nearly five years of occupation, many of them showed up with inadequate clothing and shoes with holes, or even in slippers. Beyond bullets, they needed boots and blankets, and at Sylla they required beds and cutlery. Guy appealed to London for help, but he also led a local scavenging effort. As a result, their weapons would become a hodgepodge of Sten guns, Lee-Enfield rifles, and Brens, their uniforms an eclectic mélange of American jackets and sweaters, French shorts, pants, and berets, English infantry trousers, and even German shirts. This too came with risk, with at least one incident in the region where two men were picked up because they were wearing British boots.

Among the mountains of materiel that started arriving, almost nothing was as valuable as blankets—which were so precious that any man lucky enough to score one often wore it constantly over his shoulders. Vehicles too were coveted, with fuel, parts, and tires all in short supply; there was also a shortage of all manner of medicine. Guy and his deputies tapped every possible local contact for any supplies that could be spared. Business owners, farmers, bakers—they either provided supplies or joined as fighters.

Within weeks, Sylla began to resemble a makeshift military base. Guy organized the maquis in line with standard British and Canadian military organization: platoons, companies, battalions, and even, eventually, the equivalent of an officers' training course. Before long he had created a strictly controlled base, with visiting rules, observation posts, and a twenty-four-hour security patrol. Everything was camouflaged, including the observation huts, which were shrouded with shrubs and equipped with binoculars to keep an eye on the terrain below. There was a shooting range where Guy would train the men on the weapons that were dropped by parachute. Later there were toilets, showers, and kitchens that employed several men who laboured, shirtless, all day in the summer heat. In time, several of the luckier German prisoners would be put to work peeling potatoes. The maquisards also managed to scavenge long wooden picnic tables at which the men could eat and play cards. There would be a makeshift hospital whose staff included a doctor and a nurse who wore white on the job despite the unusual surroundings. The camp would even have its own barber.

Presiding over the whole operation was Guy, a Canadian army lieutenant who would soon be temporarily promoted to the acting rank of captain while he was "specially employed." At Sylla, however, he was effectively commanding a battalion of his own creation. He may have been, in the words of the Camp X training manual, "a cog in a very large machine," but he was in charge, and it suited him to make up the rules as he went along.

Guy kept a command post in a modest house tucked away in the bush, hidden among the trees just below Sylla and removed from the camp itself. He was impressed with the young men who flocked to join his force. Despite their divided loyalties, he admired their passion for France, their fervour, their eagerness to learn. "The men were proud," Guy would say. "They also knew how to laugh, even if it's sad to have been forced to leave home. But there is strength in numbers."

Sylla was a work in progress; it wouldn't be fully up and running until mid-July. But long before then, and with modest means, Louis Lapalus still had to take down that formidable observation tower in Charolles.

He came up with a plan to lure away some of the German soldiers on duty: to cut the telephone line on which they relied, then ambush them when they arrived to fix it. That night, June 7, he severed the line right in front of his garage, and then he tried to get to sleep.

The next morning his day began with young maquisards "invading" his garage in search of their share of the arms he'd hidden on his property; they proceeded to clean them, load them, and then carry them away. Then, at about eleven o'clock, his men called to tell him that, just as he'd hoped, they had ambushed the German soldiers trying to fix the phone line. Charolles had its first three German prisoners of war.

The armed maquisards then took along one of the soldiers as they left for the lookout post. Before noon they had captured it and taken all the Germans there prisoner without a single shot being fired; they also scored arms and grenades—and, as a bonus, a "large bag of biscuits."

Meanwhile, in Suin, the task was a little more complicated, but in time René Fléchard and his men also managed to capture the observation post there, taking several German soldiers prisoner and acquiring a whole load of weapons.

Yet another group set up a checkpoint on the main road in the area, national route 79, at a spot where it intersected a railway crossing. The following day, June 8, a group led by Louis Charnay—the recipient of Louis Lapalus's wheelbarrow of weapons—intercepted a German convoy of three vehicles at the checkpoint by lowering the barrier; they killed several German soldiers. But then two more vehicles unexpectedly arrived, and their occupants opened fire.

Four of Guy's men were killed. They would be forever remembered as among the first casualties of this new phase of the war; a plaque was later installed right where they fell. The loss of these men deeply upset Guy. But after the incident, something had changed: from then on, any German forces entering Guy's area were routinely attacked.

It was the railways that mattered most, as they were the best means of transporting German men and provisions to the front. It was a challenge to keep them severed, Guy would report, because German forces had teams repairing them around the clock.

Still, these decisive early skirmishes galvanized the local population. Many more men came forward to join in. The resistance had proven its presence, though the real fight was just beginning.

Guy, suspecting it was only a matter of time before these early attacks prompted a German retaliation, advised Louis to relocate his family. Louis drove his wife and two children to his brother's house about twenty-five kilometres away.

Then, just as Guy had predicted, the next few days brought a fierce reaction from the German units nearby, who were determined to neutralize the men they labelled as "barbaric," "terrorists," and "bandits." They targeted resistance figures, capturing a few of them. They attacked Saint-Bonnet-de-Joux, bombing René Fléchard's original home, as well as the bakery, and then setting a local hotel on fire; its owner burned alive inside. The mayor in Suin, where René and his men had disabled that observation tower, was shot and his house burned.

In Charolles the Gestapo are looking for Louis Lapalus. Plain-clothed men descended on his property and set it on fire, a summary punishment the Germans were known to mete out to those they suspected of harbouring the resistance or its weapons. Louis and his family were long gone, but an unlucky member of his staff, Jean-Louis Milliat, happened by just as this was unfolding. The men accosted him in the street, beat him, and roughly interrogated him. Then, when he broke away, they chased him down and shot him. His body was only later recovered from the river in which he'd tried to escape.

The brutal reprisals left many in the resistance shaken. Guy told the maquis leaders that anyone who felt vulnerable owing to their involvement in the fight was welcome to move to the old Sylla quarry, away from their families and loved ones. Many took him up on the offer.

But not everyone approved of Guy's tactics. At a pivotal meeting he'd called at Sylla after those German observation posts were taken out, one of the more prominent local commanders, Olivier Ziegel, nicknamed Claude, complained about the lack of weapons and ammunition. Claude suggested they focus on training while they waited for the Allied forces to arrive.

Guy fumed at Claude's suggestion. It was the start of what would become a turbulent relationship. He hadn't parachuted into a war zone just to wait for Allied troops, he argued. The resistance in Saône-et-Loire, Guy insisted, could still make a difference by harassing German troops as they rushed to reinforce the Normandy front.

The weapons, he promised, would soon arrive "in abundance."

15

HIDING IN PLAIN SIGHT

Blanche/Madeleine • *Le Mans, June 6, 1944*

Inside a diminutive set-back house at No. 8 rue Mangeard, in the south of Le Mans, Sydney suddenly woke to the sound of an explosion. It wasn't the first time Allied warplanes had targeted the railway station just a stone's throw from the house he'd only recently rented. But having been wrenched out of slumber, it was hard for him to make sense of this new round of explosions thundering just down the street.

When he realized what he'd heard, Sydney got up and rushed to Sonia to reassure her. He found her in a "completely unperturbed" state.

It had been only nine days since Sonia had stumbled onto French soil, but despite the considerable pressure, she was already establishing a reputation for unflappability.

For one, since her arrival, she made the decision to live more openly than she'd intended—a way to throw off any suspicion that she might be the mystery agent who'd just parachuted in and become inadvertently separated from her fashionable wardrobe. She made the decision to start frequenting black-market restaurants and cafés, right under the noses of German officers, as if she'd always done so. With the help of Edmond and others in his sphere, she also started to get to know Le Mans and its people, finding her way to allies and quiet supporters. Now she was living a contradiction in a little French house in a quiet street away from the centre of town: French and English, fighter and civilian, in hiding but in plain sight.

It wasn't the first time Sonia had lived a double life in France. This was, of course, a dramatically different France from the one she'd known as a child: this was the France of June 1944—the France of rationing, of charcoal-fuelled vehicles, of German forces holding a terrified population hostage. It was the France of the terrible, almost unspeakable acorn coffee they were forced to drink for want of the real thing.

This was also the France where leading a double life like Sonia's meant that her life was always on the line. The Sarthe region was rife with Germans and their French collaborators. There was Rommel nearby, but Le Mans itself was home to the headquarters of the German 7th Army, led by General Friedrich Dollmann, charged with defending Normandy. The town was crawling with German soldiers.

Over time, Sonia became accustomed to walking among these men, or near them; they were impossible to avoid. She would see them during her forays into town to visit contacts, to suss out young recruits, to have lunch. And on more than one occasion she had no choice but to share a table with them in the black-market restaurants. Refusing a spot next to a German would give her away.

"You had to take that spot. If you walked away, you'd be suspected," Sonia later remarked. At the start it wasn't just uncomfortable; it was terrifying. It would take time for Sonia to accept her deception and the risks that came with it.

In one particularly memorable and horrifying instance, she was at a restaurant chatting to the German officer sitting next to her when her handbag slipped off the back of her chair and hit the floor with the unmistakable thud of a heavy object. In it she was carrying her pistol.

Sonia saw the officer reach down to pick up the bag. "Oh my God," she thought, assuming she was done for. But a breath away from being found out, she got to it first.

"He would have known that there was something unusual by the weight of it. I picked it up and I was just so thankful that he hadn't." She would later discover that the officer was the head of the local Gestapo.

She was often mistaken for a German girl on account of her blond hair and fair complexion, or at least a collaborator or a German officer's girlfriend. Leaving those restaurants, it wasn't unusual for her to be spat on for just that reason. And while none of those people had any clue who she truly was, she was quietly working to find young men who wanted to fight for France.

In those early days, Sonia was still in a great deal of pain from her landing. She remained generally unwell, too, undernourished and tired. The throb in her back hurt so much that she found it hard even to reach her bicycle's handlebars—something she had to do daily as a courier for the HEADMASTER circuit. The pain was so acute that at one point she made the decision, despite the risk, to visit a local doctor.

The sharp-eyed physician quickly concluded that there was no way she was twenty-six, as "Suzanne Bonvie" claimed to be. His confident pronouncement terrified Sonia, and so she never returned for the X-ray the doctor had arranged. She preferred to suffer in silence rather than risk blowing her cover. It would be a choice she'd be forced to make over and over. Faced with either pain or survival, she chose pain every time.

Sonia had just turned twenty, one of the youngest SOE agents sent into the field. She'd just been separated from her husband after a whirlwind romance that mirrored the hurried training program that had taken her away from everything and everyone she knew. Now she was in a war zone trying to stay alive while struggling to make sense of the twist of fate that had brought her and Sydney back together. Part of her believed it was almost fated to be. That they'd been reunited in this remarkable way certainly made it seem so.

Just as he was when she first met him, Sydney was married and the father of a little girl—a significant factor in Sonia's decision to steer clear of him the first time. Now, unlike then, she too was a married woman. Once she was over the shock of seeing Sydney, Sonia told him she had married Guy. He wasn't happy to hear the news.

Yet there was now a growing distance between her and Guy, with no measurable end in sight. Would she ever see him again? By contrast, and by necessity, Sonia and Sydney were spending a lot of time together at a dangerous moment and in a dangerous place. This time, their feelings for each other would prove impossible to ignore.

Sydney took to calling her Madeleine. Sonia called him Michel. She recalled how she "became more or less a cover" for Sydney: "It was always good for the leader [of a circuit] to have a woman agent along with him as a cover." With each day they spent posing publicly as a couple, dining out and cycling together, the line between fiction and reality began to blur. Sonia found herself making room for the growing feelings she had for the person right there by her side. But if the fictional retelling that Sydney would later write—one loosely based on their story—is anything to go by, he was probably the one who made the first move, beginning with a declaration that he was already in love with her.

Among their fellow agents and the maquisards, they were careful to keep their relationship very quiet. Living together alone would make it infinitely easier, and so, by the time D-Day arrived, Sonia and Sydney had given up the grounds of the Château des Bordeaux and moved into the small house on rue Mangeard in Le Mans. The move also spared them the long bicycle trips in and out of the city and all the risks that came with that.

On the morning of June 6 Sydney left on his bike for the Château des Bordeaux to meet his wireless operator, George Jones, at eleven o'clock. George informed him that the Allied troops had landed. He reacted the same way many SOE agents on the ground did—with "a tinge of disappointment."

"What a pity," he said, "that we could not have had more time to improve our organization and stage more drops of arms and possibly agents."

But there was no point in regret. The message from London was clear: Step up the action. Sabotage the rail lines. Cut their communications. Slow down the German forces. Help win the war.

In the weeks he'd been on the ground, Sydney had cobbled together a force of a few hundred men, organized into small groups of a handful each, hidden away on farms. Now he ordered them to escalate their sabotage attacks against German forces.

And all the while, Sonia and Sydney continued recruiting. They sought keen, loyal, ordinary young (mostly) men—and finding them took effort and time. It required invitations to quiet gatherings, outings, and lunches during which Sonia would be introduced to acquaintances who could, perhaps, be the right sort of young men, or at least connect her to some. She would then take them out for a picnic, where she felt safer asking them directly to join the fight. Sonia reportedly excelled at recruiting. Sometimes she'd arrive at Sydney's camps "with half a dozen rookies trotting at her heels." Soon they'd be tested with small tasks and given false information to observe how they handled it before they were taken fully into the fold.

Trying to find allies among a population that had been terrified into submission was difficult and fraught. Sonia and Sydney took a risk every time they knocked on a farmer's door looking for shelter, and then nursed a gut punch every time they were turned away. Sonia could understand why people said no. She knew that local French citizens would be risking everything—family, loved ones, livelihoods, their very survival. And so she lionized those who, despite that outsized risk, were willing to help a stranger, a decision that often meant their lives would never be the same again.

News of the Allied landings, oddly, made it more challenging for Sydney to recruit. "A considerable number of people, seeing the possibility of action approaching, began to get cold feet and to think of their responsibilities to their families," he would later report. Still, a steady increase in the number of fighters joining them meant that Sydney also badly needed weapons and ammunition. He also needed a place beyond the Château des Bordeaux for both the men and the arms.

The Forêt de Charnie was an attractive option. It was only forty kilometres west of Le Mans, with the Château des Bordeaux halfway between the two. And with plenty of trees and shrubbery standing guard, it was an ideal staging ground for groups preparing attacks. It had sizable clearings for parachute drops, and George could regularly operate his radio there without fear of the mobile detectors roaming the streets. It was also a convenient place in which to hide several RAF officers who'd bailed out over the area and were trying to find a way home.

It took some organizing, but about twenty-five men were finally gathered in the forest, sleeping under the tall trees, sustained by food arranged through sympathetic local villagers. Eugène Bec, who'd parachuted in with Sonia, would be the main instructor, even though Sydney had reservations about him. Although he had good technical skills, he wasn't up to the job of leading. And so Sydney appointed Edmond Cohin, the owner of the Château des Bordeaux, to lead the Forêt de Charnie maquis, with Eugène as "technical adviser."

Sonia was also very wary of Eugène. He was loud and indiscreet and would break into English at the most inopportune moments. She came to the conclusion that he should never have been deployed. But under the circumstances, Eugène would likely cause the least harm while dwelling in a thick, dark forest.

Working with him was Claude Hilleret, who at twenty-one was the second eldest of five brothers and a student of art in Paris. His mother, Evelyn Guthrie Easson Mackie, like Sydney, was from Scotland, and his father, René, was a French professor of history. With the entire family having long supported the resistance, the brothers were able to provide Sonia with leads on other possible trustworthy recruits. Their home also served as an occasional safe house and letterbox for Sonia and Sydney.

Sonia too would occasionally join the Charnie faculty, sharing some of the skills she'd learned at SOE school: how to take apart guns, clean them, and put them back together; how to shoot; and—one of her specialties—how to blow things up.

Inevitably, some of the men were awkward about being instructed by a woman, and a young, pretty one at that. "I know I am only a girl but we are short-handed," she would say, acknowledging their embarrassment as she showed them how to use and clean a Bren gun. "This weapon takes a bit of figuring out. But when you know it, you will be able to use it better than I can."

Sonia persisted, sometimes using actual German convoys for target practice. With time, the men grudgingly began to appreciate her expertise, her way with a pistol, her ambidexterity.

Sonia was now sleeping out in the forest with the others, unless she was travelling, and then she'd find shelter wherever she could. Like clockwork she'd wash her face every morning in whatever water was available, and then, in a small reach for normalcy, put on a spot of lipstick. The group would often start the day with weapons training; after lunch, they might have an afternoon target-practice session. Late afternoons were reserved for going over plans for that night's operations and preparing the explosives needed to blow up a rail line or a bridge. After an early supper they'd sleep until midnight. Like many others in the resistance across France, it was in the hours between midnight and dawn that they were most active.

Most immediately within their means were disrupting phone lines and small-scale ambushes of German convoys that could, with minimal effort, inflict damage and destabilize their enemy. There was an art to pulling them off. A small band of men would hide along a road, and at the sight of a German convoy they'd open fire at the lead vehicle, spray the rest of the convoy, throw some grenades into the mess, and then moments later disappear.

Sonia occasionally joined in. She had no qualms about firing at the convoys; she even admitted enjoying the rush of it. You just sprayed and killed faceless soldiers. It wasn't personal. It was a task that had to be done. The distance, she admitted, made it easier.

But it was a very different story up close. In one encounter involving a German staff car whose exact details are lost to history, Sonia came face to face, in the light of day, with one of the occupants.

"There was one officer who was still alive. He was aiming at me, and I shot him," she said.

"I shook after that. It was him or me. I shot him in cold blood."

One evening in June, another message came over the BBC: "*Le chacal mange les chevaux*," meaning "The jackal eats the horses." It was a signal to Sydney's HEADMASTER circuit that weapons would be parachuted in to the Charnie maquis the following night.

In the meantime, a relatively new contact by the name of Philippe had promised to bring over a dozen or so more men to join the maquis in the forest. On the appointed day, Philippe failed to show. That was worrying enough. But what no one yet knew was even worse. The previous night, Philippe had been picked up by a patrol of Germans. He was captured, then beaten into revealing what he knew about the maquis, including its location in the Forêt de Charnie.

The following day, Sonia and Sydney were making their way there when they learned that German forces were on the attack. Some two hundred soldiers and *milice* descended on the maquis, catching the men by surprise, men who did not yet have the means with which to defend themselves. They began to flee.

Eugène Bec and young Claude Hilleret were armed with Sten guns. Within moments they put themselves between the attacking Germans and the fleeing maquisards and opened fire, spraying bullets in an apparent effort to provide cover that would allow the other men to scatter.

When it was all over, the losses were devastating. Eugène and young Claude had been killed. Several fighters were taken prisoner; the RAF men had gone missing. And three cars, a million francs, weapons, a number of bicycles, and the precious radio were gone, now in German hands.

The Germans also lost several men. But they managed to receive the containers of weapons dropped from the sky, the ones intended for the maquisards. That suggested they knew something about the SOE's signalling. And that too was deeply troubling.

Sydney was sick with regret. As he would later write, "I should also have foreseen that the Germans would do their utmost to eliminate such a large and dangerous body of men as the maquis in Charnie might have become, so close to the Normandy front."

It was a terrible start to a battle that had barely begun.

16

OPERATION CADILLAC

Guy • *Sylla, July 14, 1944*

Bastille Day, 1944, was no time for celebration. Yet early that morning a handful of people were gathered next to an open field north of Cluny, not far from where Guy had landed back in May. They weren't as numerous as Guy would have liked, but many French people were understandably nervous, especially in daytime. "The argument was always that if they were caught, they would be shot," explained Guy. Yet some had shown up anyway and were standing on the side of a country road, their eyes fixed on the sky. Someone started the requisite fires. Now all they had to do was wait.

Just before nine o'clock the loud roar of an engine announced the arrival of the first wave of thirty-six aircraft to fly over that day. In a moment they emerged from the horizon, gliding through at low altitude, starting an orchestrated dance that swiftly made way for the next batch and for the seemingly countless parachutes that began to elegantly float down from the sky.

That it happened in broad daylight was a first, and extraordinary enough. But then something even more extraordinary happened. As they unfolded, the parachutes falling from the sky transformed, chameleon-like, into a celebratory cascade of *tricolore*: blue, white, and red parachutes carrying weapons and supplies drifted down like languid droplets of summer rain. It was a breathtaking display, the closest thing to the sight of fireworks in daylight. People had come expecting provisions, but at the magnitude of the morale boost they cheered in appreciation. It had turned into a celebration after all.

"It was like a fair, a party. London was very, very smart," said Guy. "They started to cry, laugh, and dance."

At the sight of this airborne salute, dozens more volunteers suddenly materialized. Men, young and old, as well as women came to help collect the containers. And in record time "they emptied the whole field," said Guy. "They had woken up. It was a matter of emotion."

Guy, who felt safe enough to appear at such events in his "staff car," was also touched by the gesture and emboldened by the sizable delivery. By the end of that day he would have much of the equipment he needed for three whole battalions. In all, thirty-six aircraft dropped four hundred and thirty parachutes in the DITCHER area that day, providing tonnes of weapons and ammunition, clothing, and medical and other supplies for Guy and Albert to equip their men. Guy's promise to Claude and the others had been kept.

Operation Cadillac was the largest weapons drop to date since the war began, and the first mass drop to be delivered while the sun was up. It involved more than three hundred aircraft delivering more than thirty-seven hundred containers in various parts of France at a key moment. The world had not forgotten France.

There was jubilance wherever the sky rained weapons. But the sight of their national colours defiantly unleashed into daylight was balm for a nation's battered soul.

Subsequently, some of them literally wore that joy on their sleeves. In the hands of housewives, the satiny nylon of the parachutes turned into shirts, even underwear. The red, blue, and white parachutes were also, inevitably, turned into more than a few flags, some of which were mounted on Sylla's growing fleet of trucks. And at a time of severe shortages of everything, the white ones were especially coveted as natural material for a wartime wedding dress.

Nothing was wasted. Even the broken containers could be salvaged: While full, they were heavy, up to four hundred pounds each, requiring at least two or four men to lift them into trucks and carts. Once emptied, Guy had the containers filled up with rocks and used in roadblocks.

The weapons themselves were transported and stored elsewhere, but then once the non-maquis helpers had left, Guy had the weapons moved again in order to protect against "loose lips."

By mid-July, German forces were rather scarce in Guy's triangle of the Charolles district. But there was still a sizable German presence in the wider region, including in Mâcon, over the rolling green hills east of Cluny. And German garrisons remained in most of the small cities on the western flank of Saône-et-Loire.

Sylla was crucial to the job ahead, and by mid-July it was fully up and running. It was now the official home of a nascent 1st Charollais Battalion, which Guy led directly. Of its four companies, the first two, led by Lieutenants Charles Herbé and André Barraud, were based at the Maquis de Sylla. The other two were led by René Fléchard and Gaston Lévy in Saint-Bonnet-de-Joux and Saint-Julien-de-Civry, respectively. "I always had a company, 150 men in all, ready for action," said Guy.

In all, Guy had helped train and equip three battalions in the Charolles region, with nearly three thousand men benefiting from his organization and expertise. The exact number of fighters was, of course, kept a closely guarded secret. But in a bold attempt at wartime propaganda, Guy let the word out that Sylla's numbers had swelled to five thousand, even to over thirty thousand, all to dissuade attacks on the hilltop sanctuary.

To round out his arsenal, Guy had asked his trusted lieutenant Jean Tabourin to lead a group dedicated to security, ferreting out collaborators. He put Louis Lapalus in charge of maintaining Sylla's weapons and the vehicles at their disposal, some of which had been commandeered from civilians or stolen from German convoys, then painted with white stars to guard against friendly fire from the Allied planes above.

Throughout, sabotage operations were ongoing. Sometimes, derailing a train brought a windfall for the maquisards; René and his men once scored cattle, another time it was shirts, and yet another a whole load of cigars—after which the fighters were suddenly walking around chomping on them.

With the attacks stepping up, Sylla became a cauldron of activity. The companies were on a steady rotation of exercises, weapons training, target practice with Guy in the quarry, parachute reception duty, and sabotage missions. They were always planning ahead, with groups taking turns conducting reconnaissance for future sabotage operations. Guy spent much of his time training his men, then bought twenty bicycles, on which he'd send some of them to hiding places outside Sylla to pass on their newly acquired skills in sabotage and explosives. Sylla was a training ground, a kitchen, a refuge—and a place of learning.

None of this would have been possible without the assistance of the people of Martigny-le-Comte, just down the hill from Sylla, who seemed to have thrown in their lot with Guy and his maquisards. Guy felt safe enough to put his headquarters at the edge of their town, and safe enough to hang the flags of the Free French, Britain, and Canada out front, even appointing a man whose duty it was to raise and lower them.

But nowhere was the support of the local citizens more notable than in keeping the men fed. Pierre found himself in charge of feeding two thousand people every single day, fighters and civilians alike, managing with the help of Martigny-le-Comte to acquire the needed quantities of meat, bread, wine, and even tobacco, often paid for at market value but at other times acquired by force. Donations frequently came their way: One day it was a barrel of rum; another it was heaps of meat from a local farmer. On yet another it was a Madame Bettremieux bringing a batch of twenty-nine shirts that locals had made using parachute fragments. On the eve of France's biggest battle yet, the generosity of Martigny-le-Comte seemed to know no limits.

Local women, however, did a lot more than bring food or sew a few shirts. Some joined as fighters. Others became members of Guy's intelligence group—staffed mostly by young women on bikes who roamed the area on the pretext of gathering food but instead gathered information about German troop movement and numbers. Organized and recruited with the help of Maman Lucienne, they were said to be "devoted to the dashing commander whom they knew as 'Michel le Canadien.'"

Other women played even more crucial roles in Guy's organization. There was, of course, Maman Lucienne herself, whom Guy described as "a true French woman who was 40 and still looked like a girl. She fed me and housed me and protected me."

There was the mysterious woman by the name of "Annie," who was assigned by Maman Lucienne to pose as Guy's wife "for security purposes." "She shot a German officer down 'like that,'" Guy said of Annie. Yet other women moved weapons around in baby carriages—the best way, according to Guy—at great risk to themselves.

"I believe personally that the women of France did more than their men. I say that is true for my sector," Guy once noted. He was often in awe of people's willingness to contribute despite the enormity of the risk. Their passion could move him to tears.

Guy was proving to be an organized and creative leader, perhaps even an eccentric one. On the advice of his security group, he ordered the kidnapping of wealthy collaborators and then exchanged them for ransom, helping raise, in his estimate, a million francs to plow back into operations.

Guy was also a leader with a keen sense of occasion. For one, he ensured that much of the activity in his sector was photographed. As an avid photographer he would occasionally snap the pictures himself. But many of them were taken by others, anonymous photographers who captured rare snapshots of life at Sylla—of the men playing cards or sweating in front of the kitchen, squinting in the sun. There were dozens of photos: of the parachutes, the damage after a battle, a group shot of the fighters, and even of the dead, eyes closed, their arms resting on their chests. Another captured the otherwise forgotten face of a man Guy described as his "favourite saboteur," a miner, he said, who knew all about explosives and never let him down, no matter the mission. "Whether it was bridges or roads, he blew up everything." Guy might have been seized with trying to win the war, but he was also seemingly adamant about preserving memories of it for the future.

Although he was strict and demanded discipline from his men, Guy often took his own risks and admitted to going on some ill-advised adventures. He once commandeered a charcoal delivery truck in order to enter a German base near Charolles, pretending to be an oaf and ignoring directions from the men there, just so that he could build a picture of the base in his mind. Against Maman Lucienne's advice, Guy would also occasionally join his men on some of their operations, including cutting rail lines—he was, after all, the resident explosives expert. She would be furious with him. "You're irresponsible! What if you get killed?"

But perhaps even more dangerously, Guy would travel all the way to Lyon, likely more than once, purely for a "vacation," frequenting cafés and restaurants in a town rife with Gestapo. On one of these trips to another nearby town, he agreed to meet some local contacts at a café. Somehow the local German unit found out about the *résistant* gathering and machine-gunned the place from the outside, killing several people. It was assumed that Michel le Canadien was dead—but he hadn't yet arrived when the shooting occurred.

All along, Guy had no idea about Sonia's whereabouts, whether she was safe or even alive. He went to sleep every night worrying about her. Sonia had been his wife for only six weeks. Beyond the SOE training houses and the hotel room they had shared as newlyweds, they'd never lived together. But they had seen each other virtually every day for nearly six months. Now they were fighting the same war but were worlds apart. Guy wished he could glimpse her beautiful face. But for security reasons he could not even bring a single photograph. All that remained of Sonia with Guy was the faint echo of her laughter and the vivid picture of her he had in his mind.

Still, Guy embraced the temporary life he was now living among the French—he said he felt at home the moment he landed. He especially appreciated their taste for food and wine and the necessity of pausing to enjoy them. "These good people don't eat to live, they live to eat," Guy said of the Charolais. "This is very difficult. But in the end, you have to apply yourself," he joked. "I know no one here who does not drink wine . . . . Just because we're in the woods doesn't mean we didn't eat well."

One day Albert Browne-Bartroli, or Toto, as he was nicknamed, dropped by to see Guy at Sylla only to find his lieutenant hosting a lunch in the woods—"with tablecloth, silverware, flowers," Albert wryly noted, making no effort to conceal his envy; he hadn't so much as had his shoes shined in weeks.

Albert appreciated his new lieutenant and his energy—and his penchant for dark suits—and he still saw Guy as the "perfect soldier" and "courageous to the point of imprudence." But the two did have an occasionally bumpy relationship. Albert was once nonplussed to find out that Guy was trying to lure Joseph, his long-awaited radio operator, away from him.

Albert told Guy, "If it's attention you're looking for, you'll have time and occasion enough later, if you survive, that is." In Albert's estimation Guy was "not very diplomatic," a "hard-kicking and loud voiced man" who "does not mince his words." He certainly did not when he clashed with Claude (whose real name was Olivier Ziegel), the head of a fourth battalion in the area. Their arguments were "famous in the region."

Like Claude, there were those who were antagonistic toward Guy from the start, describing his 1st Battalion as "*vendu aux Anglais*," or "sold out to the English." Many others in the French resistance shared that sentiment, distrustful of British intentions and openly cold toward their agents, questioning not only their actions but even their very presence. Charles de Gaulle and his Free French and *Armée secrète* were already supplying their own men from London, and they too were suspicious of Allied intentions—despite the fact that after D-Day, all SOE agents and the maquis were now ostensibly part of the French Forces of the Interior. Other groups among the local *Armée secrète* leadership were put off by Guy and Albert's refusal to supply them with arms at all. Still others decried Guy and Albert's relative independence, accusing them of acting without consulting local public opinion. And while Guy was praised by de Gaulle's representative on the ground, he also said that Guy "unfortunately, unlike his leader he lacks flexibility. And like all good Americans, (which he claims to be though he is Canadian,) he looks upon our moral war as if it were a real war, as if a military enterprise."

Guy was aware of the sensitivities, but he was convinced that being an outsider was his strength—that it enabled him to bring the various factions, right and left, together. And in an effort to allay some of the concerns he also played up the fact that he was French Canadian, and for much of that summer refused to wear his military uniform.

When D-Day arrived and Buckmaster had uniforms parachuted in for the final battle, many SOE agents surprised their followers when they suddenly appeared in them. Not Guy, who preferred his dark suits. The uniforms ostensibly gave the agents some protection if they were caught by the enemy. The irregular, outlaw maquisards had no such protection, if any truly existed, of appearing to belong to a conventional military force. "If my men were caught," Guy noted, "they were shot. So what was good enough for them was good enough for me. I didn't wear my uniform, and they were thankful for that. That's why they backed me so well."

Despite his uncompromising attitude, and the concerns of his instructors back at SOE school, Guy did develop a following among the men of the maquis, who believed in his plan and accepted his lead. In time, men such as Louis Lapalus, Jean Tabourin, René Fléchard, and Pierre Jandeau all became acolytes and trusted confidants.

"I did not accept orders from anyone, my only chief was Michel le Canadien," René said.

If Guy stepped too heavily on anyone's toes, Albert, his circuit organizer, was "always there afterwards to put ointment on the sore spots."

And Guy was always there to lend a hand in the tough ones.

Sometime later in the summer of 1944, Albert summoned Guy to discuss a sensitive matter. He told him that, just as he'd feared, Alcide Beauregard, the Canadian radio operator helping their circuit from Lyon, had been exposed.

Alcide was arrested in mid-July by the Gestapo at his mediocre hideaway, along with the host who'd hidden him in plain sight for weeks. For the DITCHER circuit, it was a significant setback. For Alcide, it was catastrophic.

He was taken to the notorious Montluc prison in Lyon, where witnesses later reported he'd been mercilessly interrogated over and over. The torturous treatment seemed to take a toll. One of those witnesses reported that Alcide was still alive on July 22, but that "his reason is believed to have been unhinged by the tortures to which he was subject."

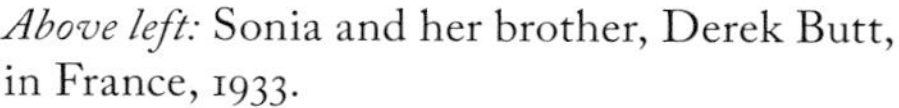

Above left: Sonia and her brother, Derek Butt, in France, 1933.

Above right: Sonia Butt at school in London, age five or six. Circa 1930.

Right: Guy at his first communion, age seven or eight. Circa 1924.

Below: Hockey at Collège Jean-de-Brébeuf. Guy's team was called "team London." Guy is second from the right, around thirteen years old, 1930.

Guy in England, likely at the No. 1 Convalescent Depot base at Dolphin Camp in Brixham, England, 1940–42.

Guy d'Artois in an undated photo.

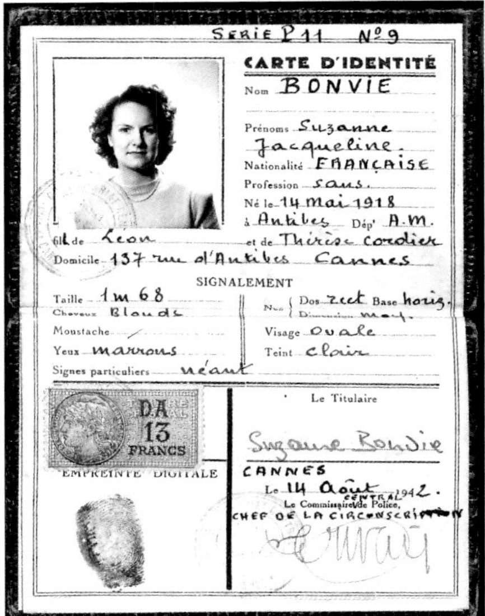

SERIE P11 Nº 9

CARTE D'IDENTITÉ

Nom BONVIE

Prénoms Suzanne Jacqueline

Nationalité FRANÇAISE

Profession sans

Né le 14 mai 1918

à Antibes Dép' A.M.

fils de Leon et de Thérèse Cordier

Domicile 137 rue d'Antibes Cannes

SIGNALEMENT

Taille 1m 68

Cheveux Blonds

Moustache —

Yeux marrons

Signes particuliers néant

Nez Dos rect Base horiz. Dimension moy.

Visage Ovale

Teint clair

DA 13 FRANCS

EMPREINTE DIGITALE

Le Titulaire

Suzanne Bonvie

CANNES

Le 14 Août 1942

Le Commissaire Central de Police, Chef de la circonscription

Sonia's SOE-issued doctored French document identifying her as Suzanne Bonvie.

Feldpoststempel.

Personalien

Zuname : Nom — Jaubert

Vorname : Prénoms — Henri

Staatsangehoerigkeit : Nationalité — Française

Geburtsort : Lieu de naissance — Miallet Dordogne

Geburtstag : Date de naissance — 25. 1906

Jetzige Wohnung : Domicile — Bourges Cher

Strasse u. Nr. : Rue — 64 bis Bd. Lamarck

Beruf : Profession — chauffeur

One of several fake French ID documents in Guy's possession while he was serving in Saône-et-Loire in France.

Sonia and Guy in London around the time of their marriage in April 1944.

Wedding day. Guy and Sonia are joined by family and friends, including other SOE agents and staff, April 15, 1944.

A rare photo of Guy in France and in uniform, likely August 15, 1944, during formalities to welcome his French counterpart, Captain C. Deprez.

Sydney Hudson in 1936.

Guy and Sonia reunited at the Bonaventure Station in Montreal on December 19, 1944, after she crossed the Atlantic to join him. With them is Guy's niece, Claudette Courchesne.

A group of Canadian SOE agents on their return to Canada from war. *L to R first row:* Lieut. J.E. Fournier, Lieut. P.E. Thibault, Capt. H.A. Benoit. *L to R second row:* Major P.E. Labelle, Capt. L.I. Taschereau, Capt. L.G. d'Artois, Capt. J.P. Archambault.

Above: Captain Guy d'Artois just after rescuing Anglican missionary Canon John Turner in the Arctic. Guy had a camera with which he chronicled their work, pictures that were later published by the *Globe and Mail*. July 7, 1948.

Guy d'Artois standing next to General Charles de Gaulle, who decorated him with the Croix de Guerre while on a visit to Ottawa, August 29, 1945.

Canadian Special Air Service Company officers and senior NCOs at Rivers, Manitoba. Guy is on the bottom left.

Sonia d'Artois posing in a staged photo with a wedding ring and a revolver.

Sonia d'Artois near her home in Québec City with her four children, 1953.

During his final visit to Charolles in 1984, Guy was gifted this Sylla flag. Guy donated the flag to Musée Royal 22e Régiment at La Citadelle de Québec where it is currently on display.

Sonia d'Artois receiving the Légion d'honneur in 2007.

Sonia marking the fiftieth anniversary of the D-Day invasion with other Canadian veterans in Normandy, France, 1994.

Above: Guy and Sonia with their six children at Nadya's wedding in 1976.

Right: Sonia d'Artois in later life.

Sonia with her grandchildren in the early 2000s.

According to Guy, the SOE in London was trying to save Alcide and six other *résistant* figures in custody by arranging to pay a ransom to their German captors. In an SOE ledger back in London a two-million-franc drop to DITCHER was noted for July, though no mention is made of its purpose.

Albert asked Guy to join him for the rendezvous and witness the money exchanging hands. It was an unusual request, but Guy readily agreed. He arrived with his lieutenant Jean Tabourin and several other men in tow. They accompanied Albert to a spot near Bois Clair, en route to the German stronghold of Mâcon. Guy's understanding was that sometime after the money was handed over, only six of the prisoners would be released. The seventh would be killed, to avoid suspicion.

At the agreed spot, two German officers arrived in a vehicle. Guy and Albert alone approached them while the others stayed behind. Only one of the men emerged from the car. "All is understood," Guy heard Albert say. Then, "All is understood. It's settled," he heard the German respond.

Guy then saw Albert rip open one of the two big canvas bags in order to prove there was money inside. He handed them over, "to who, I don't know. No names, nothing," said Guy. The man returned to the vehicle. Then it sped away.

"We didn't give a damn about those two million francs, especially since London approved the operation," Guy said later in an interview about the matter. "In the worst case, we'd lose the money. In the best case, we'd save the lives of six people."

But "from there on, I've never heard a thing," Guy said later. No hint of whether the German officers had lived up to their side of the bargain or just pocketed the cash. Weeks went by, and there was still no word on the fate of fellow Canadian Alcide Beauregard.

Alcide Beauregard was just one agent who went missing after D-Day. This was yet another catastrophic period for F Section and its personnel, especially for a number of female agents rounded up by German forces.

In early July, unbeknownst to the rest of the world, four captured female SOE agents were executed at the Natzweiler-Struthof concentration camp: Andrée Borrel, Vera Leigh, Sonya Olschanezky, and Diana Rowden. In captivity they were dealt the most extraordinary pain, and then, one by one, given a lethal injection. Their bodies were then incinerated.

Also in July, SOE agents Henri Frager and Lilian Rolfe, once Guy's love interest, were arrested and disappeared without a trace.

Alleged spies or agents who were captured were treated brutally in Nazi hands. But so were ordinary soldiers in uniform. Dozens of Canadians were taken prisoner just after D-Day by soldiers of the German 12th SS Panzer Division, northwest of Caen in the town of Authie in Normandy. Over the course of several days, twenty Canadians—who had been in uniform—would be taken outside the Abbaye d'Ardenne and shot. It became known as the Abbaye d'Ardenne Massacre, one of a series of massacres during the battle of Normandy in which more than a hundred and fifty Canadian and British soldiers were summarily executed.

German prisoners and French collaborators could also expect harsh treatment at the hands of some parts of the resistance in France. Sometimes, those who were captured were simply shot. Such instances were reported by several who served in the Saône-et-Loire region, including Guy. He reported to HQ that of the hundred and fifteen suspected collaborators that his security group had arrested, "some 22 were shot, mostly *miliciens* and people who worked openly with the Germans." Guy would also later recount the story of a beautiful Polish woman he believed was sent specifically to entrap him, but "we soon found her out." She too, he said, was shot.

There was one other particularly explosive episode to which both Albert and Guy were privy, in which more than fifty German prisoners were executed in retaliation for killing members of the maquis. But the outside world wouldn't hear about that until the war was over.

17

AWAY

Sonia • *Le Breuil Saint Michel, July 1944*

Sonia was alone again, heading south toward the city of Chédigny, about a hundred and twenty kilometres away from Le Mans, rhythmically pumping her pedals past the infinite meadows of green that make up the French countryside. By then she'd become such a practised cyclist that she was likely to cover the distance in a single day, the pain in her back and shoulder now diminished by the passage of time. On the quiet roads south of Le Mans, Sonia could truly breathe. This route seemed of small concern to the occupying forces. There was little German presence to speak of, few patrols or undue delays. And anyway, a young woman alone with proper identification wouldn't be seen as much of a threat, even if she were to be stopped for a check. Still, Sydney had seen her off with some misgivings.

Sonia's destination was a place called Château du Breuil, an immense, centuries-old castle set well away from the road, over a soft hill covered in thick bush that made it all but invisible from the property's outside edge. That also made it an ideal SOE safe house and, for Sonia, a place where she might at least temporarily find some peace.

Her host and the owner of the château was Marthe Dauprat-Sevenet. She'd been married to Louis Sevenet, who was killed in the First World War when their son, Henri, was barely a year old. Carrying on Louis's legacy in this subsequent world war, Henri and his mother had been heavily involved in the resistance. And when Henri was recruited to the SOE in 1942, he clandestinely travelled to Britain to undergo an abbreviated version of the usual SOE course. Later he returned to France by parachuting onto his family's property, with Marthe leading the group that received him.

When Sonia arrived at the family château that July, it had been only a few days since Henri was killed in a battle with German forces in the south of France. Marthe, who'd been widowed and now made childless by war, was in the depths of mourning, but she greeted Sonia warmly. She was a motherly, deeply devout, and exceptionally melancholy woman. Sonia was drawn to her from the start.

It had been a month since the Forêt de Charnie disaster, and HEADMASTER had been operating without a wireless radio. Sonia had come a long way in the hope that Marthe could connect her to Philippe de Vomécourt, that SOE old hand who'd helped get the SOE off the ground at the start and something of a legend. Saint Paul, as he was nicknamed, could get the message to London on their behalf.

Following the catastrophe in the Forêt de Charnie, Sydney had had to change tactics. To avoid another disaster he'd decided to keep the groups small, placing just five or six men in different sectors around Le Mans, separate and independent of each other.

They stayed at various farms and did most of their sabotage at night, making do with whatever arms and ammunition they still had at their disposal.

Sonia the courier, the practised cyclist, had become the main connection between the groups, carrying money and weapons or ammunition back and forth. "You knew that you were vulnerable all the time," she said later. "You knew that you were in danger. But you learned to live with that, just like you did in Britain during the raids. You just got used to things."

And now, after the longest of bicycle rides, it was her task to reconnect HEADMASTER to London. But in what would be an unexpectedly lengthy sojourn, her main occupation was simply waiting for Philippe to appear.

Over several long, quiet conversations, Sonia and Marthe grew fond of each other. They would often sit on a circular wood bench surrounding the gnarled trunk of an ancient tree that anchored the vast property. They shared stories, and Marthe generously shared her space and her meals. She even gave Sonia a pair of shoes, which were notoriously hard to get in those days, and prohibitively expensive on the black market. And in a moment of uncommon optimism, Marthe declared that while she may have lost a son, God had sent her a daughter.

Philippe knew everyone involved; he had worked with Marthe's son, Henri. He was also one of the agents who, with Sydney, had escaped the d'Eysses prison in 1944. Now he had only to show up—or send a delegate. Sonia and Marthe waited and waited, and yet there was no sign of Philippe.

Back in Le Mans, Sydney grew concerned. It would have been lonely without Sonia after weeks of constantly being together. "As the days went by I became more than ever anxious as to what might have happened to her. However, there was nothing I could do," Sydney later recalled.

He was far from idle, however. Sydney and his men kept up their attacks. They had repeatedly cut the telephone lines, although the German forces were adept at quickly fixing them and in mid-July had even installed a new "distribution centre" for all their telephone lines in the basement of the Le Mans post office, right across from German headquarters, the *Feldkommandantur*. But the night before it became operational, on July 24, Sydney himself along with Claude Hureau, a local resistance stalwart, cycled over, each with a bag of plastic explosives. They entered the building with the help of a contact who worked there. They rigged the distributor with explosives, then quietly exited and cycled away. Around midnight, an almighty explosion eviscerated the building. Sydney, by then, was back at home and fast asleep.

Sonia, meanwhile, was in a whole other world, whiling away the hours talking to Marthe, who would otherwise spend her time praying in a small chapel. Their conversations inevitably turned to religion. Sonia told Marthe of her marriage to Guy, who, like Marthe, was Catholic. The mourning mother persuaded Sonia to be baptized into the Catholic Church, into the religion of her husband and future children. Marthe volunteered to act as her godmother. And volunteering to be her godfather, Sonia later recalled, was Philippe de Vomécourt, who had finally appeared—just in time to attend the baptism.

On July 30, Sonia was baptized, at the age of twenty, at the Église Saint-Pierre-ès-Liens in Chédigny. The *abbé* provided her with a pink piece of paper on which he declared, in timid handwriting, that she had renounced Protestantism and embraced Catholicism "without conditions." Sonia signed it as "Sophie Butt, *épouse* d'Artois."

She had clearly misidentified herself, possibly out of fear of leaving behind a paper trail with her actual name.

The ceremony meant a great deal to Marthe, coming as it did just ten days after her son was killed. She gained a goddaughter that day, just as Sonia had found a kind of mother figure. For the same reasons that war accelerated love it also electrified friendships, in short order creating the kinds of bonds that could withstand the distractions of a lifetime. The two women would remain in touch long after Sonia finally made her way back to Le Mans.

Sonia had also forged deep bonds among the maquisards. The closest was with Suzanne Rebouche, an insightful and unusually philosophical young woman with a wicked sense of humour and a natural wisdom that drew Sonia in. She was only a year older and an underground fighter herself, so the bond was instant. Suzanne's whole family, including her brother as well as her boyfriend, Lucien, were also involved with the resistance. Her father, Raymond Rebouche, nicknamed Pépé, was a wealthy local who'd been in the army in the First World War. Now he had a transport business and ran a café and hotel, putting all of it at the resistance's disposal. Sonia would sometimes stay at his hotel, talking with Suzanne late into the night. Pépé donated his trucks to help move weaponry and explosives, and he even did it himself, his passage through checkpoints made easier by the fact that he also delivered food to German forces. On one occasion, Sonia recalled, he hid her along with a load of weapons under a mound of hay in one of his vehicles. When they'd reach German checkpoints, Pépé would ably talk his way through—they were not searched once.

Sonia became very fond of the entire family, especially Suzanne, and the two formed an alliance in what was mostly a male milieu. Sonia would sometimes use the black market to buy her new friend small treats like perfume, which was, like most luxuries at the time, difficult to find or far too expensive.

Money was a constant issue for most people in Le Mans, but when HEADMASTER lost its treasury in the Forêt de Charnie ambush, Sydney needed to somehow find money locally to keep his men fed, clothed, and mobile.

Edmond Cohin, leader of the ill-fated Charnie maquis and owner of the Château des Bordeaux, proposed that they approach his uncle, l'Abbé Chevalier—since, as treasurer of the Le Mans Catholic Church, he could be in a position to lend them money. Sonia went along with him and told the *abbé* that she was a secret agent and that she needed to borrow a substantial sum, one that would be duly paid back by London when the war was over. To back up her claim, she asked him to choose a message that she would arrange to have read on the BBC's *messages personnels*.

The *abbé* chose "The meek shall inherit the Earth." Sonia managed to get word to London, and the message was broadcast just as she'd promised. Sydney subsequently visited and provided an IOU for two hundred thousand francs, signed with both his real and code names. That sum represented a substantial boost to the HEADMASTER organization. They were back in business.

Sonia and Sydney were the only members of their circuit who were in touch with all the groups involved. Although she'd been sent in as courier, Sonia was taking on far greater responsibility, carrying out whatever tasks were necessary to facilitate their work. The two of them worked well together. Sydney was in love with Sonia, but he was also increasingly in awe of her. "She became in function though not in title my second in command," he would later write. "I believe her to be absolutely fearless."

After their lengthy separation, Madeleine and Michel would spend most of that summer working closely together. While she was away she had missed his thirty-fourth birthday, but she did not forget it. In her solo travels she'd taken the time to find him a rare gift: a brand-new watch.

When the Allies eventually fought their way out of Normandy, Le Mans was one of the first cities to be liberated. On August 8, 1944, as German forces retreated, American forces entered the city, flooding the roads in their jeeps and on foot, marching single file, weapons hoisted on their shoulders. The people of Le Mans, many of them dressed up for the occasion, lined the streets in celebration, waving wildly to the Americans and some even stealing a kiss or two. Others held out food and wine, drawing clumps of soldiers around them like bees to roses. Being situated just down the road from Rommel's headquarters had come with a price for Le Mans, but now that position also came with a reward: compared with the rest of France, a relatively early liberation.

In the melee, however, scores were being settled. People were turning against known collaborators and dragging them into the squares in crude attempts to exact instant justice. A number of women were rounded up and marched into town for a public humiliation. And, for a terrifying few minutes, Sonia was among them. She had, after all, been repeatedly spotted at the black-market restaurants and taken for a German officer's girl. And so she too was dragged off by two armed men to add to the pile of women whose hair would be shaved off as punishment. But as luck would have it, Sonia spotted some of the maquisards she'd worked with and, in a panic, yelled at the top of her lungs to get their attention. Mercifully, they were able to pry her away from the mob.

Although their sector had been liberated, Sydney and Sonia weren't yet ready to leave, believing that there was much more they and their men could still offer the Allied effort. Nor were they ready to part ways, to return to the lives they'd led before this war had brought them together. "We wanted to continue working or we didn't want to break up our relationship," Sonia said hesitantly in hindsight.

And so, on the very day U.S. forces entered Le Mans, Sonia and Sydney found their way to a Major Batey, who worked in intelligence for the 5th Armoured Division of General George S. Patton's Third Army. Since Sonia and Sydney could still pass for locals and knew the terrain well, they offered to gather intelligence on the Americans' behalf. Persuaded, Major Batey wrote them a note dated that same day, in what appears to be pencil, stating simply that they had "permission to pass through U.S. troops for purpose of obtaining information for the U.S. army."

In time, they would collect a number of these letters and authorizations to travel, armed, through American lines. "You will render every assistance possible to this party and will place yourself at Albin's disposal," wrote Lieutenant-Colonel Robert I. Powell of the 11th Special Force Detachment, adding that "a small fighting unit may have to be provided," revealing the extent of the trust placed in Sydney and Sonia—and the desire to obtain information about German movements.

Travelling through the countryside gave Sonia and Sydney a disturbing look at how the end of the occupation was playing out in smaller villages and towns.

Bearing witness to the aftermath of conflict is uniquely unsettling; there is the deluge of refugees, civilians who've been uprooted by the new violence and have walked away, on foot, leaving everything behind. Then there are the unspeakable remnants of human conflict: Sonia recalled seeing bodies, including those of children, "everywhere." All those civilians who'd just fallen victim to the withdrawing forces had survived four years of occupation but would never know the joy of living on the other side of it.

Sonia and Sydney were prepared for all eventualities, carrying not only their French identification papers and the letters of support they'd secured from the Americans, but also a set of German papers that presented them as collaborators who were permitted to circulate freely and carry arms. They'd lucked into the latter set, complete with photos and proper stamps, in the chaos of the German withdrawal. In both cases they presented themselves as a couple. Sonia always carried the documents, hidden in a specially made, SOE-issued girdle that had an inside pocket. She'd pull out the appropriate papers as needed. It didn't always go smoothly.

In late August Sydney and Sonia set off in a rare petrol-fuelled Renault to search for an intact bridge over which to cross the River Seine. Their assignment was to gather intelligence on the movements of the retreating German forces, now massed on the other side of the river, and report back to the American units parked about two hundred kilometres southeast of Paris.

Driving south, the couple came across one destroyed bridge after another; they had to go some distance before they found a small, unguarded but intact bridge near the village of Bar-sur-Seine. There they crossed over to the "German side," and with the assistance of helpful locals were able to assess the situation. The next day Sonia and Sydney left to return to the other side. As they neared the bridge they'd crossed only the day before, they pulled out a French flag to hang in plain sight, anticipating that the next time they saw troops, they would be American.

Instead, at the foot of the bridge they came within full view of about a dozen "fully armed" German soldiers manning a checkpoint. In what was a very fluid military zone, the German forces had taken the area overnight.

Sonia and Sydney had managed to deftly weave in and out of German-held areas nearly a dozen times, mostly untouched, gathering valuable intelligence and relaying it back to the Americans. But now, with the checkpoint immediately ahead and the wrong flag and papers on hand, their luck seemed about to run out.

There was just one possible course of action. "The only thing to do was to just go for it," said Sonia. "The car was in third gear. I put my foot down and accelerated," Sydney recalled. The car's sudden acceleration took the Germans by surprise, and they immediately opened fire.

Sonia and Sydney instinctively ducked as they careered across the bridge. Sonia's jacket was riddled with bullets, but she was miraculously unscathed. Sydney wasn't as lucky. He felt a "stinging blow" to his left shoulder. He'd been hit.

Clearing the bridge brought no respite. There were Germans down the main road. Sonia and Guy turned in the other direction and decided to ditch the car and run into the woods. There they buried their Sten guns and started walking back toward the village.

Bar-sur-Seine had been "completely pillaged" and was entirely deserted; there was no one in sight except the occasional group of soldiers passing by.

Their aim had been to blend with the population to shake any suspicion they were the couple who'd just driven through the checkpoint. They spotted an open café and walked in, but there was no one there either. Sydney set down his coat, which had a tiny bullet hole in the right shoulder where the bullet had grazed him. Thankfully, while painful, it was only a superficial wound.

Another German patrol walked by, marching along a group of locals. The soldiers spotted Sydney and Sonia and signalled to them to join the group. They had no choice but to acquiesce, hoping the papers that proved them collaborators would keep them out of trouble. As they left the café, Sydney inadvertently left his coat behind.

"We were marched off and taken to the schoolyard where there must have been four or five hundred men, all the male civilians in the town, who had been taken hostage by the Germans," said Sonia.

It didn't take long before Sonia was released; it was clear that they wanted only the men. Sydney remained, his identity papers still in the hands of the Germans. Sonia decided to use the time to return to the café to retrieve Sydney's coat and try to come up with a plan for how to proceed.

As she walked away, she heard footsteps behind her.

Sonia looked back. Two German soldiers seemed to be following her. She thought for a moment and decided to keep going, to just carry on and do what she had planned to do. The streets were mostly deserted as she made her way to the café.

She kept walking and in a few minutes was taking the stairs up to the café where she and Sydney had been just a few hours earlier. The soldiers' footsteps again, now coming up the stairs, confirmed they were following her. And then, at gunpoint, they were upon her.

As a weapon of war, sexual assault is among the most devastating and the most shockingly routine. It is every woman's worst nightmare. And in the chaos of a war zone, it is a whole other level of torture.

"My first reaction was to put up a fight," Sonia said years later when discussing it openly for the first time. She had the American papers on her, hidden in the secret pocket of that girdle. If her attackers learned her true identity the result would be certain torture, a one-way trip to a concentration camp, or worse. Never mind what it might mean for Sydney.

In that moment, Sonia was forced to make a rapid calculation. She decided not to fight back. Not this time. She was no doubt engaged in battle, however: a battle for dignity, and for survival, and one that she fought bravely. As injurious and damaging as it was, this was a battle for self-preservation.

Sonia waited a long time after the soldiers left. Then she grabbed Sydney's coat and walked back, "shaking like a leaf."

She found Sydney still waiting along with dozens of other men. He'd since met the school principal and arranged for Sonia to wait with the man's fiancée within walking distance of the school.

Sonia, still in shock, went over and knocked for several minutes before anyone answered. Finally the fiancée came to the door. She was naturally hesitant to let in this beautiful but dishevelled stranger, but the young woman's mother sensed Sonia's distress and allowed her to follow them down to the cellar. They'd been hiding there, along with about ten other women and children, all waiting for word of the fate of their brothers, fathers, husbands in German custody. Together they sat on the floor. Devastated, Sonia leaned against the wall, "not knowing what was going to happen."

The hours dragged on; Sydney's wound was throbbing. It dawned on him that this was no routine identity check, that he was a hostage—and along with the rest of the men there, likely a bargaining chip, maybe even a human shield against the approaching Americans. There was also every chance that whatever their captors were planning could be scuttled by a failed negotiation or a surprise attack by the resistance.

"It could have gone either way," said Sonia.

The morning after an agonizing night, a senior German officer appeared at the school, and soon he agreed to release the town's baker so that he could make bread. Sydney decided to approach the officer too, to underline his status as a collaborator, as his papers clearly indicated. It worked. The officer waved him off. He immediately set out to find Sonia.

She was relieved to see him, comforted by the sight of his familiar, gentle face. But she was still in terrible shape, still shaking.

Sonia told Sydney what had happened to her. Then, as though to ease the shock, she told him that luckily her assailants had never discovered the American passes hidden close to her body.

Sydney was very upset. For all his declarations of love, he'd been powerless to protect her when she needed his protection most. "I was speechless," he later recounted. Nothing he said could possibly take away Sonia's obvious distress. He realized then that his most important task was to get them out of Bar-sur-Seine as soon as possible.

They walked for two days, joining the thousands who'd been displaced by a world conflict at its height. Eventually they ran into American troops, who in turn held them briefly so they could verify they were indeed who they claimed to be. That didn't take long, thanks to the U.S. Army passes that Sonia had fought to conceal.

18

TRIUMPHANT MINUTES

Guy • *Charolles, August 1944*

On the night of August 10, Louis Lapalus was in Martigny-le-Comte, lying down under a table where a secret telephone had been installed that allowed direct communication among the resistance. At around one in the morning, he was startled by the voice of the operator on duty addressing all combat units in the Charolles region. German forces were on the move, the voice said, and they appeared to be en route to the city of Cluny. "*Please urgently send all available reinforcements.*"

An estimated three thousand German soldiers, equipped with heavy guns, armoured vehicles, and planes, were on their way to attack the city in a major counteroffensive aimed at stamping out the men they called "terrorists," on a route that was crucial for German forces.

Albert Browne-Bartroli's men arrived too late; the German force had already advanced beyond the hills into the valley that leads into Cluny. Albert rang the alarm and called on Charolles for reinforcements.

Guy happened to be away for talks in Autun, about seventy kilometres north of Martigny-le-Comte. According to Albert he'd gone there to meet the bishop, a known collaborator with the German forces, to appeal for an end to attacks on civilians.

And yet in short order Guy had been notified of the fight brewing near Bois Clair, a key mountain gateway between Cluny and the Mâcon area where German forces were concentrated. A short while after that Guy's operators were calling René Fléchard with a message from him: "The Germans have arrived in large numbers en route to Cluny, they have already arrived at Bois Clair. You must act as quickly as possible to get there with a hundred men." Guy also ordered his men from Sylla to head there, ready for a fight.

René and his men were on the road within fifteen minutes. And soon almost all the units in the area, of all political stripes, would be embroiled in what would come to be known as the Battle of Cluny.

Once they were face to face in the valley among the vineyards, it was an all-out, "savage" fight between the German forces and the maquisards of the DITCHER circuit. The Germans twice came within a hundred yards of the train station before fighters managed to push them back. And three times that day German planes appeared overhead, unleashing explosives on Cluny itself. Such an attack from the air was an ominous development; the resistance had no way to fight back against the enemy in the sky. The aerial strikes started fires and sent a procession of dazed civilians walking through the city—and yet several women who worked the "secret" telephone network "continue[d] at their posts heroically."

That secret telephone network was one of the most potent weapons in DITCHER's arsenal. Guy, with the direct involvement of Maman Lucienne and her husband, Jean Sarrazin, and up to a dozen sympathetic employees of the Postes, Télégraphes et Téléphones administration, worked to develop the network, which extended to towns large and small throughout the DITCHER area of operations. It was entirely independent of the regular phone system, providing more than forty lines through two exchanges and connecting the main resistance hubs in the region, each of which was assigned a code name: Charolles was inevitably Quebec, Cluny was Lyon, and Martigny-le-Comte, where Louis Lapalus was resting, was Bruxelles. Sylla, puzzlingly, or perhaps perfectly appropriately, was named Tokyo. The point was to throw off anyone who might be listening.

Here again women proved indispensable. Housewives working in their kitchens and homes surreptitiously kept the lines operational twenty-four hours a day, allowing Guy and others in the resistance to communicate freely, safe from German ears. In Charolles, according to Louis Lapalus, the central exchange was entrusted to a Mrs. Perrin, a supervisor at PTT working in a disused railway building. Guy said he had between six hundred and nine hundred kilometres of telephone wire at his disposal. At the sight of any significant German movement, the young women out there gathering intelligence, or anyone for that matter, would call it in. Guy insisted on having every call logged.

> *German column at present (2330) at place called de Charnoul,*
> *making for Cluny. Number about 200."*
> *"Prepare lorries."*
> *"All companies to take position.*

"I was everywhere," Guy would recall. "I had telephones hidden in hedges, in vacant lots, and everywhere, and could keep in contact with my agents and they could contact me." It was, Guy reported to his superiors, the "basis of all the success I had in the

Saône-et-Loire." Albert agreed. "This was to prove . . . responsible for most of our success."

But ultimately, the battles on the ground had to be won through sheer brute force. And at Bois Clair, by early evening, the resistance fighters had pushed the German ground force back toward Mâcon.

It was a turning point in the fight, but it came with a heavy toll. The resistance fighters lost a dozen men. And the city itself was pockmarked with mounds of twisted rubble where restaurants, shops, and people's homes had once stood. The retreating German forces left behind two "47 mm guns, 2 armoured cars, several trucks and more than 400 dead." The maquisards took over the Bois Clair mountain pass, which meant German forces could no longer easily threaten Cluny. "From that day till the end, no German entered our triangle . . . except as prisoner," reported Albert.

"Those who can walk pick up the dead and lay them in a 'chapel of rest,'" Albert wrote of that day. "Those who can think, think of what tomorrow may bring; those who can dream cannot imagine more triumphant minutes."

Cluny became the first city in the region to be successfully defended by the resistance. It was an important victory. But ultimately, the resistance would have to dislodge the German garrisons town by town. Those fights were still to come.

19

CONSTERNATION

Guy • *Sylla, August 1944*

Early on the morning of August 18, Guy ordered the men of the Maquis de Sylla to put on their finest dress. On that day, Sylla was hosting a rare military ceremony, what was described as a "change of command." And for once, Guy would cast aside his dark suit and put on his Canadian uniform—along with the distinctive maroon beret that marked him as a paratrooper.

A few days earlier, Guy's men had welcomed a team of uniformed Allied officers who had arrived by parachute: one of many so-called Jedburgh teams deployed to help smooth the Allies' final push into the rest of France. A French captain by the name of Deprez was to share power with Guy and jointly lead the 1st Charollais Battalion. Captain C. Deprez was a "tall blond man from Lille, incredibly strong, with hands as big as beaters, and yet at once able to be gentle as a child." He would now be Guy's French counterpart.

Guy took the formalities very seriously. The ceremony featured a march-past by the men of Sylla, and a photographer captured it all, including the moment when all the military officers stood together in uniform, stiffly saluting.

Then, once it was over, everyone turned their attention back to the battles at hand.

The fight right across France was reaching a crescendo. The battle for Paris began from within. It was an unprecedented challenge to the forces of German occupation, and it was the resistance, under the banner of the French Forces of the Interior (Forces françaises de l'intérieur, or FFI), leading the way. The fate of the capital was hanging in the balance, and the world was watching.

Far from such limelight, the skirmishes in Saône-et-Loire were also escalating as August progressed. But Tuesday, August 22, was a day that would remain in the minds of the region's people for decades.

On that day, fighting broke out in several of the towns on the western edge of Guy's district. In an agreement among Guy, Deprez, and other leaders, elements of the 1st Charollais Battalion attacked Génelard, La Gravoine, and Pallinges. The objective was to halt the movement of German forces along the strategic western edge of their district—from Paray-le-Monial in the south to Montceau-les-Mines farther north—and ultimately, to dislodge the German garrisons in all those towns.

The battle of Génelard appeared to require the most complex operation and the most men. The objective was to sever the railway line, take the station, and dislodge the German soldiers based at a nearby school.

Guy recalled setting out at daylight with a group of about two hundred and fifty of his Sylla battalion. As the bulk of the group engaged with the German garrison in town, Guy split off with eight of the men to take care of destroying the railway. When a train of reinforcements arrived, it was derailed. The men took the Germans on board prisoner, blew up the train, then joined the rest of his group in battle.

When they heard through the telephone system that more German reinforcements were on their way, Guy ordered René Fléchard's company to intercept them. It was a fight that would continue on several fronts, with casualties sustained on both sides.

Meanwhile, in town, Sylla's men had encircled the school amid another exchange of fire. Then the maquisards managed to blow through the wall using a bazooka, demolishing part of the building. The Germans inside held out until the end; when they did finally surrender, Guy's men took yet more prisoners. But the fight wasn't entirely over. German forces would return to Génelard on subsequent days to wreak more destruction on the town hall, on farms, and on homes. Génelard was ultimately liberated, but it was "horribly mutilated."

Also on August 22, at least two civilians reported that a train of deportees had arrived at the Paray-le-Monial train station. Thousands of citizens, most of them Jewish, were being routinely deported to Germany and its concentration camps, to be murdered en masse. Gaston Lévy's Saint-Julien-de-Civry group was ordered to liberate the prisoners. They would bear the brunt of what came next.

Their battle to liberate the deportees was underway when an armoured train arrived full of additional German troops, who opened fire to repel the attack. Many of the maquisards managed to escape. But others were cut down instantly, and those who weren't killed in the battle were shot at close range. Twenty-nine among the fighters were killed. Only two of the youngest maquisards were spared in one of the bloodiest and most ill-advised battles in which the resistance of Saône-et-Loire had engaged.

The train of deportees, meanwhile, was stuck for three days, after which it continued its journey on to Dachau concentration camp. It was exactly the fate the fighters of the 1st Charollais Batallion had tried to prevent.

For the deportees and for the young men who died there it was an especially tragic end, just as the fight for France was nearing its final stages. The funerals were arranged quickly, young bodies garlanded with flowers and the French flag and carried by their heartbroken compatriots through town on one final journey.

"In a way, the dead must look at us from above and say: 'Poor people, you're still at it,'" Guy once said. "But the honour to be a warrior, to wear the uniform and bear arms and do as you're told—that's worth something."

Surely some among the young men who survived that terrible battle would have disagreed. The massacre caused "consternation" among some of them. There were those who blamed Guy for the tragic results. One *Armée secrète* commander responsible for Guy's sector said that "had liberation taken longer, I would have had to have him arrested." But opinions differ, right up until the present day, on who deserved the blame.

Even with such losses there were growing signs that the German hold on France was faltering. Around the same time, many more *résistants* were executed en masse, among them yet another F Section agent. Unknown to London or Guy or Albert, or to anyone else until much later, was that as the Allied forces made advances into France, German forces in Lyon took a hundred and twenty prisoners from their cells and ferried them in a convoy to Fort de Côte-Lorette in Saint-Genis-Laval. It was August 20, 1944, a Sunday, when the prisoners were brought in in batches, pushed up a set of stairs into a room, and then shot. When they had killed them all, the soldiers soaked their bodies with gasoline and set them on fire, then dynamited the entire building to ensure that no one remained alive.

Alcide Beauregard, the young Canadian radio operator who had disappeared more than a month earlier, was among them. He has no known grave.

20

LIBERATION

Sonia, Guy, and Sydney • *Paris, September 1944*

At the sight of American and French troops rolling into Paris, the exhausted city went wild. People lined the streets, frantically waving to the troops and offering them bottles of champagne, wide smiles, and kisses. It wasn't an entirely smooth end to the occupation: although the German garrison had signed an unconditional surrender, there had still been pockets of soldiers who opened fire and engaged in skirmishes with the Allied forces. Meanwhile the "tears, cheers and bullets" welcoming the Allied forces were captured by journalists embedded among them with film and audio that was subsequently broadcast around the world. Charles de Gaulle, that towering and divisive figure, suddenly emerged into the crowd, drawing applause and, for a moment, gunfire. Undaunted, he kept walking. The momentary hush of some in the crowd, the instinctive running for cover, briefly made audible the perils of declaring victory while the enemy was still fighting.

Do wars ever really end? At the "end" of the Great War, in 1918, even as the armistice was just seconds away, soldiers were still killing each other. The return of war to Europe in 1939 proved, as many had suspected, that the first war had never really come to a definite conclusion. There are wars that go on hiatus and then return with a vengeance. And then there are the wars that go on, but with which we can make peace. The wars within are the most enduring, and the most difficult to end.

At one point or another, wars of all kinds become a point of departure. They open the door to a new story, a rescripting, a reinvention of the lives we knew before. For a good number of the young men and women who engaged in the battles of the Second World War, however, the end of their involvement was, at the same time, a door slamming shut.

For Guy and many others who served with the SOE, their wartime "cog in the wheel" role provided an enormous sense of purpose, a sense of exceptionalism and autonomy usually unavailable to those in the lower ranks of the military—and even to some of the higher ones. For a lieutenant-made-captain like Guy, there's nothing easy about walking away from a role that, within a few short weeks, had catapulted you to the status of high rank, or, as the case may be, a Rex Imperator. It's also wrenching to walk away from the steel-strong bonds you've formed with others under the severe stresses of living through battle together.

Strong as those bonds might grow to be, parachuting into a war is an acknowledgment that you do not belong in that place. You're a transplant, a transient; you're also "a cog in a very large machine." You may thrive in the absence of rules, the excitement of doing your part to undo a gross injustice; you may fall in love, you may be revered for what you do—but you're only really welcome there until the war ends, and then you're likely to become a footnote to history.

On September 4, 1944, French forces entered Michel le Canadien's Charolles. One after another, the towns in his sphere were all released from the occupation's grip. Within days the whole of the Saône-et-Loire region had been liberated. People poured into the streets and celebrated as only the French can, handing out flowers to the soldiers and sharing whatever they had of local food and wine. As the French army swept through, someone hauled Guy and Pierre Jandeau up onto one of the army trucks, where they smiled and waved and laughed, incredulous. As Pierre wrote, "We went through the city's streets with our hands full of flowers."

In Charolles, as elsewhere, the handover from the maquis to the liberating army was, to say the least, tumultuous. Louis Lapalus later said that there was mutual suspicion and even looting in his part of France. "We were free from the occupying forces, but the war wasn't yet over."

Two days later, Guy was among several resistance leaders who attended a meeting with some of the newly arrived French officers at a hotel in Montceau-les-Mines. According to Louis, who was also in attendance, the officers were dressed in crisp uniforms and new, well-waxed boots. The mood, he said, "quickly turned cold."

"Sir! You don't belong here anymore!" Louis recalled them saying to Guy. He described their behaviour as an affront, a "disgraceful" way to speak to a man who, at great risk to his life, had left his country voluntarily to lend a hand in liberating France. "Where did they come from, these glib officers who smelled of mothballs?"

To Guy, the message was unmistakable. He prepared to leave Charolles for good. But before he did, he addressed his fighters one last time.

Guy began by congratulating them on their achievement. It was an emotional farewell—to Jean Tabourin, to Louis Lapalus, to René Fléchard, to Gaston Lévy, and especially to Maman Lucienne. They would have been shedding tears of relief, tears of grief, and tears of absolute exhaustion. This was the end of the most important achievement of their young lives, Guy included. Together they had dreamt about the end of the war, imagined it, fantasized about it, planned and fought hard for it. But it's damned hard walking away from war; you're both born again and struggling to breathe on the way out. You're grateful to be alive and you're despondent; you're energized to continue your life and yet dead, dead tired.

At the centre of a complicated swirl of emotions, Michel le Canadien's war was over. Guy d'Artois, however, had no intention of leaving Michel, or the war, behind.

Guy, along with Jean Tabourin and Pierre Jandeau, got into a car, with Guy in the driver's seat. They were heading to the south of France to find Sonia.

Guy had no idea whether she was even alive—whether she might have been among the many unlucky ones to have been arrested, tortured, transported across a border, or left to languish in a concentration camp, or executed with a single bullet. And ever since he'd landed in occupied France, Guy had no idea where Sonia was deployed. His best guess was the south, the part of France where she grew up and knew best. In any case it wasn't a bad place to take a break, especially for soldiers who'd been on non-stop duty for months.

As the three neared Avignon they heard gunshots whistling in their direction. Jean Tabourin was hit by at least one bullet. The car came to a halt, and the men shot back into the dark. Guy then detoured to find a hospital. The others were lucky. As Guy often said, "If a bullet didn't have your name on it, it wasn't meant for you."

Once assured of Jean's stability, his two comrades reluctantly bade him farewell and then left him behind to carry on to the south, where Guy hoped to pick up Sonia's trail. But there was no immediate sign of her there, and no clues as to where she might be.

F Section had meanwhile recalled its agents to Paris in preparation for their departure. And so Guy, along with a "group of rowdies," which now included Albert Browne-Bartroli, Jean-Paul Archambault, and other Canadians, got into a vehicle and headed off to the capital.

They found a battered city electrified by liberation yet torn between jubilation, retribution, and public grief, grief that would likely take a lifetime, maybe more, to fade. It was in this city waking from the dead that dozens of F Section agents returned to the world of the living, reunited with Vera Atkins and Maurice Buckmaster at their temporary office in the Hotel Cecil on rue Didier, or later, at 37 boulevard des Capucines. As a portal for their reunion with the rest of the world, Paris was, as it is always, a gregarious and willing host.

It proved no less fitting a place to say farewell.

On September 12, Sonia and Sydney were at the conclusion of their final intelligence assignment for the Americans, and they too headed in the direction of Paris, where they had some time alone together.

Nearing the end of their months together in France, there was only one conversation that mattered. Sydney wanted Sonia to stay, to divorce Guy and make her life with him instead.

Guy had not yet arrived in Paris, but Sonia had learned through Buckmaster that her husband was alive and on his way. She'd made a commitment to him before their war began. And now she intended to honour that commitment.

How persistently had Sydney tried to change her decision? Those conversations are impossible to imagine or recount. But in the voluminous unpublished novel he later wrote, Sydney might have captured a sense of their exchanges as the war in France faded and he fought a valiant battle to keep Sonia at his side.

> *"Will you leave Jean and come away with me?"*
>
> *"I hoped you would ask me that. But we both know it's impossible."*
>
> *"Why, why is it impossible?"*
>
> *"I can't abandon Jean. I won't break my promise to stay with him for as long as he wants me."*

Sonia knew that Guy needed her far more than Sydney did. She believed that Guy wouldn't have the strength to withstand her departure. "I was afraid of what would happen to him," she later said. Sydney, she rationalized, was, at thirty-four, much older. He'd spent time in prison. He'd walked over the Pyrenees and thought about the meaning of life. "He had come a lot further in life spiritually than Guy had at that time."

Sydney found it difficult to take no for an answer. *I can't accept that this is the end—that you should enter my life, that we should have such happiness together and that it should vanish without a chance of return.* To him, their love affair was more than a wartime dalliance. He wanted to spend the rest of his life with Sonia. It wasn't possible that all they'd shared in the past four months could disappear in an instant. *That's too much for me to bear.*

But Sonia was clear: She wanted to close this chapter of her life with the end of France's war. A new chapter would begin when she reunited with Guy. She counselled Sydney to return to his family too, to try to make amends.

Finally Sydney reluctantly let go: *I am doing as you say and leaving you, but I'll not give up hope.*

For ten days Sonia waited for news of Guy, returning to the SOE office in Paris day after day; repeatedly she was told there was nothing. Then, on one more of those visits, Sonia was summoned to Buckmaster's office. He led her to an "inner" antechamber, where she spotted a man reading a newspaper. When he lowered the paper, they locked eyes—it was Guy: scruffier, thinner, darker. She, markedly thinner, tired, was still a breathtaking beauty. They had fought their wars apart, and that had come at a great cost. Now those respective wars were over. It was time to come together in a hard-earned peace.

"Until that moment I didn't know if she was still alive," said Guy. But she was alive. And he was euphoric at the sight of her. Her own euphoria was tempered by what she knew and Guy didn't. How devastating to have to break the spell of that remarkable reunion. But she knew it had to be done. Sonia was determined to tell him about Sydney, and then spend a lifetime making it up to him.

"It was pretty tough. Because I thought I had to tell him as soon as possible. And I just had to take my courage with both hands and get on with it and do it."

And so, not long after that reunion, Sonia levelled with Guy: In the days after her arrival in France under cover of darkness, and for the summer weeks afterward, she had been carrying on an affair with Sydney. But now it was over.

Somewhere along the way, the three of them sat down together. Two men from opposite sides of the Atlantic, both in love with the same woman. Only one of them would walk away with her to begin the rest of their lives.

And so there they were at what had once been the most famous tearoom in Paris, confronting what Sydney described as "the most depressing moment in the lives of all three of us." "Madeleine," he went on, "did not leave Guy under any illusion as to what her relationship with me had become and yet she was totally determined to make her future life with him."

"I'm staying with Guy. I've hurt him. I've harmed him and I have to make it up to him," she reasoned at the time. "I had made the decision to make Guy my husband and I intended to live up to my commitment."

It would be the last time the three of them sat down together. After interviews with Buckmaster in Paris they all boarded the same flight, a Dakota destined for London.

Sonia was flying under the name Bonvie, the last time she would use her SOE identification. But for years to come she'd keep it anyway, a memento of who she'd once been. Sonia was now a member of one of the war's smallest clubs: women who'd served behind enemy lines. And she was among the lucky ones.

All of them were lucky to be alive, and to serve at the time they did, in the conditions that the time afforded. Their successes were made possible only by the sacrifices of those who'd gone before them, many of whom were still languishing in concentration camps awaiting their fate.

Sydney didn't remain in London long. Reunited with his wife, he admitted he'd been in love with someone else, that their marriage could no longer continue. He left her and his young daughter, Jennifer, to sign up for further SOE duties and was soon deployed to East Asia to work behind Japanese lines. Sonia and Guy, meanwhile, returned to London to pick up where their life together had been interrupted.

Left behind, often forgotten, were the countless French women and men who'd risked everything by working with the Allies. The dead among them would be remembered with memorials, with ceremonies, with the symbolic change in the name of a street. Most of them had once been ordinary people. And for those who'd survived, reclaiming that luxury would become one of the biggest fights of their lives. Ultimately, said Sonia, "the true heroes are the French people themselves."

Within minutes of takeoff, Sonia was over the English Channel, the same turbulent waters she'd crossed alone at the start of the war in 1939. Between Sonia then and Sonia now was a veritable ocean.

Sydney said it best. "In the summer of 1944 one matured quickly."

PART VI

GOING HOME

21

WAR BRIDE

Sonia • *Atlantic Ocean, December 11, 1944*

Almost a year to the day since she'd first met Guy d'Artois, Sonia began her voyage to the place where he was born. Aboard the SS *Pasteur* dozens of other war brides were embarking on their own voyage across the Atlantic Ocean to Canada, to join new husbands and start new lives. Sonia was more than likely the only British woman on board who'd seen action in France. But she certainly wasn't the only person there to have seen combat in the ongoing war. The *Pasteur* was a troopship, after all, and a regular on the transatlantic route. Boarding in Liverpool that day were hundreds of battle-weary uniformed men, many of them pilots returning from duty, making their way home after a life-altering journey that had lasted years.

For many of the courageous young women choosing to leave home, this was just the start of their own life-altering journey: a rupture from family and a way of life that, despite their bravery, still left some of them terrified. For Sonia, though, this was familiar territory.

Once again she was an escapee in search of refuge, this time traversing an infinite ocean, much bigger and far more dangerous than the English Channel—and, owing to exceptionally stormy weather, far more tempestuous and livid with movement. These waters, too, were meant to spirit her away from war—but with a much better chance of finding peace on the other side. Or at least that's what she hoped.

On board the *Pasteur*, Sonia saw for the first time the hazy horizon blurring the Atlantic with the sky, a vista Guy had come to know well after four separate crossings to and from Canada. They'd planned to cross the ocean together, but with Sonia's paperwork delayed and Guy only on a brief leave, he'd sailed ahead. She wasn't to know it yet, but this pilgrimage to Guy's homeland was a maiden voyage into a life in which he would often be absent and she left alone to make do.

It had been only five years since Sonia made her solo passage across the English Channel at the start of the war. This time, even without Guy, she wasn't really alone. Sonia was eight days from a new home and almost exactly seven months from giving birth to her first child.

Her way in the world so far had been marked by a series of separations and reunions—in many ways it had been one long quest for belonging, for home. She'd just risked her life for one home; now she was turning her back on another and crossing an ocean in pursuit of yet one more.

"I was leaving my home and my country, pregnant and married to a man I hardly knew. Since we'd been married I'd only spent a few weeks with him. I was terrified, wondering what we'd talk about now."

The voyage was courtesy of an ongoing Canadian military operation to bring war brides "home"—possibly the largest centralized effort in the country's history to keep its men honest. There to greet the women were Canadian Red Cross workers, among others, who would help them navigate their first hours in a place they'd never been. In the early days of the operation, the arrival of war brides attracted cheering crowds and proclamations that the women, mostly of British and Dutch stock, were a "welcome addition to our country." The wives, from all strata of British society, had waited on the strength of a promise, and now they were coming to claim their new lives, some of them already with babies, and some of those already old enough to walk.

It was a difficult eight days at sea, the rough waters accentuating the effects of Sonia's pregnancy, leaving her "sick as a dog," dizzy, and nauseated throughout. Beyond that it was a blur of crying babies, diapers, tired mothers, and exhausted young airmen. Plus a handful of women, Sonia recalled, who defied the rules on board and spent the crossing consorting with the men. Sonia couldn't get to solid land quick enough.

Sonia arrived carrying Guy's unborn child and his name, inscribed in Canadian Travel Certificate No. 2624, issued by the High Commissioner for Canada—a document "valid for a single journey to Canada direct or via the United States of America." No mention of a return journey. Should one become necessary, a war bride was presumably on her own.

Despite her wartime experiences, Sonia was in every sense also a "war bride"—reducing her identity to the adjunct of a Canadian soldier-husband. It would have been uncomfortable for someone who'd led a dangerous secret life behind enemy lines to officially become the charge of her mother-in-law—because she was not yet twenty-one. Sonia had yet to be fully recognized for the lonely landing she'd made in France, for the bullets she'd dodged, for the countless times she'd put herself, body and mind, in harm's way. Now she was Mrs. d'Artois, full stop.

And upon her arrival in Halifax on December 19, Sonia also officially became a landed immigrant. Once she'd cleared the border, she was ushered onto a "war-bride train" heading west. That night she managed to send a telegram to Guy:

ARRIVING CENTRAL STATION MONTREAL WEDNESDAY AFTERNOON ON SPECIAL TRAIN ALL LOVE.

That train ride would take the better part of another day, its passengers immersed in the same wailing, chattering soundtrack to which they'd tried to sleep for the past eight days. "We were just a bunch of wives and screaming children off the boat," she said. "We were all new to Canada."

Canada became the third country Sonia called home in five years. Her journey widened the aperture on her impressions of the New World, a world she'd only ever seen though Guy's eyes. Now she could test that version against the real thing. The train took its passengers away from Pier 21—the gateway to Canada for many an immigrant—and likely through Truro, Amherst, Moncton, and Quebec City, down along the fabled St. Lawrence River, and finally to Montreal. The sporadic houses that occasionally interrupted endless expanses of snow, the dreary grey-and-whiteness of it all, was like nothing she'd seen in Europe. "The train ride from Halifax . . . nearly made me regret having come," she said. "It was just so bleak."

The next day Sonia managed to send one more telegram to Guy.

ALL MY LOVE DARLING LONGING TO BE WITH YOU.

They finally pulled into Montreal's Bonaventure Station under a steady snow. Then, amid a sea of tears and joyful reunions, Sonia finally laid eyes on Guy again. He was in dress uniform, with a sharp trench coat and a cap, a wide smile, and a deer-in-headlights look in his eyes. Guy "raced 25 yards" and greeted his wife in a "crushing embrace" while she left her luggage and "rushed into his arms." Guy's niece, Claudette, presented her with roses. Antoinette, Sonia's mother-in-law, welcomed her with an embrace of her own. Reporters stood ready and onlookers cheered when the couple appeared. And although she'd just crossed an ocean and a large swath of a large country, Sonia was well turned out in a dress and a green turban "piled high with yards of material in the latest Paris mode," clutching the flowers in one gloved hand while holding Claudette's hand in the other. The newspaper cameras captured their image as they walked away side by side: a dashing young officer and, as Antoinette described her, an "angel" war bride, taking their first few steps together into a bright Canadian future.

It was by any measure a storybook reunion, a soothing story of romance and hope for the countless inconsolable Canadians still waiting for their own loved ones to return.

After leaving Paris back in the autumn of '44, Sonia and Guy had returned to the city where they'd met and married to begin to put that marriage back together again, to try to recover something of their previous lives. After all they'd been through, both had aged rapidly; they'd grown apart in every possible way. They needed now to relearn each other, to become acquainted all over again, to move past their forced separation, their unexpected rupture. Wars change people, irretrievably. But they can also be an opportunity for a reset, a new start. Wars harden souls, too, yet they can also set the stage for forgiveness, for overcoming disappointments that in ordinary life may not be as easily forgotten. Wars can scar, they can damage, and they can lead to infinite second chances. No one will ever be privy to the discussions that saved Sonia and Guy. They alone knew what it took to arrive at their peace.

Meanwhile, they sat through hours of yet more debriefings at London's SOE office. There were reunions with friends and family, including Sonia's mother, Thelma, who'd reached out to her and then met Guy for the first time. They were also reunited with the things they'd left behind: documents, pictures, clothing. Sonia had little of the latter, and it took an intervention from Vera Atkins to have her and other newly arrived agents issued eighty coupons each with which to buy new clothes. "Treat this as urgent," wrote Atkins.

Then, less than a month after Sonia and Guy returned, they were given an opportunity to make one final trip back to France, this time together. On October 25, using their real names at last, Captain L.G. d'Artois and Section Officer S.E. d'Artois boarded a military plane carrying a briefcase full of French bills. The aim was to pay off debts and to visit both Le Mans and Charolles, giving each of them a chance to get better acquainted with the adventures of the other. It would never make up for that summer lost at the very start of their marriage, but it was a second chance, and they made the most of it. They found the time to stop and play tourists-in-uniform, with Guy snapping some photos of Sonia in the fading autumn sun. He captured her profile against the famous palace in Versailles, a wide smile playing on her lips. And in a gesture symbolic of the second chance they'd been given, at some point along the way they finally bought Guy a wedding ring, at Cartier in Paris.

In Charolles, Guy was overjoyed to be back among his men so soon—and to introduce them to Sonia, whom they embraced as one of their own. While there, the couple were personally invited by the city's mayor to attend the first November 11 remembrance ceremony since liberation. The wounds of war were raw, and both Sonia and Guy had lost friends and comrades. And there were others they didn't yet know they'd lost.

Their main mission, however, was to pay back debts, including the money Sonia and Sydney had borrowed from the Catholic Church diocese in Le Mans. When they did reach Le Mans, as a gesture of welcome they were lodged in the archbishop's bedroom.

After the distracted exit in early October, this had been an unexpected opportunity to say a proper farewell together to a country and a people who had touched them at the core.

Elsewhere in Europe and in East Asia, the war continued unabated. And it beckoned still. Sonia and Guy—among many other agents, including their friend Jean-Paul Archambault—decided to remain with the SOE and volunteer for service in French Indochina.

But then Sonia discovered she was pregnant. She had always hoped to have a large family with many children, and here was the start. But it meant that deploying again was no longer an option; as Sonia later put it, "They drummed me out of the army." Guy was slated to leave for his new mission in the new year, and she would have to stay behind.

However, London was officially still at war. The new German campaign of rocket attacks on the city made life unpredictable, and Sonia had had enough of the shortages and the rationing. Nor did she relish facing any of it without Guy with a baby on the way. Sonia and Guy decided their future was in Canada.

Any lingering doubts about leaving the U.K. vanished in the rubble after yet another German air raid. One day, Sonia had wanted to stay at her hotel to rest, but her father persuaded her to take a train over and visit the family. While she was gone the hotel was hit; her decision to visit her father had saved her life. That narrow escape confirmed that she simply had to leave. "We didn't know, then, how much longer the war was going to go on," she said. "My little brother, who was about two at the time, had yet to know what a banana was," she added, describing the effect of rationing. "I thought, 'I've got to give [my] child a good start.'"

In the weeks before she left, Sonia was invited to a reception given in her honour at the home of Sir Alexander Hay Seton and his wife in Knightsbridge.

Sonia would have beamed on recognizing the beautiful, warm redhead who rescued her from a French hospital when she was only a child of five.

Flavia, now Lady Seton, was still on good terms with Leslie, and she hadn't forgotten Sonia either.

"She is so young to be a heroine," Flavia told one newspaper. "But she deserved all the credit she has received."

22

THE LIMELIGHT

Sonia and Guy • *Canada, December 1944*

"Scores of daring young French-speaking officers of the Canadian Army parachuted into France before D-Day, last June 6, to lead groups of the Maquis in special perilous tasks which the Allied High Command required to be performed before the main invasion blow was struck, it could be disclosed today."

It was through this Canadian Press report that the public learned for the first time of Canadians working behind enemy lines. These same reports also disclosed that the vast majority of the men recruited for "dangerous and heroic work" were "listed as 'missing.'"

The news spread just as Guy d'Artois and several other SOE agents on leave arrived in Halifax on December 14 aboard the same ship. Among them were Jean-Paul Archambault, Jacques Taschereau, Paul Meunier, and Joseph Benoit. The men posed together dressed in uniform, each with their parachute wings on display, for a photo that was widely reprinted in Canadian newspapers. They were described as having "performed one of the most dangerous jobs of the war—a pre-invasion liaison with French patriots."

"What strikes you most when you see these dare-devils is their young-old faces—young physically, but old in the deep piercing look in their eyes and the way they stick together," Ronald Williams wrote from Montreal that day. "Not one is over 30, most are little over 20, yet in their short military careers has been packed an eternity of living."

Captain Guy d'Artois, smiling mischievously, really did still have a baby face. He was, according to his mother, "much more serious" than when he'd left for the war, but otherwise "hasn't changed a bit." Guy was quoted extensively in the press coverage recounting some of his experiences.

In the course of those interviews, Guy also revealed that his British wife, Sonia, soon to arrive in Canada, was no ordinary war bride but a fellow agent. Sensing a perfect wartime romance story, the press lapped it up. Sonia's own story—and her image—had made several Canadian papers even before she arrived in the flesh.

"Parachuted Behind Nazi Lines for Their Honeymoon" was the headline in the *Toronto Daily Star*'s December 18 edition. An accompanying photograph of Sonia in uniform, smiling at Versailles, was clearly supplied by Guy. In the cutline, though, she's simply labelled as "d'Artois Bride." The writer describes her as a "blonde, hazel-eyed girl" in the same breath as "British agent." He also notes her height and weight, while remaining silent about Guy's measurements.

In the article, Guy describes Sonia's experiences in detail and with apparent pride. "She has so much guts it amazes me," Captain d'Artois is quoted as saying. "She can handle weapons as well as any soldier I know. Besides that she is very pretty. Need you ask why I fell in love with her?"

Two days later, *The Globe and Mail* published a more detailed story about Guy's exploits in France. The writer, Kenneth C. Cragg, describes him as a "slender bit of officer, who calls himself Canadian," likening him to the Three Musketeers. However, the story opens with a jaw-dropping claim, attributed to Guy:

"We lined up 58 Germans up against the railing of a bridge and then we shot them, one here and one there, until they were all dead. And then we sent word to the [German] commandant and told him that if he killed any more of our wounded we would kill twice 58 Germans. He did not kill any more of our wounded."

Cragg doesn't question the veracity of his claim in the article, nor does he suggest that he'd questioned Guy about the ethics of such action.

Guy repeated the explosive claim in a *Toronto Daily Star* interview:

"The Germans considered our maquis as an outlaw army and killed our wounded prisoners, so we retaliated once by lining up 52 of their men and shooting them one by one. They killed a total of 59 of my men . . . . Their favourite method was to club them to death with their rifle butts."

Guy would later clarify that he was aware of the killings but had not been directly involved. These were still shocking revelations. They raised alarm bells among military officials both at home and abroad, prompting a sustained flurry of correspondence between officials at the British War Office and the ranking intelligence officer at the Canadian military headquarters in Trafalgar Square.

A Major I.K. Mackenzie from the War Office bluntly dismissed Guy's claims as "open to grave doubt." He further concluded that "they are the product of Capt. d'Artois' imagination for the purpose of obtaining publicity." But, he added, the publication of such statements, "even if true, would seem to be a grave mistake as, if they were quoted by the Germans, they would surely help in the defence of any war criminals when brought to trial and, in any event, they could not but harm the Allied cause in the eyes of such neutrals as still remain."

Mackenzie heaped blame on Canadian censorship authorities for allowing the story to be published at all, but concluded that there was no point in refuting the statements in public. His security people had taken "an extremely poor view" of Guy's indiscretions, and had he returned to the U.K., "it is probable that they would have pressed for disciplinary action to be taken against him."

Another intelligence official, possibly from the F Section itself, refuted a second disturbing claim attributed to Guy in the same article: "they shot nearly 50 French women during that six months." The official contended that the statement was "certainly not a statement of fact and I feel very strongly that it should form the object of a court of enquiry."

There was yet more to raise the ire of British officials. With Sonia's story already in the news, requests began pouring in for the opportunity to tell more of it. "WILL YOU ACCEPT ONE HUNDRED DOLLARS FOR EXCLUSIVE RIGHTS TO YOUR STORY OF ADVENTURES IN FRANCE FOR SHORT MAGAZINE ARTICLE" read one telegram that arrived on the same day as Sonia did.

When Sonia learned that there were journalists waiting for her in Halifax, she refused to come out of her cabin. She did agree later to give some interviews. But some of the headlines could be cringe-worthy. "She Ate with Gestapo. Killed Some? Why, Sure."

The *Globe and Mail* fared no better: "Packing Favourite Gun, Sonia Shot Up Nazi Car." In another *Globe* piece published on December 22, the writer, Kenneth C. Cragg again, describes Sonia as "slender and blond" while Guy is "dark and wiry." Cragg appears to have interviewed both of them for the piece.

"You, I take it, used your Sten quite seriously?

'Yes, quite seriously,' she said."

He went on:

"'You were on combat duty?'

'Oh yes, I used to go out with them every night.' And then a bit indignant: 'It would be a funny thing to do, instruct them and merely watch them do the actual fighting.'"

This particular revelation raised yet more alarms back in London, but for far different reasons.

By admitting she'd engaged in combat, Sonia was contradicting the official line that female members of the British armed forces were banned from "operational duties" that included combat. In a flurry of internal letters on the subject, one official noted that the revelation would "inevitably" lead to trouble when it was picked up by other media. As a result, "steps" had been taken to "prevent the BBC from giving other publicity to this question."

There was also concern that the matter would be raised in Parliament, given that "the employment of females in operational duties of this nature is contrary to pledges given by the Service Ministers earlier in the war by the House of Commons."

Officials still recommended that no action be taken. However, Sonia was asked—it is unclear by whom—to explain herself. In a handwritten letter sent back to the U.K. and later included in her file, she said she'd been "pestered" by reporters who already knew the general nature of her story, but that she'd disclosed no more than the fact that "shortly before D-Day, I had been parachuted into France as a military adviser and I praised the show that the French had put up."

After all the consternation Sonia and Guy's reports caused, Lieutenant-Colonel Felix H. Walter, the ranking intelligence officer at Canadian Military Headquarters, assured London that they'd been interviewed by military officials in Canada "and have been given a strong warning against any continuance of such publicity."

It was also decided very shortly afterward that Guy's stint as a "loan" from Canada to the War Office would be terminated—effective December 8, the day he left for Canada—and that his assignment to the East be revoked. Part of the reason given, noted in his file, was a less than optimal health assessment.

At the time, Guy did report that he'd hurt his back once while "jumping" and that "it only bothers me when I bend forward." He added, "I don't sleep well."

A doctor concluded that Guy, who was experiencing occasional lower back pain, had a problem in his spine, early arthritis "due to the fact that he has sustained a [severe] spine trauma while training as paratroops."

But in the exchange between Canadian and British officers, there is the impression that Guy's health was a minor consideration when compared to the issues raised by the publicity.

Still, the press requests continued to come from far and wide. A firm named FJ Mankey Ideas Inc. telegrammed Guy and Sonia offering to send a New York representative to discuss terms for the release of screen and radio rights, describing their romance as the "greatest of this war."

Their romance was indeed one of the "greatest of this war." An "extraordinary story," a "storybook" reunion. One article featured a series of photographs, and in one of them, Guy and Sonia are in the midst of a deep kiss. Another paper mused whether Sonia was not the "Queen of the Amazons, Antiope, incarnate?" while another had the couple recreate the moment they were together in the plane—in full parachuting gear—capturing Sonia's wink at Guy before she jumped.

Yet another photographer had Guy picking his teeth with a commando knife. Sonia was snapped in a staged photo with a pistol and the wedding ring she had bought at Marks and Spencer for her final training exercise.

In yet another article, a photo of the couple is titled "Hero and wife." A writer for *La Presse*, meanwhile, mentions Guy showing reporters his "trophy," a flag he'd brought home from France, signed by all the maquis leaders. At the end of the piece, the reporter retorts that "The most beautiful trophy, Captain, will always be Madame d'Artois."

These experiences with the press left Sonia deeply disillusioned. Seeming to tire of the limelight, she backed away from the attention, partly also in deference to her husband. And in shifting her focus to her new life, and to preparing to be a new mother, Sonia tried to make her priorities clear in the interviews she did give.

"I feel that I can settle down to a quiet life again," she said in one of them.

Canada, she told *Le Samedi* magazine, is "a country that I love very much."

"From now on I will only be a Canadian whose first duties are her husband, her children, and her new country."

The rest, she told the interviewer, "is the past" A past she said she wanted to forget.

At the dawn of a new-found peace, just two days after the war officially ended, a group captain with the initials B.R. wrote Sonia a letter from London. In it, he announced His Majesty the King's approval to honour Sonia as a Member of the Order of the British Empire, an honours system that rewarded citizens of service in both civilian and military worlds. The recommendation cited her bravery and courage, quoting Sydney Hudson describing her as "utterly fearless." Fittingly, Sonia was awarded the MBE, in the civilian category, at the same time as Paddy—her old WAAF friend Maureen O'Sullivan—and Pearl Witherington, as well as Phyllis Latour, who had all served bravely in France.

What Sonia didn't know was that her decoration had been a matter of some debate. An unsigned letter in her file, likely from the SOE office, "strongly recommended" that Sonia be awarded a Military Cross, a decoration usually reserved for military personnel. In making the case, the writer, likely Vera Atkins, cites that she worked "untiringly and fearlessly" and "became in function though not in title the second in command of the [HEADMASTER] circuit." It also mentions that even after being fired at and attacked and sexually assaulted by two German soldiers, "she did not allow this incident to affect her nerves or to shake her courage and she completed her mission with calmness, efficiency and success."

An argument then played out in the document itself. Someone noted that the award committee had "made no decision about grant of M.C. to women." Two more written comments endorsed different courses of action, one supporting an M.C., the other an MBE or the higher ranking OBE (Officer of the Order of the British Empire).

Sonia was finally honoured with an MBE, not in the military but the civilian division. The decision again reflected a reluctance to recognize women like Sonia as combatants. It was still an honour and a recognition of her work, but men who'd done equivalent jobs had been given more prestigious honours.

This refusal to recognize women for their military contributions prompted Pearl Witherington to reject the honour altogether. As she wrote to Vera Atkins, "I spent a year in the field and had I been caught I would have been shot or, worse still, sent to a concentration camp. . . . I personally was responsible for the training and organization of three thousand men for sabotage and guerilla warfare."

"There was nothing civil about what I did."

Other female SOE agents piled on, and two more declined the civilian MBE. The growing controversy made it into the British Parliament and then into a newspaper article in which Sonia was mentioned and pictured next to a photo of Paddy.

"The interesting thing about these girls is that they are not hearty and horsey young women with masculine chins. They are pretty, young girls who would look demure and sweet in crinoline . . . . They have to be able to pass themselves off as tough country wenches, and smart Parisiennes."

The noise made a difference. A year later, on August 31, 1946, Sonia's award, along with a number of others, was amended. The King approved the transfer of those women who'd been awarded the MBE in the civil division over to the military one. That included Latour, O'Sullivan, and Assistant Section Officer Sonia d'Artois, "for services in France during the enemy occupation." A minor victory, but a victory nevertheless.

Guy, too, received a letter, stating that the King had approved the Distinguished Service Order for gallant and distinguished services in the field. The recommendation for the award, made by F Section, cited his work in equipping, organizing, and instructing three battalions, and that he "personally led many attacks on enemy troops with conspicuous gallantry."

His award had also been the subject of some debate. One official suggested that Guy was being considered for the DSO only because he had "'told the tale' rather elaborately."

An unsigned document in Guy's file dated April 21, 1945, also objects to the proposal: "We maintain strongly that it would be a grave error for d'Artois to be awarded the DSO, but we feel equally strongly that an M.C. (Military Cross) is justified."

This argument was overruled, and Guy was awarded a DSO anyway.

Guy was also decorated by the French government. In August of 1945 Charles de Gaulle was on a brief state visit to Canada to ask for help in reconstruction. At a small ceremony at the French embassy in Ottawa, he towered over Guy d'Artois as he decorated him with a Croix de Guerre with Palm. Guy was photographed smiling next to de Gaulle, the very leader who wanted the SOE out of France the moment it was liberated.

Both Sonia and Guy had far exceeded F Section's expectations. As they returned from the field, there were given one final assessment to be included in their files.

The bottom line on Guy: "An unexpectedly great success in the field."

On Sonia: "she was damned brave."

"I am so pleased to hear of your award. . . ."

It was Vera Atkins, in London, at the start of only the third full week of peace, opening a congratulatory letter to Sonia on her appointment as a Member of the Order of the British Empire.

"All members of the old section send you their heartiest congratulations, particularly Colonel Buckmaster," she added.

Sonia, now twenty-one, was nearly a year removed from Europe and the life she'd lived before crossing the pond. Her apartment with

Guy on rue Laviolette in Saint-Jérôme, just an hour northwest of Montreal, couldn't be farther from the old country—from the blackouts, the curfews, the shortages, and the unceasing distress. Like the thousands of immigrants who'd arrived in Canada in 1944–45—half of them British war brides like her—Sonia was a newcomer, still becoming accustomed to Canadian ways. With one Quebec winter behind her, including a belated wintry honeymoon with Guy in the Laurentians, she had already acquired a pair of proper winter boots and wanted to learn how to ski. In September of 1945, for the first time in her life, Sonia would behold the colourful spectacle of a Quebec autumn. She would also finally experience the miracle of becoming a mother. Her bright post-war future in Canada with Guy was now her present.

But the past came knocking at regular intervals. And the news was often devastating.

The year 1945 may have marked the end of the war, and it may have brought the accolades and decorations, but the subsequent months were cruel for SOE agents and their families and friends, some of whom had already started publicly demanding answers.

Atkins was as fastidious about staying in touch with her former charges as she'd been about her work. She saw to it that agents like Sonia received official recognition and honours. She also made it her post-war mission to find out the fate of the missing.

After the war she travelled to France and Germany, and in a persistent, methodical pursuit, she slowly documented the whereabouts and ultimate fate of each of the missing agents she'd helped to send in.

"I went to find them as a private enterprise," she said. "I wanted to know. I always thought 'missing presumed dead' to be such a terrible verdict."

In Germany, Atkins sought out interviews with men in British custody who'd been in charge of concentration camps at Sachsenhausen and Ravensbrück. She was given permission to interrogate them at length.

"I stayed there until I had traced every agent we had lost."

What she learned shocked even the most hardened veterans.

Albert Browne-Bartroli's little sister, Eliane Plewman, was one of four female SOE agents executed on September 13, 1944, at the Dachau concentration camp. She was just shy of her twenty-seventh birthday. The others were Madeleine Damerment, twenty-six, Noor Inayat Khan, thirty, and Yolande Beekman, thirty-three. Yolande's organizer, Canadian Guy Biéler, was executed earlier at a different concentration camp by firing squad. He was said to have been escorted by a guard of honour after impressing his captors with his grit in the face of repeated torture.

Also in September, Lieutenant Roméo Sabourin, twenty-one, and fellow Canadians Frank Pickersgill, twenty-nine, and John K. Macalister, thirty, as well as thirteen others, many of them victims of the PHYSICIAN/PROSPER collapse, were executed at Buchenwald—slowly strangled by piano wire.

In early 1945, thirty-year-old Lilian Rolfe, Guy's first SOE love interest, and Sonia's friend Violette Szabó, twenty-three, were executed at Ravensbrück concentration camp. Their bodies were then disposed of in the crematorium, all evidence of their brief, tortured, and valiant existence incinerated beyond recognition.

Stanislaw Makowski, the Polish officer who'd shown an interest in Sonia in training, was wounded, arrested, and interrogated. His mutilated body was dumped by his captors, recovered by resistance fighters, and given a proper burial. He was thirty.

On May 2, 1945, the War Office confirmed in a letter to Canadian Military Headquarters that Alcide Beauregard had been executed by the Gestapo. Buckmaster penned a letter to Beauregard's wife, in which he wrote that her husband had "demonstrated great courage and great fortitude until the end . . . . You can be very proud of him." Alcide's work, he added, helped save the lives of many soldiers and French civilians. "I hope this will be of some comfort to you." In one of the final steps to close his file, there was the matter of the £1 that was found among his personal effects. A request was made in writing to credit his account.

The death of Jean-Paul Archambault in Burma (later Myanmar) would have been especially devastating for Guy and Sonia. He was their friend, the other Montrealer on their training course, Sonia's prank partner in crime, and Guy's co-agent in Saône-et-Loire. He died in May 1945 while working with explosives in his tent.

Given the grim fate of so many agents and local *résistants* in France in particular—as well as the repeated instances of German infiltration and impersonation, F Section masters had a lot to answer for, and the criticism came from many corners.

"It is well known that S.O.E. was mainly an amateurs' organisation," Jean Overton Fuller, a friend of captured radio operator Noor Inayat Khan, wrote in one of her books on the subject. "But was it right that an organisation of this kind should be given into the hands of amateurs?

"Who except amateurs could have thought it suitable or right to send into the field some of the very young and inexperienced people who they did?"

Maurice Buckmaster often argued back that it was not fair to blame some kind of fatal flaw in the SOE. "Our organization was human, so were its judgments, its failures, its achievements. The heroism was all the agents', but the faults were not all ours."

The criticism was especially harsh where the women agents were concerned.

Buckmaster, whose own version of the story of F Section was now also being questioned, rejected the suggestion that women should not have been deployed. Women are "as brave and as responsible as men; often more so. They are entitled to a share in the defence of their beliefs no less than are men."

Those who knew their work, he added, "can only feel anger and contempt for those who try to denigrate Baker Street by questioning the ability of women to fight alongside men and who impugn the efficiency of headquarters by doubting the readiness of brave women to face perils and, if necessary, to die for their countries.

"These women did an invaluable job and one for which, whatever people may say, they were admirably suited. Coolness and judgement were vital qualities; none lacked them. Courage was their common badge."

General Eisenhower, it is said, claimed that the larger efforts of the SOE had shortened the war by nine months. His staff reported that "without the organization, communications, training and leadership which SOE supplied . . . resistance [movements] would have been of no military value."

The efficacy of the SOE had always been hotly debated, even by its own agents, and it was often played down, no less by some members of the French resistance who resented their presence on French soil.

Philippe de Vomécourt offered a more even-handed view, concluding that "The French resistance was not a romantic and glorious battle of wits between heroic individuals, dropped by parachute from London, and the German army.

"The French people would have been less effective in their resistance had it not been for the arms and materials, the instructors and organizers, sent from London.

"But there would still have been a resistance. The agents from London, on the other hand, would have been helpless without the never failing help and courage of the ordinary people of France."

Vera Atkins and Maurice Buckmaster put considerable effort into ensuring that those ordinary people were also recognized for their work, asking their own agents to make recommendations for British awards: people like René Fléchard and Maman Lucienne, and Claude Hilleret and Edmond Cohin were all recognized in one way or another for the extraordinary support they lent to Guy and Sonia respectively.

Atkins and Buckmaster also started a campaign to ensure that those SOE agents who'd been lost were recognized posthumously, among the awards Alcide Beauregard's mention in dispatches (a written military recognition of admirable action); Violette Szabó's George Cross, awarded to her daughter; and Noor Inayat Khan's Croix de Guerre.

The SOE would be disbanded in January 1946. But Atkins and Buckmaster spent subsequent years defending their actions. The debate about the SOE's tactics, the loss of life, and its true efficacy continues to this day.

23

LETTERS

Guy and Sonia • *Canada, 1945–46*

Though far removed from post-war France, Guy and Sonia were forming an intimate portrait of the state of affairs in the country for which they're risked their lives, thanks to letters from friends and colleagues who were anxious to remain in touch.

The recovery in France had been difficult and unsteady. Scores were still being settled. The economy was shaky, and new political fault lines were emerging from the war's ashes.

Louis Lapalus wrote prodigiously, in wrenching prose, decrying the situation.

"Our recovery remains fragile," he wrote in one letter. "We must hope that it'll heal but brace ourselves for a difficult recovery after so many hardships."

Louis was trying to restart his business after the Gestapo had burned it down. He also went on to lead a group for veterans of the resistance. Months later, without a response from Guy, Louis wrote again, still struggling to restart his business. He told Guy he'd managed to help inaugurate a monument to some of the first maquisards killed on Guy's watch just after D-Day.

In such letters, Michel le Canadien remained alive and well.

"We speak often of 'our Michel,' of whom we all hold such fond and lasting memories. We'll never forget what you did for us and for our country, a country that holds a special place in the heart of [a] 'd'Artois,'" wrote Louis.

Gaston Lévy, whose Saint-Julien-de-Civry maquis had been devastated in the disastrous Paray-le-Monial operation, also wrote.

"We are thinking of you, dear Michel (for us, this name will always carry meaning), as you are the one who armed us and taught us how to use modern weapons.

"You are the one who encouraged us to take our place amongst the Allies, and you who really taught us how to fight a war."

Many among Guy's former charges were seeking a new life. They were also seeking recognition for the work they'd done as members of the resistance, sometimes an uphill battle, and they would write to Guy looking for letters and attestations to help document their involvement—so that they could serve in the French forces or receive assistance.

Guy did reply to some letters, and sent at least some of the requested attestations. And in the months following liberation, Guy and Sonia responded to the requests for provisions—for coffee and tea, for rice, and even for chocolate, all short in supply or high in price in post-war France. Letters came back carrying gratitude. "You won't believe how much fun I had tasting all of them," Paul Carret writes to thank Guy for a package of sweets, while pointing out that he never received the attestation he'd requested. Maman Lucienne sadly reports that of a whole parcel of goods they sent her, only a lone packet of coffee arrived after the package had apparently been tampered with. Marthe Dauprat-Sevenet was grateful for the pair of shoes she picked out from a box of donated goods that Sonia appears to have sent, and which also helped "support a number of families."

"Remember when I gave you a pair? I haven't been able to get any shoes since. This pair from Canada is my lucky break."

In Canada, Sonia and Guy were looking to break with their past, with the war, and to start a fully civilian life. First, they had to welcome their first child.

Guy was about to leave for military manoeuvres when Sonia called the base to let him know that she was feeling the first signs of labour. He made his way home.

"He was furious with me," said Sonia. "So typical, so typical," she recalled him saying. They rode to Montreal to the home of Guy's mother, Antoinette, so they could be closer to the hospital. Sonia's labour was slow, and Guy was frustrated with the wait, so he left, promising he'd check in regularly.

On one of those calls Sonia could hear that he was at a bar. He'd run into an old friend and the two of them were catching up over drinks. Sonia told him the doctor had advised her to proceed to the hospital. Guy suggested that he meet her there, but an outraged Antoinette intervened.

"Give me the telephone," she demanded. She told her son to return promptly. He came back with his friend in "high spirits."

It was several hours of difficult labour, but by early morning Sonia finally gave birth to a healthy boy, whom they named Robert—a nod to one of Guy's first aliases as an SOE agent, and the first of the baby names to come that worked in both languages. Guy was overjoyed, "very proud," but he was not the kind of father who was going to change diapers. He was, however, the kind of husband who would do whatever it took to ensure his wife had whatever she needed to recover from a difficult birth. That meant he insisted, on their way home from the hospital, that Sonia stay in the car while he marched into a lingerie shop on Saint Catherine Street, in full uniform, to buy her the girdle that the doctor had recommended.

Robert d'Artois was born in Montreal on July 6, 1945. He was just under seven pounds, healthy, and with an easy disposition. Sonia's transformation was complete: "I went from mixing explosives to mixing baby formula."

Three days later her father, Leslie Butt, sent a telegram.

> WELCOME YOUNG ROBERT, AND CONGRATULATIONS TO YOUR DISTINGUISHED MOTHER AND YOUR FATHER ALSO ON AWARD DSO. LOVE TO YOU ALL FROM GRANDFATHER, GRANNY ANN AND UNCLE MIKE BUTT.

Two months later, Guy left the Canadian Army and became a reservist, just as he had promised Sonia. He accepted an appointment at the Ministry of Labour as superintendent of vocational training, and hoped to parlay that into a position at the Ministry of Trade and Commerce that would take him abroad.

But it didn't take long for both of them to discover that Guy, admittedly undisciplined, was deeply unhappy out of uniform and at the whims of the civilian world.

"It was the first and only time I pushed Guy to do something for my sake," said Sonia. "He was miserable. After eight months I suggested he go back into the army. He did, like a shot."

Guy's parents had had bigger ambitions for him. "My father wanted me to go into law. My mother wanted me to go into medicine. And in the end, I became a military man."

Back in uniform, Guy was now also bound to a system that would repeatedly uproot the growing d'Artois family. His first posting, to help lead parachute training at the Canadian Joint Air Training Centre, played to his skills, but it was based in the west, in the town of Rivers, Manitoba. He left quickly to take up the job, leaving Sonia, now pregnant again, to sort out the details of their move to the Canadian prairies.

Sonia arrived later with Robert only to discover that home would be the Shilo military base in frigid southern Manitoba that was some sixty-five kilometres from where Guy actually worked every day.

At his job, Guy was in his element, his reputation preceding him. "Everyone knew who Guy was," said one young soldier who was based in Rivers at the same time.

But in every possible way, Sonia had never been so far from home. Worse, there were no dedicated married quarters on the base. At their request, the army converted some barracks into accommodations, where they were forced to sleep on army cots until their own furniture arrived. But with Sonia and Guy cajoling the military bureaucracy and scavenging materials bit by bit, Hut A-19 slowly evolved into a comfortable and inviting place to raise a family.

Sonia made friends and found community among the few families based there. In fact, she and Guy learned to love Shilo, its lively parties, its silent winters, and the generally relaxed atmosphere away from the bustle of the big city. You need to be a dreamer in such a place, Guy once said, "because all you see is the horizon."

Sonia did all she could to make the most of it. That became especially important as Guy's work took him further afield—on training courses and parachuting demonstrations. It was how Sonia learned to navigate life on a Canadian military base, a skill she was clearly going to rely on over and over.

It was also how Sonia and Guy started the habit of writing letters to each other.

"According to my calculations, you should receive this letter on Tuesday, April 15, that's to say, the day of our wedding anniversary.

"I want to repeat again, my love, how much I love you, and how happy I've been these three years. If I had to do it all over again, I would do it without hesitation. You too, I hope."

It was Sonia, writing to Guy from Shilo, mid-morning on April 12, three years after their wedding in London. "I wouldn't give you up for all the men in the world, and there are many. I love you as you are, and for what you are."

Guy was often away: in Regina, in Winnipeg, in Quebec and beyond. Sonia frequently found herself alone, with Robert as her only company. Once, while Guy was away, she had a nap in which she dreamt that he'd suddenly come home. "If only it were true!" she wrote in that day's letter as she watched Robert playing nearby. She signed off with "Robert sends you a big hug. So does his mother."

There was only the occasional burst of amusement—in Shilo, going to the cinema, catching up after church on Sundays, and playing bingo at the mess counted as top entertainment. Joining a book club ranked as significant news; the latter, Sonia promised Guy, would be a good way to shore up their library with good books. In her frequent letters, sometimes two in a day, she tells Guy all about it, keeping a constant count of how much time remained before he came home.

One evening she was playing bingo, she told him, staying out until midnight. Still, she admitted, she was bored. "Frankly for me it was not very fun, there was no life at all," she confided to Guy. This was not London, nor Montreal. Her battle to stave off loneliness on a military base in the middle of nowhere gave the words "war bride" a whole new meaning.

Reunions with Guy, however brief, would often become another honeymoon, and with every resulting pregnancy Sonia would be plunged into the now-familiar throes of illness, the nausea staying with her virtually every day until she gave birth. In those days in 1947, Sonia would write to Marthe Dauprat-Sevenet, the owner of Château du Breuil and her godmother, to tell her about the coming baby. It seemed fitting to ask her to be her second child's godmother, too.

"You don't know how much this means to me, and how pleased I am to accept wholeheartedly," Marthe wrote back. "My only sorrow is in being so far away, unable to either see my godchild, or spoil the child since everything remains so scarce here.

Still, I will pray for this dear little soul with all my heart."

Marthe gave her the only other gift she could: a reminder of her own son, who was killed during the war just before Sonia visited in 1944.

"If you wish, you can add Henri or Henriette as a middle name, so that my son can watch over the child from above. He'll surely be a devoted guardian."

Sonia and Guy named their child Michel. An ode to "Michel le Canadien."

Sonia gave him Henri as a middle name—and somewhere in France a grieving mother took some comfort in knowing that her son's name lived on.

24

NORTH

Guy • *Moffet Inlet, October 4, 1947*

Michel Henri d'Artois was only three months old when his father, Guy d'Artois, glided down in the familiar sway of a parachute, rapidly approaching frozen ground. He landed with a soft thud on a thick layer of snow that covered a much thicker one of ice; there was nothing but a blanket of white extending as far as the eye could see.

During his wartime mission, Guy had been one of hundreds of thousands of soldiers tasked with rescuing an entire nation. On this mission, he was leading a team of four tasked with saving a single life. And as the first attempt at a search-and-rescue operation in Canada's hostile North, this assignment would also prove especially challenging.

Canon John Turner was an Anglican missionary and an old Arctic hand who travelled by dogsled; he knew how to live off the land and keep himself safe in Baffin Island's hostile terrain. But late that September, he'd accidentally shot himself.

The bullet streaked straight up through Turner's lips and then through his nasal bones, fracturing his skull. Miraculously, he survived the hit, but his spine was badly injured in the subsequent fall. His wife, Joan, and their assistants managed to pull him into the house and stabilize him. But for a chance at surviving what could surely be a fatal mishap, he needed the kind of medical help that was unavailable so far north—even to white missionaries. He had to be evacuated before it was too late.

It was a job made for Guy d'Artois: he knew how to operate in cold, hostile environments, and thanks to his experiences in France with its shortages, he knew how to problem-solve on the fly. He also knew how to get himself to the ground, though less so about how to safely get everyone out.

Within days of the accident, on their second attempt, Guy, along with three others and their equipment, floated down to a drop zone on the frozen lake just east of Turner's mission on Moffet Inlet.

Back in Shilo, Sonia was alone again, now with two young boys to care for and the added weight of worry as Guy jumped once more into the unknown. "It was completely uncharted territory. And it was a hell of a risk jumping into that area," she said. From then on, her daily routine included a visit to the signals office to check for any news.

It was always lonely for her without Guy. But robbed of the opportunity to exchange letters, these would have been Sonia's loneliest days in Shilo yet. And with her children too young to appreciate the situation, whenever worry consumed her she'd find catharsis in the act of scrubbing the floors.

Having arrived safely on the ground and at the mission, the rescue team apprehended the gravity of the situation. They found Turner awake, his left side paralyzed, in pain from his spine injury and bedsores. To stave off infection, Doctor Ross Willoughby immediately started him on penicillin. Guy turned his full attention to coming up with an exit plan.

However, the radio that was to be their main connection to the outside world had been damaged. The weather was uncooperative. The patient was also unstable. And Guy had to find a safe spot that was compacted enough, long enough, and safe enough to accommodate a landing aircraft within striking distance of Turner.

The story of this daring rescue attempt riveted the country. In addition to rescuer, Guy played the role of chronicler. Not only did he bring his camera along, he also wrote dispatches about what he and his team were going through. One ran on the front page of *The Winnipeg Tribune.*

"We must remember that the patient is paralyzed and cannot stand too long a trip by dog team," Guy wrote. A bedsore had also become gangrenous. To prevent the worst, the doctor, with Guy's help, had to perform a crude operation with no anesthetic.

In the article, Guy explained how he went out daily in search of the right place for an evacuation. After a morning coffee he'd join his Inuit guides, along with their team of howling sled dogs, and take off for hours, sometimes days, on end.

On one of his excursions Guy believed he might have found a suitable spot, but to be certain he camped there to monitor the conditions. A blizzard moved in. It was so intense that Guy's local assistant was unable to reach him with supplies and he was forced to spend several days exposed to the elements without heat or light. To survive, he remained in his sleeping bag for two days waiting out the blizzard, then remained for several more gathering enough data to ensure that the landing could happen safely. At the end of it, he'd found his landing strip.

The plane landed successfully. It was November 22, almost two months after Turner had been injured. He was placed on a sled, then loaded onto the plane with his family, Guy, and the rest of his team. Within hours they were in Winnipeg, where they were met by a large team of doctors. Guy and the others were hailed as heroes.

Guy stayed in Winnipeg for a night of rest before making his way home. When Sonia finally saw him, she was shocked at the state he was in. He had a beard and his skin was weathered and rough. He was spent, both physically and mentally. Still, Guy was back on familiar ground, collecting praise as well as the newspaper articles published about his daring rescue. The Canadian Army even released some of his photographs, and several were featured in *The Globe and Mail*, including shots he took inside the Dakota when Turner was finally airborne.

But weeks later, on December 9, Guy was crushed to learn that Turner had succumbed to his injuries and died.

For his efforts, Guy received the George Medal, the first to be awarded at peacetime. In the citation he was lauded for his courage, his determination, and his disregard for personal safety.

Guy was a soldier made for risk-taking and experiments. So it seemed fitting to put him in charge of a short-lived Canadian Special Air Service (SAS) Company based at Rivers. Comprising about 125 men drawn from a number of regiments, its mission was not entirely articulated. That did not deter Guy, who saw it through his SOE lens, training his men in everything from parachuting to ropework to demolition. Even Morse code was included in the training syllabus.

Guy was increasingly gaining a reputation for being the sort of man who liked to do things his own way. He became the "absolute despair of the Senior Officers at Rivers."

"Captain d'Artois didn't understand 'no.' He carried on with his training regardless of what others said," one veteran of the SAS told a historian.

When SAS work and demonstrations repeatedly took Guy away from Sonia, their letter writing resumed.

"It feels very good to be back in civilisation," Guy wrote on July 1, 1948, from Ottawa, where he stayed in a double room at the Château Laurier. "My only regret is not having my family with me.

"I always think of you and love you more each day . . .

"I'd love to have you all close and tell you how much you mean to me. At least another day has gone by, and I'm a little closer to you."

That fall, their family grew yet again. Guy stayed at home as Sonia gave birth to their first girl, Nadya. But even though Guy had help, Sonia returned to chaos: an empty freezer and not a single diaper. Guy was many things, but he was helpless with the children.

Yet he proved a popular teacher with the men he led. Popular, but tough.

The SAS found some purpose in the rescue of an American couple whose plane had crashed near Winnipeg, and in the spring of 1948 Guy's men were put to use during floods in British Columbia.

But with each of the army's infantry regiments adding airborne units, the SAS was eventually disbanded. Guy was now to lead airborne training within his own regiment. He was posted to Valcartier, but he would live with his family in nearby Quebec City, also the home of the Royal 22e Régiment, the "Van Doos."

But there, too, it would be a challenge to escape the past.

Sonia and Guy's arrival in Quebec coincided with a divisive moment that, given their shared history, would have been upsetting, and too close for comfort.

Dozens of prominent Quebecers had signed a petition asking the federal government to stop the deportation of a French citizen, a known collaborator with the Nazi occupation. Jacques de Bernonville had slipped into Canada with a fake passport after he'd been tried and convicted in absentia in France—sentenced to death for being a traitor and a vicious wartime persecutor of his own countrymen. He was once a member of the Waffen SS, the head of the hated collaborationist Milice française, and a right-hand man to Klaus Barbie, the "Butcher of Lyon." Now he was officially seeking asylum in Canada.

Like Guy d'Artois, from May 1944 onward de Bernonville had been based in the Saône-et-Loire region of France, operating just down the road from Guy—in Chalon, and later in Lyon. He could have been implicated in attacks against Guy's own men—maybe even the terrible fate that Alcide Beauregard had met in the summer of 1944. As a notorious collaborator, he was "responsible for the deaths of members of the Allied forces, probably including Canadians," one federal minister said at the time.

Shortly after they arrived in Canada following France's liberation, Sonia and Guy were bewildered to discover that there were Canadians who supported Philippe Pétain, the collaborationist leader who had presided over Vichy France. In those quarters, the former Free French were dismissed as communists who had overturned a legitimate government.

After everything they'd been through, Sonia struggled with all this. Both she and Guy sometimes felt as though they'd lost the war, that all those risks they took had been in vain.

Guy had felt a strong compulsion to set the record straight. He had all those photographs from the war. He'd also been handed pictures that contained evidence of atrocities committed in Germany's concentration camps. He wanted to go on tour and show these across the country and he wanted Sonia to come along. But at the time, she was pregnant with Robert, and in any case was adamant about leaving the past behind. Guy gave some lectures without her.

It still upset Sonia that there were Canadians "in total denial," that Canadians were actively lobbying on a Nazi collaborator's behalf.

As the de Bernonville affair escalated, Sonia and Guy were approached by members of the Free French who lived in Quebec, looking for support in lobbying to oust de Bernonville. Sonia responded that they had no interest in getting involved in "anything political." Nonetheless, "We said yes. We would be there." It's not clear, however, whether in practice that meant anything beyond moral support.

In the end de Bernonville left Canada for Brazil of his own accord—after being warned that he was about to be deported. Several years later, at seventy-four, he was found murdered in his flat, gagged and with his hands bound behind his back.

PART VII

WAR AGAIN

25

GOING EAST

Guy and Sonia • *Korea and Quebec City, March 1952*

At exactly six p.m. on March 29, 1952, a ship carrying the 1st Battalion of the Royal 22e Régiment began its journey from Seattle to Korea. On board was a very different Guy d'Artois from the one who'd undertaken his first intercontinental crossing in 1940, back when he was an untested acting sergeant on his first voyage abroad. Now, six trips across the Atlantic Ocean and four children later, Guy at thirty-five was a newly promoted major, commanding the support company of the 1st Battalion, a decorated soldier, and an itinerant father. He was again heading into war, but this time he was heading to the East.

By now the Korean War was well into its second year and had forcibly uprooted or taken the lives of hundreds of thousands, most of them civilians. As a result of Japan's defeat in the Second World War the nation had surrendered its rule over the Korean peninsula, leading to its partition along the 38th parallel, with a communist Soviet client state in the north and one in the south, renamed the

Republic of Korea, supported by the U.S. and allied countries. In late June of 1950 North Korea's Korean People's Army overran the border in a bid to take over its southern counterpart, seizing Seoul, the capital, within days. The United Nations authorized action in support of South Korea to repel the invading forces, paving the way for the United States to forcefully intervene and lead forces from sixteen countries including the U.K. and Canada.

The Van Doos were called on again to lend soldiers, young and old, to what was the first major proxy conflict between two superpowers battling for supremacy. Once allies of convenience, the United States and the Soviet Union were now engaged in a "cold" war that nevertheless would claim millions of lives and violently shape most of the rest of the century.

That is how Guy and Sonia found themselves, in the spring of 1952, once again separated by war.

Guy's role would be largely conventional; he was stationed at the de facto border that had more or less become fixed after months of fighting between forces north and south backed by their respective patrons, which by then also included Chinese troops, who'd entered the fray in support of the North. Sonia was staying home this time, although raising four children alone in an unfamiliar city represented a battle nevertheless.

It helped that she'd fallen for Quebec City. North America's only walled city charmed her with its old-world beauty, its cobbled, dimly lit streets, and its picturesque port, unparalleled in her adopted country. "I fell in love with it," she said, "the minute I got there." Whether it was the cozy, contained feel of the old city or its aura of a transplanted corner of Europe, to Sonia it felt comfortable.

Tina became the first of her children to be born there, in 1950. The growing family started out in a flat but then moved to a sprawling stone property on rue Saint-Louis, steps from the Quebec Citadel, the home of Guy's Royal 22e Régiment. The house was a historic fixture inside the old city, part of a structure built by the French regime in the early eighteenth century, then sold to the British, who used it as officers' quarters. Now it was designated as permanent married quarters, known in the military as PMQs. Adding to its unique charm were the two old cannons standing guard just outside. It was ideally situated for the kids, as Robert (also known as Bob) was just starting nursery school, with the younger ones soon to follow. It was also just a few minutes' walk to the Château Frontenac hotel and the skating rink set up there every year. In summer the children could wander the neighbourhood's quiet streets without a worry and mix with the other "army brats" who lived nearby. For Sonia it was an ideal place to raise a family: safe and familiar enough to call home.

It was therefore fitting that Quebec City was the place where Sonia's two families finally came together. Her father, Leslie, was still working with Caltex Oil and living in Algeria at the time, and while visiting his company's New York headquarters in 1950, he took the opportunity to travel up north by train with his wife and young son, to meet his grandchildren for the first time. They arrived with more than twenty pieces of luggage, including dolls for the girls and a rocking horse for the boys. Michael, Sonia's youngest sibling, was only seven or eight, not much older than his nephews and nieces, and had few real memories of his older, adventurous sister. At that point Sonia seemed more like an aunt to him than a sister, and Guy an affable uncle.

In those days, before his Korea deployment, Guy trained paratroopers at the Valcartier military base about half an hour away. He'd leave the house and return each day in uniform—he was always in uniform. And when he'd come home, exhausted and resigned to the couch after a long day at work, Bob and Michel would compete for the chance to unlace his long boots. Every Sunday he'd wear his dress uniform and the family would go together to Sunday Mass before heading to the officers' mess. The children were well aware by then that their father was a military man. They'd internalized his rigidity about the way he wanted them to behave, and that if they pushed him to the limit, which the boys sometimes did, he might resort to spanking. Guy was the kind of father who'd help flood an ice rink for his kids in the backyard and, as a good skater himself, occasionally join them. He wasn't the kind of father to tell his children he loved them. But he was the kind to feel it deeply, channelling it into guidance, instruction, and occasionally tough love.

Three years after moving to Quebec City in mid-1949, Guy was deployed clear across the world to East Asia for a full year. Living within minutes of the regimental headquarters did come with advantages for his family, though; the regiment was always supportive of its "war widows."

However, no one but Sonia could handle the family's tight finances, take the girls to ballet lessons and the boys to hockey games, care for their scraped knees and bruised shins, impose discipline, and mete out punishment. At best, she had the help of a nanny. Ultimately, Guy was not essential to the day-to-day running of the d'Artois household. Sonia would have missed his presence, but the family's chaotic life had a certain amount of order that frankly worked best without him.

Once settled into the routine of separate, busy lives an ocean apart, Sonia and Guy tried to write letters daily: nothing too long, just numbered missives that kept them connected and facilitated the time-honoured practice of a military family clocking time until their reunion. Phone calls were difficult and expensive—and impractical anyway. On one occasion Guy tried to call just when Nadya was crying because of a broken collarbone and one of the other children was screaming from an earache. "Writing was better," Sonia admitted.

Guy's letters occasionally had a confessional quality—sometimes a nod to his frustration about their modest means, or an attempt at an apology for his occasionally volatile temperament. "I know I can be disagreeable at times, but I think it's because I can't provide the way I would like to," he once wrote. "I hope to be able to do so one day, and that you'll always be mine regardless."

Their letters also expressed the depth of love and regard they had for each other in a way that may not have been possible in the routine of daily life.

"It was destiny itself that brought and kept us together. If you look back over the years, it's so clear that, against all odds, we were made for each other," Guy wrote on one wedding anniversary.

"I may not be the most expressive or extroverted, but what I feel for you and the family makes my heart beat.

"To me, you have always been the kindest, most beautiful woman . . . . I'm confident that one day I'll be able to give you everything you desire, because I believe in the future and in God's will."

Any letters Guy received in return, especially while he was away in Korea, and especially at Christmas, were precious to him, "like gifts fallen from the sky."

"When you'd get a letter," he once said of his time there, "you'd read it ten, twenty, fifty times. You'd constantly be waiting for the next one, re-reading the old ones in the meantime."

The end of 1952 would be an anomaly for the d'Artois household, the first time Guy would be away for the holidays. Normally he was home for a very British celebration, with Christmas crackers, turkey or ham, and many gifts of clothes, for the girls especially, that Sonia would make herself. But that year Sonia had to get creative to bring Guy into the family's Christmas fold. She made him a Christmas fruitcake that she'd fed to the gills with cognac. And although she wrapped it with cheesecloth and tucked it into a parcel to send abroad, it still reeked of the booze hidden within. The postal clerk noticed, and told her that the "bottle" inside had clearly broken. She assured him it was no bottle. The cake made it all the way to Korea, where Guy happily shared it, the same way he had the year before when Sonia mailed him a cake for his birthday. Guy, meanwhile, sent gifts for the kids, among them a Japanese doll that Nadya adored.

A few days before Christmas Sonia also headed over to the telegraph office and dictated a no-frills holiday telegram: "MERRY CHRISTMAS AND HAPPY NEW YEAR DARLING FROM YOUR LOVING WIFE AND CHILDREN." Short and to the point. Telegrams were, after all, charged by the word.

Antoinette, Guy's mother, and his older sister Lorraine remained in touch with Sonia during Guy's absence. Beyond that, Sonia made friends among the wives, some of whom also had husbands at war and were similarly left alone to carry on with the day-to-day battles of running a household. But one day Sonia's social network expanded in an unexpected way.

It was mid-morning when someone knocked on the door unannounced. Sonia went to open it and was shocked to find Suzanne Rebouche standing before her. Suzanne, the young-old wise soul, the fellow resistance fighter, Sonia's only real friend in Le Mans. And it wasn't just Suzanne on her doorstep but the entire Rebouche family: her parents and her now-husband, Lucien.

"They all immigrated to Canada," said Sonia. "They all survived the war."

Suzanne's sudden appearance provided Sonia with a closeness she'd found otherwise impossible in her adopted home. Suzanne had known Sonia before all this—before the kids, before Quebec City, before the war was over. She was part of her chosen family, and a reminder of the formative years that still defined her. Anyone else who fit that description was abroad and out of reach, Guy included. Suzanne settled close by, first in Sherbrooke, then in Valleyfield—close enough for the two women to remain in close touch and occasionally see each other. It was enough that Suzanne was in the same time zone and easily reachable by phone. It made Sonia very happy, and helped deepen her roots in Canada.

Back when Sonia was new to the country, she'd also been thrilled to discover she had an uncle who was already a Canadian. He wrote her a letter not long after her arrival from the U.K., no doubt having seen the frenzied media reports. "Are you Leslie Butt's daughter? If so, you're my niece." She replied right away. Jack Butt was one of the younger siblings who'd been left behind when Leslie was whisked away for a better life with his grandparents. As a young man during the First World War he'd come to British Columbia with the merchant navy, and then stayed.

Sonia's circle was steadily expanding in this vast land she now called home—and for someone who'd long sought belonging, this was especially important. She was a woman who had many homes, as one astute Canadian writer noted, all important in their own way. "Austen Chamberlain once observed that every Englishman had two countries—his own and France," McKenzie Porter wrote in *Maclean's* magazine. "Today Sonia has three and finds no conflict in her triple allegiance. She has lived according to the best traditions of the English ballad and the French *chansons de geste*. Few new Canadians have got off to a better start."

Few new Canadians have got off to a better start.

Sonia herself was fully bilingual, and her children were a reflection of Canada itself. Having spent their formative years in friendly, frozen Manitoba, the boys were largely anglophone. The younger girls, meanwhile, identified more closely with French-speaking Quebec and weren't educated in English until high school. "The boys go to an English-language school because English is more useful. The girls will go to a French-language school because French is more becoming," Sonia once explained. The parents spoke both languages to the boys and mostly French to the girls. The boys too spoke French to the girls, while Guy and Sonia almost always spoke and wrote to each other in French. It was a truly bilingual household where either language would get you heard—if you spoke loudly enough.

Still, the children were a handful, and it was a battle keeping order at the house on Saint-Louis.

Sonia's other big battle was her health.

The old back injury she sustained during SOE training had shadowed her ever since. Each of her difficult pregnancies created pressure on her spine for nine-month intervals that seemed to make matters worse. After Tina was born, Sonia's doctor told her she shouldn't have any more children. But a tubal ligation wasn't an option, was Sonia's retort; the Church forbade it. The doctor warned her, "You could become paralyzed if you have any more."

With Guy on the move once again, there was no immediate prospect of Sonia's getting pregnant. It would be an entire year before she saw him again.

On July 1, 1952, an overcast, windy day, Guy was in his tent when he heard shots outside. Within a moment someone came running to get him. He got into his jeep and drove off.

Guy arrived to find a crowd of his soldiers gathered near twenty-year-old Private Joseph Émile Hector Sanscartier of Cantley, Quebec, who was visibly drunk and waving a rifle. He'd just completed a training course and had just returned to his unit.

"I found Sanscartier standing on a small hill, holding a .303 rifle and taking shots at the young Canadian soldiers who were nearby. He had fired several rounds," said Guy. Sanscartier had already "nicked a chap in the ear."

By that time Guy had been in Korea for about three months and was leading the support company. And now, with the summer's heavy rains and humidity and a recent spike in Chinese activity, the terrain had turned doubly hostile.

According to Captain J.P. Savary, who was on the scene, Guy approached Sanscartier and asked him to put the rifle down. The young private refused, telling Guy that "if he came any nearer, he'd get it."

Guy later said: "I doubt if Sanscartier even knew what he was doing." He was concerned that someone might get seriously hurt.

Guy asked Captain Savary to get his pistol. He kept talking to Sanscartier while slowly moving up the hill. Then suddenly someone ran over, blundering onto the scene, disrupting Guy's plan, inadvertently picking "one hell of a time to arrive."

Guy noticed Sanscartier turn toward the runner. "I knew Sanscartier was about to pull the trigger."

Guy aimed and fired a single shot. The bullet hit Sanscartier in the left side. A short while after, he was dead.

Two days later Guy was swapped out from the support company. The military then issued a release about the incident, announcing an inquiry into whether Guy's actions warranted a court martial. All over Canada, Guy was once again back in the headlines.

"A 20-year-old Quebec soldier who was threatening his comrades was shot and killed in Korea July 1," began one Canadian Press article, "by Maj. Guy D'Artois, G.M, D.S.O., one of Canada's most renowned soldiers and a hero of the wartime French resistance movement."

"I hated to kill him," Guy told an interviewer later. "But I wasn't given much choice.

"I took him in my arms and my sergeant-major took the rifle away. There was one shell in it. We called an ambulance but it was too late.

"Then I gave the men hell and told them that they had just seen what happens when you drink too much." Sanscartier was buried in the United Nations cemetery in Busan, at the southern tip of the Korean peninsula.

Back in Quebec, when Sonia heard the news, she went back to scrubbing the floor. It was a reliably productive way to cope with her worries about Guy.

And then the phone calls to the house on rue Saint-Louis began.

Sonia would pick up the receiver and listen as the voice at the other end uttered threats. She had no idea whether they would act on those threats. There were the ordinary stresses of living as a military wife, but this . . . this was traumatic.

"I couldn't let the children go to school alone, they had to be escorted." And at night, Sonia recalled, Van Doo officers living nearby would take turns guarding her house.

Guy remained in Korea as a supernumerary officer, a post without specific responsibilities, while a court of inquiry investigated.

It was two uneasy weeks for him, for his company, and for the entire Canadian force in Korea.

Finally, in mid-July, the answer came. There would be no court martial; Guy was cleared of wrongdoing. An internal report concluded that Sanscartier had "consumed unknown quantity of native liquor during afternoon 1 Jul 52 . . . . Major d'Artois acting in performance of duty and not to blame for death of Sanscartier . . . . Sanscartier was himself to blame in that his actions resulted in his death."

The Major, newspapers reported, "remains on duty with his regiment."

Guy was in fact given a new position as "director of training" and shipped off shortly thereafter. Within a month he was on his way to the British Commonwealth Battle School in Hara-mura, Japan—a centre for training troops to be deployed in Korea. Intended or not, his assignment there would have made for a cooling-off period, given the charged atmosphere around Sanscartier's death. But even in this new role, Guy was a source of concern for his superiors.

The battle school had been established as a British and Australian institution; the Canadians were added later. Within weeks, Guy, as second-in-command of the school and commander of the Canadian component, was noted for improving the training and efficient running of the school. However, his superiors also noted his "lack of cooperation," expressed in a "tactless manner."

"I have nothing against his efficiency," wrote the school's commander, "and I like him personally, but being the great individualist that he is, he just does not fit in here, where everyone, to a certain extent, has to forget one's nationality and work for the common good." He recommended that Guy be replaced "at the earliest moment."

After three months in Japan, Guy was transferred back to Korea. There he resumed command, this time at the helm of B Company, an infantry rifle company. In the field again, Guy was once more in his element, regaining a degree of the independence he'd enjoyed so much in France. He also seemed to gain his men's trust.

Guy and his men held a defensive line, keeping watch for Chinese activity, improving their position, and patrolling to keep the enemy on their toes. Bunkers dotted this line, offering the best protection against sporadic enemy shelling.

Guy's headquarters were in one such dugout in what was called Hill 133, near the border between the two Koreas. Andrew C. Moffat, a gunner who worked closely with Guy, shared the space for three months and so had a close-up view of Guy's leadership style. Moffat remembered Guy waking up each day before dawn and visiting all his men deployed along the line, no matter where they were working. While he was out, his batman would put together a breakfast table from two wooden crates that were then covered with a white tablecloth and cutlery—reminiscent of the meals Guy liked to have back in the quarry of Sylla. Guy and Moffat would then dine on cereal, toast, perhaps an egg, and coffee. Guy's dinner table was set up similarly but more formally, and he'd often have an aperitif before dinner. Afterward it was a cognac and a game of dominoes. Then he'd go out one last time around midnight for another round of the men on patrol.

"He did little to openly display his love for his men, but that love was never in doubt," Moffat later wrote. "He never asked anything of his men that he did not first do himself . . . he set high goals and high standards, which he too lived by."

At that post, come Christmastime "you'd lose a bit of the fighting spirit, but being together helped," said Guy. The cake from Sonia would have been a bright moment in an otherwise "painful day" away from family, a day that "could not end quickly enough."

It had been a challenging posting, during which Guy also began to struggle with a health condition that confounded doctors for years afterward. He discovered that he was unable to keep his balance in the dark or when his eyes were closed, a kind of vertigo that could leave him nauseated and at risk of falling, always to the left. It was just one more consequential development of several in Korea that would make its mark on Guy and the rest of his career.

Guy completed a full year in Asia before returning home. It would be his final deployment as a commander in a war zone.

Reunited again in Quebec City, it was another honeymoon for Sonia and Guy. Within months of his return, Sonia was pregnant again. In 1954 a girl arrived, and then in 1955 a boy, named respectively Lorraine, after Guy's sister, and Guy, after himself.

Even after Guy's tour was over, the threats over Sanscartier's death continued.

"We know where you are," the anonymous callers would say. "Don't think you're going to get away with what you did."

"It wasn't very pleasant," Sonia admitted.

By then Sonia had had six children in the span of a decade. She knew it was only a matter of time before she'd need to have an operation to save her back.

But again it had to wait.

26

REUNIONS

Sonia and Guy • *Werl, Germany, October 1955*

Of all the places Sonia thought her marriage to the army might take her, Germany was unlikely to have been high on the list. From the moment she received the news from a far more enthusiastic Guy, Sonia was palpably uneasy with the idea of living in a country and among people she'd grown up regarding as the enemy. Her horrifying wartime experiences, indeed, the very nature of her wartime role, had primed her for a deep distrust of and aversion to all things German. And yet here she was, contemplating life at a Canadian army base within its very borders.

It had been only a decade since its defeat, but the Germany emerging from the ashes of the Second World War was different from the one that had violently started it. This was no longer Hitler's Germany. It was the Germany of the Marshall Plan, one where American, British, and Canadian military bases were taking root on its soil to ensure that nothing like the atrocities of the war would ever be permitted to happen again.

Sonia would have been aware of the concerted international effort to track down Nazis responsible for the regime's heinous crimes, and that many perpetrators and sympathizers had nonetheless simply melted into the population. Meanwhile the revelations about the full scale of brutality in the concentration camps horrified many Germans, as they did people around the world.

The reckoning was ongoing. Still, Sonia could barely imagine having everyday interactions with anyone who might have had the slightest connection to that murderous history.

But Sonia would also have been well aware that the posting to the Canadian base at Werl was an unmissable opportunity for Major Guy d'Artois, one he could perhaps parlay into another promotion. The children would have the unique experience of living abroad for the first time and mixing with fellow "army brats" from across Canada, from Halifax to Regina to Vancouver. Returning to Europe would also be a homecoming of sorts for Sonia—living there again, even in Germany, would allow her and her new family the opportunity to travel and perhaps reconnect with family and old friends.

Sonia had become accustomed to the upheaval of army-driven moves, but preparing to leave Canada entirely presented an altogether new order of complexity. Adding to the challenge was that their youngest, Guy, was still a newborn and had been unwell for weeks.

He would in fact end up in hospital—and was still there as his father sailed to Europe with Canada's 2nd Infantry Brigade. Sonia stayed behind to pack up the six children. When it was time for the family to leave, little Guy's doctor had to provide permission for him to board the ship that would take the first tranche of the battalion's wives and children—a reported total of 625 dependants—to Europe.

Army officials at the time described the voyage as "unique in Canadian history. It is the first time army dependents have been transferred overseas en masse, and probably the biggest mass movement of children from Canada," and as such it was worthy of press coverage. The Canadian Press article, published on October 20, 1955, derisively called it the Diaper Division, on its way to "rejoin its paternal unit."

"Dependents of officers and men in the NATO brigade . . . sailed for Rotterdam," offered the observant news service reporter, singling out the d'Artois family for leading the others in size with six children.

"It will be a homecoming for Mrs. d'Artois," the writer added.

The ship chartered for the task, it so happened, was the *Empress of Australia*, the same ship that had taken Guy to Europe for the first time back in 1940. This marked the first of a series of coincidences that seemed like the closing of a giant circle in Sonia and Guy's lives. Although she was heading to an unfamiliar, possibly uncomfortable life in Germany, in many ways this voyage was taking Sonia back to the beginning.

Fort Saint-Louis, the Canadian base there, was already well established, with a church, a cinema, and a mess for the officers, complete with rooms where they could sleep when the need arose. But it couldn't accommodate families, who were instead housed in living quarters just outside the village of Werl. Married officers, such as d'Artois, lived in townhouses or large apartments that served as PMQs. The neighbourhood was wholly Canadian and mostly French speaking, a place where wives easily socialized and children played in the streets. "You'd never know you were in Germany," recalled Bob.

On Sundays—every Sunday—the d'Artois family would pile into Guy's small Ford Taunus and make the short drive to the church tucked away at the base, where they would attend Mass. Then they'd join the gathering at the mess with all the other officers, wives, and children for a big roast beef lunch. Inevitably, the officers would retreat for a session of drinking and skittle pool, after which some of them, including Guy, would repair to their rooms to sleep it off before going home.

Located in the northwest of the country, about forty kilometres from Dortmund, Werl was off the beaten path. And yet it became the address for a most important reunion between Sonia and her childhood companion, her partner in crime, her most treasured ally.

Since the last time Sonia saw him as a teenager, her brother Derek had fought his own war, apart from family and apart from most Allied soldiers of his generation. He'd first been deployed to India with the Royal Scots, then he switched to the Indian Army. He served in the Pakistan–Afghanistan border area and later in Burma (Myanmar today), among other areas. Unlike Sonia, he had remained in regular touch with their mother, Thelma, who had settled in the U.K.

When he learned that Sonia was on the Continent, Derek arranged to take a holiday and travelled to Germany to see her.

On the day of his arrival, Sonia made her way to the little train station nestled in the heart of Werl to welcome her brother. After so many years, she worried that they might not even spot each other. "I thought, 'Will he recognize me? Will I recognize him?'" She hadn't needed to worry: "As soon as he stepped off the train it was instant—he hadn't changed at all."

No one knew young Sonia as well as Derek did, and yet he knew so little of the married woman with six children she'd become. They went on to spend time together, just the two of them, recalling the innocence of the idle days of their youth before the scars of a world war altered them forever.

And despite the passage of time, they retained some vestiges of those childhood days. Sonia was now going mostly by the name Tony, the nickname her brother had given her as a child. And Derek, the mischievous but generous older brother, became the same as an uncle.

Obscure, sleepy Werl had made it possible for the two to get reacquainted. It then subsequently allowed them to reunite with their father, the three of them together for the first time since they were teenagers. By then Leslie Butt had moved to Rome with his wife, Mina, within a day's train journey of Werl. And so Derek and Sonia headed south by train to visit their father in Italy.

This time, Guy was staying behind with the children, supported by Sophia, their full-time housekeeper. For a few brief days Sonia and Derek were transported to the past—when the two of them were often the sum total of all that was beautiful in her world, and when seeing their father on his trips back from Africa was the only time of real peace. Now they were writing a new chapter in the story of a family that had been dismembered by acrimony and scattered by war.

Leslie would have been immensely proud of his now adult children, and in awe of Sonia, the teenage girl he'd reluctantly sent off to fight a secret war, hoping against hope it would end before she deployed.

To the extent that he could, Leslie had kept tabs on her while she was in France, exchanging letters with the War Office. But given what he knew of her mission, "We continue to have good news of your daughter" was hardly enough. The worry must have consumed him. The jacket riddled with bullets from Bar-sur-Seine—Leslie would keep it for decades, a testimonial to the risks of his daughter's "war work."

"My father said that I had gone to war as a girl and come back as a woman," Sonia recalled. How grateful he was that she had come back alive, that somehow all three of them had donned uniforms and then left the armed forces intact. Many others, of course, were far less fortunate.

That special reunion in Rome unfolded in an extraordinary place that Leslie called home. He and Mina were living in a flat in a large house with a roof garden on the estate of the grand Villa Doria Pamphili, a sprawling seventeenth-century villa nestled in a vast landscaped park in the Monteverde quarter. It was an inspiring setting for a journey into the past—children playing about the "gorgeous fountains" and green as far as the eye could see.

Because of his extended absences, Sonia had put her father up on a pedestal. There were yawning gaps in their relationship. It was time to make up for them now.

"It was just the four of us—my father, Ann [another name for Mina], Derek, and me. It was probably early autumn and it was just party time all the time," recalled Sonia. She appreciated Rome's ancient beauty and the silence embedded within its din. It had been some time since she could focus on being only a sister and a daughter and nothing else.

But her moment of peace and freedom was fleeting. Sonia was supposed to be gone for only a week, but "I was having too good a time," she said, and had stayed longer. Guy made a few frantic calls.

"When are you coming back?" Even with the help of Sophia, caring for the children was, at times, too much for Guy, especially when one of them fell ill, which—invariably with six children—happened with alarming frequency.

"He wasn't very good at handling the children. So I had to go back to my duties."

Oddly, the posting in Germany was enabling opportunities that weren't usually available in an international military posting. Most significantly, it allowed Sonia and her children to accompany Guy and live together full time as a family. But sometimes being together had to be encouraged and engineered, as when Sonia had to send one of the boys to fetch Guy after he stayed too long at the drinking sessions at the mess, falling asleep in his room there afterward. At other times it came more naturally, like when she made Sunday dinner and everyone was required to be present. And although across the Atlantic Ocean was a long way to go for such togetherness, given their record thus far, it was worth it.

Their life at Werl also made it possible—and affordable—for Guy to reunite with his maquis family for the first time since 1944. With the children safely in Sophia's care, Sonia and Guy had once set off for the south of France to see friends when they decided to make a stop at Charolles. Having informed no one of their visit, they went directly to Maman Lucienne's café in the town's main square.

It was a busy Friday night. After sitting down at the table they'd been offered, Sonia and Guy asked the server to summon the owner, who was busy behind the bar serving drinks. Maman Lucienne was taken completely by surprise, and was so overjoyed that she promptly announced, *"Messieurs-dames, le café est fermé jusqu'à nouvel ordre, sauf pour les résistants!"* (The café is closed until further notice, except to the *résistants*!)

News of their visit spread quickly. For the rest of the week Sonia and Guy were feted, one raucous gathering after another. They were put up in a hotel and weren't allowed to pay for anything. "We were treated like royalty," said Sonia.

It was early May 1956. At one of those gatherings, it seems, Guy announced, surprisingly, that this would be his last visit to Charolles.

"This is the last meal that I will share with you," he said. "The current circumstances mean I will not be returning here, and despite the deep friendship I have for you all, you will never see me again in Charolles."

The former resistance fighters told Guy of their admiration for him and their hope that he would still return so they could give him "the warmest of welcomes."

Werl's proximity made it hard to resist going back—and in any case it was hard to imagine Guy staying away for long. And so, in a final act, the unsuspecting town became the staging ground for one last d'Artois reunion, another meeting of worlds old and new. After two years in Germany, on his way to his new posting to attend a staff college in Italy, Guy returned to Charolles in his Ford, this time with his eldest children, Bob, Michel, and Nadya. Sonia would pack up their things and, along with the three younger children, fly to meet them in Rome.

The children, until then, had been only "mildly aware" of their parents' wartime exploits. They would occasionally hear stories and would sense the special place their parents had in military circles when anyone discovered they were children of the d'Artoises. But mostly, "as far as we were concerned, Dad was Dad. And Mum was Mum," said Bob d'Artois. That changed perceptibly when the eldest children visited Charolles with their father en route to Italy. They were "able to at least get some grasp on the adoration from others for my dad." They perceived it in the warm reception they received at Maman Lucienne's café, and at the lavish dinner they enjoyed at Gaston Lévy's home, where Bob was promptly smitten with his beautiful daughters. "I could just see how much these people adored my father," said Nadya. For Guy, introducing his children to his maquisards would have been a head-bending reminder of the march of time. It was a special moment: a chosen family meeting his real one.

Another circle closed.

After that, it was Italy's turn to bring Sonia and Guy's old world together with the new. When Guy was offered a year at the Italian staff college at Civitavecchia, he accepted. For three months of that year he'd be away from his family and with the Alpini, Italy's mountain infantry corps.

But Italy allowed Sonia a chance to spend long hours with her father for the first time in her adult life. And her two families could now build new bonds across the generations: Leslie and his grandchildren got to know each other and make memories together while Sonia and her half-brother Michael, now a teenager, became closer than they'd ever been. Italy was also the place where the older children learned independence, where the girls acquired yet another language, where Bob had his first kiss. It was a special year of reunions, of family gatherings and picnics. And it had been the posting to that obscure little German village that made it all possible.

Another circle closed. But there was yet one more waiting.

To finish off their sojourn in Europe, Sonia and Guy decided to loop back to the very beginning, to London, for the first time since they'd left for Canada in December 1944. Once again Guy would drive his Ford, which he was planning to ship back to Canada, and Sonia would fly with all six children and most of the luggage. Arriving at the other end with everyone and every bag accounted for was a feat in itself. At the airport Guy was there waiting, and with him was Thelma, Sonia's mother.

Sonia had returned to London partly with the idea of reconciling with her mother. When she reunited with Derek in Germany he had told her, "It's time you made peace with Mother." And perhaps some part of Sonia wanted her mother to meet her grandchildren, to see what had become of the daughter for whom she had caused so much pain.

It was an exhausting journey for all involved, but Sonia and Guy couldn't leave Europe without returning to the place where they first met, where they married, where they separated for the war, where they started their life together afterward. Now they could see London for the first time together in peacetime. And a decade later, the city was an altogether happier place than when they'd left it. In their week-long visit they made time to return to Marylebone, to recall the long nights they'd partied with their fellow agents on the eve of their departure to occupied France. They also made time to visit St. James's Church, where they had exchanged their vows.

Thelma, now almost sixty, lived alone with Sonia's younger sister, Bunny, who'd grown into a fragile adult, in and out of hospitals. Sonia and Guy did spend time with them but Thelma didn't make the visit easy. She questioned their plans. She was suffocating; she wanted to be included in everything. By the end of it, Sonia believed that her mother hadn't really changed. She couldn't wait to return to Canada. To head home.

There she would fight another battle for her life.

27

SURGERY

Sonia • *Montreal, 1960*

Sonia watched anxiously as the doctors began putting her in a cast. She was stunned as they wrapped an increasingly larger portion of her injured body, and from there on in she couldn't sit. That meant she'd have to eat on her side; she could not properly wash, or even scratch an itch. And she was to remain in that imprisoned state at the Montreal Neurological Institute for three long months.

Sonia's wartime injury had long demanded its due—and it was about to rule her movements, her life, and the life of her family. She'd been only nineteen when she fell from that cable during training. Now, at thirty-six, she was finally forced to pay her body some attention. The operation took eight and a half hours, during which she underwent a spinal fusion and a laminectomy, in which part of a vertebral bone was removed.

Sonia had long known that one day she'd need a spinal fusion. But it became a necessity when, at home in Montreal, she bent over while doing laundry and suddenly could not straighten up. She had to crawl upstairs on all fours to get to a phone and call her doctor. The office told her to come in as soon as she could. And when she got there, the doctor told her that two of her discs had ruptured.

As d'Artois family upheavals went, Sonia's sudden absence was of the highest order. Guy was up in the Arctic, where he once again had an unconventional assignment. He was spending up to seven months a year training a group of Inuit as Canadian Rangers, to help protect Canada's northern flank against the Russian threat.

The doctors had to contact him to get consent—the surgery, any surgery, could not proceed without a husband's authorization. Sonia even told her doctor that she was worried about Guy's reaction. When Guy returned, the doctor had him come in and he explained the problem in detail, that there was no way to avoid the surgery. And so it was arranged. Suzanne, Sonia's old *résistante* friend, immediately agreed to stay with the children until Guy could find longer-term help. Still, Guy would have to stay close to home and take care of their affairs until Sonia was strong enough to return to the family's helm.

Guy was consumed with worry for his wife, making him an especially anxious and sometimes edgy caretaker. Occasionally that anxiety translated into the Major getting tough on the children. Making matters worse was that Sonia's recovery would be slow, complicated by other health issues that required yet more surgery. She'd been so accustomed to the agility and speed required of a mother of six that she struggled with the limitations, the muscle spasms, the infuriating immobility of life in a body cast. And although the ordeal hadn't stemmed from a battlefield injury, it was nevertheless a legacy and a consequence of the war. The past that Sonia had tried so hard to put behind her had finally caught up with the present.

For the family, it was a time of recalibration. The entire time they'd been together the d'Artoises had lived the restless life of a military family—a life of displacement, of constant impermanence, of packing and unpacking—and of all the questions about belonging that came with it. For Sonia herself it had simply been a continuation of her early nomadic life as the child of divorcees with unpredictable lives.

Yet, while it may have been familiar, it was growing tiresome. Guy and Sonia decided to put an end to all that, to make a bold move away from the city and into a beautiful lakeside cottage they'd once rented for the summer near the town of Hudson, Quebec. For the first time since Bob was born, Sonia wouldn't be involved in the family's latest house move. But Sonia had already fallen in love with the place. She would have been able to imagine her future there, and she liked what she saw.

28

HOME

Sonia • *Como, 1961*

Cedar Cottage, on rue Main in the village of Como, was exactly as advertised: an inviting turn-of-the-century cottage-house on an acre of land, with a wraparound porch, two storeys, and a lush, well-kept garden that stretched all the way back to the very edge of the Lake of Two Mountains. Sonia and Guy had never stayed long enough in one place to buy a house—and could never afford one on Guy's salary even if they wanted to—but renting Cedar Cottage was the closest they'd come to having a permanent place to call their own. In its warm kitchen, cozy confines, and idyllic location near the water, Sonia had found a true home. It was an ideal place for a still-young woman to recover, to set down roots, to thrive anew.

Sonia, an early riser, began countless mornings by stealing a quiet moment to gaze out her kitchen window at the peaceful lake, occasionally embellished by the glide of a canoe or sailboat. She flourished as the steward of Cedar Cottage, immersing herself in a life of cooking for big groups and socializing with everyone who walked through the door. She was an easygoing mum, and yet strict in her own way. Outsiders would remark on how everyone in the family had the same smile—and it was unmistakably Sonia's smile. Her children, the eldest of whom were teenagers now, were very quickly escaping the constraints of life as army kids, growing up in a decade shaped by the Kennedys and the Beatles. And as they branched out and formed their own social networks, Sonia's home became a gathering place, a drop-in, and her kitchen the welcoming safe haven that back in her childhood she'd imagined kitchens to be. Cedar Cottage had a constantly open door. Sonia's father and Mina came to visit, along with Sonia's younger brother, Michael. He too fell in love with Como, with the idle afternoons spent among nephews and nieces who were his contemporaries, cycling up and down the road, swimming, and stalking the Hudson yacht club.

There was little evidence in Sonia's life of her wartime adventures—beyond the household, she kept busy with knitting, swimming in the lake, and caring for several dogs and cats, including two German shepherds. She avoided sharing those old stories, even with her own family. Some of her children believed it was partly out of deference to Guy, that she was wary of upstaging him. Nadya became aware of her mother's feats only when they showed a film at school about Violette Szabó, Sonia's wartime friend. Nor had Sonia spoken of her wartime past to Michael, for whom it was always second-hand. "I'd read about it," he said. "It wasn't a big subject of discussion." But like everyone else in her family, he admired her for it.

Still, while Sonia may have been a mild-mannered, community-minded mother, her skills as an agent would occasionally seep into ordinary life. In one incident, Bob was driving along with his friend Fred Langan when three men in a taxi cut them off and started taunting and threatening them. Sonia happened to be visiting a friend nearby, and someone alerted her to the tense standoff unfolding in the street. She came out and demanded to know what the men were up to. They told her off, but when one of them opened the car door to step out, "she grabbed the car door and she smashed it on his leg," Fred recalled. "And then she smacked him right in the head and he fell back into his seat. She then pointed at the others in the car and warned, 'Don't you move.' They were scared shitless." The men drove away, defeated—and the story became legendary among family friends.

As Sonia approached her fortieth year, little else in her life spoke of her wartime experiences. There were few hints left of the irreverent teenager who first joined the SOE, of the young woman who lived under bombardment, or of the agent handling guns and explosives as part of her daily existence. And there was nothing at all that hinted at the difficult choices she had made in 1944: her determination to stick with her marriage and her courage in owning up to her involvement with another man. Thoughts of Sydney had receded well into the past, superseded by Sonia and Guy's mutual devotion, the busyness of life, and time itself.

"As far as I was concerned, the war was a period in my life, not my whole life," she once said.

That past did briefly interject, however, in the form of letters.

Suzanne's husband, Lucien, was in Europe when he ran into Sydney at an airport. Sydney had remarried and had worked for years at the Bank of Scotland. Naturally, he asked for news of Sonia.

After that, Sydney started to write Suzanne. And occasionally he would enclose a letter for Sonia.

"I let him do it for a little while," said Sonia, recounting the story decades later, "and then I just couldn't do it any longer.

"I felt that it just wasn't right.

"I said to Suzanne to ask him to please stop, which she did. I said, 'If he does write again, don't give me the letter.'"

"But I always knew that we would somehow meet up again."

1963

At Como, it was time for another farewell. Guy was ordered deployed to Asia as part of an effort to monitor ceasefires and help implement a treaty that divided Vietnam and Laos from the former French Indochina. Again Guy would be absent for a full year. Of course by then both he and Sonia were well practised at long separations. And in a house full of heavy traffic, those absences for Sonia were far less jarring. Still, they weren't easy.

This time when Guy returned a year later, there were no more babies. But there was the usual awkward adjustment required to bring him back into the family fold. The first week or two would be awash with the joy of reunion and the love engendered by distance. Then things would get darker.

"I was able to cope when he was away. But then when he came back, I had to revert to being the subservient little housewife again," said Sonia. She'd go from having all the responsibility, all the control, to "absolutely none at all." And this time, when Guy learned that Sonia had started taking driving lessons, he put a stop to it. Later, though, she would quietly start them up again.

Whenever he returned, Sonia and Guy would always slip back into their social circle. They were a popular couple. They enjoyed dressing up and attending the military balls, and they loved to dance together—moments during which their love for each other was plain as day.

After he returned from Laos, most of their entertaining happened at Cedar Cottage, with a parade of old friends and family coming over for a night of chatter, drink, and food. Guy was always sharply dressed, always with a cigarette—in those days he smoked as much as three packs a day—and often with a beer in hand. Guy always made time for lunches with fellow war veterans, during which he would hold court—a habit that became less endearing when he drank too much.

With the children Guy was generous with both his possessions and his knowledge. When Bob turned seventeen, Guy handed him the keys to his beloved Ford Taunus as a gift. And on his many trips into Montreal from Como, he'd give Nadya impromptu lessons in how to drive defensively. He also taught young Michael, Sonia's little brother, how to drive, how to fence, and, along with Bob, how to play chess. Guy was still a prolific photographer, even once building a darkroom at home. He was a voracious reader, too, always with a book in his hands, sometimes reading out loud to himself.

Guy liked to ponder life's bigger questions, including the legacy of war and conflict.

"Did we really need to kill each other? Did we change anything at all?" he once asked in a newspaper interview.

"We fought in pursuit of an ideal, and watched friends die trying to win that war. You have to wonder whether the fight, and the loss of life, were worth it when we seem to be in an even greater state of decline today.

"We've never achieved a just society, so we've justified the use of force instead."

Guy was always a thinker. But when he drank, he became a dark thinker.

His doctors noted that he drank "more than occasionally." Beer was his drink of choice. Later, his family would find empty bottles of the harder stuff hidden around the house. When Guy was sober he was gentle and charming and kind. Unbelievably kind. But after his mission to Korea, and in his later years, his drinking would cloud his personality. He'd become sharp-tempered and angry. The children were sometimes afraid of him.

By 1965 Guy was ready to retire, this time of his own accord. On September 22 he was officially "struck off strength" from the Canadian Army, twenty years after the first time he tried to leave. He was only forty-eight, and still a major. Guy was also still a man best motivated by challenge, by conflict. And now that he was no longer living the military life that had shaped him, he began to withdraw into himself. "I was irritated. I realized that living in society is the hardest thing to do. Everyone does as they please," he once said. He delegated most things to Sonia. "Go ask your mother, she's the boss," he would say.

She really was the boss, and as they grew older, some of her children might go so far as to describe her as controlling. She was decisive and resilient, and she had strong opinions about her children and her place in their lives. As the years wore on, Sonia became increasingly sure of herself, more independent and more vibrant, while Guy found it increasingly harder to cope.

He didn't retire completely. At first he worked in civil protection with the City of Montreal, a job he seemed to enjoy. But the drive back and forth to Como took its toll, especially in the winter. It was time for another move.

This sparked a period of great change for Sonia too. Guy was around a lot more. One by one her children were leaving home, travelling and starting careers, scattered at times across Europe, Canada, the United States, even the Bahamas. The two youngest, however, were still in high school. It made sense for Sonia and Guy to move to Montreal.

Sonia wasn't ready to leave Cedar Cottage behind. It was her favourite home, her safe haven, everything that was beautiful about her world. She would have loved to buy the property and always regretted not doing it, especially when it was sold just a short while after they left. It was so wrenching for her to leave, she shed tears on her way out.

Over the next decade, so much more of what was familiar in Sonia's life would change. Her father, Leslie, died on April 11, 1973. A month after that heartbreak she welcomed her first grandchild, Stephanie, born on exactly the same day as Sonia, forty-nine years later. Time was swiftly marching on. But as a middle-aged woman, Sonia's world was still expanding. Change seemed to fuel her.

It was in that period that Sonia began working for the first time. She'd always been engaged in some manner of volunteer work, but now she was a caregiver, assisting people with terminal illnesses in their own homes. It had once, as a child, been her dream to be a nurse. The care Sonia now gave others was immensely rewarding work that also afforded her some independence and space after so many years devoted to her own family.

But Guy struggled with all the change. He never lost his charm—he remained gallant in an old-fashioned kind of way. And yet there was bitterness and anger growing within him that would occasionally bubble to the surface.

Soon after they moved to Montreal, the October Crisis erupted. The Quebec Liberation Front had unleashed a barrage of explosions, and by 1970 it had carried out more than two hundred attacks. When a British diplomat and a Quebec politician were kidnapped, then Prime Minister Pierre Trudeau controversially invoked the War Measures Act—a first on the domestic front and outside of wartime—suspending civil rights and allowing police greater powers to arrest and imprison people. Trudeau deployed the army into a tense Montreal to end the attacks—men in fatigues, wearing helmets and carrying guns on the streets. Such scenes would have been disturbing for any Canadian, but for Guy and Sonia it would have been devastating to see at home, after everything they'd experienced abroad.

Guy was a proud Quebecer, but the separatist movement bewildered him. As the head of a bilingual household he disliked tribalist and nationalist tendencies. When he'd returned from the war in 1944, he'd even had to defend himself for fighting in a "British" war.

"I have been told by my compatriots 'Oh you have fought for England.' I say to them to hell with England. I fought for Canada and England is my ally . . . . It is not a matter of being French Canadian or an English Canadian. It is a matter of being a Canadian. I am just a Canadian."

"We have got to help each other or we will be sunk. I did not marry my wife because she was English or French. I married her because I loved her and she has guts. That's the truth of it."

Guy's words warranted an editorial in *The Globe and Mail* titled "Real Basis for Unity":

> The key to unity between French and English speaking Canadians has been given by a young Quebecer who just returned to his native land after fighting France with the Maquis. This Canadian, of whom all are proud, Capt. Guy [d']Artois, through his experiences with all manner of citizens united in their resistance to the German oppressor, has read a lesson in unity to all men of goodwill.
>
> Understanding unity born of mutual danger and aspiration, men of the type of Capt. [d']Artois, French-speaking and English-speaking, can bring healing to a disunited nation.

Guy was a fighter at heart. He was more at home in times of conflict, more optimistic, more present. In peacetime he was a glass-half-empty kind of man, aimless and distracted. Conflict focused him. And the military was his family first; he had friends across the ranks, even in the upper echelons of the organization. But those who knew him could sense Guy's underlying impatience with the military brass—and his frustration that he'd never been promoted beyond major. He believed he was in line for a promotion after Vietnam, but, as he put it, he'd "told the generals certain things" and "the promotion never came through."

Bob d'Artois remembers a close friend of Guy's, Major-General John "Rocky" Rockingham, telling him that his father could have "easily" gone right to the top of the military. "Except he was a shit disturber," Rocky had said, and his advancement was "stifled" as a result.

Guy had served, and served well, being tasked with some of the tougher jobs. But he didn't suffer fools gladly, and wouldn't take orders from just anyone.

Guy's other likely challenge was an inability to get past the war and his role in it. He could never quite outdo Michel le Canadien. Guy had been lauded in many corners, and certainly had the medals to prove his accomplishments, but it seemed it was never enough.

Like Sonia, Guy rarely spoke of his exploits with his family, and if he did it was with the boys, not the girls—out of a desire to protect them. He was more willing, even eager, to recount his experiences to newspapers, friends, fellow veterans at the mess—some of whom would say that he relived his battles *ad nauseam*, to the point of tedium, leaving some among them grumbling whenever he spoke; or he would talk to friends like Fred Langan, Bob's good friend, with whom he would wax nostalgic over a chess board.

Still, in a moment of humble reflection, Guy once said, "We are privileged to be able to talk about these things, because there are many who can no longer do so. But we are not the only ones. We [Guy and Sonia] were two out of hundreds."

He still wanted his story told, and he at one point planned to write it—who better to tell it like it was, to capture all that had made it so compelling? Cognizant of the momentous times they'd lived through together, several of Guy's maquis friends had written up their own memoirs. Some were published, others were not. Guy had always intended to do the same; later in life, he even bought a typewriter with that purpose in mind. And as a prodigious collector of his life's artifacts, he'd been building a vast archive of his accomplishments: newspaper articles, notes, a deep stack of photos he and others had taken that bore witness to all he'd experienced during the war—everything that related to his military career and especially his time in France.

Guy never wrote his book. But in the mid-1980s, an opportunity finally came along for Guy and Sonia to tell their story in its entirety. Producer Ronald Cohen and writer Rob Forsyth proposed a three-part, six-hour television miniseries based on Guy's and Sonia's adventures. It would have a $7.5 million budget and was to be delivered to the CBC by Christmas of 1986. The couple agreed. The script was written and the pitch was made: "What we propose is a spy story, a Canadian spy story. All of it is true. It is a story with a romantic beginning, an exciting middle and a happy ending."

But the series fell victim to CBC funding cuts, and the project was scrapped. That too made the papers.

PART VIII

PEACE AT LAST

29

ONE FINAL VISIT

Guy • *Charolles, June 9, 1984*

On June 9, 1984, just before one, a Canadian military vehicle stopped at Louis Lapalus's front window. A silver-haired Guy d'Artois emerged and walked into the welcoming arms of his old friend.

It was the first time Louis had seen his "brother and friend" in more than a decade. He too had aged, his now three daughters fully grown women. Charolles had also changed appreciably. Guy would be staying at the Lion d'Or, situated on what was now called "avenue de la Libération." The war was a dying, distant memory, though one that Louis worked tirelessly to keep alive: in the countless plaques and memorials he'd helped inaugurate as the founder of an association for veterans of the maquis and the resistance, and in the regular commemorative events he planned and executed. Having Major Guy d'Artois attend the fortieth-anniversary commemorations in Charolles, on an official trip organized by the Canadian Armed Forces, seemed to invigorate Louis, who'd been planning the occasion for months.

Between them Louis and Guy had been to dozens of remembrance ceremonies marking the ruthless passage of time. On every occasion they gathered, the veterans were a little older, a little more removed from—and perhaps more philosophical about—those momentous and terrifying days, a little more caught up in the mundane matters of ordinary life. But once again they would put on their medals, berets, ties, and jackets and join old friends to ritually remember the trying days gone by.

These were not celebrations of war. A procession of old soldiers is, in a sense, a show of gratitude for survival. These ceremonies, in some ways, are also funerals, occasions to mourn lost youth, the ones who didn't make it.

> *They shall grow not old, as we that are left grow old:*
> *Age shall not weary them, nor the years condemn.*
> *At the going down of the sun and in the morning*
> *We will remember them.*

And we do remember them. In speeches, in song, in prayer. With blood-red poppies and the Last Post, and then, most eloquently perhaps, in the subsequent two minutes of silence.

It had been forty years since Europe began to comprehend just how many of its children had been victims of book-burning authoritarians, of populism gone murderously awry, of blind and violent intolerance; forty years since Canadians, Britons, Americans, and their allies landed in France, many of them never to return. It had been forty years since Alcide Beauregard went missing, shot point-blank during a massacre that casually took the lives of a hundred and twenty people in the dying days of an occupation. Forty years since several young women were secretly sent off to war, their short, tortured wartime journey coming to a premature and cruel end.

And for many who survived, it had been forty years of recovery, of tears, of ailments, of occasional triumphs, and of the many disappointments of an ordinary life. They would never wish for war to return, but they could never really get beyond it.

In the summer of 1944, one matured quickly . . .

In the summer of 1984, one would have felt distinctly the vast distance from the old days. One would have been struggling to remember all the details and fighting the urge to shed the weight of memory once and for all. In the summer of 1984, one might have been surprised and pleased and sad that everyone in Charolles still remembered and appreciated all that had been accomplished—the victories the rest of the world had forgotten. Every act of remembrance, however, forced open one's emotional vault to mark the occasion, inviting back ghosts one might rather forget.

It was hard for Sonia and Guy to avoid such events entirely, given their history, though Guy was more drawn to them that she was. On his previous visit to Charolles, Guy had been asked to place a plaque on the front of Maman Lucienne's house, baptizing it "Villa des Alliés" in recognition of its role as a welcoming refuge for SOE agents during the war.

Guy and Sonia also returned together to London to be reunited with Vera Atkins and Maurice Buckmaster and several other SOE agents, who gathered at the Special Forces Club in Knightsbridge to mark the anniversary of victory in Europe.

Sonia took that opportunity to visit Horley, mostly to see her sister Bunny, who was still living a fragile life, suffocated by her illness and by their controlling mother. It saddened Sonia to see her little sister's life so constrained by both, constantly breathless and bluish in the face. The timing had been fortuitous for a final farewell. It was only a few months later that Bunny died. She was only thirty-six.

When in 1984 Guy travelled to France with the help of the Canadian government to mark the fortieth anniversary of the liberation of France, he went without Sonia.

"When Major d'Artois opened the door of the car, in a fraction of a second, he became Michel le Canadien," a local reporter wrote. Guy recognized and hugged everyone, seeing past the wrinkles and the grey hair. "Forty years have faded away."

In that ceremony in Charolles, Louis Lapalus took the microphone to welcome a crowd of a few hundred people, among them many familiar, time-worn faces: René Fléchard, Pierre Jandeau, and Maman Lucienne. The mayor, Jean Devron, spoke next. He declared Guy an honorary citizen of Charolles, presenting him with the city's medal to warm applause.

Guy, in a grey three-piece suit adorned with his many other medals, took the podium, silent at first. Then he addressed the aging fighters. "You, resistance fighters, do you know who you are?"

He reminded them of Eisenhower's often-quoted assertion that the work of the resistance helped shorten the war by nine months.

"Think of the human lives that have been saved."

Over the next few days Guy retraced every step of his time there. He wanted to see the field where he and young Joseph had landed and searched for hours in the dark, trying to find Albert Browne-Bartroli and his reception committee. He visited Pierre Jandeau's farm, where he was given shelter and his nickname—Michel le Canadien. He returned to the Villa des Alliés, where he'd spent many of his early nights in the wise counsel and under the protection of Maman Lucienne. By then she was eighty-two years old and overjoyed to see him. He visited René Fléchard, now seventy-two, in his house atop the hill in Saint-Julien-de-Civry, since baptized the "maquis house," and where the old maquisards gathered every year for yet another ceremony of remembrance. He met with his old confidant and first trusted lieutenant, Jean Tabourin. And he finally had a chance to see the Charolles region from the sky in daylight, forty years after he'd dropped from it in the dead of night. He barely recognized the terrain spread out beneath him. It took fifty-five minutes in a small plane to see it all.

In another ceremony, Guy helped René Fléchard inaugurate a monument commemorating the lives of the twenty-nine young men from the maquis of Saint-Julien-de-Civry who died in the catastrophic battle of Paray-le-Monial. Guy shed tears for those men.

At a cemetery in Charolles, Guy and Louis placed a rose at every one of the nineteen graves of young fighters cut down during the war.

They shall grow not old.

When speaking of those days, Guy would often tell younger soldiers that it could all happen again, that history could repeat itself. They too could be called on to make life-or-death decisions.

"One day, you might be called up and asked: Are you ready?

"You never know what the days will bring."

In those summer days of 1984, Guy was received like a hero. He was also presented with a precious gift: an old wartime Sylla flag that had been sitting in a small museum. Inscribed on one side of it are the names of all the familiar places: Cluny, Génelard, Pallinges. On the other is the cross of Lorraine, used as a symbol by the FFI, the Forces françaises de l'intérieur, as well as the words "Honneur et Patrie." *Honour and country. Maquis de Sylla. 1944.* The gesture left Guy again in tears. He promised that the flag would have a home at the Royal 22e Régiment's home at the Quebec Citadel.

His hosts were not to know it yet, but this really would be Guy's final visit to Charolles. And even if they had known, they couldn't have planned a better send-off.

The year 1984 also marked a significant milestone for Sonia and Guy. Their big wedding anniversaries necessarily intersected with those of the war—they were, after all, married in 1944. And that year, just before Guy left for Charolles, they celebrated their fortieth.

Throughout those years they'd spent almost as much time apart as they had together. But now, with Guy in retirement, they were together most of the time. No more missions, no more deployments or absences. And while they both took jobs later in life, requiring yet another move to Quebec City, Guy was fully there for the first time since they married.

It had never been an easy relationship. But four decades, six children, several grandchildren, and more than a dozen moves later, Sonia and Guy could still regard each other with love and overt affection.

"Love Story Outlasts Dangers of War" was the headline in the *Montreal Gazette* just ahead of St. Valentine's Day in 1985.

It was one of the final times they made the paper together to talk about the old days. The main photo shows a greying, smiling Guy with his arms encircling Sonia at the waist. Two small insets feature youthful photos of them in wartime, each enclosed in a heart-shaped frame.

"From the way their eyes frequently link, from the affectionate barbs they toss in each other's direction, it's clear that Blanche and Dieudonné don't need Valentine cards, chocolates and roses to remind them why they fell in love."

Memory. It is one of life's most precious and fraught gifts, and yet it's one we begin to lose late in life, just when we might have more time and reason than ever to recall and appreciate past experience. As he aged, Guy's memory faltered faster than most, and by the time Sonia embarked on her own solo trip of remembrance in 1994, he was showing signs of early dementia.

30

REMEMBRANCE

Sonia • *Normandy, France, 1994*

On a bright, sunny day in early June 1994, tens of thousands of people descended on Normandy to mark the fiftieth anniversary of D-Day. As organizers went all out with the preparations, leaders from all the Allied countries were en route to attend, including Queen Elizabeth—who, later in the war, had at nineteen worn a uniform and served with the Auxiliary Territorial Service, the women's branch of the British Army. Several world leaders joined her on the *Britannia*, her royal yacht, as part of a thirty-vessel flotilla that crossed the English Channel that day, stopping briefly to watch as a Lancaster that had been in action on D-Day dropped two million blood-red poppies into the sea.

Once on shore, Queen Elizabeth and Prince Philip rode atop a Range Rover to greet the crowds. President Bill Clinton regaled American veterans with reverential words: "We are the children of your sacrifice. We are the sons and daughters you saved from tyranny's reach."

"We stand on sacred soil," he said, where the miracle of liberation began fifty years ago "to end the enslavement of Europe."

Fifty years and nine days earlier, unbeknownst to most of the world and probably to most attending the commemorations that summer, Sonia had parachuted into the Sarthe in the middle of the night. It was, by necessity, a secret endeavour. But that secrecy led to a lifetime of unfair obscurity for most of the men and women of the SOE who, like Sonia, risked body and mind to "end the enslavement of Europe."

Admittedly, over the years Sonia was far less interested in marking such anniversaries than Guy was, and she had happily eschewed the attention often given to former female agents of the SOE. But her interest grew as she aged. So when she was finally asked to be part of an official Canadian delegation to mark the fiftieth anniversary of D-Day, she accepted the invitation. Her daughters Nadya and Tina, then living in Washington and France respectively, travelled to Normandy to join her.

Sonia was one of only two female veterans to attend the ceremony on the beach at Courseulles-sur-Mer as participants. The other was Major Elizabeth McIntosh, a former nurse in the Canadian Army, who came wearing her uniform. Sonia, the forgotten SOE agent, dressed in white and wore diamond earrings. Elizabeth had landed in Normandy on June 19, 1944. Sonia landed by parachute nine days ahead of the Canadian men sitting in front of her, who were taking in the usual deserved praise.

"Two women in a sea of men weighed down by medals, each discreetly bearing witness to a facet of the war that goes unmentioned too often," said an article in *Le Monde*.

"Neither of them batted an eyelid when a prestigious speaker, Senator Gildas Molgat, wanted to 'pay tribute to the young Canadian men because, unfortunately, there were no women in the army as there are today.'"

"No women?" continued the unnamed writer. "What could Sonia d'Artois, the youngest SOE agent who parachuted into occupied France to train the maquis, have said to him?"

And what would Elizabeth McIntosh, of the Nursing Sisters Association of Canada, have said?

Sonia and Elizabeth were accustomed to the exclusion; as women, they had never truly been given their due. Remembrance ceremonies came and went, lionizing the shrinking group of men who'd risked their lives on those beaches. But Sonia and the other Canadian women involved in the war were often forgotten—as were SOE agents as a whole in France, where they were infrequently mentioned in French history books and eliminated entirely from some museums and even from the official memory.

In Normandy, Sonia, the veteran and mother, was more preoccupied and deeply moved by the sight of the vast cemeteries, the resting places of thousands of soldiers who'd lost their lives in battle. She and they, children of the same generation, had shared this terrain ever so briefly. *J.R. Gregoire, age 22. B.L. Tinney, age 18. H. Stolar, age 21.* Sonia shed tears for all those young lives cut so short. Against the odds she had survived, and they had not.

Just a few days earlier, Sonia had marked her seventieth birthday. By then she'd had three spinal fusions. She had finally learned how to drive. And, to Guy's consternation, she'd taken up a job managing and buying for a series of clothing stores, something she thoroughly enjoyed. Sonia was thriving, and yet she was also embarking on what might be the toughest battle of her life: caring for her ailing husband.

With his dementia worsening, Guy was becoming more forgetful and, on occasion, angrier. He would become disoriented and sometimes lost. He was difficult with doctors, even staging a hunger strike at the hospital following a triple bypass surgery that he'd tried to avoid. Although the doctors advised walking, at one point Sonia couldn't even persuade him to leave the house. Meanwhile the children tried to persuade them both to move back to Montreal, but neither Sonia nor Guy wanted to return to the big city.

Instead Sonia reached out to family living in Hudson, Quebec, where Sonia had so many fond memories of Cedar Cottage. They helped pick out a couple of places, and when Sonia went to take a look, she found a smaller house that would suit them. Daunted by change, Guy wasn't too enthusiastic, but he did not resist. Sonia and Guy finally bought their first house together, only a short distance from the cottage in Como that Sonia had loved so dearly. Once more it was left to her to pack up their things. By April of 1990 Sonia and Guy were finally together in their very own home.

In that home, she cared for him for five long years. Throughout that time Guy became increasingly erratic, sometimes asking her, even as they played cards together, when his wife was coming home. Minutes later he'd be lucid, as if nothing had happened. Finally aware that he was suffering from Alzheimer's, Sonia learned a whole new language, a whole new way of dealing with Guy and cajoling him to do the things he needed to do. She tried to be patient, but sometimes it was beyond even her capacity. When he became intolerable, the doctor would remind Sonia that "it was the illness talking," not Guy. But she could see his personality changing.

There was one upside. Over time, the anger and aggression that had inhabited Guy since he'd returned from Korea simply melted away. When he was lucid, he was the Guy whom Sonia had first met and fallen in love with all those years ago.

It also seemed clear that Guy was increasingly tormented by reliving his wartime memories. He became overly security conscious, locking all the windows and doors every night. He would sometimes hide under tables. In his mind, the invisible fence that Sonia had installed outside to keep the dogs in was the work of Germans. Sonia knew that another drastic change would soon be unavoidable.

One day after she returned from Normandy, Sonia found herself sitting inside the house while Guy sat in the car outside for several hours. By then his driver's licence had been taken away, and he could no longer drive. But somehow he found the keys and then went out and sat in the car, refusing to talk to her.

Sonia had reached her limit. Nadya called her mother from Montreal. She listened as Sonia told her the time had come. It was time to take Guy to Ste. Anne's Hospital for full-time care.

"It was a very difficult decision," said Sonia. "But I knew that it was going to come eventually."

Luckily, it was a relatively smooth transition. It was a hospital that cared mostly for veterans and, as a result, Guy felt at home there. He made friends at the hospital. He was still physically very fit and tried to help others—pushing wheelchairs, getting patients to lunch—so the staff adored him. But he did seem to be living in two worlds: sometimes he'd see it as an army posting and tell Sonia he'd be back in a week.

Sonia stayed by his side, visiting almost every single day. But she was also able to spread her wings a little wider. She visited her younger brother, Michael, in Bermuda, where he lived. She was also determined to finish paying off their house. She increased her mortgage payments, and in February 1999 finally made the last one. What was supposed to take twenty-five years she'd paid off in nine. Sonia and

Guy finally fully owned their very first home. It was a bittersweet achievement; Guy would never see it again.

With time, his cognition faltered. With further health setbacks, his references to the war increased. Then he lost his ability to speak. Sometimes he couldn't quite recognize Sonia, or confused her with someone else. For a while he referred to Nadya as his sister. But somehow his eyes never stopped sparkling, even through the fog.

Sometime in March of that year, Sonia realized that Guy was slipping through her fingers, this time for good. She joined him at the hospital for a few days.

"Let go," she said to him. "You're tired. Have a nice long sleep." And so, eventually, he did.

Guy, at eighty-one, died on a Monday around noon, leaving Sonia one final time. She was quietly holding his hand. After a lifetime of wandering, of adventure, of boundless then frustrated ambition, after a lifetime of fighting, he was finally at peace.

In attendance at Guy's military funeral in Hudson were Chief of Defence Staff General Maurice Baril and Finance Minister Paul Martin. Two of his grandchildren, Annabelle and Patrick, spoke to memorialize him. "One day, perhaps we will learn the secret behind your charm. Maybe one day we will also understand the strength and wisdom buried within your crushing handshake. We might even come to know the same charisma, spirit of adventure and energy of life that so mysteriously expresses itself in the glint of your eyes . . . . But even when that day comes, Pappy, you will still hold an enduring space in our hearts," said Patrick.

On that day, Sonia received Guy's medals and a maroon beret. The Sylla maquis flag he'd been given on his final visit to France was carried as part of the procession.

Sonia felt a profound sadness. She felt guilty about his final years, about his difficult time in hospital. In his memory she began to plant a flowerbed, right outside her kitchen window in the only house they had ever owned.

Months went by. Then, just as she finished it, a white dove appeared at the bird feeder. It stayed for ten days, then flew away.

"That's Guy telling me he's at peace now. That helped me. His demons had gone."

31

ÇA FAIT LONGTEMPS

Sonia • *London, December 2001*

The world in late 2001 had been turned inside out, seized by 9/11, a new war, and a new round of killing and destruction. By December the Taliban had been routed in Afghanistan; they'd finally surrendered Kabul, the city they'd held captive for five years; and Al-Qaeda were on the run. American forces, backed by a "coalition of the willing," were hunting Osama bin Laden in the wilds of Tora Bora, a rotation of air strikes pounding the mountains nearby. British and American soldiers were on the ground. And within weeks Canadian soldiers would begin to arrive in the south, in Kandahar. News of their casualties would soon follow.

"It makes you wonder if there's ever going to be a time when we aren't going to have wars. Are we ever going to reach that time?" Sonia said when asked about the latest wars. "Every big war we have, we say, 'This is the last one.' But we don't seem to learn any lessons from it, and we start all over again."

It had also been a tough year for Sonia on the personal front. Her beloved brother Derek had died. She was devastated. How could time be so cruel?

She flew across the Atlantic again with Nadya to London for the funeral, held at Southwark Cathedral near the Thames. Now seventy-seven, Sonia had a chance to meet her brother's family anew: in his children, and his grandchildren, she would have caught glimpses of the Derek she had adored, the Derek with whom she shared a deep trove of memories. The Derek with whom at times she also shared a treehouse, an allowance—and a mother.

It would have been hard to avoid thinking of Thelma. When she died two decades earlier, it had been left to Derek to tell Sonia that Thelma had left explicit instructions denying her any inheritance and barring her from attending the funeral.

Those injuries, the likes of which Sonia had begun to sustain in childhood, ran deep. They were part of her foundation before it was set. But even war-damaged London had managed to heal. It had once rained incendiaries there. It was once a terrorized city inhabited by terrorized people, but now traffic flowed again. The scars had been patched up—not healed, but patched up. The lively theatre crowds, the swarms of pub-goers, were bigger than ever.

Yet the threat of a flare-up was omnipresent, especially as first-hand witnesses of the war moved on, taking those memories with them; and especially as old, intolerable ideas were made new, and palatable again.

London was as vulnerable as ever, yet it still somehow stood as testament to the possibility of survival and reinvention post conflict.

The war was a period in my life, not my whole life.

With Derek and Bunny gone and both her parents deceased, Sonia was all that remained of her first family. Michael, her much younger half-brother, was the only sibling left. She would begin to spend more time with him and his family in the south of France, where they lived. For weeks at a stretch there she'd walk, read endlessly, and learn to become more of the (sometimes mischievous) big sister that sheer distance had prevented her from being before. "As soon as she thought I was getting pompous or out of order or pedantic or telling people what to do too much . . . she would tear in and pull me apart," said Michael. "And she loved doing it."

There were serious moments, too, when Sonia wondered out loud to Michael's wife, Zoe, and within his earshot, what her world might look like had she not married Guy and moved to Canada. Underlying the question, Michael thought, was whether her life might have been "easier."

Sonia had led a peripatetic life, ruled first by the troubles of a broken home and then by the army, along with all the constraints that came with raising six children, in large part on her own. In her final years, however, Sonia was unencumbering herself of all that had constrained her. Since Guy left her she'd become more open about sharing what remained of her memories of the war, memories that were fading in a world consumed by new conflicts and moving at warp speed.

Sonia had been disillusioned by decades of journalists, writers, and historians wanting to tell her story and either failing or getting it wrong. And in the background, always, were her concerns about outshining Guy. But in 2001 she agreed to take part in an interview about her life and career at the SOE.

A Hollywood film starring Cate Blanchett was in the works, based on a novel about the SOE by British writer Sebastian Faulks. The story concerned a young Scottish woman who travels to France and joins the resistance in the hope of finding and saving her wartime lover, an RAF pilot. The film was to be titled *Charlotte Gray*. The main character was to be a composite of several well-known SOE agents, including Violette Szabó and Sonia's longtime friend Nancy Wake, who by then had been recognized as one of the most decorated agents of the Second World War.

As part of the run-up to that film, a major television documentary on the women of SOE was also in the works, titled *Behind Enemy Lines: The Real Charlotte Grays*, by director Jenny Morgan. The documentary would feature interviews with four surviving female SOE agents: Pearl Witherington, Nancy Wake, Lise de Baissac, and the youngest, Sonia d'Artois.

With the camera trained on her, Sonia looked relaxed as she related some of what had happened all those years ago. She spoke about growing up a tomboy and a daredevil. She spoke about getting bored in the WAAF and asking her father to intervene on her behalf. She talked about her arduous training, about meeting Guy for the first time, about getting shot with Sydney in the car at Bar-sur-Seine.

During a break in the filming Sonia and Nadya were taken by car to go for lunch. It took longer than Sonia had anticipated, but finally the group walked into a hotel. A door was opened for Sonia and she walked into the room, where someone was already sitting with their back to the door. When she noticed that there were cameras and that they were already filming, she understood she was being reunited with someone—perhaps an old hand from Buckmaster's office.

Then she walked around the couch and came face to face with him—and "just couldn't believe it."

His shoulders were a little hunched over, his hair white, his face soft with wrinkles. He was ninety-one now, but she recognized him immediately. In an instant she was embracing him with a wide smile.

"*Oh, bonjour, comment ça va?*" she whispered, her chin resting on his stooped shoulder. She was simply beaming.

Sydney Hudson was crying. "*Ça fait longtemps?* It's been a long time?" he asked.

She nodded. "*Ça fait longtemps. Très longtemps.*"

It had been more than fifty-seven years since they'd last laid eyes on each other. Sonia was stunned to see what had become of that broad, athletic man she'd loved all those years ago, but she was "very happy" to see him. On his wrist was the watch she'd given him for his thirty-fourth birthday. Sydney still had a sense of occasion. And he was so obviously still in love with Sonia.

There were tears shed around the room. No one yet knew they were witnessing a reunion of former lovers.

A keen-eyed cameraman, however, noticed the incredible warmth between them, the way they looked at each other. He brought it to Jenny Morgan's attention. She quietly approached Nadya to ask an awkward question: Was it possible that Sonia and Sydney had had a relationship?

Nadya told Jenny that she would never ask her mother such a question, but why didn't Jenny?

The next day, she did ask. Sonia looked at Nadya and said, "I always thought the circle would close."

Then she admitted that it was true; they had been in love. Sonia had never discussed this with her family, but now that the question was asked, now that Guy and his mother had passed away and she couldn't cause them distress, it was time.

There would be no mention of it in the documentary. But Sonia later told Nadya the whole story.

Nearly sixty years after they first met, Sonia and Sydney struck up a new friendship, spending a long time together remembering the old days. She met his second wife, Ruth, with whom she felt an instant kinship. Ruth had grown up in Essen, Germany; her family had lost everything in the Allied bombardment of that city. Her Jewish mother was reported to the authorities, incarcerated in a Gestapo prison, and then, in the final days of Nazi rule, shot along with dozens of other prisoners. Sydney had met Ruth when he worked in Germany after the war, and they married soon after.

The three of them—Sonia, Sydney, and Ruth—even travelled to France together. On the meandering roads of Le Mans, Sonia and Sydney walked in their own, much younger footsteps. They visited the Château des Bordeaux and, thanks to its new owner, they had a chance to walk its grounds and the forest out back where they'd once camped out, fearful of German soldiers showing up.

They stopped at No. 8 rue Mangeard, that little house where they'd woken up to explosions, heralding the arrival of D-Day. They wandered around narrow streets that were entirely unaware of their story, of the youthful versions of themselves who'd come to know the city by heart. In a few days Michel and Madeleine were ready to say farewell to Le Mans one last time, never to return.

After years of their stories being sensationalized and criticized, Sonia could finally see evidence of genuine recognition of their work. The names of the fallen were inscribed on the SOE Memorial's Roll of Honour at Valençay, where the first SOE agent had landed.

And in London, her lost friends were immortalized with a statue overlooking the River Thames. The face that stares out from that monument was—and remains—that of Sonia's friend Violette Szabó.

In the autumn of one's life, there is very little time left. Sydney decided late in life to write a memoir, and since Sonia figured prominently in its pages, he asked her to read it. He'd also written a novel based on his SOE days and partly on his love affair with Sonia. It was never published, but he shared a copy with her as well, all 425 pages of it.

Sydney Hudson, DSO, died in Scotland in 2005. He was ninety-four years old.

32

SONIA'S WAY

Sonia • *Salt Spring Island, March 2002*

On the 20th of March, 2002, Sonia d'Artois was sitting in her daughter's spacious living room on Salt Spring Island and looking out over the placid ocean, trying to keep warm in the morning chill. Outside, the verdant surroundings were dotted with dormant ferns still waiting to come to life. It wasn't unusual for the odd deer to pass nearby. And the stillness of the water would sometimes be punctuated by the occasional log or an otter poking its head up. The silence lent itself to reflection. There, Sonia would have felt at peace.

Cognizant that Sonia was getting on in years, Nadya had cajoled her mother to sit down and tell her story from beginning to end. It had taken years to persuade her that it was important for the family to know, for the grandchildren and great-grandchildren to hear the whole story directly from her. This would be a different experience from the fleeting interviews she'd given the press. Nadya had found a professional interviewer by the name of Robin Fowler, who agreed to conduct the interview and produce a book of Sonia's recollections for the family.

From the start, Robin tried to put Sonia at ease. She made it clear that this would be Sonia's interview. She could say as much or as little as she wanted.

Once they settled in, Robin started at the beginning.

"I would like to know your full name at birth," she said.

"Sonia Esme Florence Butt. I was supposed to be Florence. But I found out forty years later that it was Juliet."

Sonia was referring to the belated discovery that she'd been living for decades with the wrong middle names. She had long believed them to be Esme Florence, but the surprise unearthing of her birth certificate revealed that she was in fact Sonia *Juliet* Esme Butt. Juliet was one of the names of her maternal grandmother, who'd passed away long before she was born.

And from there, Sonia's story unfolded, from one surprising turn of events to another. Robin was riveted from the very beginning. Sonia seemed to her confident, comfortable—even excited—and at peace. "Sonia had an incredible story to tell, and she knew that," Robin said.

Over five days, a Wednesday to a Sunday, in two sessions a day, Sonia spoke about her family, her early days, her constant displacement; about crossing the English Channel, about training, about fighting, and about falling in love—twice—in a time of war. She spoke about a partnership with Guy that was tested early, by distance and indiscretion, about a marriage she said was best described as "turbulent" and yet stood the test of time. About the bond they built and maintained even across vast distances, one letter at a time.

When speaking about her painful childhood, Sonia was matter-of-fact. When she spoke about her own family, she was thoughtful and loving and warm. Throughout there was a lightness in Sonia's telling, punctuated often with her distinctively gentle, warm giggle.

By then, Sonia was almost seventy-eight years old, a grandmother several times over. In the face of countless challenges, she had largely been the author of her own life. But for the first time she was fully recounting her past victories and mistakes, her sacrifices, her choices. In her own voice, she was finally telling her story. On her own terms.

EPILOGUE: NEVER TOO LATE

Montreal, 2007

Sonia was dressed in a white shirt tucked underneath a black velvet jacket, her brilliant grey-white hair softly framing her face. She stood solemnly, staring at the shoulder of the uniformed man who pinned the medal on her chest while a handful of people began to clap.

It was now sixty-three years since Sonia d'Artois had landed by parachute into France, an underestimated, poorly understood, sick, and injured young woman still bent on doing her part. The country she helped liberate was only now acknowledging the achievements of her twenty-year-old self. She was being appointed a Knight of the Order of the Legion of Honour (Légion d'honneur).

Together, Sonia and Guy had become one of the most decorated couples of the Second World War. But Sonia wasn't counting. And she dismissed any notion that hers was any greater a generation than those who have come since.

"We didn't know we would rise to the occasion. We didn't know any more than you guys know," she once told an interviewer.

But she had defied all expectations. She thrived when they predicted she would fall apart. She upheld a marriage some said would unravel in months. She lived in the present while other survivors, including her husband, were diminished by the weight of the past. She also imbued the next generation with the belief that they too could do anything.

Sonia, the former agent, the immigrant, mother, grandmother, and great-grandmother, died in 2014 at ninety years old. She was buried next to Guy. The unlikely couple, from two sides of an ocean, now share a headstone. Below Guy's inscription is Sonia's:

SONIA F. ESME BUTT, MBE, L. D'H

1924 – 2014

WAAF, FANY, SOE

ÉPOUSE DU MAJ. L.G. D'ARTOIS

A NOTE ON SOURCES

I came to the story of the Special Operations Executive very late. It was only in 2019 that I began to understand its unique role in the Second World War—and the significant role of women, as well as Canadians, within it.

Though my endeavour began many years after both Sonia and Guy d'Artois had passed on, from the start I wanted to write a book that told their version of events to the extent possible. That meant relying on pre-existing interviews with Sonia and Guy, with all the limitations that inevitably entails, including the inability to interrogate, ask follow-up questions, and probe deeper into their thoughts and recollections. The result is a book of non-fiction about their lives together and apart, reconstructed from dozens of sources and brought all together for the first time.

Incredibly, thanks to Nadya Murdoch and her determined efforts, Sonia's voice and story, from start to finish, are preserved in a taped conversation with professional interviewer Robin Fowler, then of Speak Memories Publishing. After a lifetime of disappointments in the many attempts to tell her story, Sonia had the opportunity to correct the record. Nadya and Robin encouraged her to tell the story in whatever way she wished, giving her agency to include or omit whatever details she wished. That makes the interview both authentic and selective, and yet it remains an incredibly rich glimpse into Sonia's life and thoughts and personality.

Sonia's telling inevitably contained some errors, and even some contradictions with some of her own earlier versions of certain events, or those of others who were also witnesses. By comparing her stories and consulting other sources I tried to approximate the events as they happened. If contradictions remained, I mentioned them in the notes.

Luckily, an audio recording of Guy speaking of his exploits in France is also preserved by the Musée Royal 22e Régiment at La Citadelle de Québec. It was only thanks to the talented archivist Jason Thiffault that we learned of the audio's existence. This recording was more of a lecture—a "show-and-tell" monologue apparently aimed at younger officers that was meant to be accompanied by some of the hundreds of photographs he'd ordered taken or took himself while he operated as an agent and military organizer in France. To hear Guy, in his own voice, describing his life and work in France in his first language was invaluable, and the recording was an important resource in telling his story.

Both Guy and Sonia were also both interviewed, in the early 1980s, by writer Rob Forsyth, with an eye to making a mini-series with producer Ronald Cohen that was to run on CBC Television. Sadly, *The d'Artois Story*, a three-part series that was to cost $7.5M CAD to make, was scrapped because of CBC funding cuts. But a dossier of the notes from those interviews survives in the Rob Forsyth Fonds at the Clara Thomas Archives and Special Collections at York University in Toronto. Again, this resource came with limitations. Direct quotes were scarce (and sometimes it wasn't clear whether Sonia or Guy was speaking), and the notes were only a résumé of what was heard in the interviews. But again, they were nevertheless rich with information and helped confirm several facts and scenarios.

Beyond those sources, I mined book chapters and articles in various newspapers and magazines for Sonia's and Guy's words over the years. Some of those articles were riddled with errors. Teasing fiction from fact was arduous and sometimes impossible. Nevertheless, I was able to uncover wonderful detail about places and events that would have otherwise been unavailable. The extensive coverage of their story after they arrived in Canada in 1944 in itself painted a picture of the incredible reception they were given as heroes.

Sydney Hudson's book, *Undercover Operator*, was a key source in telling Sonia's story, as they worked closely together throughout the summer of 1944. Sydney wrote the book later in life, and after their reunion, he asked Sonia to look it over to review the sections that told stories she knew. Even then, their accounts of some events differed, sometimes in the timing, sometimes in more substantial aspects. Again, this is occasionally nodded to in the notes.

Several French resistance figures who worked alongside Guy d'Artois have also written memoirs (published and unpublished) and kept notes about their extraordinary experiences. Sadly, none of those witnesses is alive, and I could not interrogate their stories. Thanks to each of their families, I accessed those documents and mined them for anecdotes, stories, and descriptions of key events during the summer of 1944. But the stories and the battles they fought were complicated. Sometimes they didn't add up. Still, to the extent possible, I tried to cross-reference the stories they contained and compared them to those Guy had told, in an effort to approximate true events. To further verify certain stories, I also consulted published local histories.

It is important to note here that countless original SOE documents are missing, thanks to "weeding and a fire" at the SOE headquarters in 1945, according to the National Archives. All of the Camp X files are also said to have been destroyed in a fire, and the camp itself subsequently razed to the ground. Countless books have been written about the SOE, which were helpful in filling the gaps. But there are facts that will never be known.

Still, documents and articles and personnel files and military records as well as several war diaries were graciously made available by the Musée Royal 22e Régiment in Quebec City, as well as Library and Archives Canada, the Canadian War Museum, and the National Archives and the Imperial War Museum in the U.K.

Nadya Murdoch also made available an invaluable collection of documents, newspaper clippings, photographs, and other records that Guy and Sonia and the family had amassed relating to their story. Guy had meticulously kept documents pertaining to his career. Some of them were only photocopies, but they were valuable nevertheless.

The story was rounded out through several conversations, some on the record, others on background, with family, family friends, surviving veterans, colleagues, historians (professional and amateur), and archivists.

I travelled to the U.K., France, and Quebec City, to several locations important to Guy and Sonia's story—from the church at Marylebone in London where they married to the little house Sonia and Sydney rented in Le Mans and, with Nadya's guidance, to the streets of Charolles and the café and villa hideout that Maman Lucienne ran and where Guy stayed and held court. Most physical descriptions of these places are largely based on my own observations. I have gathered fragments of documents from a number of sources, written either by local historians or the players themselves, some of them obscure and messy and difficult to decode.

Names were incredibly challenging. Agents had code names and aliases—often more than one. I tried to simplify where I could. Even non-agents emerged in this story with multiple names. To simplify those, I tried to only use legal names while nodding to nicknames in the endnotes.

Everything in quotations either came from an interview (on tape or in a newspaper/television/radio piece) or represents a person's recollections of what was said in dialogue. Any hint at inner thoughts or temperament is based on a statement or observation.

There are, indeed, many aspects of this story that I simply could not fit into one book—players who would have been interesting to explore further, events that had a direct effect on Sonia's and Guy's lives, and ones that loomed large in the background—but naturally I had to overlook or just nod to many of them in the interest of focusing on Sonia and Guy's story, and in the interest of finishing the book. Where errors occur—and surely there will be some, given the gaps—they are unintended and I made every effort to avoid them.

The final result, then, is an amalgam, based on snippets of stories that have been brought together for the first time in one document. But it is still an approximation. My driving motivation and hope are that even in its imperfect state, this book can be of value to future students of history, and a starting point on which others can build.

NOTES

PROLOGUE: LUNCH IN PARIS, 1944

1 **most popular tearooms:** Sydney Hudson, *Undercover Operator: An SOE Agent's Experiences in France and the Far East*, p. 116.
thirty pounds in four months: Rob Forsyth, *d'Artois Interviews*, notes from interviews with Guy and Sonia d'Artois, p. 53. Rob Forsyth Fonds, F0545, Clara Thomas Archives and Special Collections, York University.
2 **for a frank conversation:** Sydney Hudson, *Undercover Operator*, p. 116.
3 **for a debrief:** Report on Judex mission, p. 8, HS7/134, The National Archives, United Kingdom
"the most depressing moment": Sydney Hudson, *Undercover Operator*, p. 116.

1: SEEKING REFUGE

8 **this late summer day:** It's not entirely clear from the existing documentation whether Sonia's voyage happened just before or just after Britain's declaration of war.
made it on board: Sonia d'Artois, interview with Robin Fowler. Speak Memories Publishing, 2002.
"a horrendous journey": Ibid.
"does not include tip": Ibid.
"clear conscience": Neville Chamberlain's Declaration of War, September 3, 1939. Text accessed at www.theguardian.com/world/2009/sep/06/second-world-war-declaration-chamberlain.
9 **Hundreds of thousands of children:** Allan Allport, *Britain at Bay: The Epic Story of the Second World War, 1938–1941*, pp. 427–428.

10 **"You're completely alone":** Sonia d'Artois, interview with Robin Fowler.
The crowds and queues disappeared: Allan Allport, *Britain at Bay*, pp. 427–428.
11 **Nothing, it seemed, was immune:** Ibid., p. 35.
one attack every other day: Tony Craig. "Sabotage! The Origins, Development and Impact of the IRA's Infrastructural Bombing Campaigns 1939–1997, Intelligence and National Security, 25:3, 309-326, 2010.
"sabotage and subversion": M.R.D. Foot, *SOE in France: An Account of the Work of the British Special Operations Executive in France, 1940–44*, p. 7.
"elementary theory": Ibid., pp. 3–8.
12 **to do their part:** For a basic outline of women's participation in the Second World War see https://www.gov.uk/government/news/the-women-of-the-second-world-war.
Thelma Esme Florence Gordon: There are various spellings of Esme in both Thelma's and Sonia's names, sometimes with an extra "e." In this book I have opted to use Esme, with one exception to come.
she was raised in India: Most of the details on Thelma's life and history were provided by Sonia d'Artois, in an interview with Robin Fowler.
13 **daughter was concerned, cruel:** Sonia d'Artois, ibid.
dead on the train tracks: *The Sutton Coldfield News*, January 1, 1910, p. 12.
"his family and friends": Ibid.
14 **"suicide while temporarily insane":** *Birmingham Daily Gazette*, January 1, 1910, p. 7.
"unhingements of the mind": *Dudley Chronicle*, January 8, 1910, p. 6.
left his young wife, Sarah: According to a family history written by Janet Upton and Heather Brown. D'Artois family private papers.
join the Indian Army: Ibid. Impossible to verify from documents provided by the RAF as the documents pertaining to first years of his career are illegible.
May 14, 1924: Sonia Butt birth certificate, d'Artois family private papers.
"to marry a third time": *Yorkshire Post and Leeds Intelligencer*, November 17, 1928, p. 13.
15 **"a decent girl":** Justice Hill, quoted in ibid.
"by his own request": L.A.K. Butt, "Record of Service in the Royal Air Force." Entry dated: January 1, 1929. Royal Air Force, RAF Disclosures—Veterans.
antipathy for her daughter: Sonia d'Artois, interview with Robin Fowler.
"beating and starving Sonia Butt": *Daily Herald*, June 13, 1930, p. 1.
16 **"I was in London":** Sonia d'Artois, interview with Robin Fowler.
as Auntie Vi: Her real name was Violet.
"I loved it there": Sonia d'Artois, interview with Robin Fowler.
"he just couldn't prevent": Sonia d'Artois, ibid.
17 **"a hole in her heart":** Ibid.

18 **who lived there for seventeen years:** See a list of celebrities who lived there at Office de Tourism de Saint-Paul-de-Vence, www.saint-pauldevence.com/en/history/celebrities.

to get her on the train: Rob Forsyth, *d'Artois Interviews*, notes from interviews with Guy and Sonia d'Artois, p. 90. Rob Forsyth Fonds, F0545, Clara Thomas Archives and Special Collections, York University, and Sonia d'Artois, interview with Robin Fowler.

2: FINDING A WAY

19 **attacked it with a torpedo:** *Coventry Evening Telegraph*, September 4, 1939, p. 1.

main course: Francis M. Carroll, *Athenia Torpedoed: The U-Boat Attack That Ignited the Battle of the Atlantic*, p. 24.

inaugurated its casualty list: Ibid., p. 25.

20 **in the West:** Ibid.

nearly sixty thousand: "Canada at Britain's Side: 1939–1942," *Canada and the Second World War*, Canadian War Museum, https://www.warmuseum.ca/cwm/exhibitions/chrono/1931britains_side_e.html.

twenty-two-year-old Guy d'Artois: "Love Outlasts Danger of War," *Montreal Gazette*, February 9, 1985, p. H1.

21 **The Battle of Vimy Ridge:** Tim Cook, *Vimy: The Battle and the Legend*, p. 64.

"the birth of a nation": Ibid., p. 436.

gave birth to her second child: Copy of Guy d'Artois's baptism certificate, noting birthdate on April 9 and baptism on April 15, d'Artois family private papers.

In 1912 she'd married: Marriage certificate. D'Artois family private papers.

thirteen years her senior: d'Artois family history, d'Artois family private papers.

and settled in Quebec: According to family tree by Pierre Courchesne. D'Artois family private papers.

22 **Calixte Lionel Alsace d'Artois:** Guy d'Artois, baptism certificate. D'Artois family private papers.

an offer of funding: This came from a delegation led by a wealthy francophone Canadian Dr. Arthur Mignault. Serge Bernier, *The Royal 22e Regiment, 1914–1999*, p. 16.

Royal Canadien-Français: Ibid., p. 17. The official date for the start of recruitment was October 20, 1914, and it became the 22nd battalion in the Canadian Expeditionary Force.

Montreal and Quebec City: Ibid., p. 17

"Enrolez-vous dans les régiments Canadiens-Français": "Enrol in the Canadian-French regiments." Recruitment poster circa 1915, at Musée Royal 22e Régiment, La Citadelle de Québec.

23 **Royal 22e Régiment:** Serge Bernier, *Royal 22e Regiment,* p. 16.
more than sixty thousand Canadians: G.W.L. Nicholson, *Canadian Expeditionary Force, 1914–1919: Official History of the Canadian Army in the First World War,* p. 535.
Thousands and thousands of veterans: Ibid.

24 **a chauffeur-driven car:** Bob d'Artois, eldest son of Guy and Sonia, interview with author.
"to see your little Guy": Guy d'Artois, letter to father, undated. d'Artois family private papers.
Petit Guy was among the first students: Guy d'Artois, "Dossier d'étudiant," Les archives du Collège Jean-de-Brébeuf.
French Jesuit missionary: College history, www.brebeuf.qc.ca/le-college/jean-de-brebeuf.
Trudeau, who attended three years after Guy: John English, *Citizen of the World: The Life of Pierre Elliott Trudeau, Volume One: 1919–1968*, p. 26.
Guy enrolled in classical studies: In some of the Brébeuf documents and photos, Guy is named as "Guy Artois" with the "d" dropped.

25 **294 out of 900:** Guy d'Artois's report card, d'Artois family private papers. Also, in a document titled "Anciens du Collège Jean-de-Brébeuf" it is noted that "*au premier semestre, 1931–32, en Syntaxe, il a obtenu 294 sur 900—donc, descendu de classe.*" Les archives du Collège Jean-de-Brébeuf.
a good practical joker: La page des anciens, October 1943, Les archives du Collège Jean-de- Brébeuf.
the nearby airport: Michel Gariepy and Renée Hudon-Auger, "Major Guy d'Artois du Royal 22e Régiment." *Gens de Mon Pays*. Archives Radio-Canada. Broadcast. October 23, 1977.
Guy's father lost everything: Bob d'Artois, interview with the author.
re-establish a legal practice: Sonia d'Artois, interview with Robin Fowler.
"and what about tomorrow?": Michel Gariepy and Renée Hudon-Auger, "Major Guy d'Artois."
Guy joined the militia: Corps école d'officiers canadien was the French-Canadian universities' equivalent of the Canadian Officers Training Corps. Guy d'Artois' "États de Service, Armée du Canada," d'Artois private papers.

26 **"among our young people":** J. Paré, recommendation letter, dated November 2, 1937, d'Artois family private papers.
"very energetic, serious": Illegibly signed recommendation letter from the "Gérant-Directeur" of J.L. Guay & Frère, Limitée, dated August 5, 1936, d'Artois family private papers.
for sixty dollars a month: Letter of offer, J-Ernest Laforce, sous-ministre at the Ministère de la colonisation, dated January 14, 1939, d'Artois family private

papers. The letter indicated that he should report to a Jean-Joseph Levesque, a chemist in the ministry, based at L'École des hautes études commerciales à Montreal. Another handwritten letter, from a Gérard Delorme, "professeur de chimie," dated October 5, 1938, says that Guy was taking courses in physics and chemistry at L'École des hautes études commerciales. Guy's military record often mentioned that he was a student. However, in a search via Université de Montréal and L'École des hautes études commerciales, archivists could not produce any documentary evidence that he formally attended the university.

company sergeant major: État du service dans l'armée canadienne, indicating he worked his way up to sous-officier breveté de 2e classe. D'Artois private papers.

On June 29, 1938: "Physician's or Coroner's certificate for Canadian National Railways, Transportation of Corpse." Document stamped July 1, 1938, d'Artois family private papers.

age fifty-six: "Inhumation de M. J.-V. Artois" (the spelling of d'Artois is the paper's). *La Tribune*. July 4, 1938, p. 7.

27 **completely off the table:** J.L. Granatstein, *Canada at War: Conscription, Diplomacy, and Politics*, p. 108.

seven days after Britain's: David Bercuson. *Our Finest Hour: Canada Fights the Second World War*, p. 28

to the tune of fifty dollars a month: "Particulars of family of an Officer or soldier of the Canadian Active Service Force." Dated 22 January 1940. d'Artois military record. Library and Archives Canada.

3: LEAVING HOME

31 **soldiers headed to war:** Documents titled "Troops Convoys from Canada" and "Ships Carrying Canadian Troops" (Appendix C), both appended to CMHQ 45: Major C.P. Stacy (historical officer CMHQ), *Situation of the Canadian Forces in the United Kingdom, Summer 1941: Part IV*, accessed online at www.canada.ca/content/dam/themes/defence/caf/militaryhistory/dhh/reports/cmhq-reports/cmhq045.pdf. See also War Diary, Convalescent Depot No. 1, Royal Canadian Army Medical Corps, December 39 to June 41. Entry dated January 31, 1940. Library and Archives Canada. RG24-C-3, Volume number 15981, File number 283.

32 **Troop Convoy No. 3:** "Troops Convoys from Canada."

They held morning parade: War Diary, Convalescent Depot No. 1. Entry dated January 26, 1940.

arrival in Halifax, at four: Ibid.

Empress of Australia: The ship, incidentally, was German made, destined to become a royal yacht for Kaiser Wilhelm II before it was seized by the British in 1919, acquired by Canadian Pacific, then finally served as a royal yacht—but instead for King George during his 1939 visit to Canada. With the outbreak of war it was transformed into a troop-carrying ship, retrofitted with a lone 76 mm gun to complement its new, less frolicsome purpose.

33 **The infantry rejected him:** Sonia d'Artois, interview with Robin Fowler.

necessitated surgery in his late teens: d'Artois medical record, Library and Archives Canada.

No. 1 Convalescent Depot: Guy d'Artois, military record, Library and Archives Canada.

On January 20, 1940: Ibid., and War Diary, Convalescent Depot No. 1. Entry dated January 22, 1940. It said Guy to be "A/Sgt, effect 20 jan 40." Also see d'Artois Attestation paper, military record, Library and Archives Canada.

physical training instructor: Michel Gariepy and Renée Hudon-Auger, "Major Guy d'Artois du Royal 22e Régiment." *Gens de Mon Pays*. Archives Radio-Canada. Broadcast. October 23, 1977. Title also noted in "Extract from a summary of the Military Career of Major Guy d'Artois." D'Artois family private papers.

34 **not a single survivor:** *Daily Mirror*, January 24, 1940, p. 1.

"very capable": War Diary, Convalescent Depot No. 1, Royal Canadian Army Medical Corps, December 39 to June 41. Entry dated January 31, 1940. Library and Archives Canada. RG24-C-3, Volume number 15981, File number 283.

"This must cease forthwith": "Daily Orders" dated January 31, 1940. Ibid.

"closely guarded secrets": *Northern Whig*, February 9, 1940, p. 5.

on their fifth day: War Diary, Convalescent Depot No. 1.

including U-boats: War Diary, Convalescent Depot No. 1. "We were without our escort for quite a while," wrote Captain D.L. Darey in the unit's war diary. February 7, 1940.

35 **Major-General Andrew G.L. McNaughton:** *Birmingham Mail*, February 8, 1940, p. 10.

a "wee girl" handed out chocolates: *Daily Record*, February 9, 1940, p. 10.

"sang themselves hoarse": Ibid.

"has arrived in this country": Ibid.

36 **"skates over his shoulder":** *Daily Mirror*, February 9, 1940, p. 1.

wearing their First World War ribbons: *Nottingham Evening Post*, February 9, 1940, p. 6.

St. Valentine's Day, 1940: d'Artois military record, Library and Archives Canada.

37 **"seen in an intoxicated state":** Daily Orders, dated April 30, 1940. War Diary, Convalescent Depot No. 1.

Guy was confirmed as sergeant: d'Artois military record, entry dated April 20, 1940, Library and Archives Canada.

Britain's new wartime prime minister: Erik Larson, *The Splendid and the Vile: A Saga of Churchill, Family, and Defiance During the Blitz*, pp. 11–16.

"This should cause some action": War Diary, No. 1 Convalescent Depot. Entry dated May 9, 1940.

38 **wrote Captain Darey:** Ibid. Entry dated May 28, 1940.

and their kit: Major C.P. Stacy, CMHQ031. No. 1 Canadian Convalescent Depot, Brixham, Devon, June 7, 1941, p. 4. Accessed online at www.canada.ca/en/department-national-defence/services/military-history/history-heritage/official-military-history-lineages/reports/military-headquarters-1940-1948/no1-canadian-convalescent-depot-brixham-devon.html.

39 **Canadian Red Cross:** War Diary, No. 1 Canadian Convalescent Depot. Entries dated September 13 and October 1, 1940.

"I wish you the same": Guy d'Artois, postcard to his mother, October 10, 1940. d'Artois family private papers.

another on orderly duty: War Diary, No. 1 Canadian Convalescent Depot, Daily Orders, December 6, 1940.

"throughout the course": Letter titled "Extract of Report of Command Course Physical Training," dated May 27, 1940, at Aldershot. From Colonel L. Henshaw at Aldershot. d'Artois private papers.

"intelligent and very popular": Major G.D. Kersley, GSO for Physical Training Southern Command at Salisbury. Letter titled "Extract from Report of Remedial P.T. Course," stamped April 2, 1941. Course was held at the depot from March 17 to 29, 1941. D'Artois family private papers.

40 **"Wars are not won by evacuations":** Erik Larson, *The Splendid and the Vile*, p. 58.

fiery Churchill intoned: Ibid.

41 **"enormous":** As quoted by Odette Coupal, *Le Petit Journal*, December 27, 1942, p. 19.

One day, at nine-fifteen a.m.: War Diary, Convalescent Depot No. 1. Entry dated May 20, 1941.

a visitor from Canadian military headquarters: The visitor was Major John P. Page. His report, "Defence Scheme—No. 1 Convalescent Depot, RCAMC," is Appendix A to CMHQ031, Major C.P. Stacey, No. 1 Canadian Convalescent Depot, Brixham, Devon, June 7, 1941. Accessed online.

"as a guide for enemy aircraft": Ibid.

42 **"defeat and humiliation":** Philippe de Vomécourt, *An Army of Amateurs*, p. 14.

Behind the scenes: M.R.D. Foot, *SOE in France: An Account of the Work of the British Special Operations Executive in France, 1940–44*, p. 8.

4: FINDING HOME

43 **enlisting in the armed forces:** Sonia d'Artois, interview with Robin Fowler. Also in *d'Artois Interviews*, notes from interviews with Guy and Sonia d'Artois, p. 2. Rob Forsyth Fonds, F0545 Clara Thomas Archives and Special Collections, York University.

blackout order in effect until 5:27: *The Daily Herald*, May 12, 1941, p. 1.

44 **"a constant procession":** Ibid.

lives of at least fourteen hundred people: Erik Larson, *The Splendid and the Vile: A Saga of Churchill, Family, and Defiance During the Blitz*, p. 478.

"the most wanton raid of the war": *The Daily Herald*, May 12, 1941, p. 1.

Churchill's becoming prime minister: Erik Larson, *The Splendid and the Vile*, p. 480.

six high-explosive bombs: Ibid.

The chamber itself: Ibid.

Big Ben suffered a direct hit: Ibid.

mechanism remained intact: Ibid.

"have been crowned": *The Daily Herald*, May 12, 1941, p. 1.

45 **between the rails below:** *News Chronicle*, September 20, 1940, p. 4.

plan for how to decide: Sonia d'Artois, interview with Robin Fowler.

suited her best: Ibid.

46 **in exactly this way:** At least one source indicates as much: "Due to many women not knowing what to expect of the different services open to them, the aesthetic appearance of the uniforms was known to have played a large role in the selection process." See "Women of the Second World War: Wrens." Accessed at https://twmuseumsandarchives.medium.com/women-of-the-second-world-war-wrens-e6d395812476.

Sarah Churchill: Sonia d'Artois, interview with Robin Fowler.

"knew you'd come through": Sonia recalled her father saying, in interview with Robin Fowler.

47 **his new wife, Mina:** Mina Gascoigne Butt, also known as Ann, or later, Granny Ann, likely the genesis of her nickname "Gan." She is the mother of Michael Butt, Sonia's youngest sibling.

classic custody battle: Sonia d'Artois, interview with Robin Fowler.

"hurt you and haunt you": Ibid.

48 **"making of butter and cheese":** Copy of Certificate, Wiltshire School of Domestic Science, Trowbridge, dated May 1940. d'Artois family private papers.

British Red Cross Society: Copy of British Red Cross Society certificate in home nursing, dated March 19, 1940. d'Artois family private papers.

Derek had enlisted: Derek Butt, record of service, courtesy of Johnny Butt, via email.

acting squadron leader: L.A.K. Butt, "Record of Service in the Royal Air Force," Royal Air Force, RAF Disclosures—Veterans.

49 **"shall not be extinguished":** General Charles de Gaulle, speaking on the BBC, June 18, 1940. Quoted in "French May Raise Arms Here," *The Daily Mirror*, June 19, 1940.

5: A CHANGE OF DIRECTION

50 **exactly six months:** According to a document in SOE file she joined the WAAF on 14.11.41.

the seaside town of Morecambe: Sonia d'Artois, interview with Robin Fowler.

"road to victory": WAAF recruitment poster, Second World War, Imperial War Museum, accessed online at www.iwm.org.uk/collections/item/object/9763. Similar posters by the same artist are from circa 1941.

51 **joined the Land Army:** Sonia d'Artois, interview with Robin Fowler.

food to recovering pilots: Ibid.

Churchill happened to be: Erik Larson, *The Splendid and the Vile: A Saga of Churchill, Family, and Defiance During the Blitz*, p. 485.

52 **"all in the same boat now":** Ibid., p. 486. Also see James MacGregor Burns, *Roosevelt: The Soldier of Freedom, 1940–1945*, p. 362.

"saved and thankful": Ibid, p. 487. See also Winston S. Churchill, *The Second World War*, Volume 3, p. 608.

"date which will live in infamy": James MacGregor Burns, *Roosevelt*, p. 368.

mass murder of Jews: Patrick Montague. *Chelmno and the Holocaust: The History of Hilter's First Death Camp*, p. 6.

53 **as an aircraftwoman, 2nd class:** Sonia d'Artois, interview with Robin Fowler.

an aunt in Belgium: Kate Vigurs, *Mission France: The True History of the Women of SOE*, p. 171.

54 **wartime would allow:** Sonia d'Artois, interview with Robin Fowler.

55 **was named Michael Todd:** Sonia d'Artois, ibid.

felt sorry for him: Rob Forsyth, *d'Artois Interviews*, notes from interviews with Guy and Sonia d'Artois, p. 7. Rob Forsyth Fonds, F0545, Clara Thomas Archives and Special Collections, York University.

56 **"He had a direct connection":** Sonia d'Artois, interview with Robin Fowler and in interview with Rob Forsyth, ibid. It was impossible to independently verify this, but in various interviews Sonia said that her father was aware of the SOE and was helping to recruit on their behalf.

while he lived in France: Maurice Buckmaster, *They Fought Alone: The Story of British Agents in France*, p. 16.

"highly embryonic": Ibid., p. 18.

57 **Ford Motor Company:** Ibid., p. 15.

"boycotts and riots": Hugh Dalton, *The Fateful Years: Memoirs, 1931–1945*, p. 368.

left to civilians: Hugh Dalton, letter to Clement Attlee, July 2, 1940. Dalton Papers.

"set Europe ablaze": David Stafford, *Britain and European Resistance 1940–1945: A Survey of the Special Operations Executive, with Documents*, p. 46. Also see M.R.D. Foot, *SOE in France: An Account of the Work of the British Special Operations Executive in France, 1940–44*, p. 241.

"designed to bring Hitler down": Ibid., p. 44. Also see M.R.D. Foot, "Was SOE Any Good?" *Journal of Contemporary History*, January 1981, Vol. 16, No. 1, *The Second World War*: Part 1, pp. 167–181.

58 **On May 5, 1941:** Major Robert Bourne-Paterson, *SOE in France 1941–1945*, p. 133.

George Noble: He is also known as George Begue, or George the first. The property he landed on is owned by a "close personal friend" of "a certain Maurice Buckmaster."

"The British had sent us the tools": Philippe de Vomécourt, *An Army of Amateurs*, p. 38.

Service travail obligatoire: Leo Marks, *Between Silk and Cyanide: A Codemaker's War, 1941–1945*, p. 359.

***maquis*, meaning "underbrush":** www.larousse.fr/dictionnaires/francais/maquis/49319

59 **recruiting French citizens:** Marcel Ruby, *F Section SOE: The Story of the Buckmaster Network*, p. 10. There was another SOE French section called RF Section, which worked with de Gaulle's Free French. F Section did not at the outset.

trained to do extraordinary things: Maurice Buckmaster, *They Fought Alone*, p. 102.

"How do you get there?": Sonia d'Artois, quoted in *Behind Enemy Lines: The Real Charlotte Grays*, directed by Jenny Morgan.

paperwork to be filled out: Application for engagement or transfer, dated December 4, 1943, Sonia d'Artois Personnel File, HS9/56/7, The National Archives.

preferred cover for women: Sarah Helm, *A Life in Secrets: Vera Atkins and the Lost Agents of SOE*, p. 5. See also Kate Vigurs, *Mission France,* p. 51, and J. Selwyn, *Forgotten Voices of the Secret War: An Inside History of Special Operations in the Second World War*, p. 68.

"in the field after training": Application for engagement or transfer, dated December 4, 1943, Sonia d'Artois Personnel File, HS9/56/7, The National Archives.

official transfer date: Ibid.

60 **pick up the pieces:** Sonia d'Artois, interview with Robin Fowler.

6: ANOTHER DETOUR

61 **the storied Royal 22e Régiment:** Guy d'Artois, military record, Library and Archives Canada.

62 **"again in hope":** Churchill's speech to the U.S. Congress. Text and partial audio accessed at https://www.nationalchurchillmuseum.org/churchill-address-to-congress.html.

a fight with the enemy: Neville Thompson, *The Third Man: Churchill, Roosevelt, Mackenzie King, and the Untold Friendships That Won WWII*, p. 531.

"a battle on British soil": Ibid. Also see British Pathé video report on Churchill's speech in Ottawa, with excerpts, at www.youtube.com/watch?v=y6JxSHmVB5g. There is a longer version at https://www.youtube.com/watch?v=2jtOGDjlM10&t=144s.

***The Roaring Lion*:** Churchill was defiant, even combative in that address, a mood captured moments afterward in the speakers' chambers by Yousuf Karsh, an Armenian Canadian photographer. When Churchill refused to set aside his cigar for the photo, Karsh took matters, and the cigar, into his own hands, then quickly captured a scowling Churchill. It would become an iconic image of wartime Churchill and Britain, hung in government offices, embassies, and schools all over the U.K., Canada, and beyond for generations to come.

"secret service": Soldiers Qualification Card, dated February 5, 1942. From Guy d'Artois's military record, Library and Archives Canada.

"like to be in paratroops": Ibid.

63 **"Good material for an officer":** Ibid.

becoming a paratrooper: Guy d'Artois, audio recording, AV2_172_044_B. Musée Royal 22e Régiment, La Citadelle de Québec.

officially posted to Brockville: Guy d'Artois, military record, Library and Archives Canada.

pulling in around noon: War Diary, 2nd Canadian Parachute Battalion, 1st Special Service Force. August 1 to August 31, 1942. Volume 1. Library and Archives Canada. Entry dated August 6.

aggressiveness, and self-reliance: Bernd Horn, *We Will Find a Way: The Canadian Special Operations Legacy*, p. 27. Produced for CANSOFCOM Education and Research Centre, 2018.

64 **parachute out of a plane:** Ibid.

"American army. Goodbye": Guy d'Artois, audio recording, AV2_172_044_B. Musée Royal 22e Régiment, La Citadelle de Québec. He is more than likely referring to the R22eR's J.P.E. Bernatchez.

the Devil's Brigade: Bernd Horn and Michel Wyczynski, *Of Courage and Determination: The First Special Service Force, "The Devil's Brigade," 1942–44*, p. 7
to be kept secret: Ibid., p. 97.
"and desert warfare": Ibid., p. 97
"quick-witted, sharp mind": Guy d'Artois, as quoted by Odette Coupal, *Le Petit Journal,* December 27, 1942.

65 **"lead us to victory":** Ibid.
promoted to lieutenant: Guy d'Artois, military record, Library and Archives Canada.
by December 15, 1942: War Diary, 2nd Canadian Parachute Battalion, August 1 to August 31, 1942, Volume 1, Library and Archives Canada and Bernd Horn and Michel Wyczynski, *Of Courage and Determination: The First Special Service Force, "The Devil's Brigade," 1942–44,* p. 102.
was likely on August 14: War Diary, 2nd Canadian Parachute Battalion, August 1 to August 31, 1942, Volume 1. Entry dated August 14. Library and Archives Canada.
"uncontrollable prickle of fear": Guy d'Artois, as quoted by Odette Coupal, *Le Petit Journal*, December 27, 1942.
two dollars per day: Guy d'Artois military record. August 15, 1942, is the date when he qualified as a parachutist. The pay adjustment came as soon as he was taken on by the 2nd Parachute Battalion.
brass back in Ottawa: Bernd Horn and Michel Wyczynski, *Of Courage and Determination*, p. 98.

66 **"is likely to be shot":** War Diary, 2nd Canadian Parachute Battalion, January 1 to January 31, 1943, Volume 6. Entry dated January 21. Library and Archives Canada.
dubbed Operation COTTAGE: Bernd Horn and Michel Wyczynski, *Of Courage and Determination,* p. 310.
"EXPECT ME AROUND 15-": Telegram sent September 4, 1943. d'Artois family private papers.
an unusual invitation: Roy MacLaren, *Canadians Behind Enemy Lines, 1939–1945*, p. 95.
answered in the affirmative: Rob Forsyth, *d'Artois Interviews*, notes from interviews with Guy and Sonia d'Artois, pp. 5–6. Rob Forsyth Fonds, F0545, Clara Thomas Archives and Special Collections, York University.
a woman who drove him: Ibid.

7: COG IN A LARGE MACHINE

67 **Department of National Defence:** Lynn-Philip Hodgson, *Inside Camp X*, p. 104.
"*consistently maintained*": "Camp Arrangements," p. 1. Lecture Folder STS 103, Part I. HS7/55. 1943–44, The National Archives.

farm owned by a family: Lynn-Philip Hodgson, *Inside Camp X*, p. 98.

68 **A single jeep patrolled:** Ibid., p. 34.

Special Training School 103: For official purposes in Canada, it was known as "Project J." In Canadian military records it was also referred to as 25-1-1. That is how it is referred to in Guy d'Artois's military record for the period he was at Camp X.

American support of the war: Henry Hemming, *Agents of Influence: A British Campaign, a Canadian Spy, and the Secret Plot to Bring America into World War II.*

presided over training: David Stafford, *Camp X: SOE School for Spies*, p. 257.

multicultural Canada for help: F.H. Walter, *"Cloak and Dagger,"* p. 3.

69 **"a global affair":** Eric Curwain, *"Almost Top Secret,"*, unpublished manuscript, p. 95, Royal Canadian Military Institute. Eric Curwain, who sometimes went by the name Bill Simpson, was a prolific recruiter for Camp X and may have been the man who recruited Guy—but I could find no conclusive proof that it was him he met in Montreal. Curwain was a former British secret agent who was based in Poland, the man who told the world through Morse code, from the attic of the British embassy, that the German invasion of Poland had begun. He moved to Canada afterwards, to become the chief recruiter for the SOE.

even a priest: Ibid., p. 96.

forty-nine French Canadians: F.H. Walter, "Cloak and Dagger,", p. 5. Also see David Stafford, *Camp X*, p. 210.

"strain of clandestine war": Ibid.

"pre-invasion phase": Opening address, dated September 3, 1943. "Objects and Methods of Irregular Warfare," p. 2. Lecture Folder STS 103, Part I. HS7/55. 1943–44, The National Archives.

70 ***"efficiency of your performance"*:** Ibid.

just over four weeks: Guy d'Artois, military record, Library and Archives Canada.

"couldn't wait to tell Britain": As told to historian Lynn-Philip Hodgson and related to the author.

"soldier of fortune": F.H. Walter, *"Cloak and Dagger,"* p. 14.

On November 23, 1943: "Reply to access request re: Major Lionel Guy d'Artois. Dated May 19, 2016." and Guy d'Artois' military record. Both Library and Archives Canada.

8: AGENTS-TO-BE

73 **small room:** Rob Forsyth, *d'Artois Interviews*, notes from interviews with Guy and Sonia d'Artois, p. 4. Rob Forsyth Fonds, F0545, Clara Thomas Archives and Special Collections, York University.

about mundane things: Ibid.

Party 27AG: Various HS personnel files, The National Archives.

74 **effectively two masters:** Maurice Buckmaster, *They Fought Alone: The Story of British Agents in France*, p. 181.

75 **"the racket":** Noreen Riols, *The Secret Ministry of Ag. & Fish: My Life in Churchill's School for Spies*, p. 25. Guy also used that term to refer to the organization.

wasn't for him: Rob Forsyth, *d'Artois Interviews*, notes from interviews with Guy and Sonia d'Artois, p. 7.

firmly in one or the other: Sydney Hudson, unpublished novel, p. 69-70, d'Artois family private papers.

"the conflict within": Ibid., p. 70.

the promise of adventure: Rob Forsyth, *d'Artois Interviews*, notes from interviews with Guy and Sonia d'Artois, pp. 5–6.

76 **desperately wanted to be there:** Ibid., p. 4.

self-reliance: Noreen Riols, *The Secret Ministry of Ag. & Fish*, p. 73.

77 **spectacular collapse in mid-1943:** For the initial, official accounting of these events, see M.R.D. Foot, *SOE in France: An Account of the Work of the British Special Operations Executive in France, 1940–44*, pp. 273–308. For a more recent, investigative account, see Francis J. Suttill, *PROSPER: Major Suttill's French Resistance Network*. This was written by Suttill's son.

security lapses, both in the field and at HQ: M.R.D. Foot, *SOE in France*, p. 273.

Frank Pickersgill and Ken Macalister: For a thorough account of their story, see Jonathan Vance, *Unlikely Soldiers: How Two Canadians Fought the Secret War Against Nazi Occupation*.

Noor Inayat Khan: An incredible story that has generated a number of accounts, including Shrabani Basu, *Spy Princess: The Life of Noor Inayat Khan*.

78 **were repeatedly missed:** Ibid., pp. 291–92.

"be more careful next time": Ibid., p. 291.

the German *Funkspiel*: M.R.D. Foot, *SOE in France*, p. 290.

"a hopeful improvisation": David Stafford, "Churchill and the SOE," a chapter in Mark Seaman's *Special Operations Executive: A New Instrument of War*, p. 49. The official was Bickham Sweet-Escott.

amateurish and irresponsible: David Stafford, *Britain and European Resistance 1940–1945: A Survey of the Special Operations Executive, with Documents*, p. 17.

protect D-Day: For an account of this version of events, investigated long after the fact, see Patrick Marnham, *War in the Shadows: Resistance, Deception and Betrayal in Occupied France*.

"or that man Buckmaster": Maurice Buckmaster, *They Fought Alone*, p. 60. This is quoted in a number of books but none I have come across has pointed out a primary source.

Vera May Rosenberg: Sarah Helm, *A Life in Secrets: Vera Atkins and the Missing Agents of WWII,* p. 130.

79 **in April 1941:** Ibid., Introduction, Kindle location 217.

intelligence officer: Ibid.

"very conscientious:" Vera Atkins, quoted in Roderick Bailey, *Forgotten Voices of the Secret War: An Inside History of Special Operations in the Second World War*, p. 70.

80 **"Good luck to you":** David Stafford, *Ten Days to D-Day: Countdown to the Liberation of Europe*, p. 168. Also J. Selwyn in Roderick Bailey, *Forgotten Voices*, p. 68.

one staffer as "a lech": Sarah Helm, *A Life in Secrets*, p. 7.

81 **"Attractive looking":** Sonia d'Artois personnel File, HS9/56/7, National Archives.

on the security front: Vera Atkins interview with Conrad Wood, January 6, 1987, Imperial War Museum, Catalog number 9551.

"happy days lay ahead": *Montreal Gazette*, February 9, 1985, p. H1.

82 **"looks like a Christmas tree":** Sonia d'Artois, interview with Robin Fowler.

"Stately 'Omes of England": Beryl E. Escott, *The Heroines of SOE F Section: Britain's Secret Women in France*, p. 9.

83 **student assessment board:** History of the training section of SOE, 1940–1945, SOE history file 30, compiled by Major G.M. Forty, London, September 1945. HS7/51, p. 19. The National Archives.

who were testers: Ibid.

***Where are the exits?*:** Sonia d'Artois, interview with Robin Fowler. Also see McKenzie Porter, "Sonia Was a Spy," *Maclean's*, February 15, 1953.

called "the cooler": Noreen Riols, *The Secret Ministry of Ag. & Fish*, p. 40.

84 **lived in Marseille:** For a full account of her story see Nancy Wake, *The White Mouse: The Autobiography of Australia's Wartime Legend.*

"knit them balaclavas": Ibid., p. 91.

his time and hers: Ibid.

or the Looney Bin: Sonia d'Artois, interview with Robin Fowler. Also see McKenzie Porter, "Sonia Was a Spy."

edge of her bed: Sonia d'Artois, interview with Robin Fowler.

85 **landed hard on the ground:** Ibid.

"no organic damage to herself": Doctor's note, undated, Sonia Butt Personnel File, HS9/56/7, The National Archives. It was handwritten on letterhead labelled Royal Surrey County Hospital.

86 **got herself stuck inside:** Rob Forsyth, *d'Artois Interviews*, notes from interviews with Guy and Sonia d'Artois, p. 7.

"quite reckless and fearless": Student Assessment Board report. Sonia Esme Florence (Née Butt) personnel File, HS9/56/7, entry dated December 16, 1943, The National Archives.
"low, but pass": Major G.M. Forty, "Appendix II (b)." This appears to be a grading form for staff of STS 7 (Winterfold) Student Assessment Board, p. 138. London, September 1945. HS7/51. The National Archives.

9: LOVE IN A TIME OF WAR

87 **Paddington station:** for an image of the memorial please see https://www.warmemorialsonline.org.uk/memorial/112234.
88 **two days of rest:** Rob Forsyth, *d'Artois Interviews*, notes from interviews with Guy and Sonia d'Artois, p. 7. Rob Forsyth Fonds, F0545, Clara Thomas Archives and Special Collections, York University.
hide a secret army: M.R.D. Foot, *SOE in France: An Account of the Work of the British Special Operations Executive in France, 1940–44*, p. 53.
89 **rolled into one:** Sonia d'Artois, interview with Robin Fowler.
reassemble them: Ibid., and M.R.D. Foot, *SOE in France*, p. 53.
"quite well with pistol": "Para-Military Report" from STS 23a. Dated January 22, 1944, p. 1. Sonia Butt Personnel File, HS9/56/7, The National Archives. The comment continues by saying that her handling is "poor."
could outshoot: Sonia d'Artois, interview with Robin Fowler.
"on special dummies": History of the training section of SOE, 1940–1945, SOE history file 30, compiled by Major G.M. Forty London, September 1945. HS7/51, p. 19. The National Archives.
how to blow one up: Lieutenant Robert Ferrier, SOE instructor, Scotland, in Roderick Bailey, *Forgotten Voices of the Secret War*, p. 81, and also "the use of explosives" in M.R.D. Foot, *SOE in France*, p. 55.
"for a bilingual secretary": M.R.D. Foot, *SOE in France,* p. 54.
90 **in constant mourning:** Sonia recounts this story in her interview with Robin Fowler. One of either Guy or Sonia also tells the story to Rob Forsyth, although in those notes the man Lilian marries is Belgian. I did not manage to independently confirm this story.
one May Talbot: Ibid. I could not independently confirm her name.
in Guy's company: Rob Forsyth, *d'Artois Interviews*, notes from interviews with Guy and Sonia d'Artois, p. 7.
impossible not to: Sydney Hudson, *Undercover Operator: An SOE Agent's Experiences in France and the Far East*, p. 77, and Noreen Riols, *The Secret Ministry of Ag. & Fish: My Life in Churchill's School for Spies*, p. 219.
91 **she steered clear:** Sonia d'Artois, interview with Robin Fowler.

"his relations with others": SOE assessment at Student Assessment Board. Guy d'Artois, personnel File. HS9/56/7, entry dated December 16, 1943. The National Archives.
an audible giggle: Rob Forsyth, *d'Artois Interviews*, notes from interviews with Guy and Sonia d'Artois, p. 10.
back to the lodge: Robert Ferrier, SOE instructor, in Roderick Bailey, *Forgotten Voices of the Secret War: An Inside History of Special Operations in the Second World War*, p. 82.
happily seized it: Rob Forsyth, *d'Artois Interviews*, notes from interviews with Guy and Sonia d'Artois, p. 10.

92 **it was all "innocent":** Ibid.
encouraged to have fun: Ibid.
assessed at fifty-fifty: Vera Atkins, interview with Conrad Wood, January 6, 1987, Imperial War Museum, Catalogue number 9551.
only around six weeks: Various, including Maurice Buckmaster, *They Fought Alone: The Story of British Agents in France*, p. 5.

93 **"from motives of romance":** Acting Lieutenant Gordon, December 24, 1944, Sonia d'Artois Personnel File, HS9/56/7, The National Archives. Gordon is likely William Gordon, who witnessed one of Guy's signatures in his file.
shield herself from the cold: "Love Outlasts Danger of War." *Montreal Gazette*, February 9, 1985, p. H1.

94 **raids on the city yet:** "Berlin Again." *Birmingham Evening Mail.* December 24, 1943, p. 2.
"peace on Earth, goodwill toward men": The full text of Roosevelt's Christmas message can be accessed online on Newsweek.com, at https://www.newsweek.com/peace-earth-and-goodwill-toward-men-will-be-realized-535672.
"may be long": Franklin D. Roosevelt, "FDR's 1943 Christmas Address: Peace on Earth and Goodwill Toward Men Will Be Realized," www.newsweek.com/peace-earth-and-goodwill-toward-men-will-be-realized-535672.

95 **refused to speak to her:** Sonia d'Artois, interview with Robin Fowler.

96 **"but very young":** Acting Lieutenant Gordon, December 30, 1944, Sonia d'Artois Personnel File, HS9/56/7, The National Archives.
"she cannot concentrate": Ibid.
"understanding between them": Ibid.
named Gustave Biéler: F.H. Walter, *"Cloak and Dagger,"* p. 9.

97 **five-year prison sentence:** Sydney Hudson, *Undercover Operator: An SOE Agent's Experiences in France and the Far East*, p. 36.
French-controlled Maison centrale: Ibid., p. 37.

98 **over the border to Spain:** Ibid., p. 47.

99 **"that I must be there":** Ibid., p. 58.

"on sex appeal alone": Acting Lieutenant Gordon, January 7, 1944, Sonia d'Artois Personnel File, HS9/56/7, National Archives.

of another sex: Acting Lieutenant Gordon, entry dated Jan 12, Sonia d'Artois Personnel File, HS9/56/7. The National Archives.

"truly in this work": Commandant's Report. Entry dated January 22. Sonia d'Artois Personnel File, HS9/56/7, The National Archives.

called her in for a meeting: Sonia d'Artois, interview with Robin Fowler.

100 **"I was sure of myself in that":** Ibid.

most thoroughly trained Canadians: Roy MacLaren, *Canadians Behind Enemy Lines, 1939–1945*, p. 95.

"for anything else": Acting Lieutenant Gordon, entry dated December 24, Guy d'Artois Personnel File, HS9/56/7. The National Archives.

"natural leader here": Unidentified writer, entry dated December 30, Guy d'Artois Personnel File, HS9/56/7. The National Archives.

"The armies of General Wallenstein": Assessment, dated January 7, 1944, Guy d'Artois Personnel File, HS9/56/7, The National Archives.

for parachute training: Sonia and Guy stayed in Altrincham at Dunham Massey House, a classic red-brick Georgian mansion with a moat and vast grounds—an ideal setting for an evening stroll.

101 **"terms of this declaration":** "Declaration" signed by Guy d'Artois, dated January 24, 1944. Guy d'Artois Personnel File, HS9/56/7, The National Archives.

a promising SOE recruit: For a thorough account of Violette Szabó's story, see Tania Szabó, *Young, Brave and Beautiful: The Missions of Special Operations Executive Agent Lieutenant Violette Szabó.*

"good fun, warm, gutsy": *You Magazine*, *Mail on Sunday*, February 3, 2002.

time partying together: Tania Szabó, *Young, Brave and Beautiful*, p. 342.

"first class": Entry dated 29 January 1944, Guy d'Artois Personnel File, HS9/56/7, The National Archives.

"nervous throughout the course": Assessment dated January 1, 1944. Sonia d'Artois personnel File, HS9/56/7, The National Archives.

102 **"looking at me and laughing":** "She winked, jumped, I said 'marry me,'" *Toronto Daily Star*, December 18, 1944, p. 15.

a fear of heights: Sonia d'Artois, interview with Robin Fowler.

"never see her again": "She winked, jumped, I said 'marry me,'" *Toronto Daily Star*, December 18, 1944, p. 15.

"ask her to marry me": Ibid.

to begin his mission: Chronology of SOE Operations with the Resistance in France during World War II. Originally produced in London, December 1960, by Lieutenant-Colonel E.G. Boxshall. Sheet 17. Imperial War Museum.

103 **"three days before":** Sonia d'Artois in interview, *Behind Enemy Lines: The Real Charlotte Grays*, directed by Jenny Morgan.

"stood up to interrogation very well": Assessment by one "Ensign Davenport," undated. Sonia d'Artois personnel File, HS9/56/7, The National Archives.

"*in modern warfare*": Special Operations Executive Manual, *How to Be an Agent in Europe*. Published by The National Archives, pp. 3, 12–13.

"cannot guarantee your safety": Ibid., pp. 12–13.

104 **"picked up is very small":** Ibid.

no significant financial incentive: Noreen Riols, *The Secret Ministry of Ag. & Fish,* p. 40.

thirty-nine women deployed by F Section: Here again numbers differ. Sometimes it is counted as forty-one, other times a number in the fifties when you add women of the RF section.

"*prepare a story of your past life*": Special Operations Executive Manual, *How to Be an Agent in Europe*, pp. 3, 12–13.

105 **a real-life scenario:** "Report on 96 hours scheme–3/27/150," Sonia d'Artois Personnel File, HS9/56/7, The National Archives.

questioned by Nottingham police: Ibid., p. 2.

"considerably in her work": Assessment by Ensign Davenport, undated, Sonia d'Artois Personnel File, HS9/56/7, The National Archives.

"book learning": Commandant's report, dated January 22, 1944. Sonia d'Artois Personnel File, HS9/56/7, The National Archives.

"brain-work": Assessment by Ensign Davenport. Undated. Sonia d'Artois Personnel File, HS9/56/7, The National Archives.

106 **"as though she were baking a cake":** Beryl E. Escott, *The Heroines of SOE: Britain's Secret Women in France*, F Section p. 204.

meticulous notes in pencil: Handwritten notebook of Sonia d'Artois, private papers of Mrs. S.E.F. d'Artois, Imperial War Museum.

"do most of the work": Untitled assessment; in pencil it says "home-made explosives." Undated. Sonia d'Artois Personnel File, HS9/56/7, The National Archives.

"now operationally ready": Application for Commission dated 17th March, 1944. Sonia d'Artois Personnel File, HS9/56/7, The National Archives.

Halfway House: David Stafford, *Ten Days to D-Day: Countdown to the Liberation of Europe*, p. 77.

107 **Their connection was instantaneous:** Sonia d'Artois, interview with Robin Fowler.

108 **"for breaking up a marriage":** Ibid.

10: FIRST DISAPPOINTMENT

109 **friends began to disappear:** Chronology of SOE Operations with the Resistance in France during World War II. Originally produced in London, December 1960, by Lieutenant-Colonel E.G. Boxshall.

110 **deployed to France as a team:** Sonia d'Artois, interview with Robin Fowler.

111 **"learn English":** Sonia remembers her father saying so, in interview with Robin Fowler.

"*ET DIEU DISPOSE*": Ibid.

"doubtful whether she would be employed": Assessment from an unnamed instructor at Beaulieu (STS 33), dated February 29, 1944. Sonia d'Artois Personnel File, HS9/56/7, The National Archives.

"interested him more": Report from Ensign Davenport, from STS 33, undated, Sonia d'Artois Personnel File, HS9/56/7. The National Archives.

112 **"were they to work together":** Unsigned assessment from Beaulieu, STS 33, dated February 29, 1944. Guy d'Artois Personnel File, HS9/56/7, The National Archives.

wasn't even worth trying: Sonia d'Artois, interview with Robin Fowler.

On April 15, 1944: Marriage certificate, d'Artois family private papers.

113 **"before the wedding":** The note, from a Mrs. King, reads: "Miss Butt is being married tomorrow, she will require a new FANY Identity Card in the name of d'Artois." Sonia d'Artois Personnel File, HS9/56/7, The National Archives.

11: FROM THE HEAVENS

117 **Over France, May 23, 1944:** Operations Record Book, RAF 138 Squadron Tempsford, "Summary of Events." Reference AIR 27/956/1, p. 19. "Entry dated May 23, 1944, Flight piloted by S/L Wilding," downloaded from The National Archives.

at twenty minutes out: Rob Forsyth, *d'Artois Interviews*, notes from interviews with Guy and Sonia d'Artois, p. 38. Rob Forsyth Fonds, F0545, Clara Thomas Archives and Special Collections, York University.

some cognac and cigarettes: Ibid. Also in Guy d'Artois handwritten notes. D'Artois family private papers.

were two Canadians: The other Canadian was Capt. Joseph H. A. Benoit. He was slated to join the SILVERSMITH circuit.

the lone woman on board: The story of Madeleine Lavigne is told in brief in Kate Vigurs, *Mission France: The True History of the Women of SOE*, pp. 192–193.

Madeleine Lavigne: Her code name was Isabelle, but her alias on the ground was Henriette. Albert Browne-Bartroli, *Mémoires d'un résistant en Saône-et-Loire*, p. 67.

118 **four months earlier:** Kate Vigurs, *Mission France*, pp. 192–193.
toward British airspace: Operation DITCHER 38A, Squadron 406th, dated 15/16 May [1944]. Operation was not completed. In the captain's personal report he says he "circled target area for 8 minutes but saw no reception." Website of The Carpetbaggers." Accessed online at 801492.org.
slammed the door behind her: Sonia d'Artois, interview with Robin Fowler.
at the RAF Tempsford airfield: Operations Record Book, RAF 138 Squadron Tempsford, "Summary of Events." Reference AIR 27/956/1, p. 142. "Entry dated May 23/24, 1944. Downloaded from The National Archives.

119 **half a million francs:** *Operation instruction No. F. 126*, prepared for Guy d'Artois. Dated April 26, 1944, p. 4. D'Artois family private papers.
600 francs a month: Ibid.
a .32 pistol: Rob Forsyth, *d'Artois Interviews*, notes from interviews with Guy and Sonia d'Artois, pp. 25, 39.
good luck: Ibid, p. 25.

120 **twice over:** Ibid, p. 88.
RAF Halifax bomber: Operations Record Book, RAF 138 Squadron Tempsford, "Summary of Events." Reference AIR 27/956/1, p. 19. Entry dated 23/24 May 1944. Downloaded from The National Archives (U.K.). Also see Pierre Tillet, *History of WWII Infiltrations into France*, accessed online at http://www.plan-sussex-1944.net/anglais/infiltrations_into_france.pdf, p. 59, via Paul McCue.
"I felt absolutely bereft": "Love Story Outlasts Dangers of War." *Montreal Gazette*, February 9, 1985, p. H1.

121 **as previous employment:** Joseph Gerard Litalien Personnel File. HS9/928/6. The National Archives.
been born in Canada: Ibid.
"impossible to forget the danger": As quoted by Odette Coupal, *Le Petit Journal,* December 27, 1942.

122 **"Something new":** Rob Forsyth, *d'Artois Interviews*, notes from interviews with Guy and Sonia d'Artois, p. 57.
"*the maximum effectiveness*": "Operation instruction No. F. 126," prepared for Guy d'Artois. Dated April 26, 1944. The operation was called Decorator. D'Artois family private papers.

123 **between Marseille and Barcelona:** Albert Browne-Bartroli, *Mémoires d'un résistant en Saône-et-Loire*, p. 2. Published online, 2020. Accessed at https://cortevaix.fr/wp-content/uploads/2021/02/Me%CC%81moires-Albert-Browne-Bartroli-.pdf
"Penchant for poetry": Ibid.
without news of her: Ibid., p. 65. Also Kate Vigurs, *Mission France,* p. 174.

intolerant of discipline: Guy himself would say that he was "undisciplined." Michel Gariepy and Renée Hudon-Auger, "Major Guy d'Artois du Royal 22e Régiment." *Gens de Mon Pays*. Archives Radio-Canada, October 23, 1977.

124 **or king emperor:** Rob Forsyth, *d'Artois Interviews*, notes from interviews with Guy and Sonia d'Artois, p. 40. Rob Forsyth Fonds, F0545, Clara Thomas Archives and Special Collections, York University.

"great drive": Student Assessment Board report, Guy d'Artois Personnel File, HS9/56/7, entry dated December 16, 1943, The National Archives.

"*all around them*": Operation instruction No. F. 126, prepared for Guy d'Artois. Dated April 26, 1944. The operation was called Decorator. Guy d'Artois Personnel File, HS9/56/7, The National Archives.

***Pont d'Ain*:** Ibid., p. 5.

125 **"approach the abyss":** *Le Petit Journal*, December 27, 1942.

"from there on in": "Romance of 'Michel le Canadien' Started in Air, Grew in France," *Montreal Gazette*, December 20, 1944, p. 11.

had spotted the Halifax: Albert Browne-Bartroli, *Mémoires d'un résistant en Saône-et-Loire*, p. 69.

126 **and then disappeared:** Ibid.

"white as a ghost": Ibid.

about three kilometres: Guy d'Artois, "report of Dieudonné, known as Michel." Dated October 7, 1944, Guy d'Artois Personnel File, HS9/56/7, The National Archives.

yelled out "Halt!": Rob Forsyth, *d'Artois Interviews*, notes from interviews with Guy and Sonia d'Artois, p. 39.

pointing at his chest: Albert Browne-Bartroli, *Mémoires d'un résistant en Saône-et-Loire*, p. 71.

127 **speaking in French, asked drily:** The dialogue is from ibid., p. 71. The circumstances of the encounter told separately by Albert and Guy are very similar; however, Albert never says whether it was Guy who was questioning him. He did say, at the end of his description, that he had found his missing agents, and he said there were three of them. Those were Guy and Joseph and possibly Benoit, but neither account clarifies this (nor does Benoit's after-mission report make it clear either). Guy's version can be found in: Rob Forsyth, *d'Artois Interviews*, notes from interviews with Guy and Sonia d'Artois, p. 39. He also discusses it in a Radio-Canada interview: Michel Gariepy and Renée Hudon-Auger, "Major Guy d'Artois du Royal 22e Régiment."

a hail of questions: Rob Forsyth, *d'Artois Interviews*, notes from interviews with Guy and Sonia d'Artois, p. 39.

as Albert watched: Albert Browne-Bartroli, *Mémoires d'un résistant en Saône-et-Loire*, p. 72.

128 **Jean-Paul's:** That is Jean-Paul Archambault, also from Montreal and who joined Guy and Sonia's training cohort and a friend.
"a regular stop": "Pierre Jandeau handwritten recollections, Written in Saint-Quay-Portrieux on September 9th, 1985." Jandeau family private papers. Courtesy of his daughter, Mme Paule Jandeau.
"hour of day or night": Ibid.
anointed him Michel: Ibid. Also in Rob Forsyth, *d'Artois Interviews*, notes from interviews with Guy and Sonia d'Artois, p. 39.

129 **the corner bedroom:** According to Mme Paule Jandeau, on a visit to her former home with author.
red terracotta rooftops: Michel Gariepy and Renée Hudon-Auger, "Major Guy d'Artois du Royal 22e Régiment." *Gens de Mon Pays*. Archives Radio-Canada, October 23, 1977.
Robert Guy d'Artois: Operation instruction No. F. 126, prepared for Guy d'Artois. Dated April 26, 1944. The operation was called Decorator. D'Artois family private papers.
despised historical figure: Possibly Comte d'Artois, who became Charles X and reigned as an absolute monarch in the nineteenth century.
a pile of others: Copies of these can be found in Fonds Guy d'Artois, FPA018, Archives at the Royal 22e Régiment Museum, La Citadelle de Quebec, Quebec City, Canada.
"Who am I today?": Rob Forsyth, *d'Artois Interviews*, notes from interviews with Guy and Sonia d'Artois, p. 25.
wouldn't expose him: Ibid., p. 40.

130 **spotted the woman:** Ibid.
called her Maman Lucienne: According to various figures, including Guy, involved in the resistance in Charolles.
the centre of town: As seen on a tour of Charolles in 2022, courtesy of Louis Lapalus's daughters, Jeanine and Francoise.
would attract attention: Report on after-mission briefing, Albert Browne-Bartroli, dated November 25, 1944, p. 6.
impeccably polished floors: Albert Browne-Bartroli, *Mémoires d'un résistant en Saône-et-Loire*, p. 30.

131 **Villa des Alliés:** According to historian Jérémy Beurier, co-author of *Les Téméraires: une histoire neuve de la Résistance*, in conversation with the author. Also mentioned in Louis Lapalus, private notes, p. 9. Courtesy of Jérémy Beurier and the Lapalus family.
"the best woman I have ever seen": Kenneth C. Cragg, "French-Canadian's Maquis Clubbed So 58 Germans Lined Up and Shot," *The Globe and Mail*, December 20, 1944, p. 11.

"nobody tried very hard": Report of Dieudonné, known as Michel. Dated October 7, 1944. Guy d'Artois personnel file, HS9/56/7, The National Archives.
willing to work with him: Rob Forsyth, *d'Artois Interviews*, notes from interviews with Guy and Sonia d'Artois, p. 40.

132 **"as quickly as possible":** Ibid. Also Sonia d'Artois, interview with Robin Fowler.
"field for some weeks": Document signed by A.G/Med. May 23, 1944. Sonia d'Artois Personnel File, HS9/56/7. The National Archives.
"should take the risk": The undated handwritten note was scribbled below the doctor's note; the initials were illegible. Sonia d'Artois Personnel File, HS9/56/7. The National Archives.

12: A "GIRL" COURIER

133 **Halifax III LK810:** W.R. Chorley, RAF *Bomber Command Losses of the Second World War*. Volume 5. 1944. Details of the mission and crew can be found at https://aircrewremembered.com/la-porte-edmund-elie.html. Pieces of the stricken aircraft are in the possession of a local historian, Tony Chisserez of Association AOK7, who showed them to author.
all of twenty: Laporte's personal information accessed online at https://www.veterans.gc.ca/eng/remembrance/memorialsesistann-virtual-war-memorial/detail/2846540.

134 **Sergeant Robert McGowan:** Ibid.
north of central Le Mans: The details of where all the fallen are buried in Le Mans are listed in a document titled "Post Presumption Memorandum No. 1276/47," accessed at www.veterans.gc.ca/eng/remembrance/memorials/canadian-virtual-war-memorial/detail/2846540.
one hundred thousand people: That was the approximate population of Le Mans just after the war, according to the French National Institute of Statistics and Economic Studies. An Associated Press report at the time of its capture in 1944 put the figure at 84,525. The Associated Press. "War Touches Le Mans Again." Published in *The Charlotte News*, August 8, 1944, p. 1.

135 **"important junction":** Operation Instruction No. F. 139, Part I. Dated May 24, 1944, p. 1. d'Artois family private papers.
bunkers that sprang up: "*Un bunker apparaît sous la cité administrative démolie.*" Actu.fr. December 26, 2019. Accessed online at https://actu.fr/pays-de-la-loire/le-mans_72181/video-mans-bunker-apparait-sous-cite-administrative-demolie_30418079.html.
agent code-named Albin: Chronology of SOE Operations with the Resistance in France During World War II. Originally produced in London, December 1960, by Lieutenant-Colonel E.G. Boxshall. Sheet 6.

136 **Muriel Byck:** For more on her story see Kate Vigurs, *Mission France: The True History of the Women of SOE*, p. 179.
found each other: Sydney Hudson, *Undercover Operator: An SOE Agent's Experiences in France and the Far East*, p. 66.
twenty-sixth birthday: Kate Vigurs, *Mission France,* p. 307.
stashed away until it was time: David Stafford, *Ten Days to D-Day: Countdown to the Liberation of Europe*, p. 20.
"they certainly were now": Sydney Hudson, *Undercover Operator*, p. 75

137 **contacts in Le Mans:** Ibid., p. 74.
leaving on a mission: Sarah Helm, *A Life in Secrets: Vera Atkins and the Missing Agents of WWII*, Kindle location 691.
"Black Maria": Anne Fromer, "I Was a Woman Spy," *Coronet Magazine*, May 1954, p. 162.
to 'almost worship' her: David Stafford, who had interviewed Sonia, in conversation with author.
she terrified some among the staff: Noreen Riols writes that Vera "terrified me," *The Secret Ministry of Ag. & Fish: My Life in Churchill's School for Spies,* p. 114.
"the family situation": Vera Atkins, interview with Conrad Wood, January 6, 1987, Imperial War Museum, catalog number 9551.
a silver cigarette case: Sonia d'Artois, interview with Robin Fowler. Also in Robyn Walker, *The Women Who Spied for Britain: Female Secret Agents of the Second World War*, p. 96.

138 **"rely on my wits":** Sonia d'Artois, interview with Robin Fowler.
two other agents: "Blanche's Report," post-deployment report by Sonia d'Artois, undated. HS 9/56/7. The National Archives. Exact Details provided in Chronology of SOE Operations with the Resistance in France During World War II. Originally produced in London, December 1960, by Lieutenant-Colonel E.G. Boxshall. Sheet 6. Entry dated May 28. Imperial War Museum.
"*take all your instructions from him*": Instructions for Sonia d'Artois. May 24, p. 1. HS 9/56/7. The National Archives.

139 **1918 instead of 1924:** Sonia's SOE-issued forged identification. Mrs. S.E.F. d'Artois Private Papers, Imperial War Museum.
and extra nourishment: SOE-issued doctor's note for "Suzanne Bonvie." Found, oddly, among Private Papers of Lieutenant-Colonel C.S. Hudson DSO, Imperial War Museum.
"*chèvre à vendre*": Another copy of operating instructions for Sonia d'Artois, dated May 24, which contains this particular instruction on p. 2, redacted in other copies. Found in "d'Artois-Notes," Rob Forsyth Fonds.
"the upper-middle-class standards": McKenzie Porter, "Sonia Was a Spy," *Maclean's*, February 15, 1953.

"as moderate as possible": Operating Instructions for Sonia d'Artois, May 24, HS 9/56/7.

and eight packages: Flight log, Squadron 26, Aircraft 501, Operation named HEADMASTER 4. Accessed online at "Wesbsite of the Carpetbaggers," www.801492.org.

140 **"six more packages":** Ibid.

rough landing: Flight log, Squadron 26, Aircraft 501, Operation named HEADMASTER 4. Accessed online at www.801492.org.

her back and shoulder: Sonia d'Artois, interview with Robin Fowler.

distant rumbling sound: Sonia d'Artois, as told to Anne Fromer, in "I Was a Woman Spy,". *Coronet Magazine.* May 1954, p. 162.

.32 Colt pistol: Ibid. David Stafford, *Ten Days to D-Day*, p. 13.

"is a woman": Ibid.

to send in a woman: Ibid.

141 **apple brandy:** Ibid., pp. 43–44.

goods company Lancel: a copy of typewritten partial SOE instructions, prepared for "Miss Butt" and Operation "Biographer," found in *d'Artois-Notes*, Rob Forsyth Fonds, F0545, Clara Thomas Archives and Special Collections, York University. Several other tellings, including by Sonia herself, suggest she was pretending to work for Louis Vuitton.

could cure any ailment: In the opinion of the author upon visual inspection of the château.

l'Abbé Chevalier: Sydney Hudson, *Undercover Operator*, p. 88.

142 **convoys driving by:** Sonia d'Artois, interview with Robin Fowler.

"the rule in France!": Sydney Hudson, *Undercover Operator*, p. 71.

her circuit leader: Sonia says, "I had no idea he would be there. All I had been told was that his code name was Albin; I wasn't given his real name." Sonia d'Artois, interview with Robin Fowler.

"how am I going to handle this?": David Stafford, *Ten Days to D-Day*, p. 127.

13: THE MOMENT HAS ARRIVED

145 **he'd just unearthed from hiding:** Louis Lapalus, *Ma vie, ma guerre*, p. 158.

146 **a book he wrote:** Ibid.

some two million Allied soldiers: "More than 2 million Allied soldiers, sailors, pilots, medics and other people from a dozen countries were involved in the overall Operation Overlord." The Associated Press. June 5, 2023. Accessed online at https://apnews.com/article/d-day-invasion-normandy-france-nazis-07094640dd7bb938a23e144cc23f348c.

left his post in Normandy: Andrew Roberts, *The Storm of War: A New History of the Second World War*, p. 1099.
in the immediate future: Andrew Roberts, Ibid., pp. 1098–1099.

147 **the order to proceed:** Ibid., pp. 1099, 1100.
messages personnels: M.R.D. Foot, *SOE in France: An Account of the Work of the British Special Operations Executive in France, 1940–44*, p. 102.
action on the ground: Ibid.
"V" for victory in Morse code: Three dots and a dash (also the opening of Beethoven's Fifth).

148 **"Tell fourteen the Queen's terrace is wide":** Louis Lapalus, *Ma vie, ma guerre*, p. 157, and Albert Browne-Bartroli, *Mémoires d'un résistant en Saône-et-Loire*, p. 79.
cousins visiting from Lyon: Ibid., p. 153.
Guy asked Louis Lapalus: Louis Lapalus, *Ma vie, ma guerre*, p 157.

149 **"could give a certain and apolitical result":** Louis Lapalus, letter to Guy dated July 2, 1946.
they had at their disposal: Pierre Jandeau, notes, from Jandeau family private papers, p. 3.
quartermaster: Ibid. Also see Rob Forsyth, *d'Artois Interviews*, notes from interviews with Guy and Sonia d'Artois, p. 91.
how to command a unit: Ibid.

150 **One of those meetings:** René Fléchard, *Le Maquis de Saint-Bonnet-de-Joux*, p. 84.
nearby Saint-Julien-de-Civry: Ibid., p. 19 onward, and p. 53.
who were both there on June 4: Ibid., p. 79.
with his family nearby: Ibid., p. 79.
"unfortunate country": Ibid., p. 85.

151 **Michel le Canadien's orders:** Ibid., p. 85.
protection of a bodyguard: Debrief of Brown-Bartroli, Albert, dated November 25, 1944, p. 4. Circuit and Mission Reports and Interrogations. HS6/567. The National Archives.
He was recruited: "Lieutenant (Joseph) Alcide Beauregard." Paul McCue, Secret WW2, from an ongoing project titled "Roll of Honour of F Section," p. 2. Dated December 28, 2022. More of Paul's work can be found at www.secret-ww2.net. Though his name was Alcide, he went by André. As in other cases, I use his legal name, Alcide, throughout the text.
"listless and bored": SOE assessment of Alcide Beauregard, dated August 27, 1943, Beauregard personnel file, HS9/111/1, The National Archives.
fast-tracked to parachute training: Ibid., August 25, 1943.
by Lysander: "Lieutenant (Joseph) Alcide Beauregard." Paul McCue, "Secret WW2," www.secret-ww2.net, from an ongoing project titled "Roll of Honour of F Section," p. 2. Dated December 28, 2022.

to help handle: Roy MacLaren, Canadians Behind Enemy Lines 1939–1945, p. 91.

152 **"conscientious and faithful":** Albert Browne-Bartroli, *Mémoires d'un résistant en Saône-et-Loire*, p. 67.

"tightening around him": Ibid., p. 79.

some two hundred and twenty SOE agents: Maurice Buckmaster, *They Fought Alone: The Story of British Agents in France*, p. 52.

three hundred and six of them: Ibid., p. 192.

153 **"before we have had anything to drink":** Albert Browne-Bartroli, *Mémoires d'un résistant en Saône-et-Loire*, p. 79.

14: MOTHER OF ALL MAQUIS

154 **dotting the horizon with parachutes:** Tim Cook, *Fight to the Finish: Canadians in the Second World War 1944–45*, p. 281.

First Canadian Parachute Battalion: Ibid.

fourteen thousand young Canadian men: Mark Zuehlke, *Assault on Juno*, p. 19.

155 **stretch code-named Juno Beach:** Tim Cook, *Fight to the Finish*, p. 301.

lasted mere minutes: Ibid., p. 304.

More than three hundred and fifty Canadians: http://www.warmuseum.ca/cwm/exhibitions/chrono/1931d_day_e.html.

soldiers met a similar fate: "A total of 4,414 Allied troops were killed on D-Day itself." Associated Press, June 5, 2023, accessed online at https://apnews.com/article/d-day-invasion-normandy-france-nazis-07094640dd7bb938a23e144cc23f348c.

"on the Normandy coast!": Louis Lapalus, *Ma vie, ma guerre*, p. 161.

be attacked the following day: Ibid., p. 162.

to keep people away: Ibid.

"everything on the roads": Guy d'Artois audio recording, AV2_172_044_A, Musée Royal 22e Régiment, La Citadelle de Québec.

156 **"Charolles would be set on fire":** Louis Lapalus, *Ma vie, ma guerre*, p. 162.

first military mission: René Fléchard, *Le Maquis de Saint-Bonnet-de-Joux*, p. 87.

sixteen trains: Guy d'Artois, "Report of Dieudonné, known as Michel," after-mission report dated October 7, 1944, p. 1. Guy d'Artois Personnel File, HS9/56/7, The National Archives.

"was not Berlin": Ibid.

"protect them first": Guy d'Artois audio recording, AV2_172_044_A, Musée Royal 22e Régiment, La Citadelle de Québec.

157 **"natural means of defence":** Louis Lapalus, "Petit résumé historique du maquis de Sylla," p. 2, Musée Royal 22e Régiment, La Citadelle de Québec.
former miners, who were numerous: André Jeannet, *La Seconde Guerre Mondiale en Saône-et-Loire: Occupation et résistance*, p. 177.
"I can tell you that": Guy d'Artois audio recording, AV2_172_044_A, Musée Royal 22e Régiment.
English infantry trousers: Louis Lapalus, *Ma vie, ma guerre*, p. 193.

158 **British boots:** Albert Browne-Bartroli, report on after-mission briefing, dated November 25, 1944, p. 5, Circuit and Mission reports and Interrogations, HS6/567, The National Archives.
officers' training course: Albert Browne-Bartroli, report on after-mission briefing, dated November 25, 1944, p. 3, Circuit and Mission reports and Interrogations, HS6/567, The National Archives.
visiting rules: The description of Sylla here is assembled from a variety of sources, including Guy himself, but also Louis Lapalus and André Barraud in a document titled "Maquis de Sylla, Historique, Origines," p. 53, provided courtesy of Jérémy Beurier. Barraud was commander of the second company of the 1st Charollais battalion under Guy.
"specially employed": Letter of promotion. Guy d'Artois Personnel File. HS9/56/7, The National Archives.

159 **"strength in numbers":** Guy d'Artois audio recording, AV2_172_044_A, Musée Royal 22e Régiment, La Citadelle de Québec.
tried to get to sleep: Louis Lapalus, *Ma vie, ma guerre*, p. 193.
three German prisoners of war: Ibid., p. 164.

160 **"large bag of biscuits":** Ibid.
capture the observation Post: René Fléchard, *Le Maquis de Saint-Bonnet-de-Joux*, pp. 87–89.
occupants opened fire: Rob Forsyth, *d'Artois Interviews*, notes from interviews with Guy and Sonia d'Artois, p. 47. Rob Forsyth Fonds, F0545, Clara Thomas Archives and Special Collections, York University. Also see a slightly different description of this incident in André Jeannet, *La Seconde Guerre Mondiale en Saône-et-Loire*, p. 177.
deeply upset Guy: Ibid.
routinely attacked: Recommendation for DSO for Guy d'Artois, Personnel File, HS9/56/7, The National Archives.
keep them severed: "Report of Dieudonné, known as Michel." Dated October 7, 1944. p. 1.

161 **about twenty-five kilometres away:** Louis Lapalus, *Ma vie, ma guerre*, p. 164.
"terrorists," and "bandits": Guy d'Artois audio recording, AV2_172_044_B, Musée Royal 22e Régiment, La Citadelle de Québec.

and his house burned: René Fléchard, *Le Maquis de Saint-Bonnet-de-Joux* pp. 93–94, and André Jeannet, *La Seconde Guerre Mondiale en Saône-et-Loire*, p. 298.

when he broke away: Louis Lapalus, *Ma vie, ma guerre*, p. 174.

162 **a turbulent relationship:** Albert Browne-Bartroli, *Mémoires d'un résistant en Saône-et-Loire*, p. 99.

arrive "in abundance": Louis Lapalus, *Ma vie, ma guerre*, p. 166.

15: HIDING IN PLAIN SIGHT

163 **Sydney suddenly woke:** Sydney Hudson, *Undercover Operator: An SOE's Experiences in France and the Far East*, p. 77.

"completely unperturbed" state: Ibid.

164 **she'd always done so:** Sonia d'Artois, interview with Robin Fowler.

General Friedrich Dollmann: Samuel W. Mitcham and Gene Mueller, *Hitler's Commanders*, p. 122.

165 **"thankful that he hadn't":** Sonia d'Artois, interview with Robin Fowler.

local Gestapo: David Stafford, *Ten Days to D-Day: Countdown to the Liberation of Europe*, p. 246.

spat on for just that reason: Rob Forsyth, *d'Artois Interviews*, notes from interviews with Guy and Sonia d'Artois, p. 53. Rob Forsyth Fonds, F0545, Clara Thomas Archives and Special Collections, York University.

visit a local doctor: Ibid., p. 30.

166 **made it seem so:** Ibid.

"along with him as a cover": Ibid.

167 **loosely based on their story:** Sydney Hudson, unpublished novel, d'Artois family private papers.

to keep their relationship very quiet: Sonia d'Artois, interview with Robin Fowler.

George informed him: Sydney Hudson, *Undercover Operator*, p. 77.

"tinge of disappointment": Ibid. pp. 77–78.

168 **asking them directly:** McKenzie Porter, "Sonia Was a Spy," *Maclean's*, February 15, 1953.

"at her heels": Ibid.

taken fully into the fold: Rob Forsyth, *d'Artois Interviews*, notes from interviews with Guy and Sonia d'Artois, p. 22.

he would later report: As quoted by David Stafford in *Ten Days to D-Day*, p. 348.

169 **"technical adviser":** Sydney Hudson, after-mission report, titled "From 8.4.44 to Date, by Albin," undated, p. 2, The National Archives.

never have been deployed: Sonia d'Artois, document titled "Blanche's Report," undated after-mission report, p. 2, HS9/56/7, The National Archives.

of five brothers: Joseph Estevès, "Biography of Claude Hilleret," Unpublished article courtesy of the author. Estevès is the author of four books about the resistance and deportations in Sarthe, http://jesteves.online.fr/.

letterbox for Sonia and Sydney: McKenzie Porter, "Sonia Was a Spy," *Maclean's*, February 15, 1953.

how to blow things up: Kate Vigurs, *Mission France: The True History of the Women of the SOE*, p. 211.

170 **"better than I can":** McKenzie Porter, "Sonia Was a Spy," *Maclean's*, February 15, 1953.

sleep until midnight: Beryl Escott, *The Heroines of SOE: Britain's Secret Women in France, F Section*, p. 205.

moments later disappear: Sydney Hudson, *Undercover Operator*, p. 80.

The distance, she admitted: Rob Forsyth, d'Artois Interviews, p. 34.

171 **"in cold blood":** Ibid.

les chevaux: Sydney Hudson, *Undercover Operator*, p. 83. Important to note here that Sydney's dates for this and subsequent events related to the forest differ wildly from those provided in several other sources. I have opted to use the date most often cited in local sources—June 20—including in André Pioger, *Le Mans et la Sarthe pendant la 2e guerre mondiale*, pp. 522–526.

Forêt de Charnie: Sydney Hudson, *Undercover Operator*, p. 84.

descended on the maquis: Ibid. And Lieutenant-Colonel E.G. Boxshall, Chronology of SOE Operations with the Resistance in France During World War, Sheet 6.

They began to flee: Sydney Hudson, *Undercover Operator*, p. 84. Details of the events of this day can also be found in André Pioger, *Le Mans et la Sarthe pendant la 2e guerre mondiale*, pp. 522–526.

172 **Claude had been killed:** Sydney Hudson, after-mission report, titled "From 8.4.44 to Date, by Albin," undated, p. 2, The National Archives.

now in German hands: Ibid. For another detailed telling of this incident, see Edmond Cohin's account in "Groupes Mobiles Franco-Anglais," in *Les Cahiers du Maine Libre: Récits de la Résistance et de la Libération dans la Région*, January 1945, p. 12–13

"so close to the Normandy front": Sydney Hudson, *Undercover Operator*, p. 86.

16: OPERATION CADILLAC

173 **"they would be shot":** Guy d'Artois audio recording, AV2_172_044_A, Musée Royal 22e Régiment, La Citadelle de Québec.

174 **"celebratory cascade of *tricolore*":** René Fléchard, *Le Maquis de Saint-Bonnet-de-Joux*, p. 109.

"very, very smart": Rob Forsyth, *d'Artois Interviews*, notes from interviews with Guy and Sonia d'Artois, p. 72. Rob Forsyth Fonds, F0545, Clara Thomas Archives and Special Collections, York University.

"They started to cry, laugh, and dance": Guy d'Artois audio recording, AV2_172_044_A, Musée Royal 22e Régiment, La Citadelle de Québec.

"a matter of emotion": Ibid.

four hundred and thirty: René Fléchard, *Le Maquis de Saint-Bonnet-de-Joux*, p. 109.

the sun was up: M.R.D. Foot, *SOE in France: An Account of the Work of the British Special Operations Executive in France, 1940–44*, p. 360. See more details at https://resistancefrancaise.blogspot.com/2015/12/operation-cadillac-le-parachutage.html.

175 **shirts, even underwear:** Rob Forsyth, *d'Artois Interviews*, notes from interviews with Guy and Sonia d'Artois, p. 72.

Even the broken containers: Guy d'Artois audio recording, AV2_172_044_B, Musée Royal 22e Régiment, La Citadelle de Québec.

"loose lips": Ibid.

including in Mâcon: Ibid. Also see Albert Browne-Bartroli, after-mission report, dated October 24, 1944, p. 2. The National Archives, HS6/567 Circuit and Mission reports and Interrogations.

176 **Maquis de Sylla:** Another noteworthy figure at Sylla was Captain Raoul Lamiral, who led the battalion under Guy's control.

Saint-Julien-de-Civry, respectively: René Fléchard, *Le Maquis de Saint-Bonnet-de-Joux*, p. 84.

"ready for action": Guy d'Artois audio recording, AV2_172_044_A, Musée Royal 22e Régiment, La Citadelle de Québec.

attempt at wartime propaganda: Guy d'Artois audio recording, AV2_172_044_A, Musée Royal 22e Régiment, La Citadelle de Québec.

Allied planes above: Ibid.

once scored cattle: René Fléchard, *Le Maquis de Saint-Bonnet-de-Joux*, p. 85.

Guy in the quarry: André Barraud, unpublished notes, p. 53, courtesy of Jérémy Beurier.

177 **sabotage and explosives:** Pierre Jandeau, unpublished notes, Jandeau private family papers, p. 5.

wine, and even tobacco: Ibid., p. 8.
seemed to know no limits: René Fléchard, *Le Maquis de Saint-Bonnet-de-Joux*, p. 92.
women on bikes: Pierre Jandeau, unpublished notes, Jandeau family private papers.
"Michel le Canadien": F.H. Walter, "Cloak and Dagger," p. 13. Historical section file 760.013 (D1). Courtesy of Stephen Harris, Chief Historian, and Emilie Vandal, Chief Archivist, both from the Directorate of History and Heritage, Department of National Defence.

178 **"housed me and protected me":** Guy d'Artois, as quoted in *The Globe and Mail*, December 1944, p. 11.
"shot a German officer down": Guy d'Artois, as quoted by Kenneth C. Cragg in "French-Canadian's Maquis Clubbed So 58 Germans Lined Up and Shot," *The Globe and Mail*, December 20, 1944, p. 11.
at great risk to themselves: Guy d'Artois, as quoted in "Capt. G. d'Artois Recalls Life in German-Occupied France as British Agent and Leader of a Maquis Unit," *Sherbrooke Daily Record*, September 13, 1945, p. 3.
"for my sector": Kenneth C. Cragg, "French-Canadian's Maquis Clubbed," *The Globe and Mail*, December 20, 1944, p. 11.
plow back into operations: "Report of Dieudonné, known as Michel," October 7, 1944, HS9/56/7, p. 1, The National Archives.

179 **"favourite saboteur":** Guy d'Artois audio recording, AV2_172_044_A, Musée Royal 22e Régiment, La Citadelle de Québec.
a picture of the base in his mind: Rob Forsyth, *d'Artois Interviews*, notes from interviews with Guy and Sonia d'Artois, p. 75.
"What if you get killed?": Ibid., p. 60.
"frequenting cafés and restaurants": Ibid., pp. 66–67.
when the shooting occurred: "Capt. G. d'Artois Recalls Life in German-Occupied France," *Sherbrooke Daily Record*, September 13, 1945, p. 3.

180 **felt at home:** Michel Gariepy and Renée Hudon-Auger, "Major Guy d'Artois du Royal 22e Régiment." *Gens de Mon Pays*. Archives Radio-Canada. Broadcast. October 23, 1977.
"they live to eat": Guy d'Artois audio recording, AV2_172_044_A, Musée Royal 22e Régiment, La Citadelle de Québec.
"doesn't mean we didn't eat well": Ibid.
his shoes shined in weeks: Albert Browne-Bartroli, *Mémoires d'un résistant en Saône-et-Loire*, p. 105.
"if you survive, that is": Ibid., p. 107.
"famous in the region": Ibid., p. 105.

181 **"*vendu aux anglais*":** René Fléchard, *Le Maquis de Saint-Bonnet-de-Joux*, p. 105.

their very presence: Patrick Veyret, *Histoire de la résistance en Saône-et-Loire*, p. 80.

French Forces of the Interior: Albert Browne-Bartroli said he received a message after D-Day that resistance forces in the DITCHER area were now officially under the umbrella of the French Forces of the Interior, under the leadership of General Marie-Pierre Koenig in London. The move was aimed at unifying interior resistance forces and nominally placing them under de Gaulle's control. Albert Browne-Bartroli, after-mission report, dated October 24, 1944, p. 2, The National Archives.

181 **"local public opinion":** Patrick Veyret, *Histoire de la résistance en Saône-et-Loire*, p. 80.

"a military enterprise.": George de la Ferté-Sénectère, appointed by de Gaulle to lead a united resistance in the region under the French Forces of the Interior, quoted in Ibid.

being an outsider: Guy d'Artois, as quoted by Pierre Vennat in *Les héros oubliés*, p. 76.

182 **"backed me so well":** Kenneth C. Cragg, "French-Canadian's Maquis Clubbed," *The Globe and Mail*, December 20, 1944, p. 11.

"Michel le Canadien": René Fléchard, *Le Maquis de Saint-Bonnet-de-Joux*, p. 111.

"on the sore spots": Albert Browne-Bartroli, *Mémoires d'un résistant en Saône-et-Loire*, p. 105.

Albert summoned Guy: Robert Pelletier, "2 millions de francs n'ont pas réussi à sauver la vie d'un agent secret québécois," *Le Journal de Montréal*, March 24, 1983, p. 40. Also see "7 membres de la resistance," *Le journal de Québec*, March 24, 1983, p.4.

his mediocre hideaway: "Behind Enemy Lines," *The Fifth Estate*, by Hana Gartner, et. al., aired October 27, 1987. Canadian Broadcasting Corporation (CBC) Archives.

"to which he was subject": F.H. Walter, "Cloak and Dagger," p. 11, Historical section file 760.013 (D1).

183 **their German captors:** Robert Pelletier, "2 millions de francs," *Le Journal de Montréal*, March 24, 1983. p. 40.

made of its purpose: "History of F section by Colonel Buckmaster/Personnel dropped by F Section. Expenditure in field," HS7/121, SOE History 86, 1943–1945, The National Archives. Also see Roy MacLaren, *Canadians Behind Enemy Lines*, p. 97.

other men in tow: Rob Forsyth, *d'Artois Interviews*, notes from interviews with Guy and Sonia d'Artois, p. 49.

"All is understood": Robert Pelletier, "2 millions de francs," *Le Journal de Montréal*, March 24, 1983, p. 40.

saw Albert rip open: Rob Forsyth, *d'Artois Interviews*, notes from interviews with Guy and Sonia d'Artois, p. 66.
"No names, nothing": Guy d'Artois, interviewed in "Behind Enemy Lines," *The Fifth Estate*, by Hana Gartner et. al., aired October 27, 1987. Via CBC Archives. In the interview he gave to a Canadian newspaper, Guy could not rule out that one of the men was Klaus Barbie—the German SS officer who was labelled "the butcher of Lyon" and was responsible for the death and torture of countless resistance figures in the region. There is no way to independently verify either this fact or the entire story.
"lives of six people": Robert Pelletier, "2 millions de francs," *Le Journal de Montréal*, March 24, 1983, p. 40. There is no available evidence confirming whether London okayed the exchange, but it would not have been the first time the SOE had negotiated and paid ransom for the release of captured agents. A Polish SOE agent who came to be known as Christine Granville successfully freed two other agents in France by paying the Gestapo a ransom of two million francs, money that was apparently parachuted in from London for the purpose.
"never heard a thing": d'Artois, Guy, interviewed in "Behind Enemy Lines," *The Fifth Estate*.

184 **Andrée Borrel, Vera Leigh, Sonya Olschanezky, and Diana Rowden:** For a thorough accounting of the story of these four women, see Rita Kramer, *Flames in the Field: The Story of Four SOE Agents in Occupied France*.
were then incinerated: Ibid., p. 115.
disappeared without a trace: Kate Vigurs, *Mission France: The True History of the Women of SOE*, p. 250.
were summarily executed: Tim Cook, *Fight to the Finish: Canadians in the Second World War* 1944–1945, p. 264.

185 **"worked openly with the Germans":** Guy d'Artois, "Report of Dieudonné, known as Michel," October 7, 1944, HS9/56/7, p. 1, The National Archives.
"we soon found her out": Kenneth C. Cragg, "French-Canadian's Maquis Clubbed," *The Globe and Mail*, December 20, 1944, p. 11.
fifty German prisoners: Ibid.
until the war was over: Ibid.

17: AWAY

186 **with some misgivings:** Sydney Hudson, *Undercover Operator: An SOE's Experiences in France and the Far East*, p. 95.
a place called Château du Breuil: Sonia d'Artois, interview with Robin Fowler.

187 **involved in the resistance:** Paul McCue, from an ongoing project titled "Roll of Honour of F Section," "Biography of Captain Henri Paul Sevenet." January 4, 1921, unpublished document. More of Paul's work can be found at www.secret-ww2.net. Also see letter from Maurice Buckmaster dated June 4, 1946, in which he describes Marthe Dauprat-Sevenet as supporting the resistance from 1941, and whose work "tangibly contributed to liberation." Courtesy of Paul McCue.
group that received him: Ibid.
the south of France: Sydney Hudson, *Undercover Operator*, p. 100, and https://fusilles-40-44.maitron.fr/spip.php?article163956.
"off the ground": See Philippe de Vomécourt, *An Army of Amateurs*.
London on their behalf: Sonia d'Artois, document titled "Blanche's Report," undated after-mission report, p. 1, HS9/56/7, The National Archives. It is important to note that there are several discrepancies in dates between Sydney's and Sonia's versions, with Sonia's appearing to be more in line with the available documentation.
just five or six men: Sydney Hudson, after-mission report, undated, p. 2, The National Archives.

188 **"you were in danger":** Rob Forsyth, *d'Artois Interviews*, notes from interviews with Guy and Sonia d'Artois, p. 49. Rob Forsyth Fonds, F0545, Clara Thomas Archives and Special Collections, York University.
a pair of shoes: Marthe Dauprat-Sevenet, letter to Sonia, May 10, 1947, d'Artois family private papers.

189 **"nothing I could do":** Sydney Hudson, *Undercover Operator*, p. 95.
"headquarters, the *Feldkommandantur*": Ibid.
Claude Hureau: One historian, Joseph Estevès, identifies his real name as Maurice Hureau, and Claude Hurteau as his code name. Biography of Eugène Bec, courtesy of the author. Estevès is the author of four books about the resistance and deportations in Sarthe, http://jesteves.online.fr/.
Around midnight, an almighty explosion: André Pioger, *Le Mans et la Sarthe pendant la 2e guerre mondiale*, p. 109.
to attend the baptism: Sonia d'Artois, interview with Robin Fowler.
"without conditions": Handwritten baptism certificate dated July 30, 1944, d'Artois family private papers.

190 **misidentified herself:** Ibid.
late into the night: Rob Forsyth, *d'Artois Interviews*, notes from interviews with Guy and Sonia d'Artois, p. 49.
talk his way through: Sonia d'Artois, interview with Robin Fowler.

191 **treasurer of the Le Mans Catholic Church:** David Stafford, *Ten Days to D-Day: Countdown to the Liberation of Europe*, p. 245.

BBC's *messages personnels*: Sonia d'Artois, interview with Robin Fowler.
provided an IOU: Sydney Hudson, *Undercover Operator: An SOE Agent's Experiences in France and the Far East*, p. 89.
two hundred thousand francs: Ibid. "Debts incurred by the Headmaster Circuit in the Region of Le Mans," dated March 11, 1944, The National Archives. This document indicates the Abbé is owed 250,000 francs; that, along with various other debts that needed to be paid back, totalled more than two million francs.

192 **"to be absolutely fearless":** Sydney Hudson, after-mission report, undated. Contained in Circuit & Missions Reports & Interrogations (H), dated March 11, p. 6, HS6/572, The National Archives.
brand-new watch: Sonia d'Artois, interview with Robin Fowler.
On August 8, 1944: Associated Press, "War Touches Le Mans Again," *The Charlotte News*, August 8, 1944, p. 1.
as German forces retreated: Sydney Hudson, *Undercover Operator*, p. 103. See also André Pioger, *Le Mans et la Sarthe pendant la 2e guerre mondiale*, p. 109. See also this British Pathé video captured as Americans marched into Le Mans: https://www.youtube.com/watch?v=kbsSbj9EUME.
Sonia was among them: Sydney Hudson, *Undercover Operator*, p. 103.

193 **by two armed men:** Sonia d'Artois, interview with Robin Fowler.
Sonia said hesitantly in hindsight: Ibid.
"for the U.S. army": Handwritten note, signed "D.M. Batey, Maj aut G2, 5th Arm'd Div.," dated August 8, 1944. Private papers of Lieutenant-Colonel C.S. Hudson DSO, Imperial War Museum.
trust placed in Sydney and Sonia: Typed letter, signed by Robert I. Powell, Lt. Col. Cav Commanding, dated September 8, 1944. Private papers of Lieutenant-Colonel C.S. Hudson DSO, Imperial War Museum.

194 **including those of children:** Rob Forsyth, *d'Artois Interviews*, notes from interviews with Guy and Sonia d'Artois, p. 89.
photos and proper stamps: Sydney Hudson, *Undercover Operator*, p. 109.
In late August: Ibid., p. 110.

195 **nearly a dozen times:** Ibid.
"go for it," said Sonia: Sonia d'Artois, interview with Robin Fowler.
"put my foot down and accelerated": Sydney Hudson, *Undercover Operator*, p. 111.
riddled with bullets: Sonia d'Artois, interview with Robin Fowler.
He'd been hit: Ibid, p. 111.

196 **"completely pillaged":** Ibid.
"taken hostage by the Germans," said Sonia: Sonia d'Artois, interview with Robin Fowler.

197 **openly for the first time:** Ibid.

sensed Sonia's distress: Rob Forsyth, *d'Artois Interviews*, notes from interviews with Guy and Sonia d'Artois, p. 50.

198 **"I was speechless":** Sydney Hudson, *Undercover Operator*, p. 114.

199 **fought to conceal:** Ibid.

18: TRIUMPHANT MINUTES

200 **the voice said:** Louis Lapalus, *Ma vie, ma guerre*, p. 182.

armoured vehicles, and planes: Lieutenant-Colonel E.G. Boxshall, "Chronology of SOE Operations with the Resistance in France During World War II," Sheet 49. Also see Albert Browne-Bartroli, *Mémoires d'un résistant en Saône-et-Loire*, p. 102.

201 **"with a hundred men":** René Fléchard, *Le Maquis de Saint-Bonnet-de-Joux*, p. 110.

Battle of Cluny: André Jeannet, *La Seconde Guerre Mondiale en Saône-et-Loire*, p. 228.

an all-out, "savage" fight: Albert Browne-Bartroli, *Mémoires d'un résistant en Saône-et-Loire*, p. 102.

German planes appeared overhead: Ibid., p. 229

"continue[d] at their posts heroically": Ibid.

in DITCHER's arsenal: Guy d'Artois, "Report of Dieudonné, known as Michel," October 7, 1944, HS9/56/7, p. 2, The National Archives.

Postes, Télégraphes et Téléphones: Louis Lapalus, *Ma vie, ma guerre*, p. 172. Also see Judex mission report, p. 66, The National Archives.

202 **was named Tokyo:** From drawing of network, d'Artois family private papers. Also see René Fléchard, *Le Maquis de Saint-Bonnet-de-Joux*, p. 6.

at his disposal: Guy d'Artois, "Report of Dieudonné, known as Michel," October 7, 1944, HS9/56/7, p. 2, The National Archives.

"*companies to take position*": "Report on Judex mission," p. 66. HS7/134, The National Archives.

"basis of all the success": Guy d'Artois, "Report of Dieudonné, known as Michel," October 7, 1944, HS9/56/7, p. 2, National Archives.

203 **most of our success:** Albert Browne-Bartroli, report on after-mission briefing, dated November 25, 1944, p. 5, Circuit and Mission Reports and Interrogations, HS6-567, The National Archives.

"more than 400 dead": Lieutenant-Colonel E.G. Boxshall, "Chronology of SOE Operations with the Resistance in France During World War II," Sheet 49, originally produced in London, December 1960, Imperial War Museum.

"except as prisoner": Ibid. Also see Albert Browne-Bartroli, after-mission report, dated October 24, 1944, p. 3, Circuit and Mission reports and Interrogations, HS6/567, The National Archives.

"more triumphant minutes": Ibid.
successfully defended by the resistance: André Jeannet, *La Seconde Guerre Mondiale en Saône-et-Loire*, p. 230.

19: CONSTERNATION

204 **on the morning of August 18:** André Barraud, "Maquis de Sylla, Historique, Origines." Barraud was commander of the second company of Sylla's 1st Charollais Battalion under Guy. Unpublished document, copy courtesy of Jérémy Beurier, p. 53.
their finest dress: Ibid.
uniformed Allied officers: "Operational Report of Team Anthony." In France – Jedburghs, Team Anthony, HS6/479, The National Archives.
"gentle as a child": Albert Browne-Bartroli, *Mémoires d'un résistant*, p. 106.
205 **uniform, stiffly saluting:** Photos courtesy of Jérémy Beurier. The same photos also appear in André Barraud, "Maquis de Sylla, Historique, Origines." Barraud was commander of the second company of the 1st Charollais Battalion under Guy. Unpublished document, copy courtesy of Jérémy Beurier, pp. 52–53.
Deprez, and other leaders: "La bataille de Génélard," document in private papers of André Barraud, p. 35. Courtesy of historian Jérémy Beurier.
the German garrisons in all those towns: Ibid, p. 38. Also see René Fléchard, *Le Maquis de Saint-Bonnet-de-Joux*, p. 117.
based at a nearby school: "La bataille de Génélard," p. 38. Courtesy of historian Jérémy Beurier. More accounts of the battle are available in a pamphlet titled "Commémoration du Cinquantenaire de la Bataille de Génelard 22 Août 1944," courtesy of historian Jérémy Beurier.
206 **his group in battle:** "Romance of 'Michel le Canadien' Started in Air, Grew in France," *Montreal Gazette*, December 20, 1944, p. 11.
sustained on both sides: René Fléchard, *Le Maquis de Saint-Bonnet-de-Joux*, p. 119.
part of the building: Rob Forsyth, *d'Artois Interviews*, notes from interviews with Guy and Sonia d'Artois, p. 82. Rob Forsyth Fonds, F0545, Clara Thomas Archives and Special Collections, York University.
"horribly mutilated": André Godot, *Histoires des Palingeois*, p. 263.
Paray-le-Monial train station: René Fléchard, *Le Maquis de Saint-Bonnet-de-Joux*, p. 115.
was ordered to liberate: A debate continues until today as to who gave the order. Some insist it was Guy, while Fléchard and others insist that it came from Deprez. Both men were involved in the battles of that day. Nevertheless, the order came to intercept the train and liberate those deportees, and that came at a great cost.

armoured train arrived: There are some accounts that say the armoured train was already in the station. Albert Browne-Bartroli wrote that the train arrived mid-attack, in *Mémoires d'un résistant en Saône-et-Loire*, p. 103.
"shot at close range": René Fléchard, *Le Maquis de Saint-Bonnet-de-Joux*, p. 115.

207 **"Dachau concentration camp":** "Anniversaire du 22 août 1944." *Le Journal de Saône-et-Loire*. August 20, 2011. Accessed online. https://www.lejsl.com/pays-charolais/2011/08/20/anniversaire-du-22-aout-1944.
one final journey: Guy d'Artois audio recording, AV2_172_044_B, Musée Royal 22e Régiment, La Citadelle de Québec.
"you're still at it": Ibid.
massacre caused "consternation": according to Louis Lapalus, *Ma vie, ma guerre*, p. 185.
for the tragic results: Patrick Veyret, *Histoire de la Résistance en Saône-et-Loire*, p. 80.
"to have him arrested": Claude Rochat, in ibid. Rochat led the Armée secrète in Sâone-et-Loire.
August 20, 1944, a Sunday: Paul McCue, "Secret WW2," www.secret-ww2.net, from ongoing project titled "Roll of Honour of F Section."

208 **no one remained alive:** Ibid. Also Colonel F.H. Walter, "Cloak and Dagger," p. 11.
was among them: Ibid.
no known grave: Ibid.

20: LIBERATION

211 **On September 4, 1944:** Louis Lapalus, *Ma vie, ma guerre*, p. 193.
"our hands full of flowers": Pierre Jandeau, handwritten notes, Jandeau family private papers, 1985.
"the war wasn't yet over": Louis Lapalus, *Ma vie, ma guerre*, p. 193.
"who smelled of mothballs": Ibid.
one last time: André Barraud, "Maquis de Sylla, Historique, Origines," September 12, p. 60, unpublished document, copy courtesy of Jérémy Beurier.

212 **to find Sonia:** Rob Forsyth, *d'Artois Interviews*, notes from interviews with Guy and Sonia d'Artois, p. 77. Rob Forsyth Fonds, F0545, Clara Thomas Archives and Special Collections, York University.

213 **to find a hospital:** Ibid., p. 76.
"meant for you": Sonia d'Artois, quoting Guy, in interview with Robin Fowler.
headed off to the capital: Rob Forsyth, *d'Artois Interviews*, notes from interviews with Guy and Sonia d'Artois, p. 78.
Hotel Cecil on rue Didier: M.R.D. Foot, *The SOE in France,* p. 371.

final intelligence assignment: Sydney Hudson, after-mission report, undated, pp. 5–6, Circuit & Missions Reports & Interrogations (H), HS6/572. The National Archives.

214 ***"as long as he wants me"*****:** Sydney Hudson, unpublished novel, p. 185, d'Artois family private papers.

further in life spiritually: Sonia d'Artois, interview with Robin Fowler.

215 ***"I'll not give up hope"*****:** Sydney Hudson, unpublished novel, p. 187, d'Artois family private papers.

"it was Guy": Rob Forsyth, *d'Artois Interviews*, notes from interviews with Guy and Sonia d'Artois, p. 78.

"if she was still alive," said Guy: Ben Rose, "She Winked, Jumped, I Said 'Marry Me,'" *Toronto Daily Star*, December 18, 1944, front of second section.

"get on with it and do it": Sonia d'Artois, interview with Robin Fowler.

216 **famous tearoom in Paris:** Sydney Hudson, *Undercover Operator: An SOE Agent's Experiences in France and the Far East*, p. 116.

"future life with him": Ibid.

"live up to my commitment": Sonia d'Artois, interview with Robin Fowler.

interviews with Buckmaster in Paris: Report on Judex mission, p. 8, HS7/134, The National Archives.

Dakota destined for London: Rob Forsyth, *d'Artois Interviews*, notes from interviews with Guy and Sonia d'Artois, p. 79. Also see Army Air Forces air transport command ticket, Paris to London, issued October 4, d'Artois family private papers.

further SOE duties: Sydney Hudson, *Undercover Operator*, p. 123.

217 **"one matured quickly":** Ibid., p. 117.

21: WAR BRIDE

221 **Dec 11, 1944:** Sonia's Canadian travel certificate stamped by immigration authorities in Liverpool as "Embarked 11 Dec, 1944." Found in Private Papers of Mrs. S.E.F. d'Artois, Imperial War Museum.

SS *Pasteur*: "Cabin Class" Immigration Identification Card, lists "Pasteur" under Name of Ship. The card is stamped by Canadian Immigration in Halifax on December 19, 1944. It is also stamped "Landed Immigrant." Private Papers of Mrs. S.E.F. d'Artois, Imperial War Museum.

many of them pilots: "34 British Brides, Nine Airmen reach City in Two Special Trains," *The Montreal Gazette.* December 21, 1944. p. 11.

222 **"what we'd talk about now":** "Love Story Outlasts Dangers of War," *Montreal Gazette*, February 9, 1985, p. H1.

Red Cross Workers: For a snapshot of the experience of war brides coming to Canada, see https://www.veterans.gc.ca/eng/remembrance/history/second-world-war/canadian-war-brides.

223 **"welcome addition to our country":** See Steve Schwinghamer, "Kinship, Inclusion and Exclusion in Canadian Immigration History." Canadian Museum of Immigration at Pier 21, accessed online. https://pier21.ca/research/immigration-history/kinship-inclusion-and-exclusion-canadian-immigration-history.

"valid for a single journey": Canadian Travel Certificate No. 2624, issued December 4, 1944, Private Papers of Mrs. S.E.F. d'Artois, MBE, Imperial War Museum.

her mother-in-law: Sonia d'Artois, interview with Robin Fowler.

224 **on December 19:** Canadian Travel Certificate, No. 2624, stamped by Canadian immigration in Halifax, Nova Scotia, on December 19, 1944, and the stamp "Landed Immigrant," Private Papers of Mrs. S.E.F. d'Artois, MBE, Imperial War Museum.

"ON SPECIAL TRAIN": Telegram dated December 19, 1944, d'Artois private papers.

"We were all new to Canada": Sonia d'Artois, interview with Robin Fowler.

"It was just so bleak": Ibid. In one newspaper interview, she described her view en route as "exquisite."

"TO BE WITH YOU": Telegram dated December 20, d'Artois family private papers.

225 a **"crushing embrace":** Ben Rose, "d'Artois Thinks Stork Too May Come by 'Chute," *Toronto Daily Star*, December 21, 1944, p. 3.

"in the latest Paris mode": Ibid.

as **Antoinette described her:** Kenneth Cragg, "Packing Favourite Gun, Sonia Shot Up Nazi Car." *The Globe and Mail*. December 21, 1944. p. 13.

226 **could buy new clothes:** Letter from F Section dated October 9, 1944, Sonia d'Artois personnel file, HS9/56/7, The National Archives. And Carole Seymour-Jones, *She Landed by Moonlight: The Story of Secret Agent Pearl Witherington, the Real "Charlotte Gray"*, pp. 347–348. Seymour-Jones attributes the letter to Vera Atkins.

On October 25: Supreme Headquarters Allied Expeditionary Force Rear Headquarters letter directing Guy and Sonia to travel by military aircraft on or about 25 October "to carry out an assigned mission." Dated October 24, 1944.

smile playing on her lips: Photograph, likely taken by Guy D'Artois; dated "October '44" on the back, d'Artois family private papers.

"at Cartier in Paris": Sonia d'Artois, interview with Robin Fowler.

227 **were personally invited:** Copy of invitation from Charolles mayor, on "Mairie de Charolles" letterhead and stamp, dated November 9, 1944. The letter is accompanied by a copy of the envelope in which it was sent, addressed to "Capitaine Michel, chez Sarrazin on Rue de la Condémine." Found in Ron Cohen's private papers related to d'Artois mini-series.
archbishop's bedroom: Sonia d'Artois, interview with Robin Fowler.
service in French Indochina: David Stafford, *Ten Days to D-Day: Countdown to the Liberation of Europe*, p. 375.
"They drummed me out of the army": McKenzie Porter, "Sonia Was a Spy," *Maclean's*, February 15, 1953, p. 46.
rocket attacks: Carole Seymour-Jones, *She Landed by Moonlight*, p. 347.

228 **"a good start":** Sonia d'Artois, interview with Robin Fowler.
Flavia, now Lady Seton: "Romance Began as They Jumped into German Lines." *The Daily Sketch.* Flavia had married Sir Alexander Hay Seton and became Lady Seton.

22: THE LIMELIGHT

229 **"disclosed today":** Fred Backhouse, The Canadian Press. "French Speaking Canadians Led Maquis in Special Work," *The Windsor Star*. December 16, 1944, p. 2.
in Halifax on December 14: Copy of "Immigration Identification Card" in the name of d'Artois, Lionel G, stamped by Canadian Immigration on December 14, 1944.
The men posed together: The men who appear in the photo are Lieutenant J.E. Fournier, Lieutenant Paul. E. Thibeault, Captain Joseph H.A. Benoit, Major Paul Labelle, Captain Jacques Taschereau, Captain Guy d'Artois, Captain J. Paul Archambault, and in some versions of the photo, Captain Paul Meunier also appears. December 16, 1944. Library and Archives Canada.

230 **"they stick together":** Ronald Williams, "60 French Canadians Blazed D-Day Trail," *Toronto Star.* December 16, 1944, p. 3.
"hasn't changed a bit": "Heroic Couple in Blackout," *The Montreal Star*. December 21, 1944. p. 3.
"fell in love with her": "Parachuted behind Nazi Lines for Their Honeymoon," *Toronto Star*, December 18, 1944.

231 **"any more of our wounded":** Kenneth C. Cragg, "French-Canadian's Maquis Clubbed So 58 Germans Lined Up and Shot," *The Globe and Mail*, December 20, 1944, p. 11.
"with their rifle butts": "Helped Line Up 52 Nazis, Shoot Them One by One," *Toronto Daily Star*, December 20, 1944, p. 3. Guy's superiors doubted the

veracity of this story. Albert, Guy's chief in Saône-et-Loire, however, would later tell a similar story. He described a moment when "the whole village" of Pallinges attacked the railway track and tore up two hundred metres of it. German forces surprised the town that evening, shooting fifty-three civilians in retaliation. In a counterattack that resembles the story Guy related, Albert recounts that fifty-three German prisoners "were lined up and were slowly killed with a gunshot to the back of the neck, one after another."

flurry of correspondence: Numerous letters on the topic can be found in Guy d'Artois personnel file, HS9/56/7, The National Archives.

A Major I.K. Mackenzie: He signs letter as "D.A.A.G.," presumably from the office of the Deputy Assistant Adjutant General. Guy d'Artois personnel file, HS9/56/7, The National Archives.

232 **"court of enquiry":** Document titled "Lieutenant G. d'Artois." Dated March 12, 1945. Guy d'Artois Personnel File, HS9/56/7, The National Archives.

"SHORT MAGAZINE ARTICLE": Telegram signed by W.A. Irwin, *Maclean's*, dated December 19, 1944, d'Artois family private papers.

"Killed Some? Why, Sure": *Toronto Daily Star*, December 20, 1944, p. 1.

"Shot Up Nazi Car": Kenneth C. Cragg again had the complete d'Artois scoop. *The Globe and Mail*, Dec 22, 1944, p. 13.

233 **"*the actual fighting*":** Ibid.

"from giving other publicity to this question": Various correspondence on the topic can be found in d'Artois personnel file, HS9/56/7, The National Archives.

"that the French had put up": Sonia d'Artois, note, d'Artois personnel file, HS9/56/7, The National Archives.

234 **"continuance of such publicity":** Appears to be an extract of a letter, dated Jannuary 3, 1945, from Canadian officials to Mackenzie in the War Office. d'Artois personnel file, HS9/56/7, The National Archives.

effective December 8: Letter from Felix Walter, dated January 26, 1945, d'Artois personnel file, HS9/56/7, The National Archives.

"when I bend forward": Guy d'Artois medical file, Library and Archives Canada.

"training as paratroops": Ibid.

"greatest of this war": Telegram, dated January 16, 1945. Copy can be found in Rob Forsyth, *d'Artois Interviews*, notes from interviews with Guy and Sonia d'Artois, p. 6. Rob Forsyth Fonds, F0545, Clara Thomas Archives and Special Collections, York University.

"Queen of the Amazons, Antiope, incarnate": "Événement unique dans l'histoire de la guerre." *La Presse*, December 22, 1944.

235 **"will always be Madame d'Artois":** *La Presse*, December 23, 1944.

deference to her husband: Nadya Murdoch, interview with author.

"a quiet life again": Kenneth C. Cragg, "Packing Favourite Gun, Sonia Shot Up Nazi Car," *The Globe and Mail*, December 22, 1944, p. 13.

"and her new country": Alberte Sénécal, "Ce Qui se Passe en France." *Le Samedi*, April 28, 1945, p. 5.

letter from London: Letter signed "B.R., Group Captain," dated September 4, 1945, d'Artois personnel file, HS9/56/7, The National Archives.

236 **matter of some debate:** Recommendation for award of the M.C. [crossed out, and replaced by "M.B.E."], undated, Sonia d'Artois personnel file, HS9/56/7, The National Archives.

for their military contributions: Carol Seymour-Jones, *She Landed by Moonlight: The Story of Secret Agent Pearl Witherington, the Real 'Charlotte Gray,'* pp. 353–355.

237 **"nothing civil about what I did.":** Ibid.

Sonia was mentioned: Squadron Leader William Simpson, "WAAF Girls Parachuted into France," *The Sunday Express*, March 11, 1945.

award, along with a number of others, was amended: Letter from Air Ministry, dated August 31, 1946, Private Papers of Mrs. S.E.F. d'Artois, MBE, Imperial War Museum.

"the enemy occupation": Photocopy of document titled "Extract from the Second Supplement to the London Gazette," September 3, 1946, d'Artois family private papers; HS 9/56/7, National Archives.

"with conspicuous gallantry": Commendation, Guy d'Artois personnel file, HS 9/56/7, National Archives.

238 **"(Military Cross) is justified":** Unsigned document titled "Honours and Awards," dated April 21, 1945, Guy d'Artois personnel file, HS9/56/7, The National Archives.

a Croix de Guerre with Palm: "Impressive Scene at Embassy When de Gaulle Speaks," *The Ottawa Journal*, August 30, 1945, p. 3. The article is accompanied by a Canadian Army photo showing Guy with de Gaulle after receiving the Croix de Guerre. It is important to note here that the award was only officially announced by Ottawa the following year, at which time it received yet more press coverage.

moment it was liberated: Foot, *SOE in France: An Account of the Work of the British Special Operations Executive in France, 1940–44*, p. 122. De Gaulle, said Foot, "viewed F section organizers as mercenaries."

"unexpectedly great success in the field": Pro-forma documents filled out post-mission for both Sonia and Guy, found in their personnel file, HS9/56/7, The National Archives.

"was damned brave": Ibid.

Order of the British Empire: Letter from Vera Atkins dated September 24, 1945, Sonia d'Artois personnel file, HS9/56/7, The National Archives.

239 **publicly demanding answers:** Jean Overton Fuller, *Double Webs: Light on the Secret Agents' War in France*, p. 239.
"such a terrible verdict": Sarah Helm, *A Life in Secrets: Vera Atkins and the Missing Agents of WWII*, Kindle location 249.
240 **"every agent we had lost":** Ibid., Kindle location 263.
in the face of repeated torture: M.R.D. Foot, *SOE in France*, p. 373.
executed at Buchenwald: Jonathan Vance, *Unlikely Soldiers: How Two Canadians Fought the Secret War Against Nazi Occupation*, p. 259.
incinerated beyond recognition: Tania Szabó, *Violette: The Missions of SOE Agent Violette Szabó*, p. 577.
a proper burial: Details about Stanislaw Makowski's death accessed at https://museedelaresistanceenligne.org/media7410-Stanislaw-Makowski.
241 **"of some comfort to you":** Maurice Buckmaster, letter to Alcide Beauregard's wife, dated April 30, 1945, Alcide Beauregard Personnel File, HS9/111/1, The National Archives.
credit his account: Letter from the "Effects Branch, Canadian Military headquarters," dated August 30, 1945, HS9/111/1, The National Archives.
The death of Jean-Paul Archambault: Jean-Paul Archambault personnel file HS9/49/1, The National Archives.
"people who they did": Jean Overton Fuller, *Double Webs*, p. 239.
242 **"faults were not all ours":** Maurice Buckmaster, *They Fought Alone: The Story of British Agents in France*, p. 184.
"Courage was their common badge": Ibid.
by nine months: Ibid., pp. 258–59.
"no military value": Bernd Horn, *We Will Find a Way: The Canadian Special Operations Legacy*, p. 13. Accessed online at https://publications.gc.ca/collections/collection_2018/mdn-dnd/D2-405-2018-eng.pdf.
243 **"ordinary people of France":** Philippe de Vomécourt, *An Army of Amateurs*, p. 31.
disbanded in January 1946: M.R.D. Foot, *SOE in France*, p. 45.

23: LETTERS

245 **"heart of [a] d'Artois":** Another Louis Lapalus letter, dated July 2, 1946, d'Artois family private papers.
"how to fight a war": Letter from Gaston Lévy, dated January 28, 1945, d'Artois family private papers.
attestation he'd requested: Letter from Paul Carret dated February 15, 1946, d'Artois family private papers.
246 **tampered with:** Letter from Laure Sarrazin (Maman Lucienne), dated October 17, 1945, d'Artois family private papers.

"my lucky break": Letter from Marthe Dauprat-Sevenet, May 10, 1947, d'Artois family private papers.

"furious with me": Sonia d'Artois, interview with Robin Fowler.

247 **"mixing baby formula":** McKenzie Porter, "Sonia Was a Spy," *Maclean's*, February 15, 1953.

"UNCLE MIKE BUTT": Telegram dated July 9, 1945, copy in d'Artois family private papers.

became a reservist: Guy d'Artois military record, Library and Archives Canada.

as he had promised Sonia: Michel Gariepy and Renée Hudon-Auger, "Major Guy d'Artois du Royal 22e Régiment." *Gens de Mon Pays*. Archives Radio-Canada. Broadcast. October 23, 1977.

"He did, like a shot": "Love Story Outlasts Dangers of War," *Montreal Gazette*, February 9, 1985, p. H1

248 **"I became a military man":** Michel Gariepy and Renée Hudon-Auger, "Major Guy d'Artois du Royal 22e Régiment."

the town of Rivers: Guy d'Artois military record, Library and National Archives.

"Everyone knew who Guy was": Andrew Moffat, *Korea Memories: A Canadian Gunner's Experience in the "Forgotten War,"* p. 128.

"all you see is the horizon": Michel Gariepy and Renée Hudon-Auger, "Major Guy d'Artois du Royal 22e Régiment."

249 **"If only it were true!":** Letter from Sonia d'Artois dated April 12, 1947, d'Artois family private papers.

250 **"I accept wholeheartedly," Marthe wrote back:** Letter from Marthe Dauprat-Sevenet dated May 10, 1947, d'Artois family private papers.

24: NORTH

252 **accidentally shot himself:** For the account of the Canon Turner story, I relied largely on Hugh A. Halliday's "Rescue Mission." *The Beaver* magazine. Vol. 75, Issue 2. April 1995, pp. 14–25. See also Whitney Lackenbauer, Operation Canon: Rescuing Canon John Turner in the Canadian Arctic, 1947. http://lackenbauer.ca/wp-content/uploads/2022/11/AOH11-OpCANON-final.pdf.

253 **"jumping into that area":** Sonia d'Artois, interview with Robin Fowler.

254 **"trip by dog team":** Guy d'Artois, "Strange Arctic Territory Hampers Turner Rescuers," *The Winnipeg Tribune,* November 4, 1947, p. 13. The article begins with a note that Guy had "radioed the following story of one typical day at the lonely arctic mission."

255 **the state he was in:** Sonia d'Artois, interview with Robin Fowler.
Turner was finally airborne: "Soldier's Camera Tells Dramatic Story of Arctic Rescue," *The Globe and Mail*, November 26, 1947, p. 17.
succumbed to his injuries: "Rescued in North, Dies of Wounds," *The Globe and Mail*, December 10, 1947, p. 8.
disregard for personal safety: "Mercy Fliers Get George Medal," *The Winnipeg Tribune*, July 31, 1948, p. 1.
not entirely articulated: Roy Thomas, "The Canadian SAS Company. A Missed Opportunity?" *Esprit de Corps: Canadian Military Then & Now*. Vol. 3. Issue 3. August 1993, p. 23.
included in the training syllabus: Ibid., pp. 22–24.

256 **"absolute despair of the Senior Officers":** Bernd Horn, "A Military Enigma: The Canadian Special Air Service Company, 1948–49," *Canadian Military History,* vol. 10, no. 1, Winter 2001, p. 25.
"what others said": Ibid.
"back in civilisation": Letter from Guy d'Artois, dated July 1, 1948, d'Artois family private papers.
an American couple: "We'll never forget rescue." *The Winnipeg Tribune*. August 26, 1947, p. 1
spring of 1948: Roy Thomas, "The Canadian SAS Company. A Missed Opportunity?" p. 24.
SAS was eventually disbanded: Ibid. and Bernd Horn, "A Military Enigma, p. 28.
posted to Valcartier: Guy d'Artois military record, Library and Archives Canada.

257 **Jacques de Bernonville:** For a thorough accounting of de Bernonville's story, see McKenzie Porter, "De Bernonville!" *Maclean's*. November 15, 1951, p. 10.
seeking asylum in Canada: Ibid.
"probably including Canadians": Ibid., p. 10, quoting Dr. H.L. Keenleyside, then deputy minister of mines and resources (responsible for immigration.)

258 **"We would be there":** Sonia d'Artois, interview with Robin Fowler.
about to be deported: David Vienneau. "King Cabinet approved order to let alleged Nazis stay in Canada." *Toronto Star*. March 21, 1985, A15. The article states that "Perhaps the best example of government collusion was an admission by former prime minister Louis St. Laurent's chief of staff that, in 1951, the prime minister tipped off Count Jacques de Bernonville – the former right-hand man of Gestapo chief Klaus Barbie – to leave Canada before he was deported."
bound behind his back: "21 Ans après avoir quitté le Québec, de Bernonville est assassiné au Brésil," *La Presse,* May 6, 1972, p. F7.

25: GOING EAST

261 **from Seattle to Korea:** War Diary, 1st Battalion, Royal 22e Régiment, RCIC, March 29, 1952, Library and Archives Canada.

262 **forcefully intervene:** For an updated look at the Korean War, see Bruce Cumings, *The Korean War: A History*.

"the minute I got there": Sonia d'Artois, interview with Robin Fowler.

263 **as officers' quarters:** 57-63 St. Louis Street, National Historic Site of Canada. Accessed at https://www.pc.gc.ca/apps/dfhd/page_nhs_eng.aspx?id=1853.

more like an aunt: Michael Butt, interview with author.

always in uniform: Nadya Murdoch, interview with author.

264 **"his long boots":** Robert (Bob) d'Artois, interview with author.

tough love: Ibid.

until their reunion: No letters of the Korea exchange survive in the family collection, short of a telegram, but Sonia spoke about those letters in her interview with Robin Fowler.

265 **"be mine regardless":** Letter from Guy d'Artois, dated March 30, 1950, d'Artois family private papers.

one wedding anniversary: Letter from Guy d'Artois on the occasion of their seventh anniversary, dated April 15, 1951, d'Artois family private papers.

"I believe in the future and in God's will": Ibid.

"gifts fallen from the sky": *Le Soleil*, December 24, 1965, p. C2.

"old ones in the meantime.": Ibid.

266 **mailed him a cake for his birthday:** Guy d'Artois letter to Sonia d'Artois, dated April 10, 1951. D'Artois family private papers.

"LOVING WIFE AND CHILDREN": Telegram to Major L.G. d'Artois dated December 20, 1952, d'Artois family private papers.

"all survived the war": Sonia d'Artois, interview with Robin Fowler.

267 **"a better start":** McKenzie Porter, "Sonia Was a Spy," *Maclean's*, February 15, 1953.

269 **and waving a rifle:** John Melady, *Korea: Canada's Forgotten War*, p. 247.

"returned to his unit.": Message from HQ 25 CND Inf BDE, dated July 12, 1952, copy found in d'Artois family private papers. "Sanscartier had consumed unknown quantity of native liquor during afternoon 1 jul 52."

"nicked a chap in the ear": John Melady, *Korea: Canada's Forgotten War*, p. 247.

leading the support company: War Diary, 1st Battalion, Royal 22e Régiment, RCIC. Ordres Quotidiens. Entry dated July 3, 1952, Library and Archives Canada.

270 **"French resistance movement":** The Canadian Press. "Army Officer Kills Private in Korea." *The Globe and Mail*. July 5, 1952, p. 3.

"I hated to kill him": Guy d'Artois quoted in John Melady, *Korea: Canada's Forgotten War*, p. 248.

"United Nations cemetery": details accessed at https://www.veterans.gc.ca/eng/remembrance/memorials/canadian-virtual-war-memorial/detail/80000407.

productive way to cope: Sonia d'Artois, interview with Robin Fowler.

271 **"resulted in his death":** Document from HQ 25 CDN INF BDE, dated July 12, 1952, d'Artois family private papers.

"on duty with his regiment": The Canadian Press, "d'Artois Gets Clearance from Army," *Sherbrooke Daily Record*, August 19, 1952, p. 3.

"director of training": War Diary, 1st Battalion, Royal 22e Régiment, RCIC, entry dated July 14, 1952, Library and Archives Canada.

Within a month: Ibid., entry dated August 4, 1952.

"lack of cooperation": Letter signed by Lt. Col. G.O. Taschereau, commander of 25 Canadian Reinforcement Group, dated October 29, 1952, d'Artois family private papers.

"for the common good": Letter illegibly signed by a Lt Col. from Comd 1 COMWEL Division, Division Battle School, dated October 17, 1952, d'Artois family private papers.

"at the earliest moment": Letter signed by Lt. Col. G.O. Taschereau, dated October 29, 1952.

272 **helm of B Company:** War Diary, 1 Royal 22e Régiment RCIC, November 1, 1952–November 30, 1952. Entry dated November 18.

called Hill 133: Andrew C. Moffat, *Korea Memories: A Canadian Gunner's Experiences in the "Forgotten War,"* p. 128.

"he too lived by": Ibid., p. 130

273 **"could not end quickly enough":** "A-t-on changer la société?" *Le Soleil*, December 24, 1965, p. C2.

always to the left: Guy d'Artois medical record, Library and Archives Canada.

Sonia admitted: Sonia d'Artois, interview with Robin Fowler.

26: REUNIONS

275 **a reported total of 625 dependants:** The Canadian Press, "Wives and Children Sail to Join Canadian Brigade," *The Globe and Mail*, October 20, 1955, p. 22.

276 **the Diaper Division:** Ibid.

already well established: Bob d'Artois, interview with author. For a hint of the setup at Fort Saint Louis and Werl, see "1er Bataillon, Royal 22e Régiment en Westphalie 1970," Musée Royal 22e Régiment, La Citadelle de Québec.

"you were in Germany": Bob d'Artois, interview with author.

277 **with the Royal Scots:** Derek Butt's military record also mentions him embarking for India on July 29, 1941. Courtesy of Johnny Butt.
"hadn't changed at all": Sonia d'Artois, interview with Robin Fowler.

278 **"good news of your daughter":** Letter to Leslie Butt from War Office. Dated July 12, 1944. Sonia d'Artois personnel file. HS9/56/7, The National Archives.
"back as a woman": Louette Harding, "My Life as Charlotte Gray," *You Magazine, Mail on Sunday*, February 3, 2002, pp. 46–50.

280 **"treated like royalty":** Sonia d'Artois, interview with Robin Fowler.

281 **"the warmest of welcomes":** unidentified newspaper clipping, dated May 5, 1956, under the heading "Le 'capitaine Michel', Canadien parachuté pendant l'occupation, n'a pas oublié la Résistance charollaise." Found in Robin Fowler's book on Sonia's interviews for the family.
"Mum was Mum": Bob d'Artois, interview with author.
"adored my father": Nadya Murdoch, interview with author.

282 **staff college:** Guy d'Artois military record, Library and Archives Canada.

283 **"peace with Mother":** Sonia d'Artois recalling Derek Butt's words, interview with Robin Fowler.

27: SURGERY

284 **three long months:** Sonia d'Artois, interview with Robin Fowler.

28: HOME

287 **She flourished as the steward:** Various interviews with family/friends conducted by the author.

288 **in love with Como:** Michael Butt, interview with author.
wary of upstaging him: Nadya Murdoch, interview with author.
about Violette Szabó: Lewis Gilbert, director, *Carve Her Name with Pride*, 1958.
"subject of discussion": Michael Butt, interview with author.

289 **among family friends:** Fred Langan, interview with author.
"not my whole life": Louette Harding, "My Life as Charlotte Gray," *You Magazine, Mail on Sunday*, February 3, 2002, pp. 46–50.

290 **"meet up again":** Sonia d'Artois, interview with Robin Fowler.
deployed to Asia: Guy d'Artois military record, Library and Archives Canada.
start them up again: Sonia d'Artois, interview with Robin Fowler.

291 **he would hold court:** According to various witnesses to such sessions with Guy.
reading out loud to himself: Observations in the preceding paragraph came from various interviews with family and friends.
"use of force instead": "A-t-on changer la société?" *Le Soleil*, December 24, 1965, p. C2.

"more than occasionally": Guy d'Artois medical record. Library and Archives Canada.

292 **after his mission to Korea:** Various interviews.

"struck off strength": Guy d'Artois military record, Library and Archives Canada.

"does as they please": Michel Gariepy and Renée Hudon-Auger, "Major Guy d'Artois du Royal 22e Régiment." *Gens de Mon Pays*. Archives Radio-Canada. Broadcast. October 23, 1977.

293 **The October Crisis erupted:** There are countless sources on the October Crisis; the basic outline of the key dates can be found at https://www.historymuseum.ca/history-hall/october-crisis/.

294 **"I am just a Canadian":** Guy d'Artois, as quoted by Kenneth C. Cragg in "French-Canadian's Maquis Clubbed So 58 Germans Lined Up and Shot," *The Globe and Mail*, December 20, 1944, p. 11.

"Real Basis for Unity": *The Globe and Mail*, December 21, 1944, p. 6.

295 **"never came through":** Rob Forsyth, *d'Artois Interviews*, notes from interviews with Guy and Sonia d'Artois, p. 6. Rob Forsyth Fonds, F0545, Clara Thomas Archives and Special Collections, York University.

"stifled" as a result: Bob d'Artois recalling the words of Rockingham, in an interview with the author.

orders from just anyone: Sonia d'Artois, interview with Robin Fowler.

was never enough: Based on various interviews with author.

to the point of tedium: Various witnesses, interviews with the author.

296 **"We were two out of hundreds":** Guy d'Artois, *L'amicale du 22e*, February 13, 1955, p. 4. Musée Royal 22e Régiment, La Citadelle de Québec.

Christmas of 1986: According to original proposal for the miniseries, titled "The d'Artois Story," courtesy of producer Ron Cohen.

"a happy ending": Draft of proposal for "The d'Artois Story." Rob Forsyth Fonds, F0545, Clara Thomas Archives and Special Collections, p. 1.

project was scrapped: Ron Cohen in conversation with the author. Also see Christopher Young, "CBC Cutbacks Cripple Canadian Film Industry," *Vancouver Sun*, February 2, 1985, p. 31.

29: ONE FINAL VISIT

299 **On June 9, 1984:** Louis Lapalus, "Rapport concernant la venue de Monsieur le Major Guy d'Artois . . . au 40ième anniversaire de débarquement allié et libération locale," dated July 3, 1984, Musée Royal 22e Régiment, La Citadelle de Québec.

300 ***They shall grow not old*:** Stanza from Laurence Binyon's poem "For the Fallen," first published in *The Times*, 1914.

301 **a fragile life:** Sonia d'Artois, interview with Robin Fowler.

302 **without Sonia:** He was accompanied by Captain G. Linteau, who wrote about the experience in "Le Maquis de 'Sylla' 1944–45," *La Citadelle*, August 1984, Musée Royal 22e Régiment, La Citadelle de Québec.

"Forty years have faded away": From *Le Dauphine*, June 11, 1984, quoted by Captain G. Linteau in "Le Maquis de 'Sylla' 1944–45," *La Citadelle*, August 1984.

"have been saved": Louis Lapalus, "Rapport concernant la venue de Monsieur le Major Guy d'Artois . . . au 40ième anniversaire de débarquement allié et libération locale," dated July 3, 1984, Musée Royal 22e Régiment, La Citadelle de Québec, p. 5.

303 **it took fifty-five minutes:** Rob Forsyth, *d'Artois Interviews*, notes from interviews with Guy and Sonia d'Artois, p. 46. Rob Forsyth Fonds, F0545, Clara Thomas Archives and Special Collections, York University.

cut down during the war: Captain G. Linteau in "Le Maquis de 'Sylla' 1944–45," *La Citadelle*, August 1984.

"You never know what the days will bring": Guy d'Artois, audio recording, AV2_172_044_B, Musée Royal 22e Régiment, La Citadelle de Québec.

at the Quebec Citadel: It was donated by Guy and it is indeed available and on display at the museum now.

304 **"Love Story Outlasts Dangers of War":** *Montreal Gazette*, February 9, 1985, p. H1.

"why they fell in love": Ibid.

30: REMEMBRANCE

306 **tens of thousands of people:** "Tears and Joy as Armada Sets Sail for a New Invasion," *Coventry Evening Telegraph*. June 6, 1994, p. 3.

blood-red poppies into the sea: Murray Campbell, *The Globe and Mail*, June 6, 1994, p. A1.

"you saved from tyranny's reach": William J. Clinton, "Remarks on the 50th Anniversary of D-Day at Pointe du Hoc in Normandy, France, June 6, 1994," Available online at Gerhard Peters and John T. Woolley, *The American Presidency Project*, www.presidency.ucsb.edu/documents/remarks-the-50th-anniversary-d-day-pointe-du-hoc-normandy-france.

307 **Elizabeth McIntosh, a former nurse:** As indicated on the list of invitees, d'Artois family private papers and in newspaper articles from the time.

on June 19, 1944: "The 50th Anniversary of D-Day," *Le Monde*, June 7, 1994.

309 **for five long years:** The description of Guy's decline is based largely on Sonia's interview with Robin Fowler.

310 **his wartime memories:** Sonia d'Artois, interview with Robin Fowler.

311 **Finance Minister Paul Martin:** Lieutenant Luc Charron, "Loss of a Canadian Hero," *The Maroon Beret*, Vol. 4, No. 2, August 1999, p. 30.

"behind your charm": Patrick's speech is from the d'Artois family private papers.

part of the procession: Lieutenant Luc Charron, "Loss of a Canadian Hero," *The Maroon Beret*, Vol. 4, No. 2, August 1999, p. 30.

312 **"demons had gone":** Sonia d'Artois, interview with Robin Fowler.

31: ÇA FAIT LONGTEMPS

313 **"all over again":** Sonia d'Artois, interview with Robin Fowler.

315 **might have been "easier":** Michael Butt, interview with author.

316 **would feature interviews:** *Behind Enemy Lines: The Real Charlotte Grays*, directed by Jenny Morgan.

"couldn't believe it": Sonia d'Artois, interview with Robin Fowler.

317 **"*Ça fait longtemps?*":** Sydney Hudson in the documentary *Behind Enemy Lines: The Real Charlotte Grays*, directed by Jenny Morgan.

had a relationship: Nadya Murdoch, interview with author.

318 **Ruth had grown up in Essen, Germany:** Sydney Hudson, *Undercover Operator: An SOE Agent's Experiences in France and the Far East*, p. 187.

married soon after: Ibid.

Violette Szabó: For an image see "The Maquis/Szabò Plaque," credit Ruth Mansergh, www.iwm.org.uk/memorials/item/memorial/57804.

32: SONIA'S WAY

321 **"your full name":** Sonia d'Artois, interview with Robin Fowler.

"incredible story to tell": Robin Fowler, interview with the author.

322 **On her own terms:** Sonia d'Artois, interview with Robin Fowler.

EPILOGUE: NEVER TOO LATE

323 **Legion of Honour (Légion d'honneur):** "Awards to Canadians." *Canada Gazette*. March 24, 2007. The exact date of the ceremony is not known, but family and French officials believe it occurred sometime in 2007.

told an interviewer: Louette Harding, "My Life as Charlotte Gray," *You Magazine*, *Mail on Sunday*, February 3, 2002, pp. 46–50.

BIBLIOGRAPHY

Adleman, Robert, and Walton, George. *The Devil's Brigade*. Annapolis: Naval Institute Press, 1966.

Allport, Alan. *Britain at Bay: The Epic Story of the Second World War, 1938–1941.* New York: Vintage Books, 2020.

Argyle, Ray. *The Paris Game: Charles de Gaulle, the Liberation of Paris, and the Gamble that Won France*. Toronto: Dundurn Press, 2014.

Bailey, Roderick. *Forgotten Voices of the Secret War: An Inside History of Special Operations During the Second World War*. London: Ebury Press, 2008.

Basu, Shrabani. *Spy Princess: The Life of Noor Inayat Khan*. Stroud: The History Press, 2008.

Bercuson, David. *Our Finest Hour: Canada Fights the Second World War.* Toronto: HarperCollins, 2015.

Bernier, Serge, translated by Phillips, Charles. *The Royal 22e Régiment, 1914–1999.* Montreal: Art Global, 2000.

Binney, Marcus. *The Women Who Lived for Danger: The Agents of the Special Operations Executive*. New York: William Morrow, 2003.

Bourne-Patterson, Major Robert. *SOE in France 1941–45: An Official Account of the Special Operations Executive's 'British' Circuits in France*. Barnsley: Frontline Books, 2016.

Braddon, Russell. *Nancy Wake: World War Two's Most Rebellious Spy.* New York: Little A, 2019.

Buckmaster, Maurice. *They Fought Alone: The True Story of SOE's Agents in Wartime France.* London: Biteback Publishing, 2014.

Burns, James MacGregor. *Roosevelt: The Soldier of Freedom (1940–1945)*. New York: Open Road Media, 2012.

Carroll, Francis. *Athenia Torpedoed: The U–Boat Attack That Ignited the Battle of the Atlantic*. Anapolis: Naval Institute Press, 2012.

Chorley, W.R. *RAF Bomber Command Losses of the Second World War*, Volume 5. Hinkley: Midland Publishing, 1997.

Churchill, Winston S. *The Second World War,* vol. 1–6. London: Houghton Mifflin, 1948–1954.

Cohin, Edmond, "Groupes Mobiles Franco-Anglais," in *Les Cahiers du Maine Libre: Récits de la Resistance et de la Libération dans la Région*. Publisher Unknown. January 1945.

Cook, Tim. *Fight to the Finish: Canadians in the Second World War 1944–1945*. Toronto: Allen Lane, 2015.

Cook, Tim. *Vimy: The Battle and the Legend.* Toronto: Allen Lane, 2017.

Cookeridge, E.H. *Inside SOE: The First Full Story of Special Operations Executive in Western Europe 1940–45*. London: Arthur Barker Limited, 1966.

Cummings, Bruce. *The Korean War: A History*. New York: Modern Library, 2011.

Curwain, Eric. *Almost Top Secret*. Unpublished manuscript, held by the Royal Canadian Military Institute. RCMI, undated.

Dalton, Hugh. *The Fateful Years: Memoirs 1931–1945.* London: Frederick Muller, Ltd., 1957.

Elliott, Major S.R. *Scarlet to Green: A History of Intelligence in the Canadian Army 1903–1963*. Victoria: Canadian Military Intelligence Association, 2018.

Escott, Beryl E. *The Heroines of SOE: Britain's Secret Women in France, F Section.* Stroud: The History Press, 2010.

FitzSimons, Peter. *Nancy Wake: The Gripping True Story of the Woman Who Became the Gestapo's Most Wanted Spy.* Sydney: HarperCollins Publishers, 2001.

Fléchard, René. *Le Maquis de Saint-Bonnet-de-Joux.* Charolles: Dumas, 1991.

Foot, M.R.D. *SOE in France: An Account of the Work of the British Special Operations Executive in France 1940–1944.* London: Whitehall History Publishing, 1966.

Fuller, Jean Overton. *Double Webs: Light on the Secret Agents' War in France.* London: Sapere Books, 2023.

Godot, André. *Histoires des Palingeois au XXe Siècle.* Pallinges: Les Amis du Passé de Palinges et sa Région, 2009.

Granatstein, J.L. *Canada at War: Conscription, Diplomacy, and Politics.* Toronto: University of Toronto Press, 2020.

Granatstein, J.L., and Morton, Desmond. *Bloody Victory: Canadians and the D-Day Campaign 1944.* Toronto: Lester & Orpen Dennys, 1984.

Helm, Sarah. *A Life in Secrets: Vera Atkins and the Lost Agents of SOE.* London: Hachette Digital, 2005.

Hemming, Henry. *Agents of Influence: A British Campaign, a Canadian Spy, and the Secret Plot to Bring America into World War II*. New York: Public affairs, 2019.

Hodgson, Lynn-Philip. *Inside Camp* X. Lynn Philip Hodgson, 2013. EBook.

Horn, Bernd. *A Most Ungentlemanly Way of War: The SOE and the Canadian Connection*. Toronto: Dundurn Press, 2016.

Horn, Bernd. *We Will Find a Way: The Canadian Special Operations Legacy*. Ottawa: Department of National Defence, 2018.

Horn, Bernd, and Wyczynski, Michel. *Of Courage and Determination: The First Special Service Force, "The Devils Brigade" 1942–44*. Toronto: Dundurn, 2013.

Hudson, Sydney. *Undercover Operator: An SOE Agent's Experiences in France and the Far East*. Barnsley: Leo Cooper, 2003.

Jeannet, André. *Mémorial de la Résistance en Saône-et-Loire: Biographie des Résistants*. Mâcon: JPM Éditions, 2005.

Jeannet, André. *La Seconde Guerre Mondiale en Sâone-et-Loire: Occupation et Resistance*. Mâcon: JPM Editions, 2003.

Jones, Liane. *A Quiet Courage: Women Agents in the French Resistance*. London: Bantam Press, 1990.

Kramer, Rita. *Flames in the Field: The Story of Four SOE Agents in Occupied France*. London: Penguin, 1996.

Lackenbauer, Whitney. *Operation Canon: Rescuing Canon John Turner in the Canadian Arctic*. Antigonish: Brian Mulroney Institute of Government, 2022.

Lapalus, Louis, and Aurélie Lavergnat. *Ma vie, ma guerre*. Lausanne: Imprimerie Chabloz S.A., 2008.

Larson, Erik. *The Splendid and the Vile: A Saga of Churchill, Family, and Defiance During the Blitz*. New York: Crown, 2020.

Linderman, A.R.B., *Rediscovering Irregular Warfare: Colin Gubbins and the Origins of Britain's Special Operations Executive*. Norman: University of Oklahoma Press, 2016.

Marks, Leo. *Between Silk and Cyanide: A Codemaker's War, 1941–1945*. Cheltenham: The History Press, 2012.

Marnham, Patrick. *War in the Shadows: Resistance, Deception and Betrayal in Occupied France*. London: Simon & Schuster, 2020.

McLaren, Roy. *Canadians Behind Enemy Lines: 1939–1945*. Vancouver: UBC Press, 2004.

Melady, John. *Korea: Canada's Forgotten War*. Toronto: Dundurn Press, 2012.

Millar, George. *Road to Resistance: An Autobiography*. Boston: Little Brown and Company, 1979.

Milton, Giles. *Churchill's Ministry of Ungentlemanly Warfare: The Mavericks Who Plotted Hitler's Defeat*. London: Picador, 2017.

Mitcham, Samuel, and Mueller, Gene. *Hitler's Commanders*. Barnsley: Leo Cooper, 1992.

Moffat, Andrew C. *Korea Memories: A Canadian Gunner's Experience in the "Forgotten War."* Ottawa: Keshet Productions, 2006.

Montague, Patrick. *Chelmno and the Holocaust: The History of Hilter's First Death Camp*. Chapel Hill: University of North Carolina Press, 2012.

Mulley, Clare. *The Spy Who Loved: The Secrets and Lives of Christine Granville*. London: St. Martin's Publishing Group, 2013.

The National Archives (U.K.). *Special Operations Executive Manual: How to Be an Agent in Europe*. London: William Collins, 2014.

Nicholas, Elizabeth. *Death Be Not Proud.* London: Cresset Press, 1958.

Nicholson, G.W.L. *Canadian Expeditionary Force, 1914–1919: Official History of the Canadian Army in the First World War.* Montreal: McGill Queen's University Press, 1962.

O'Conner, Bernard. *SOE Heroines: The Special Operations Eexcutive's French Section and Free French Women Agents.* Stroud: Amberley Publishing, 2018.

Ottaway, Susan. *Sisters and Spies: Two Remarkable Sisters Who Risked Everything as WWII Special Agents.* London: HarperElement, 2021.

Pattinson, Juliette. *Behind Enemy Lines: Gender, Passing and the Special Operations Executive in the Second World War.* Manchester: Manchester University Press, 2007.

Pioger, André. *Le Mans et la Sarthe pendant la 2e guerre mondiale*. Le Mans: Extraits de la Revue "La Province du Maine," 1976.

Riols, Noreen. *The Secret Ministry of Ag. & Fish: My Life in Churchill's School for Spies.* London: Pan Books, 2013.

Roberts, Andrew. *The Storm of War: A New History of the Second World War*. London: Allen Lane, 2009.

Rose, Larry D. *Mobilize!: Why Canada Was Unprepared for the Second World War.* Toronto: Dundurn, 2013.

Ruby, Marcel. *F Section SOE: The Story of the Buckmaster Network*. London: Leo Cooper, 1988.

Seymour-Jones, Carol. *She Landed by Moonlight: The Story of Secret Agent Pearl Witherington: The 'Real Charlotte Gray.'* Hodder, 2013.

Stafford, David. *Britain and European Resistance 1940–45: A Survey of the Special Operations Executive, with Documents*. Borough: Lume Books, 1980.

Stafford, David. *Camp X: SOE School for Spies*. Borough: Lume Books, 1986.

Stafford, David. *Churchill and Secret Service*. New York: The Overlook Press, 1998.

Stafford, David. "Churchill and SOE." Chapter 4 in Mark Seaman, ed., *Special Operations Executive: A New Instrument of War*, 47–60. London: Routledge, 2006.

Stafford, David. *Secret Agent: The True Story of the Special Operations Executive.* Borough: Lume Books, 2000.

Stafford, David. *Ten Days to D-Day: Countdown to the Liberation of Europe.* Borough: Lume Books, 2003.

Stevenson, William. *Spymistress: The Life of Vera Atkins*. New York: Arcade Publishing, 2011.

Stroud, Rick. *Lonely Courage: The True Story of the SOE Heroines Who Fought to Free Nazi-Occupied France*, 2017.

Suttill, Francis J. *PROSPER: Major Suttill's French Resistance Network*. Stroud: The History Press, 2014.

Szabó, Tania. *Violette: The Missions of Special Operations Executive Agent Lieutenant Violette Szabó*. The Stroud: History Press, 2015.

Thompson, Neville. *The Third Man: Churchill, Roosevelt, Mackenzie King, and the Untold Friendships that Won WWII.* Toronto: Sutherland House, 2021.

Vance, Jonathan. *Unlikely Soldiers: How Two Canadians Fought the Secret War Against Nazi Occupation*. Toronto: HarperCollins, 2009.

Vennat, Pierre. *Les héros oubliés: L'histoire inédite des militaires canadiens-français de la Dieuxième Guerre Mondiale*, Tome 1–3. Meridien: Montreal, 1994.

Veyret, Patrick. *Histoire de la résistance en Saône et Loire*. Lyon: Éditions La Taillanderie, 2001.

Vigurs, Kate. *Mission France: The True History of the Women of SOE*. New Haven and London: Yale University Press, 2021.

Vomécourt, Philippe de. *An Army of Amateurs: The Story of the SOE Resistance Movement in France*. New York: Doubleday and Company, 1961.

Wake, Nancy. *The White Mouse: The Autobiography of Australia's Wartime Legend.* Sydney: Pan Macmillan, 2013.

Walker, Robyn. *The Women Who Spied for Britain: Female Secret Agents of the Second World War.* Stroud: Amberley, 2014.

Walter, Col. F.H. "Cloak and Dagger." Historical Section file 760.013(D1). Ottawa: Department of National Defence.

West, Nigel. *Secret War: The Story of SOE; Britain's Wartime Sabotage Organisation.* London: Hodder & Stoughton, 1992.

Witherington Cornioley, Pearl, and Larroque, Hervé. *Code Name Pauline: Memoirs of a World War II Special Agent.* Chicago: Chicago Review Press, 2013.

Zuehlke, Mark. *Assault on Juno*. Victoria: Orca, 2012.

ARTICLES, PERIODICALS

Feasby, W.R. "Official History of the Canadian Medical Services, 1939–1945." Ottawa: Queen's Printer. https://www.canada.ca/content/dam/themes/defence/caf/militaryhistory/dhh/official/book-1956-medical-services-1-en.pdf.

Foot, M.R.D. "Was SOE Any Good?" *Journal of Contemporary History*, Vol. 16, No. 1 (January 1981), 167–181.

Horn, Bernd. *The Canadian Special Air Service Company*. Produced for CANSOFCOM Education and Research Centre. Government of Canada Catalogue Number D4-13/22-2017E-PDF (PDF), 2017.

Horn, Bernd. "A Military Enigma: The Canadian Special Air Service Company, 1948–49," *Canadian Military History,* vol. 10, no. 1, Winter 2001.

The Maroon Beret, August 1999, via the Airborne Regiment Association of Canada.

Pattinson, Juliette. "Turning a Pretty Girl into a Killer: Women, Violence and Clandestine Operations During the Second World War." *Gender and Interpersonal Violence*, edited by K. Thorsby et al., 2008.

Thomas, Roy. "The Canadian SAS Company. A Missed Opportunity?" *Esprit de Corps: Canadian Military Then & Now*. Vol. 3, No. 3, August 1993.

ARCHIVES

Library and Archives Canada, Ottawa, Canada

Various war diaries

Guy d'Artois military record

The National Archives of the United Kingdom

Circuit and Mission Reports and Interrogations: HS6/566, HS6/567, HS6/571, HS6/572, HS6/585, HS6/586

France-Jedburghs, Team Anthony, HS6/479

Lecture Folder STS 103, HS7/55

Lecture Folder STS 103, minor tactics, demolitions, and field craft lectures, physical training syllabus, 1943–44, HS7/56

Military Mission 207. S.T.S. Canada, October 1941–3 Jan 1942, WO 193/631

SOE History 91 – Report on Judex Mission, 1944–1945, HS7/134

SOE History 86 – History of F section by Colonel Buckmaster/Personnel dropped by F Section. Expenditure in field. 1943–1945, HS7/121

SOE Security/Missing Agents Index/Concentration Camps, HS8/893

Squadron Number 138 summary of events, AIR 27/956/1

Training Section 1940–1945/Industrial Sabotage Training, 1941–44, HS7/51

Training STS 103, Supplementary Reading (1944), HS7/57

The National Archives of the United Kingdom, Personnel Files

Sonia and Guy d'Artois, HS9/56/7

Jean-Paul Archambault, HS9/49/1

Vera Atkins, HS9/59/2

Alcide Beauregard, HS9/111/1

Eugène Bec, HS9/111/5

Muriel Byck HS9/250/2

Raymond Glaesner, HS6/586

Sydney Hudson, HS9/747/4

Phyllis Latour, HS9/888/9

Joseph Gerard Litalien HS9/928/6

Stanislaw Makowski HS9/978/2

Nancy Wake, HS9/1545

Imperial War Museum

Private Papers of Mrs. SEF d'Artois.

Private Papers of Lieutenant Colonel CS Hudson.

Clara Thomas Archives and Special Collections, York University, Toronto, Canada

Rob Forsyth Fonds, Inventory F0545

Archives at Musée Royal 22e Régiment, La Citadelle de Québec, Québec City, Canada

FPA018 Fonds Guy d'Artois

1er Bataillon, Royal 22e Régiment en Westphalie 1970

La Citadelle magazine archive

L'Amicale magazine archive

Guy d'Artois Audio recordings: Musée Royal 22e Régiment AV2-172-044

Centre Historique des Archives, Vincennes, France

Various documents relating to Sylla and *résistants* from the Charolles area.

Les archives du Collège Jean-de-Brébeuf

Various documents relating to Guy d'Artois' education

FILM/TELEVISION/BROADCASTS

"Behind Enemy Lines," *The Fifth Estate*, by Hana Gartner et al., Canadian Broadcasting Corporation Archives. October 27, 1987.

Behind Enemy Lines: The Real Charlotte Grays, Darlow Smithson Productions, directed by Jenny Morgan, Channel 4, 2002.

Camp X: Secret Agent School, by Yap films, 2014.

Carve Her Name with Pride, Directed by Lewis Gilbert, 1958.

Gariepy, Michel and Hudon-Auger, Renée "Major Guy d'Artois du Royal 22e Régiment." *Gens de Mon Pays*. Archives Radio-Canada. October 23, 1977.

Letter from Aldershot, by John Taylor, National Film Board of Canada, 1940.

Ten Days to D-Day miniseries, directed by Marion Milne, 3BM Television, 2004.

ONLINE RESOURCES

Stacey, C.P. Canadian Military Headquarters (CMHQ) reports 1940–1948

https://www.canada.ca/en/department-national-defence/services/military-history/history-heritage/official-military-history-lineages/reports/military-headquarters-1940-1948.html.

Imperial War Museum Sounds Archive Interviews

Vera Atkins

Maurice Buckmaster

Selwyn Jepson

British Pathé video: www.youtube.com/watch?v=y6JxSHmVB5g. Longer version here: www.youtube.com/watch?v=2jtOGDjlM10&t=144s; www.youtube.com/watch?v=kbsSbj9EUME.

Browne-Bartroli, Albert. Mémoires d'un résistant: https://cortevaix.fr/wp-content/uploads/2021/02/Me%CC%81moires-Albert-Browne-Bartroli-.pdf.

Tillet, Pierre. History of WWII Infiltrations into France: http://www.plan-sussex-1944.net/anglais/pdf/infiltrations_into_france.pdf.

57–63 St. Louis Street National Historic Site of Canada: https://www.pc.gc.ca/apps/dfhd/page_nhs_eng.aspx?id=1853.

ACKNOWLEDGMENTS

It truly takes a village to write a book. This volume is proof of the veracity of that statement.

This book would not have been at all possible without the outsized efforts of Nadya Murdoch (*née* d'Artois). She meticulously catalogued and kept her family's large private collection of documents and artifacts, provided me with unfettered access to the material on several occasions, and helped make sense of it all. Further, over countless conversations, she patiently answered my questions and provided invaluable context, as well as contacts and suggestions—all while remaining respectful of the journalistic process and my independence as a researcher. I owe Nadya an incalculable debt of gratitude. Without her there would be no book. Thanks also to Bob Murdoch, for his guidance and encouragement and for sharing his knowledge.

Several other family members helped in ways impossible to quantify: Bob d'Artois and Michael d'Artois, Michael Butt, and Johnny and Louis Butt. There were other family and friends also helping out behind the scenes, and my thanks extend to them too. Thanks also to Fred Langan and Jennifer Mattatia for conversation and context.

Thanks to Major-General (Ret.) Terry Liston for many things, especially for connecting me with other veterans among the Van Doos. Many thanks to each and every one of them for speaking with me.

In France, gratitude to historian Jérémy Beurier for his wide-ranging assistance, including reaching family members of several key players from the Charolles region. Thanks to him for also providing documents and photographs and access to his impressive collection of artifacts.

Sincere thanks to Louis Lapalus's family—his two daughters, Jeanine and Françoise, for the tour and the conversation, and especially his granddaughter, Aurélie Lavergnat, who provided me with her compilation of Lapalus's very rich manuscript. Huge thanks to René Fléchard's son, Daniel, for conversation and access to documents. Big thanks to the entire Jandeau family, especially Pierre's daughter Paule Jandeau, for sharing family documents and taking us to Ferme la Breuil.

This book would not have been published without the incredible research skills of Michelle Gagnon, who did the impossible on both sides of the Atlantic. Thanks to Jet Belgraver for additional research and support and to Stephanie Jenzer for introducing me to the d'Artois story, which inspired this entire endeavour. Thanks to Louis Butt and Marie-Hélène Hétu for research and translation help. Thanks to Deb Rutherford and Sujata Berry for enabling the writing process.

A special thanks to historian David Stafford for his invaluable advice and generosity. I also owe a debt of gratitude to Paul McCue for his generous sharing of knowledge. Also to Col. Bernd Horn and Lynn-Philip Hodgson for lending their time and expertise. Thanks to Jenny Morgan, and especially to Robin Fowler, without whose interviews this book would not have been possible.

Many archivists and librarians were integral to telling this story. Jason Thiffault from the Musée Royal 22e Régiment at La Citadelle in Quebec City went above and beyond to help; Stephen Harris,

Chief Historian, and Emilie Vandal, Chief Archivist, both from the Directorate of History and Heritage, Department of National Defence; Penny Lipman from the Royal Canadian Military Institute; Jean-Philippe Gauthier and others from the Archives at Collège Jean-de-Brébeuf; Vincent Lafond and Paul Durand at the Canadian War Museum; and Julia Holland and Michael B. Moir at Clara Thomas Archives and Special Collections at York University. A special thanks to Luc Forsyth, Rob Forsyth's son, for pointing me in the right direction. Thank you also to Ron Cohen, the original producer of Forsyth's d'Artois project, who provided yet more documents related to the project and valuable conversation. Thanks also to Seana Jones, Collections Manager at the Garrison Petawawa Military Museum. Finally, sincere thanks to the unsung heroes among the archivists and librarians at Library and Archives Canada and The National Archives in the U.K., as well as the Imperial War Museum and the Vincennes Historical Archives Centre in France, for all their assistance.

At Penguin Random House, sincere thanks to Diane Turbide, who launched this project, and to Laura Dosky for so patiently and thoughtfully seeing it through. Thanks to the whole team at PRH, and again to Dawn Kepron, and Chris Kepron, for introducing me to PRH at the very start.

Many thanks to all the CBC colleagues who helped make this book possible, especially to Raj Ahluwalia, who provided a crucial pair of eyes.

Warm and heartfelt thanks to all my loved ones and friends—too numerous to list here—who tolerated the chaos, and on top of that found countless ways to help. Your unwavering support is a lifeline. You are my rock, and my love and gratitude to you is infinite.

PHOTO CREDITS

Sonia and her brother: Courtesy of Nadya Murdoch.

Sonia Butt at school: Courtesy of Nadya Murdoch.

Guy at his first communion: Courtesy of Nadya Murdoch.

Hockey at Collège Jean-de-Brébeuf: Courtesy of Archives du Collège Jean-de-Brébeuf. ALB_SPO_1930-1931_001-039.

Guy in England: From the d'Artois family archives.

Guy d'Artois in undated photo: Courtesy of Nadya Murdoch.

Sonia's SOE-issued doctored French document: Private Papers of Mrs S E F d'Artois MBE, © Imperial War Museum. Documents.12356, I.D. card.

One of several fake French ID documents: Courtesy of Musée Royal 22e Régiment, La Citadelle de Québec.

Sonia and Guy in London: From the d'Artois family archives.

Wedding day: From the d'Artois family archives.

A rare photo of Guy: Courtesy of French historian Jérémy Beurier; photographer unknown.

Sydney Hudson in 1936: Courtesy of the Hudson family.

Guy and Sonia reunited: From the d'Artois family archives.

A group of Canadian SOE agents: Canadian Department of National Defence / Library and Archives Canada / PA-213624.

Guy d'Artois standing next to General Charles de Gaulle: From the d'Artois family archives.

Captain Guy d'Artois: Army Public Relations Photo.

Canadian Special Air Service Company officers: Courtesy of 1st Canadian Parachute Battalion Association Archives.

Sonia d'Artois posing: From the d'Artois family archives.

Sonia d'Artois near her home: Photograph by David Bier. From the d'Artois family archives.

During his final visit to Charolles: From the d'Artois family archives.

Sonia marking the fiftieth anniversary: From the d'Artois family archives.

Sonia d'Artois receiving the Legion d'Honneur: From the d'Artois family archives.

Sonia d'Artois in later life: Courtesy of Nadya Murdoch.

Guy and Sonia with their six children: Courtesy of Nadya Murdoch.

Sonia with her grandchildren: Courtesy of Nadya Murdoch.

INDEX

acting, utilization of, 104–6
agents, exposure of, 184–85
Albin, agent, 135–37
Aldershot, England, Canadian troops in, 36–38
Aleutian Islands, 66
Allied Expeditionary Force, 94
Allies, 2, 99, 131, 146, 149, 192, 204, 217, 245, 301–2
Alzheimer's, 308–12
Aquitania, ship, 32
Archambault, Jean-Paul, 90, 95, 213, 227, 241
Archambault, Montrealer Jean-Paul, 109, 229
armée secrète, 181, 207
Atkins, Vera, 136, 138, 213, 237, 301
  staying in touch with, 238–43
  taking charge of female agents, 78–81
Auxiliary Territorial Service (ATS), 12, 45–46, 306

Baissac, Lise de, 316
Baldwin, Grey Patrick, 15
Bar-sur-Seine, 195–96
Bardy, Emile, 139
Baril, Maurice, 311
Barraud, André, 140, 175
Batey, D. M., 193
Battle of Cluny, 200–203
Battle of the Atlantic, 33–36
Battle of Vimy Ridge, WWI, 21, 22
BBC
  jackal message, 171
  using, 147–48
Beaulieu, Hampshire. *See* House on the Shore, training at
Beauregard, Alcide, 151–53, 208, 241, 257, 300
  exposure of, 182–83
Bec, Eugène, 138, 140, 169, 171–72
Beekman, Yolande, 96, 240
Behind Enemy Lines: The Real Charlotte Grays (documentary), 316
Benoit, Joseph, 229
Bernonville, Jacques de, 257–58
Biéler, Gustave, 96, 240
Blanche, Butt as
  at Château des Bordeaux, 141–42
  double life in France, 163–71
  German forces on move, 171–72
  Le Mans strategic importance, 133–37
  parachuting into Le Mans, 137–41
  re-meeting Hudson, 142
Blanchett, Cate, 315
Blitz, bombing campaign, 43–45
Bonvie, 141
Bonvie, Suzanne. *See* Butt, Sonia: double life in France
Borden, Robert, 22
Borrel, Andrée, 185
Boxing Day, 61
Bracebridge Cutting, 13
British Commonwealth Battle School, 271
British Expeditionary Force, 36, 40
British Museum, 44
British Security Coordination, 68
Browne-Bartroli, Albert, 123–25, 180, 182–83, 200, 213, 302

at drop zone, 125–28
Buckmaster, Maurice, 78, 112, 181, 213, 216, 301
and Butt-d'Artois farewell ritual, 118–20
interviews by, 56–59
meeting with Hudson, 99
on SOE flaws, 41043
Butt, Bunny, 301–2
Butt, Derek, 8, 10, 277–79
Butt, Florence Juliet Walters, 12–18
Butt, Harry Percy, 13–14
Butt, Jack, 267
Butt, Leslie, 46, 278, 293
Butt, Michael, 310
Butt, Nadya, 256, 265–66, 281, 288, 307, 310–11, 314, 317, 320
Butt, Sonia, 1–3, 76
as agent-to-be, 73–86
appointing as Légion d'honneur, 323
arriving in London, 43–46
Atkins and, 80–81
background of, 7–12
baptism of, 189–90
as Blanche, 133–42
in Como, Italy, 287–92
critique of abilities of, 99–100
in custody battle, 46–48
de Bernonville affair, 257–58
death of, 324
double life in France, 163–71
falling in love with, 87–108
farewell ritual of, 118–20
final intelligence assignment of, 213–17
finishing training, 102–6
first days in military setting, 50–56
following departure of d'Artois, 132
honouring, 235–38
interviewing, 229–35
joining parachute training, 100–102
joining party 27AG, 73–76
Korea separation and, 261–68
on latest wars, 313
and Le Mans liberation, 192–99
letters of, 244–51
and liberation of Paris, 209–17
marriage of, 109–14
meeting Guy d'Artois, 89–93
milestone year, 304–5
money issues, 191–92
moving to Montreal, 292–96
parents of, 12–18
paying back debts, 225–28
postwar reunions, 314–19
pregnancy, 246–49
receiving call, 56
reentering real world, 1068
relationship with d'Artois, 93–96
relationship with Dauprat-Sevenet, 186–90
relationship with Rebouche, 190–91
remembrances, 306–12
reunions, 274–83
reuniting with d'Artois, 213–17
on Salt Spring Island, 320–22
seeking refuge, 4–18
separation from d'Artois, 109–14
sexual assault of, 197–99
speaking with Buckmaster, 59–60
and student assessment board, 81–86
in surgery, 284–86
time in Germany, 274–83
traning of, 89–93
as war bride, 221–25
Byck, Muriel, 136

Caltex Oil, 16, 263
Camp X, 67–70, 75, 124
Canada
drawn into war, 19–27
Korea and, 261–73
letters in, 244–51
limelight in, 229–43
Montreal surgery, 284–86
Salt Spring Island, 320–22
Canadian Broadcasting Corporation, 68
Canadian Expeditionary Force, 22
Canadian Joint Air Training Centre, 248
Canadian Press, 229, 270, 276
Canadian Red Cross, 39
Canadian Travel Certificate No. 2624, 223
Canadien, Michel le. *See* Dieudonné, d'Artois as
Canadien, Michel le (d'Artois), 131–32
building trust in region, 151–53
D-Day arrival and, 145–53
D-Day first phase arrival, 145–47
meeting René Fléchard, 150
visiting resistance leaders, 148–53

Carpetbaggers, 118
Carret, Paul, 245
Cedar Cottage. *See* Como, Italy
Chagall, Marc, 17
Chamberlain, Neville, 8, 10–11, 35, 37, 57
Charlotte Gray (film), 316
Charnay, Louis, 145–46, 160
Charolles, France
  and Battle of Cluny, 200–203
  conflict in, 159–62
  fortieth-anniversary commemorations in, 299–304
  and liberation of Paris, 211–12
  paying back debts in, 226–28
Château des Bordeaux, 139, 141–42, 167–69, 191, 318
Château du Breuil, 186–90, 250
Chevalier, l'Abbé, 141, 191
Choper, Emmanuel, 139–40
Christmas Eve, events on, 93–94
Churchill, Winston, 37, 51–52, 57
  addressing Canadians, 61–63
circuits
  DITCHER, 109, 121–22, 127, 148, 150–52, 174, 182–83, 201–2
  HEADMASTER, 18, 135, 137–39, 165, 171, 185, 188, 191, 236
  leader of, 138, 142
  PHYSICIAN, 77, 135, 165, 240
Clair, Bois, 201
Claude. *See* Ziegel, Olivier
Cohen, Ronald, 296
Cohin, Edmund, 141, 169, 191–92, 243
Cold War, background, 261–62
Collège Jean-de-Brébeuf, 24
Comi, Italy, 287–92
cookery school, 105–6
Coupal, Odette, 64
Courseulles, village, 154, 307
Coventon, Leonard, 17
"Cover," lecture on, 104–6
Cragg, Kenneth C., 231–32

D-Day, 2, 88, 118
  approaching, 69–70
  arrival of, 145–53
  Charolles conflict, 159–62
  determining exact date of, 109–10
  establishing Sylla base, 154–59
  eve of, 152–53
  fiftieth anniversary of, 306–12
  parachuting uniforms in for, 181–82
  people missing after, 184–85
  preparing for, 74–76
d'Artois, Bob, 281, 295
d'Artois, Calixte Lionel Alsace, 22
d'Artois, Guy, 1–3
  as agent-to-be, 73–86
  Alzheimer's of, 308–12
  at Battle of Cluny, 200–203
  beginning of D-day, 154–59
  birth of son, 246–49
  at Camp X, 67–70
  in Como, Italy, 287–92
  critique of abilities of, 100
  de Bernonville affair, 257–58
  death of father of, 26
  detour of, 61–66
  as Dieudonné, 117–32
  as director of training, 271
  at Dolphin Holiday Camp, 38–40
  early life of, 21–27
  education of, 24–25
  facing World War II, 41–42
  falling in love with, 87–108
  finishing training, 102–6
  at Génelard battle, 204–8
  heading to Halifax, 31–33
  honouring, 235–38
  interviewing, 229–35
  joining militia, 25–27
  joining parachute training, 100–102
  Korea separation and, 261–68
  leadership of, 178–82
  leaving home, 31–42
  letters of, 244–51
  and liberation of Paris, 209–17
  looking for work, 26
  marriage of, 109–14
  meeting Sonia Butt, 89–93
  milestone year of, 304–5
  moving to Montreal, 292–96
  Operation Cadillac and, 173–85
  paying back debts, 225–28
  realizing paratrooper dream of, 63–66
  receiving George Medal, 252–55

reentering real world, 106–8
relationship with Butt, 93–96
reunions, 274–83
reuniting with Butt, 213–17
running Special Air Service, 255–56
separation from Butt, 109–14
tactics of, 159–62
time in Korea, 269–73
time with children, 290–92
wife surgery, 284–86
witnessing SS *Athenia* sinking, 19–20
d'Artois, Joseph Valmore, 21–27
d'Artois, Lorraine, 22–24
d'Artois, Michel Henri, birth of, 249–51
d'Artois, Nadya, 256
d'Artois, Robert, 246–49
d'Artois, Sonia. *See* Butt, Sonia
Daily Herald, The, 44
Daily Mirror, 35–36
Daily Record and Mail, 35
Dalton, Hugh, 57
Damerment, Madeleine, 240
Darey, D.L., 37–38
Dauprat-Sevenet, Marthe, 187–90, 246, 250
Davenport, ensign, 105
Devil's Brigade. *See* First Special Service Force (FSSF)
Devron, Jean, 302
Diaper Division, 275–76
Dieudonné, d'Artois as
dropping into France, 120–25
farewell ritual of, 118–20
meeting Albert, 125–28
pre-invasion phase, 128–32
second foray into French skies, 117–18
Distinguished Service Order (DSO), 237–38
DITCHER, circuit, 109, 121–22, 127, 148, 150–52, 174, 182–83, 201–2
Dollmann, Friedrich, 164
Dolphin Holiday Camp, 38–42
DSO. *See* Distinguished Service Order
Dufort d'Artois, Antoinette, 21, 24–25, 27
Dunkirk, 40, 42, 49, 57

Église Saint-Pierre-ès-Liens, 189
Eisenhower, Dwight D., 94, 242
elementary theory, guerilla warfare, 11
11th Special Force Detachment, 193
Empress of Australia, ship, 33–34, 276
Empress of Britain, ship, 32
English Channel, 7, 38, 40, 48, 95, 146, 217, 222, 306, 321
Ensign Davenport, 105, 111
extermination camps, 52–53, 240

F Section, SOE, 56–59, 74
agent prototype, 123
disturbing claims from, 232
gender roles in, 79–81
New Year's Eve news, 96
questioning story of, 242
recalling agents, 213
weaknesses of, 77
family, starting, 246–51
Faulks, Sebastian, 315
Feldkommandantur, 189
Firm. *See* F Section, SOE
1st Battalion, Royal 22e Régiment, 261
1st Charollais Battalion, 205, 207
First Aid Nursing Yeomanry (FANY), 59
First Canadian Parachute Battalion, 154
First Special Service Force (FSSF), 64–66
First World War. *See* World War I
FJ Mankey Ideas Inc., 234
Fléchard, René, 150, 156, 160–61, 176, 206, 212, 243, 302–3
and Battle of Cluny, 200–203
Ford Motor Company, 57
Forêt de Charnie, 168–71, 187, 191
Forsyth, Rob, 296
Fort de Côte-Lorette, 207
Fort William Henry Harrison, 63
Fortress Europe, 154
Frager, Henri, 184
française, Milice, 257
France
acquiring weapons in, 147
Charolles conflict, 159–62
dropping into, 120–25
and F Section of SOE, 56–59
living double life in, 163–71
solitary confinement in, 97–99
Franco-German War, 22
Frederick, Robert, 63
FSSF. *See* First Special Service Force

Fuller, Jean Overton, 241
Funkspiel, 78

Gaulle, Charles de, 49, 57, 59, 181, 209
gender roles. *See* women
Génelard, battle of, 204–8
George Medla, receiving, 252–55
German 12th SS Panzer Division, 184
Germany
  Battle of Cluny, 200–203
  and Génelard battle, 204–8
  and Le Mans liberation, 192–99
  Sonia Butt in, 274–83
Gestapo, 77, 99, 103, 123, 161, 165, 179, 182, 232, 241, 244, 318, 135036
girl courier. *See* Blanche, Butt as
Glaesner, Pierre Raimond, 138, 140
Globe and Mail, The, 231–32, 255, 294–95
Gordon, acting lieutenant, 92, 96, 99
Gordon, Laurence George Frank, 12–18
Gordon, Thelma Esme Florence, 12–18, 47, 226, 277, 283, 314
Grand Union Hotel, 32
Great Britain, Pearl Harbor attack and, 51–53
Great Depression, 25
Great War. *See* World War I
Great Western Railway, 87
Grosvenor, 10
Gubbins, Colin, 80
Guy, Petit, 24

Hackett, Mart, 112–13
Halifax III LK810, 133
Harriman, Averell, 51
Harrington Airfield, 118
Haudenosaunee, 24
HEADMASTER, circuit, 18, 135, 137–39, 165, 171, 185, 188, 191, 236
Helena, Montana, 63–66
Herbé, Charles, 175
Hill 133, 272
Hilleret, Claude, 169, 171–72, 243
Hitler, Adolf, 8
HMS *Exmouth,* 34
Home Guard, 12
honours, postwar, 235–38
House on the Shore, training at, 102–6
Houses of Parliament, 44

Hudson, Ruth, 318
Hudson, Sydney, 97–99, 106–8, 110, 142, 236
  and Butt sexual assault, 197–99
  final intelligence assignment of, 213–17
  Germa forces on move, 171–72
  and Le Mans liberation, 192–99
  and liberation of Paris, 209–17
  money issues, 191–92
  reunion with, 316–19
  working with Butt, 163–71
Hut A-19, 248

"Ici Londres," BBC Radio, 147
interviews, 229–35
IRA. *See* Irish Republican Army
Irish Republican Army (IRA), 11
Ivy, Thea, 17

Jacquot. *See* Litalien, Joseph Gerard
Jandeau, Mme, 128
Jandeau, Pierre, 128, 149, 211, 302
Japan, d'Artois in, 272
Jepson, Selwyn, 80
Jones, George, 167
Juno Beach, 155

Khan, Noor Inayat, 77, 240, 243
King, William Lyon Mackenzie, 27
Kingsford, Leslie Acton, 13–18
Korean War, 261

Laden, Osama bin, 313
Langan, Fred, 295
Lapalus, Louis, 145–49, 161, 176, 200, 202, 212
  restarting business, 244–46
  reunion with Guy, 299–300
Latour, Phyllis, 236
Lavigne, Madeleine, 117–18
Le Mans, France, 133–35
  liberation of, 192–99
  money issues, 191–92
Leigh, Vera, 184
Lemay, J. D., 62–63
les anglais, 146, 149
letters
  forming portrait of state of affairs, 244–46
  Korea deployment and, 264–65
  starting family, 246–51

Lévy, Gaston, 150, 156, 176, 206, 212, 245, 281–82
Life magazine, 40
limelight
  honours, 235–38
  interviews, 229–35
  SOE disbandment, 238–43
Litalien, Joseph Gerard, 121
  pre-invasion phase, 128–32
London
  agents-to-be, 73–86
  change in direction, 50–60
  detour, 61–66
  finding home, 43–49
  first disappointment, 109–14
  postwar reunions in, 313–19
Looney Bin. *See* Winterford House
Lucienne, Maman, 130–32, 178, 179, 201, 212, 243, 281, 301, 302
letters of, 245–46
Luftwaffe, 43

Macalister, Ken, 77
Mackenzie, I. K., 231–32
Mackie, Evelyn Guthrie Easson, 169
Mad House. *See* Winterford House
Madeleine. *See* Butt, Sonia: double life in France
Maison centrale d'Eysses, 97
Makowski, Stanislaw, 90–91, 240
maquis, 58, 110, 119, 130, 149–50, 156, 158, 161, 169, 171–72, 175, 181–82
Maquis de Sylla, 176, 204, 303
Marshall Plan, 274
Martigny-le-Comte, 177–78
Martin, Paul, 311
MBE, 236–38
MBE. *See* Member of the Order of the British Empire
McGowan, Robert, 134
McIntosh, Elizabeth, 307–8
McNaughton, Andrew G.L., 35
McQueen, John G, 63
Member of the Order of the British Empire (MBE), 235–38
Meoble Lodge, 88–93
messages personnels, 147, 152, 191
Meunier, Paul, 229
milestone year, 304–5
Ministry of Economic Warfare, 57
Ministry of Trade and Commerce, 247
Moffat, Andrew C., 272
Molgat, Gildas, 307–8
Monarch of Bermuda, ship, 33
Montreal Gazette, 304
Montreal Neurological Institute, 284
Montreal, moving to, 292–96
Montreal, surgery in, 284–86
Morgan, Jenny, 317
Morse code, 147–48, 255
Moss Brothers Clothiers, 45

Nazi Germany, 8, 11, 52, 75
No. 1 Canadian Division Infantry Reinforcement Unit, 61
No. 1 Convalescent Depot, 32, 38
No. 1 Convalescent Hospital, 61
Noble, Goerge, 58
Normandy, France
  fiftieth anniversary of D-Day, 306–12
North Korea, 26
Nursing Sisters Association of Canada, 308

O'Sullivan, Maureen, 53–55, 236
OBE. *See* Order of the British Empire
October Crisis, 293–94
Office of Strategic Services (OSS), 69
Olschanezky, Sonya, 184
Operation Cadillac
  agent exposure, 184–85
  Alcide ransom, 182–83
  leadership, 178–82
  rounding out arsenal, 175–78
  weapons drop, 173–75
Operation Carpetbagger, 139
Operation COTTAGE, 66
Operation Overlord, 153
Operation Pied Piper, 9
Order of the British Empire (OBE), 236
OSS. *See* Office of Strategic Services

Paddy. *See* O'Sullivan, Maureen
parachute battalion, recruiting, 63–66
parachute training, 100–102
parachutiste anglais, 97
Paris, liberation of

post-battle, 209–12
saying farewell, 212–13
party 27AG, 73–76
first days at SOE, 77–78
at Meoble Lodge, 88–93
Patton, George S., 193
Pearl Harbor, attack on, 51–52
Pelham-Burn, Hamish, 70
Pensionnat de Jeunes Filles, 17–18
permanent married quarters (PMQs), 263, 276
Pétain, Maréchal Philippe, 40, 257
Petit Journal, Le, 64
Philippe, contact, 171–72
PHYSICIAN, cicuit, 77, 135, 165, 240
Pickersgill, Frank, 77, 240
Plewman, Eliane, 123, 240
PMQs. *See* permanent married quarters
Porte, Edmund Elie La, 133
Porter, McKenzie, 267
Postes, Télégraphes et Téléphones (PTT), 201–3
Powell, Robert I., 193
Presse, La, 235
prosper (SMALL CAPS), collapse of, 77–78
PTT. *See* Postes, Télégraphes et Téléphones
Pyrenees Mountains, 84, 98

Quebec City, time in, 261–73
Quebec Liberation Front, 293
Quebec, crisis in, 257–58

RAF Convalescent Hospital, 95
RAF Cosford, 53
"Real Basis for Unity," editorial, 294–95
real world, reentering, 106–8
Rebouche, Raymond, 190
Rebouche, Suzanne, 190–91, 266–68
Red Cross, 48, 222
refuge, seeking
Butt parents, 12–18
war declaration, 7–12
Republic of Korea
cold war in, 261–62
d'Artois household anomaly, 265–68
d'Atois time in, 269–73
days before deployment to, 263–64
letters and, 264–65
separating Guy and Sonia, 262–63
résistant, 150, 179, 183
reunions, 274–77
in Germany, 277–82
in Italy, 282
in London, 282–85
Ringway Airfield, Manchester, training at, 100–102
Roaring Lion, The (photograph), 62
Rockingham, John "Rocky," 295
Rolfe, Lilian, 90, 184, 240
Rome, reunion in, 278–81
Rommel, Erwin, 135, 146
Roosevelt, Franklin D., 51–52
Rosenberg, Vera May. *See* Atkins, Vera
Rowden, Diana, 184
Royal 22e Régiment, 23, 61, 256, 261, 263
Royal Air Force Club, 113
Royal Canadian Air Force, 33
Royal Canadien-Français, 22
Royal Flying Corps, 13
Royal Military Academy Sandhurst, 14

sabotage and subversion, phrase, 11
Sabourin, Roméo, 102–3, 240
Saint-Aubin-sur-Mer, village, 154–55
Saint-Bonnet-de-Joux, 150–51, 156, 161, 176
Saint-Julien-de-Civry, 150, 176, 206, 245, 303
Salt Spring Island, Canada, 320–22
Samedi, Le, 235
Sanscartier, Joseph Émile Hector, 269
Sarrazin, Jean, 155–56, 201
Sarrazin, Laure. *See* Maman Lucienne
Sarthe, region, 135, 141, 164
SAS. *See* Special Air Service
Savary, J.P., 269
2nd Infantry Brigade, 275
Séminaire Saint-Charles-Borromée, 25
Seton, Alexander Hay, 228
Sevenet, Henri, 187
Sevenet, Louis, 187
sexual assault, weapon of war, 197–99
SHAEF. *See* Supreme Headquarters Allied Expeditionary Force
SOE. *See* Special Operations Executive
South Korea, 262
Special Air Service (SAS), 255–56
Special Forces Club, 301
Special Operations Executive (SOE), 2–3, 42
assigning Butt and d'Artois, 109–14

Atkins joining, 78–81
and D-Day anniversary, 307
detractors of, 78
disbanding, 238–43
establishing, 56–59
evolution of, 73–76
F Section of, 56–59
finishing training, 102–6
and First World War memorial, 87–88
gender roles in, 79–81
honours, 2355–38
party 27AG, 73–76
radio-operating volunteers, 151–53
Ringway Airfield and, 100–102
Roll of Honour at Valençay, 318
student assessment board, 81–86
using BBC, 147–48
Special Training School 103 (STS 103). *See* Camp X
spycraft, introduction to, 104–6
SS *Athenia,* sinking of, 19–20
SS *Batory,* ship, 32
SS *Mauretania,* 70
SS *Pasteur,* 221–22
Stagg, james, 146–47
Stephenson, William, 68
STS 103. *See* Special Training School 103
STS 33, 103
STS 4. *See* Winterford House
student assessment board, SOE, 81–86
Supreme Headquarters Allied Expeditionary Force (SHAEF), 74
surgery, 284–86
Sutton Coldfield News, 13
Sylla, establishing base at, 155–59
Szabó, Violette, 106, 109, 240, 243, 288, 316

Tabourin, Jean, 131, 149, 176, 183, 212, 303
Talbot, May, 90
Taliban, 313
Taschereau, Jacques, 229
38th parallel, 261
Tiburce, agent, 122–23
Todd, Michael, 54–55, 59–60
Toronto Daily Star, 230–31
Toto. *See* Browne-Bartroli, Albert
Troop Convoy No. 3, 32
Trudeau, Pierre, 293
Trudeau, Pierre Elliott, 24
Turner, Canon John, 252–55
22nd Battalion, 22–23

U-22, submarine, 34
U-30, submarine, 19
United Nations, 270
Université de Montréal, 25

Van Doos, 23, 256, 262, 394
Vomécourt, Philippe de, 97–99, 187, 242

Wake, Nancy, 84, 86, 101, 106, 316
Walter, Felix H., 233–34
war bride. *See* Butt, Sonia: as war bride
War Measures Act, 293–94
war, declaring, 7–12
weapons drop, 174–75
Werl, Germany, 276–81
White Shoes Ball, 90
Williams, Ronald, 230
Willoughby, Ross, 254
Wiltshire School of Domestic Science, 48
Winant, Gil, 51
Winnipeg Tribune, The, 254
Winter War, 36
Winterfold House, 81–86
Witherington, Pearl, 236, 316
women
in F Section, 79–81
MBE and, 235–38
Women's Auxiliary Air Force (WAAF), 12, 45–46, 50–51, 53, 55, 59, 76, 88, 113, 236, 316
Women's Land Army, 12
Women's Royal Naval Service (WRNS), 12, 45–46
World War I, 12, 210
Guy during, 21–23
World War II, 1–3, 261–62
Battle of the Atlantic, 33–36
declaration of war, 48–49
liberation of Paris, 209–17
opening act of, 19–20
Operation Cadillac and, 173–85
switching prime ministers during, 37–38

Ziegel, Olivier, 180–81